Cultures of Defiance and Resistance

How does one achieve a sense of freedom and meaning in a confusing, over-bureaucratized, and unequal world? Scott McNall offers the compelling case that we do so by taking a stand to protect our identities and values, and by taking further steps to create a sense of community with like-minded people. Modern social movements have sprung up on the right and left, to provide this sense of community, to seek explanations for why things are the way they are, and to discover what might be done in response. At this critical juncture in American society when divisions over race, class, gender, and government influence persist, movements allow their members to feel they are not trapped by their conditions.

Cultures of Defiance and Resistance is an eye-opening account of the "Antis"—those who stand in opposition to received wisdom and power, who resist the science of climate change, who reject vaccinations, who want to ban GMOs, and those who have resisted what they see as political or cultural oppression, such as Black Lives Matter, Occupy Wall Street, and the Tea Party. McNall masterfully explores the goals, narratives, and rhetoric used by groups on the left, right, and center to understand and cope with 21st-century America in a time of mass discord, uncertainty, and hostility. In doing so, he reframes social movements for a new era in one of the first cross-comparative books reflecting the entire political spectrum.

Scott G. McNall is Emeritus Provost and Professor at California State University, Chico (CSUC) and currently an affiliated Professor in the Department of Sociology at the University of Montana. He was the founding Executive Director of the Institute for Sustainable Development at CSUC. He lives with his wife, Sally, in Missoula, Montana.

For those trying to understand the upsurging popular resistance against established authority in 21st-century America, Scott McNall's *Cultures of Defiance and Resistance* is a "must read" book. He masterfully investigates "the Antis," which are new social movements from the left, right, and center of the ideological spectrum who resist almost any form of cultural, economic, governmental, scientific, and social authority. From anti-vaxxers to Black Lives Matter, or climate change denialists to the Sagebrush Rebellion, his analysis carefully explores how these new groups create identities, build communities, and mobilize resources for their defiant networks of opposition in an era that all too often seems meaningless, oppressive, and exploitative.

Timothy W. Luke, *University Distinguished Professor, Virginia Polytechnic Institute and State University*

McNall's book will be the indispensable resource for Sociology courses in Social Movements, Social Problems, Political Sociology, and more. Students in my Social Movements class read pre-published chapters and found them to be provocative, well-sourced, memorable, and especially useful to their understanding of current and past events and movements. Highly recommended.

Janja Lalich, Ph.D., *Professor Emerita of Sociology, Author of* Escaping Utopia: Growing Up in a Cult, Getting Out, and Starting Over

Scott McNall, building on his work on social movements, and well known for his *Rapid Climate Change, The Business of Sustainability*, and *The Problem of Social Inequality*, has done it again in *Cultures of Defiance and Resistance*. Guided by a social movement theoretical framework, McNall provides a cogent analysis of important recent events such as 1999 Seattle WTO protests, Occupy Wall Street, the Tea Party, Black Lives Matter, right-wing movements, and the occupation of the Malheur National Wildlife Refuge. In addition to presenting the key social and historical contexts, he captures a lively ethnography of these events. In the concluding chapter on how to organize I especially liked the practical links to organizations provided, and his analysis of the limits of social media. A compelling and motivating read for sociology and political science courses.

Jeffrey A. Halley, *The University of Texas at San Antonio*

The current administration would have us believe that all problems facing us are simple and their solutions even simpler. With his book, *Cultures of Defiance and Resistance: Social Movements in 21st-Century America*, Scott G. McNall lays out for us the means by which the informed reader can access the complexity of problems facing us. Of equal, and maybe greater importance, McNall addresses the plurality, and often conflicting components, of proposed solutions offered from a wide range of interest groups. He accomplishes this without being didactic—informing, but leaving space for readers to find their own space.

James W. McManus, *Professor Emeritus Art History,*
California State University, Chico

Scott McNall has written an important, timely, and innovative book that allows us to understand the social, political, and economic factors that have divided the country and given rise to a range of new movements on both the left and right. He clearly portrays the dynamics of movements driven by anger, anxiety, and fear that serve to enhance peoples' sense of self-worth and belonging. He also explains what it will take for a progressive movement to succeed in today's political climate.

Kay Schaffer, *Dean and Professor Emerita,*
Oregon State University

Cultures of Defiance and Resistance

Social Movements in 21st-Century America

SCOTT G. MCNALL

Routledge
Taylor & Francis Group

NEW YORK AND LONDON

First published 2018
by Routledge
711 Third Avenue, New York, NY 10017

and by Routledge
2 Park Square, Milton Park, Abingdon, Oxon, OX14 4RN

Routledge is an imprint of the Taylor & Francis Group, an informa business

Library of Congress Cataloging in Publication Data
A catalog record for this book has been requested

ISBN: 978-1-138-23971-5 (hbk)
ISBN: 978-1-138-23972-2 (pbk)
ISBN: 978-1-315-29513-8 (ebk)

Typeset in Avenir and Dante
by Keystroke, Neville Lodge, Tettenhall, Wolverhampton

Be realistic. Demand the Impossible.
Ché Guevara

Contents

Acknowledgments

I want to thank the students in Professor Janja Lalich's spring 2017 class on social movements, at California State University, Chico, who took the time to read and comment on selected chapters. Their careful and thoughtful feedback and encouragement made this a much better book. I also want to thank those who sponsored this effort and encouraged its publication: Jeff Halley, Janja Lalich, and Tim Luke. In addition, I want to extend my appreciation to those who took the time from their busy schedules of teaching and research to read and comment on chapters: Jim Pushnik, Miles McNall, Robin Miller, and of course my wife, Sally McNall, whose critical eye and patience has informed all of my work. Finally, Dean Birkenkamp deserves to be singled out because he is an exceptional editor whose suggestions and comments are always offered with kindness and encouragement.

Introduction

When I began writing this book in 2016, Donald Trump had not yet been elected President and it seemed that Bernie Sanders had a chance to capture the Democratic nomination for President. The election eventually pitted Hillary Clinton against Trump, two candidates with the lowest approval ratings of any modern presidential contenders. Though Clinton won the popular vote by close to 3 million, with overwhelming support from voters on the West Coast and in New York, Trump took the heartland of America and reached deep into communities where peoples' fortunes had been in decline for decades. Pollsters had predicted a close race, but one Clinton was expected to win. Once people woke up on November 29 to the news that Trump was the new President, protests began. Angry voters who opposed Trump took to the streets to demonstrate. For those who supported Trump it was a day of celebration. The outcome of the election did little to unite a country divided by issues of race, class, gender, ideas of the role of government in our lives, and what we owed to one another. This book tells about people's search for dignity and the transformations taking place in American society. Today's mass mobilizations and social movements are a reaction to what people see as an assault on their values, their bodies, and their sense of self.

Disturbing Trends

A number of disturbing trends were in clear evidence *before* the upsurge of populist sentiment that sent Donald Trump to the White House. His "America First" rhetoric promised to remove restrictions on oil as well as coal extraction, replace "Obamacare," give all Americans cheaper and better health insurance, bring back jobs that had been shipped abroad, lower the cost of drugs, and make us safe by strengthening our military. He did not offer policies designed to tinker with our political and economic institutions, but "big" ideas to blow them up. These ideas appealed to many Americans who felt the economic system was rigged against them, and their political leaders had failed them. There were plenty of reasons for believing so.

Prospects are Bleak for a Number of Young Americans

For the first time since 1880, a higher number of 18- to 34-year-olds are living with their parents.[1] Jobs requiring only a high school education continue their rapid decline. Those who do go to college and graduate have an average student loan debt of $37,142, which can take years to pay off and delay home ownership.[2]

Americans are Financially Insecure

Most Americans (63%) do not have the resources to cover a $500 financial setback, and only half of those earning more than $75,000 a year have enough savings to deal with a $500 emergency.[3] Around 80 million workers in America are paid hourly rates. Of those paid by the hour, 2.6 million are paid either at the minimum wage of $7.25 an hour, or below, because they receive tips or are disabled.[4] Even worse, the minimum wage has lost 25% of its purchasing power since 1968.[5] Home ownership has dropped to its lowest level in 20 years, especially among African-Americans and young adults.[6] In January of 2015, 565,000 Americans were homeless including veterans, families, and children.[7]

In Spite of More Children Living at Home, We Are a Lonely Nation

In 1960, 75% of the population 18–64 (before widowhood kicks in) was married; today the figure is under 50%. In 1960, 13% of the population was living alone, today it is over 25%. And for those widowed, the figure is 60%.[8] This has profound implications for family structure. We have also lost our connections to one another through the workplace. We have entered a "gig" economy with people signing up as Uber drivers or seeking employment through a temp agency. Contract labor in which people work alone is increasing. Union membership, which used to bring people together after work, declined from 20.1% in 1983 (the first year for which data was available) to 11.1% in 2015.[9]

Our Economic Prospects and Opportunities for Mobility Have Declined

If you are born poor, you are likely to die poor. Since the 1970s social mobility has slowed. If you are born into the bottom one-fifth of the income distribution you have only a 9% chance of making it to the top tier.[10] Fifty-eight percent of all the real growth in wages and income, 2004–2014, went to the top 1% of earners— those making more than $1.3 million a year. Everybody else, the bottom 99%, reaped only 42%.[11] It is not just wages that differentiates us. The top 10% of U.S. households have captured *76% of all the wealth* in America. The 10% own more in stocks, bonds, houses, and so forth than the other 90% combined. The bottom 40% of all households has absolutely *no* wealth.[12]

We Are a Sick Nation and Getting Sicker

White middle-aged Americans (45–54 years of age) are dying faster than their counterparts in any other developed nation. The rising death rate is accounted for by an increase in "diseases of despair," that is, drug and alcohol overdoses, suicides, chronic liver diseases, and diabetes.[13] Drugs (opiates and heroin) killed almost 50,000 people in 2015, more than the number who died in car crashes.[14]

Decent Jobs are Disappearing

Logging, the most dangerous job in America next to commercial fishing, saw a loss of 20,000 jobs between 2005 and 2015 due to a combination of environmental regulations and the shipment of lumber from Canada made possible by NAFTA (North American Free Trade Agreement).[15] Between January 2000 and December 2014 the United States lost *5 million manufacturing jobs* as jobs were shipped abroad to countries with low wages and no unions.[16] Since 2014 the mining industry (coal, gold, copper, etc.) has lost 191,000 jobs. Coal mining was hardest hit, dropping from a high of 178,300 jobs in 1985 to just 56,600 in 2016. The drop in coal jobs is due primarily to automation and the availability of cheap natural gas.[17] Most Americans believe that in the distant future their jobs will be done by robots.[18]

We Are Not Living in a Post-Racial Society

When President Obama was elected President, the number of anti-government white militia groups surged from 42 to 334 by the middle of his presidency.[19] The

Secret Service recorded numerous threats of assassination against Obama and racist jokes about Obama and his family were widely circulated on right-wing websites.[20]

We Live in a Violent Society

More guns are in the hands of Americans than in any other country in the world, except for countries at war. Police shot and killed 289 African-Americans in 2016, 200 of whom were unarmed. In 97% of the cases, officers involved were not charged with any crime.[21] (Sixty-four police officers were shot and killed in the line of duty in 2016.) The United States, with 2.3 million people locked up in jails and prisons is, along with China and Russia, a world leader in incarceration.[22] African-Americans make up 12–13% of the population but account for 37.7% of all of those in prison.[23]

Trust in Our Public Institutions is at an All-Time Low

By 2015, only 19% of Americans believed they could trust the government in Washington to always do what is right (3%) or do what is right most of the time (16%), down from a high of 73% in 1958.[24]

We are a Deeply Divided and Tribal Nation, With Severe Consequences for What We Know

We are confined to small circles of like-mined others who get our "information" from "friends" on Twitter and Facebook. There are, worldwide, 1.13 billion websites, changing second-by-second that allow us to select only information we already agree with.[25] We all have confirmation biases. We reject facts that are threatening to our sense of self and embrace those that help us reach conclusions we already hold.[26] We have become, as Alexis de Tocqueville feared 200 years ago, a nation "shut up in the habits of our own hearts."[27]

Alternative Facts Substitute for Scientific Knowledge

There is a significant gap between the general public and scientists in terms of their views on science and society. To take but three examples, there is a 37 point gap between scientists and deniers in terms of the belief that climate change is real and caused by humans.[28] Studies not verified by the scientific community are used to bolster arguments that vaccines are dangerous and cause autism. Or, for climate deniers, an anomalous weather pattern is trumpeted to claim that the planet really isn't warming. Degrading science to "just another opinion" limits our ability to solve real world problems. Alternative facts divide people when they can pick and choose which ones support their beliefs from the internet.

These trends have given rise to anger, as well as fear and anxiety, and served as a push for people to mobilize for change on both the left and right. Pressure for change takes many different forms. Tea Party activists want to shrink government and reduce entitlement programs. MoveOn.org followers seek to elect progressive candidates who will support an expanded social safety net and put people, not corporations, first. Pressure for change can take the shape of single-issue movements such as demanding fluoride be taken out of the water supply, or take the form of big-issue movements, e.g., MoveOn.org, that focus on demands for social justice which can encompass prison reform, demands for raising the minimum wage, paid parental leave, and so forth. The landscape of social movements is vast and varied.

Cultures of Defiance and Resistance

My concern here, however, is with contemporary movements I have chosen to label *cultures of defiance and resistance*. These movements are driven by *moral shock* and outrage and anchored in fundamental ideas about what is right and what is wrong. Participants in cultures of defiance engage in *moral reasoning*, which does not necessarily yield to scientific reasoning or facts. Those who are opposed to abortion have one clear position: it is morally wrong and should never be permitted because life begins at conception. Likewise, those who support a pro-choice position believe nobody but the woman involved should have control over her body and emphatically resist the claim that a human life begins when sperm meets egg. Differing moral positions can seldom be reconciled. Further, cultures of defiance and resistance use *motivated reasoning*, a handmaid of moral reasoning. Motivated reasoning, driven by confirmation bias, involves seeking out information that fits with opinions or conclusions we already have. The climate denier will seize on even inaccurate data, which suggests the science is "unsettled." Motivated reasoning causes us to focus on trivia that supports our position, such as whether there is more sea ice than last year and how thick it is, rather than whether there is a steady warming of the planet.

Cultures of defiance and resistance are generated by fear and anger and demands for freedom and justice. These demands can be as personal as control over one's body or demands for freedom from economic, legal, and social oppression. Cultures of defiance are by their nature anti-elitist, whether government, corporate, or social. In a world of uncertainty, movement members come together to create **communities of meaning** which are designed to affirm a sense of belonging, as well as maintaining a sense of self worth and dignity.[29] They are tribal in nature, closed off from contradictions. *They are, simply put, a refusal to accept the way things are.*

Commodification of Dissent

There are a number of groups and social movement organizations that serve to channel people's anger and fear and to profit from it. Yes, there are ads which tell us we can challenge the status quo by buying a pair of "new revolutionary jeans." Google has several on display.[30] Or we are told we can be rebels by buying a particular brand of vehicle; say a pickup from which we can fly a Confederate flag. I mean something other than corporate ad campaigns designed to emphasize our difference and uniqueness by what we buy.[31]

My interest is with non-democratic organizations characterized by a small paid leadership team whose primary purpose is to raise funds to keep the organization going, and to drive people to buy an ideology. We can think of Fox News or the Democratic National Committee in these terms; both social movement organizations "selling" an ideology. I have chosen two social movement organizations to illustrate how dissent is being commodified. The anti-vaccination movement, discussed in Chapter 5, is driven and funded by a number of alternative-health sites, as well as outright quacks, who seek to profit by dispensing advice and products to allay the fears of parents who have autistic children. Likewise, the anti-GMO (Chapter 6) movement is designed in large part to scare consumers away from all but organic products and boost the market share for organic products, not out of a concern for people's health. Many social movement organizations are focused, not on social justice issues, but on maximizing fear for profit.

Purpose and Organization

I want to do several things in this work. One is to bring the concept of emotion (anger and fear) to center stage and, second, to demonstrate that *a search for dignity and freedom in our modern world is also a primary reason for mobilization.* A third intention is to bring class back into the equation. Class is not some fixed economic position but comprises the culture that springs from that position, our interactions with others, and our position relative to others. Class position determines whether or not we are full or partial participants in our own society. Many are denied dignity by the very nature of our economic institutions. As I have argued elsewhere, the greater the degree of inequality in a society, the lower the level of trust in others as well as the social institutions that govern our lives.[32] *Inequality*, understood as our ability to participate in our own society, *is a direct threat to democracy and a driver of movement creation and participation.*

The facts and trends I listed point to economic and social conditions that are clearly painful and humiliating for many Americans. If you have a family, it is humiliating to be paid a minimum wage, because even with two jobs you can't pay the rent and put food on the table. Equally important is the concept of what constitutes good work. Simply raising the minimum wage is not an answer to the indignity of holding what most Americans regard as a crummy job.

There is little pride in flipping hamburgers or serving up deep-fried chicken. We need our work to give us some sense of accomplishment and pride. We cannot fully understand why Trump was elected President without taking into account the precarious class position of many voters and the anger and shame that result from that.

The fourth goal is to bring close attention to those movements based on gender and ethnicity. The day after Trump was inaugurated, 500,000+ women marched in Washington, D.C. chanting, among other things, "Women's Rights are Human Rights!" There were another 400 women's marches in communities spread across the country, making it the largest protest march in American history (see Chapter 7). The Black Lives Matter movement grew not just out of the shooting of unarmed African-Americans but out of a long history of overt discrimination, the criminalization of the Black male population, and discrimination against the African-American LBGT community (see Chapter 3). Again, *the inability to be full participants in a society drives people to action designed to restore dignity.*[33]

While I will use concepts familiar to social movement scholars, my intention is not to construct some overarching theoretical framework that explains how all modern social movements come into being, or how and why they succeed or fail. Clearly some classical theoretical frameworks, e.g., **resource mobilization theory**, or theories that focus on **political timing and opportunity**, are helpful in explaining the evolution and dynamics of some movements. I will use these frameworks when they are. But not all of them are useful in all cases, especially when we consider new movements where people are focused on taking back control of their lives.

Classical social movement theory, as the sociologist Kathleen Blee has pointed out, has grown primarily out of the study of successful movements.[34] The reality is that many contentious movements are ephemeral; they spring up in response to some grievance and then vanish as members move on to other organizations or drop completely out of movement activity. As I'll explain in Chapter 7, there was an eruption of anti-Trump activity after his election, and an attempt by a number of previously existing social justice organizations to link their efforts to this swell of activity. There were also new groups that came into being. Some sought affiliations with existing groups; some were sustained; and some vanished.

I have chosen several contemporary groups to illustrate how our current *social-historical context* shapes their growth and development, as well as how issues of gender, race, and class affect who is drawn to a particular group and the ways in which grievances are expressed. The reader will encounter groups on the left and right, along with militia members, climate activists, the Tea Party, anti-vaccine advocates, and Trump supporters. All social movements occur within a specific historical context. To paraphrase Karl Marx, "humans create their own history but not always under circumstances of their own choosing."[35] So it is with the movements under consideration here. Whenever possible, I let the groups and their members speak for themselves. It is their stories I am telling here.

Chapter 1. Cultures of Defiance and Resistance: The Search for Dignity and Respect in 21st-Century America

Trump described his electoral triumph as the result of a "great mass movement." It was the result of long-standing tensions within American society. He took direct aim at free trade and globalization. His supporters were part of a revolt against the **Washington consensus**; the belief that free trade, the free flow of money, and a reduction in taxes for the wealthy would lead to economic growth in which everyone would share. Globalization was supposed to usher in an era of prosperity, but what it did instead was concentrate wealth and income gains in the hands of the 1%. As I will note, both the Democratic and Republican Parties made frequent use of what I would call the "Wal-Mart argument" in support of globalization and free trade. The argument goes something like this: Americans can buy cheap goods at Target and Wal-Mart, stretching their scarce dollars, because they are produced in countries like China, Mexico, and Vietnam, with lower labor costs. *Yet globalization and free trade are not about prosperity for the American worker, but about finding the cheapest labor and raw materials wherever they are in the world to maximize profit.* This comes at a heavy cost to the environment, of course.

Trump also benefitted from the **politics of resentment** which have developed alongside the Washington consensus. Racial resentment, and resentment of those whose *moral* values differed, added to social and economic divisions which pitted cosmopolitan, coastal elites against others. Racial resentment is deeply embedded in American politics, and it boiled to the surface in 2016. Resentment was fomented among a white working class that stands in opposition to those who are not white and who do not share their cultural values. *What might have been economic battles over economic and social inequality have been transformed into ones focused on values and battles over identity.*

Chapter 2. The Battle in Seattle and Occupy Wall Street Movement: The Meaning of Success and Failure

To help understand the dynamics that both lead to mobilization, as well as movement success and failure, I look at two "historic" movements: the Battle in Seattle, which took place in 1999, and the 2011 Occupy Wall Street (OWS) movement. The Battle in Seattle is important because it built on international opposition to globalization, particularly in Central and South America. It drew over 50,000 protesters who were attempting to shut down a World Trade Organization (WTO) meeting. It is also important because it underscores the importance of long-term planning to movement success and the development of a *spoke-and-hub model of protest*. The spoke-and-hub model operated with a central plan (a hub with the purpose of shutting down or disrupting the WTO meetings) and groups (spokes) that were given the autonomy to figure out how best to accomplish their objective. This model would be copied in a number of ensuing protests but not always with the same effect. Likewise the use of street theatre by Seattle protesters, which featured clowns, puppets, and ridicule of public figures, would be copied in future protests.

Seattle protesters were met with violence by a militarized police force and, even though police assaults and illegal arrests were met with condemnation, the same tactics have been employed by the police elsewhere. Police and protesters learned from one another and the tactics and strategies of each would be diffused to other settings.

OWS stands in stark contrast to Seattle because it was spontaneous and lacked the *organizational structure* and focus of the Seattle demonstrations. OWS organizers wanted the protests to model democracy in action, which meant decisions needed to be made on the basis of consensus. The goal in Seattle was achieved, the WTO meetings were disrupted. OWS, however, did not have a clear purpose other than pointing out the gross inequities that had opened up between the 1% and the 99%. With no political platform, OWS encampments across the country were eventually abandoned, some by force. However, the movement cannot be considered a failure, since Senator Bernie Sanders would use the same themes in his campaign for President.

Chapter 3. Black Lives Matter: The Evolution of a Social Movement

Black Lives Matter sprang into existence in 2013, after George Zimmerman, a volunteer watch coordinator for a gated community in Florida, was acquitted for the murder of Trayvon Martin, an unarmed teenager. Demonstrations broke out in major cities across the United States. It wasn't just the injustice of the verdict that brought protesters into the streets but years of continued discrimination against the African-American community. Alicia Garza, an Oakland-based activist, posted on Facebook: "Black people. I love you. I love us. Our lives matter, Black Lives Matter." Her friend, Patrisse Cullors, turned it into the hashtag, "#BlackLivesMatter." Garza and Cullors were joined by Opal Tometi to form the movement, which they understood as a response to the anti-Black racism that permeated American society.

The women who formed the movement wanted to move beyond traditional civil rights and Black Power movements by taking up the cause of "our sisters, queer and trans and disabled folks." They wanted it to be a woman-centered organization that took the spot-light off a few, male, charismatic leaders. As with OWS there wasn't a distinct political agenda, so other closely affiliated groups spun off from Black Lives Matter to create one. As shootings of unarmed Black men and women continued, support for the effort grew and the U.S. Department of Justice demanded and got reforms in Ferguson, Missouri and Baltimore, Maryland. There would be *counter-mobilization efforts*. Black Lives Matter would be blamed for the death of policemen and for a claimed increase in violence in minority communities, because police were reluctant to arrest potential law breakers. Police unions countered Black Lives Matter with the hashtag, #Bluelivesmatter. The success of political efforts to hold police departments accountable were rolled back when Trump's Attorney General, Jeff Sessions, took the position that the Department of Justice would support the police, not the protesters. *Historical context matters greatly in determining movement success or failure.*

Chapter 4. Cultures of Hyper-Masculinity: Guns, the NRA, and Militias

For those on the margins of power and threatened by economic forces over which they have little control, the gun can be a symbol of righteous power. Some own guns because they believe they are essential for protecting their families. They also compensate for a loss of strength that comes with growing age. Yet guns allow people to identify with a male-dominated culture and with its fantasies of threats and the need for self-defense. Guns have given rise to mass shootings, and yet efforts to ban the sale of handguns and automatic rifles and to keep them out of the hands of the mentally ill have been unsuccessful. The National Rifle Association is one of the most effective *social movement organizations* in America.

Odd as it may seem, men feel discriminated against and the more marginalized they feel, the more likely they are to identify with candidates like Trump who they think will restore men's status in society. Militias and right-wing movements spring out of this culture of guns and a desire to be tough. I closely follow the attempted takeover of the Malheur Wildlife Refuge in eastern Oregon in 2016 by a small militia whose members believe that public lands should be turned over to local control for ranching, mining, and lumbering. What is ignored, or seen as irrelevant by those involved, is that *public* lands belong to everyone. Militias favor their own unique interpretation of the U.S. Constitution, claiming it is a religiously inspired document that gives focus and purpose to their lives in a world of uncertainty. They are "called" to oppose what they see as government overreach and oppression. Those participating in the takeover showed up armed and urged others to join them and bring their guns. They vowed they would stay as long as it took for the federal government to honor their demands, and some pledged to fight to the death. But, drawing on their past experiences, federal officials simply waited them out and then prosecuted the ringleaders.

Chapter 5. The Anti-Vaccination Movement: Bounded Rationality

I ask why people would reject scientific consensus about the importance of vaccinating their child against diseases that could kill them. The answer stems in part from a desire to keep our children's bodies pure. One's child may be born with a genetic defect. A parent with an autistic child seeks for both an explanation of why their child was afflicted and what, if anything, might cure this disorder. The explanation some have arrived at is that autism is caused by vaccinations.

Vaccinations have been controversial since the mid-19th century. When the British government mandated in 1853 and 1867 that all children up to 14 years of age would be vaccinated against smallpox, people marched in protest. They had doubts about being inoculated with ooze from the lesions of another person. The greatest protests came from members of the working class who believed it was their right, not that of the government, to decide how best to protect their children. The science of vaccinations in the 19th century was rejected out of hand, because it was simply not understood at the time.

Today the science and importance of vaccinations can be explained, but is not always accepted. People seize on the "science" that supports their beliefs. One of the greatest controversies, and one which has not yet died out, were the "findings" of a British doctor, Andrew Wakefield. Wakefield claimed that he had found a direct link between vaccines for measles, mumps, and rubella (MMR) and autism, as well as "leaky gut syndrome" which caused toxins to be sent into the bloodstream. His findings were found to be fraudulent and he was ultimately barred from practicing medicine. Still, those committed to the idea that vaccines can cause autism believe he is right. The anti-vaccination movement allows us to understand how some social movement organizations function in the same way cults do; choices become circumscribed and should people fall away from the faith, they are exiled from the group.

Chapter 6. The Body as the Last Line of Defense: The Fight against GMOs

The anti-vaxxers are not the only group that has an uneasy relationship with science. Those who support the science of climate change do not always accept the science of genetically modified organisms (GMOs). As I point out, our understanding of science has little to do with whether or not we accept scientific facts. Most of us do not understand the actual science of climate change, nor the science of GMOs.[36] Support for the belief that the planet is warming and humans are responsible, and support for the idea that GMO crops are harmful to our health, both derive in part from our belief that both are caused by greedy corporations. In the case of climate change it is the fossil fuel industry and in the case of our food the villain is the agro-industrial food complex.

Chapter 7. The Revolution Will Not Be Tweeted, But It Can Be Organized

In the aftermath of Trump's election a number of groups on the left saw a surge in memberships and donations. I chose to focus on the first 100 days of Trump's administration. Drawing on my own experiences with several of these groups in my home town of Missoula, Montana, I describe the problems all social movements must solve. I show how the choices made at the outset of a group's formation and the differing needs of group members determine its future development and its chances of success. New movements face intense competition from established groups for media attention, for members, and for resources. Localized social movements spring up in response to well-defined grievances but, as I explain, most are fragile and fade quickly away.

I argue that contemporary movements of defiance and resistance are attempts to form *moral communities* that stand in opposition to the received wisdom of Washington political elites and in opposition to the bureaucratization and commodification of social life. Movements of defiance are *value-based movements* that arise in response to dissolving bonds of solidarity—faith, family, and community. Whether these movements occur on the left or the right, they are attempts to establish our humanity and our dignity.

The idea that the success and evolution of social movements depends on *social media* is challenged. *Social media is simply a tool to bring together people who already share the same values.* Drawing on the lessons learned from the different groups covered in previous chapters, I offer five lessons and suggest that movement success will depend on embracing two separate strategies. First is the face-to-face organizing advocated by Saul Alinsky; the second is the strategy of mass mobilization advocated most recently by Frances Fox Piven. Movement success depends on any number of factors (the nature of the grievance, political opportunity, and organizational strength) but courage, hard work, and persistence in the face of opposition are absolutely essential.

Notes

1 Richard Fry. May 24, 2016. "For First Time in Modern Era, Living Arrangements with Parents Edges Out Other Living Arrangements for 18- to 34-Year-Olds." Pew Research Center. Retrieved on January 6, 2017 at: www.pewsocialtrends.org/2016/05/24/for-first-time-in-modern-era-living-with-parents-edges-out-other-living-arrangements-for-18-to-34-year-olds/.

2 Kim Clark. October 18, 2016. "Student Loan Debt Hits Another Record High." *Time.* Retrieved on January 7, 2017 at: http://time.com/money/4534379/student-loan-debt-record/.

3 Kristin Wong. January 8, 2016. "Most Americans Lack Reserve Cash to Cover $500 Emergency: Survey." *NBC News.* Retrieved on January 8, 2016 at: www.nbcnews.com/business/personal-finance/most-americans-lack-reserve-cash-cover-500-emergency-survey-n493096.

4 U.S. Bureau of Labor. April, 2016. "Characteristics of Minimum Wage Workers, 2015." Retrieved on January 9, 2017 at: www.bls.gov/opub/reports/minimum-wage/2015/home.htm.

5 U.S. Bureau of Labor. April, 2016.

6 Richard Fry and Anna Brown. December 15, 2016. "In a Recovering Market, Home-ownership Rates Are Down Sharply for Blacks, Young Adults." PEW Research Center. Retrieved on January 6, 2017 at: www.pewsocialtrends.org/2016/12/15/in-a-recovering-market-homeownership-rates-are-down-sharply-for-blacks-young-adults/.

7 Meghan Henry, Azim Shivji, Tanya de Sousa, and Rebecca Cohen. November, 2015. *The 2015 Annual Homeless Assessment Report to Congress.* U.S. Department of Housing and Urban

Development. Retrieved on January 9, 2017 at: www.hudexchange.info/resources/documents/2015-AHAR-Part-1.pdf.

8 Lisa Neidert. July 6, 2015. "A Rise in the Number of Those Living Alone." *The New York Times*. Retrieved on January 8, 2017 at: www.nytimes.com/roomfordebate/2015/07/06/has-being-single-in-america-changed/a-rise-in-the-number-of-those-living-alone. See also: U.S. Bureau of the Census. 2016. "Families and Living Arrangements." Retrieved on January 6, 2017 at: www.census.gov/hhes/families/data/cps2016A.html.

9 Bureau of Labor Statistics. January 28, 2016. "Union Members Summary." Retrieved on January 6, 2017 at: www.bls.gov/news.release/union2.nr0.htm.

10 Several studies of mobility trends are summarized in *The Economist*. February 1, 2014. "Class in America: Mobility, Measured." Retrieved on January 6, 2017 at: www.economist.com/news/united-states/21595437-america-no-less-socially-mobile-it-was-generation-ago-mobility-measured. See also: Alana Semuels. July 14, 2016. "Poor at 20, Poor for Life." *The Atlantic*. Retrieved on January 6, 2017 at: www.theatlantic.com/business/archive/2016/07/social-mobility-america/491240/.

11 Emmanuel Saez. June 29, 2015. "U.S. Income Inequality Persists Amid Overall Growth in 2014." *Washington Center for Equitable Growth*. Retrieved on January 9, 2017 at: http://equitablegrowth.org/research-analysis/u-s-income-inequality-persists-amid-overall-growth-2014/.

12 Christopher Ingraham. May 21, 2015. "If You Thought Income Inequality Was Bad, Get a Load of Wealth Inequality." *Washington Post*. Retrieved on January 9, 2016 at: www.washingtonpost.com/news/wonk/wp/2015/05/21/the-top-10-of-americans-own-76-of-the-stuff-and-its-dragging-our-economy-down/?utm_term=.fcc821ddd358.

13 Anne Case and Angus Deaton. September, 2015. "Rising Morbidity and Mortality in Midlife among White Non-Hispanic Americans in the 21st Century." *Proceedings of the National Academy of Sciences*. Retrieved on January 6, 2017 at: www.pnas.org/content/112/49/15078.full.

14 Jen Christensen and Sergio Hernandez. October 14, 2016. "'This Is America on Drugs: A Visual Guide." *CNN*. Retrieved on January 9, 2017 at: www.cnn.com/2016/09/23/health/heroin-opioid-drug-overdose-deaths-visual-guide/.

15 Bureau of Labor Statistics. December 17, 2015. "Occupational Outlook Handbook, Logging Workers." Retrieved on January 6, 2017 at: www.bls.gov/ooh/farming-fishing-and-forestry/logging-workers.htm.

16 Robert E. Scott. August 11, 2015. 'Manufacturing Job Loss: Trade, Not Productivity, Is the Culprit." *Economy Policy Institute*. Retrieved on January 9, 2017 at: www.epi.org/publication/manufacturing-job-loss-trade-not-productivity-is-the-culprit/.

17 Terence P. Jeffrey. May 6, 2016. "U.S. Has Lost 191,000 Mining Industry Jobs Since September 2014." *CNS News*. Retrieved on January 7, 2017 at: www.cnsnews.com/news/article/terence-p-jeffrey/us-has-lost-191000-mining-jobs-september-2014. See also: Bureau of Labor Statistics. January 6, 2017. "The Employment Situation—December 2016." Retrieved on January 6, 2017 at: www.bls.gov/news.release/pdf/empsit.pdf.

18 Aaron Smith. March 10, 2016. "Public Predictions for the Future of Workforce Automation." *Pew Research Center*. Retrieved on January 9, 2017 at: www.pewinternet.org/2016/03/10/public-predictions-for-the-future-of-workforce-automation/.

19 Southern Poverty Law Center. January 4, 2016. "Anti-Government Militia Groups Grew by More Than One-Third Last Year." Retrieved on January 9, 2017 at: www.splcenter.org/news/2016/01/04/antigovernment-militia-groups-grew-more-one-third-last-year.

20 Gregory S. Parks and Danielle C. Heard. 2009. "'Assassinate the Nigger Ape': Obama, Implicit Imagery, and the Dire Consequences of Racist Jokes." *Cornell Law Faculty Working Papers, Paper 61*. Retrieved on April 12, 2017 at: http://scholarship.law.cornell.edu/cgi/viewcontent.cgi?article=1063&context=clsops_papers.

21 Mapping Police Violence. January 1, 2017. "Police Killed 346 Black People in 2015." *Mapping Police Violence.* Retrieved on January 6, 2017 at: https://mappingpoliceviolence. org/.

22 Peter Wagner and Bernadette Rabuy. March 14, 2016. "Mass Incarceration: The Whole Pie 2016." *Prison Policy.* Retrieved on January 9, 2017 at: www.prisonpolicy.org/reports/pie2016.html.

23 Federal Bureau of Prisons. May 27, 2017. "Inmate Race." Retrieved on June 16, 2017 at: www.bop.gov/about/statistics/statistics_inmate_race.jsp.

24 Pew Research Center. November 23, 2015. "Trust in Government: 1958–2015." Retrieved on January 9, 2017 at: www.people-press.org/2015/11/23/1-trust-in-government-1958-2015/.

25 Worldwide Internet Live. January 9, 2017. Retrieved on January 9, 2017 at: www.internetlivestats.com/watch/websites/.

26 Tim Harford. March 8, 2017. "The Problem with Facts." *FT Magazine.* Retrieved on April 18, 2017 at: http://timharford.com/2017/03/the-problem-with-facts/.

27 Alexis de Tocqueville. 1835. *Democracy in America, Vol. 1.* Retrieved on April 13, 2017 at: www.columbia.edu/cu/tat/core/tocqueville.htm/.

28 Cary Funk and Lee Raine. January 29, 2015. "Public and Scientists' Views on Science and Society." *Pew Research Center.* Retrieved on April 13, 2017 at: www.pewinternet.org/2015/01/29/public-and-scientists-views-on-science-and-society/.

29 Sam Friedman, Diana Rossi, and Gonzalo Ralón. January 7, 2015. "Dignity Denial and Social Conflicts." *Rethinking Marxism: A Journal of Economics, Culture, & Society.* Vol.27(1): 65–84. See also: Sam Friedman. 1991. "Alienated Labor and Dignity Denial in Capitalist Society," in Berch Berberoglu, ed. *Critical Perspectives in Sociology.* Dubuque, Iowa: Kendall Hunt, pp.83–91.

30 Google. 2017. "Shop for Revolutionary New Jeans on Google." Retrieved on April 14, 2017 at: www.google.com/webhp?sourceid=chrome-instant&ion=1&espv=2&ie=UTF-8#q=revolutionary+new+jeans&tbm=shop.

31 Thomas Frank. 1997. "Why Johnny Can't Dissent." Chapter 1 in Thomas Frank and Matt Weiland, eds. *Commodify Your Dissent: Salvos from the Baffler.* New York: W.W. Norton.

32 Scott G. McNall. 2016. *The Problem of Social Inequality: Why It Destroys Democracy, Threatens the Planet, and What We Can Do About It.* New York: Routledge.

33 I want to be clear that I am not making an argument which claims that economic discrimination results in mobilization. Threats to our identity and dignity result from a complex of factors that must take into account gender, race, and economic circumstances.

34 Kathleen Blee. 2012. *Democracy in the Making: How Activist Groups Form.* New York: Oxford.

35 Karl Marx. 1852. *The 18th Brumaire of Louis Bonaparte. Marxist Archives.* Retrieved on April 13, 2017 at: www.marxists.org/archive/marx/works/1852/18th-brumaire/ch01.htm.

36 Brandon R. McFadden. November 9, 2016. "Examining the Gap between Science and Public Opinion about Genetically Modified Food and Global Warming." *PlosOne.* Vol.11(11). Retrieved on June 14, 2017 at: http://journals.plos.org/plosone/article?id=10.1371/journal.pone.0166140.

Cultures of Defiance and Resistance

1

The Search for Dignity and Respect in 21st-Century America

Consider:

- Donald Trump was elected President of the United States in November 2016 in part because white working-class Americans embraced a politics of resentment.
- Fox News is an example of a social movement organization used to advance conservative candidates and causes.
- Cultures of defiance and resistance are grounded in opposition to dominant social, economic, and political institutions.
- Resistance is a way to assert one's self worth and maintain dignity.
- Protest movements are a way to test the boundaries of established norms and rules and to advance a cause.
- Our race, class, and gender determine which movements we embrace in our quest for acceptance and dignity.
- Many of today's social movements can be characterized as a Great Refusal.

"I'm mad as hell, and I'm not going to take this anymore!" shouts Howard Beale, the long-time news anchor of the fictional Union Broadcasting System (UBS). In the 1976 movie classic, *Network*, Beale is told that because of declining ratings he has only two more weeks left at UBS. He goes on the air and tells his viewers he's been fired and that he plans to commit suicide live on next Tuesday's broadcast. He is immediately terminated by the corporate brass but after apologizing profusely they give him a chance to retire with dignity. However, instead of apologizing, the next time he goes on air he engages in another rant

concluding that life is *"bullshit!"* The result of Beale's antics is that ratings spike and the network decides to keep him. In one of his ensuing diatribes, he encourages his viewers to shout out of their windows, *"I'm mad as hell and I'm not going to take it anymore."* The movie then shows listeners echoing Beale's rant leaning out of their windows across the city shouting, "I'm not going to take it anymore!" There are clear similarities between this fiction and the reality of the 2016 presidential election, which revealed a nation divided and angry.

In writing about cultures of defiance and resistance it is tempting to focus solely on the 2016 election of Donald Trump as President. Above all, he was a political outsider—a wealthy reality-television personality and real estate developer who had never before been elected to any public position or held a high military office. What he had was experience in making deals, which he claimed would "Make America Great Again." During the primaries and in the general election campaign he made provocative and outrageous comments and completely dominated the news cycle all the way through the primaries and into the general election. He was, to use the words of the social theorist Douglas Kellner, a master of the *politics of spectacle*.[1] He Tweeted attacks on a Muslim family who had lost a son fighting our wars in the Middle East. He claimed that Mexico was sending rapists and murderers across the border and Mexico would have to pay for a "beautiful" wall. He claimed that climate change was a hoax created by the Chinese to weaken American businesses. He ridiculed a former beauty queen as being too fat. He asserted with no proof that Hillary Clinton was going to abolish the 2nd Amendment and take away people's guns. He mused that maybe 2nd Amendment supporters could take care of her.[2]

The promises he made to the American people were extensive. He promised that Obamacare would be eliminated and everyone would have cheaper and better medical care. We'd get rid of environmental regulations so that jobs in coal would return, never mind that most jobs had been eliminated by automation and cheaper fuels like natural gas. Manufacturing jobs would return because he would negotiate better trade deals and impose tariffs so high that American companies would think twice before setting up shop in low-waged countries. He promised to strengthen our military (already the most powerful in the world), and wipe all traces of the Islamic State (ISIS or ISIL) from the face of the earth. He promised to give huge tax cuts to the wealthy and improve the lives of ordinary Americans. And so on.

What trends and issues caused so many (though not a plurality) Americans to vote for him? Why did the message of the Alt-right, which combines populist fervor with white nationalism and racism, become a powerful force in bringing people to the polls? The slogan, "Make America Great Again," suggested there was a point in time when things were better, but for whom?

Anxiety and Fear Revealed in the 2016 Election Cycle

The demographics of who voted for Trump, and who did not, tell an important story about existing and growing divisions within American society. Trump labeled his efforts to capture the Presidency as America's greatest mass movement ever. It wasn't, but it should be understood the same way we understand other mass movements.[3] The story of Trump's ascendancy tells an important story about why cultures of defiance and resistance exist. Trump voters tended to be male and to be older, whiter, less healthy, less educated, and living in rural areas. Clinton voters were concentrated in urban areas, tended to be better educated, younger, African-Americans, Asians, Hispanics, and women. Trump's margin of victory among whites without a college degree (67% to Clinton's 28%) was the largest for any candidate since 1980.[4] However, such demographics tell only part of the story.

> The election of Donald Trump to the Presidency can be understood as a social movement grounded in the politics of resentment.

The electoral divide was not just between red and blue states or red and blue counties but between cultures and classes. Though racists and misogynists voted for Trump, he won because millions of Americans, both Democrat and Republican, were deeply distressed about the direction of their country and felt abandoned by status-quo politicians in their parties. They were tired of being made promises that were never kept. In the words of the fictional character, Howard Beale, they were "mad as hell." Seventy-three percent said the country was on the wrong track.[5] The electorate did not trust our major institutions and did not trust the leadership of either party to help them.

Voters gave many reasons for their growing anger, but one repeated over and over was the lack of well-paying jobs. People were frightened by continued deindustrialization and their place in the overall economy. A survey by the AFL-CIO of 1,600 white working-class voters in Cleveland and Pittsburg found that "people are fed up, people are hurting, they are very distressed about the fact that their kids don't have a future." There had been no recovery from the recession.[6] There were other issues. Families reported being stuck with thousands of dollars in medical bills, some having to declare bankruptcy. The cost of drug prices had continued to soar. Retirees saw their pension plans threatened. For many Americans, working hard and playing by the rules no longer meant you could feel secure.

Republicans were more pessimistic than Democrats about the country's future and, perhaps, most susceptible to promises of change. When asked whether or not life would be better or worse for the next generation, 64% of

Republicans though it would be *worse*, compared to 39% of Democrats.[7] Confidence in the two parties' abilities to reverse this course of events was extremely low. Only 8% of voters expressed confidence in the Republican Party, while 15% trusted the Democratic Party. Only 4% of voters expressed any confidence in Congress.[8] Why not go with an outsider?

Trump hit a nerve with voters when he claimed he would "drain the swamp" of the nation's capitol by flushing out lobbyists and professional politicians.[9] As the opinion writer for the *Wall Street Journal*, Peggy Noonan, wrote, Trump's victories in the primaries signaled that people were fed up with entrenched political elites who had failed to act on the interests of white working-class Americans.[10] For most workers real wages (purchasing power) were the same in 2016 as they were in 1970.[11] Voters were highly attuned to the fact that they were stuck in place economically, while over the last four decades the 1% had grabbed most of the country's economic growth and wealth for themselves. The structural inequality that had once defined the condition of minorities was now a fact of life for a growing number of white Americans. Both Sanders and Trump, and to a lesser extent Clinton, played on these concerns but Trump would be the major beneficiary of growing anger, especially among white working-class voters.[12]

As *The New York Times* opinion writer Charles M. Blow explained, a rejection of America and its institutions occurred on both the left and right.

> There is profound disappointment. On one hand, it's about fear of dislocation of supremacy, and the surrendering of power and the security it provides. On the other hand, it's about disillusionment that the game is rigged . . . It is about defining who created this country's bounty and who has most benefitted from it.[13]

There is fear and anger about changing demographics and culture. White ethnocentrism and racial resentment were highly visible in the 2016 campaign. One measure of ethnocentrism is to ask whites to compare themselves to African-Americans, Hispanics, or other minorities in terms of whether whites are more trustworthy, intelligent, and less violent than minorities. Another way is to ask whites whether they resent gays, lesbians, and transgendered people. Combining these two measures, 41% of Democrats expressed resentment against minority Americans, including members of the LBGT community. Among independents, 56% expressed resentment while 72% of all Republicans did.[14] Just how important were these cultural factors? For some voters they were as important as their economic interests.

In Iowa, which Obama had easily won in 2012, voters went for Trump in a 15-percentage point reversal over Obama's earlier victory. A retired farmer interviewed by Trip Gabriel of *The New York Times* noted that Trump opposed the Trans-Pacific Partnership (TPP) which would have helped with the export of corn and soybeans from Iowa. People voted against their own economic interests in supporting Trump.[15] In attempting to explain this, a news director for an Iowa radio station described two young men he had known since they were children:

> They're hard workers. As a kid, one washed dishes . . . at a restaurant. Every summer, the other picked sweet corn by hand at dawn for a farm stand and for grocery stores, and then went to work all day on his parents' farm. Now one is a welder, and the other is in his first year at a state university on an academic scholarship. They are conservative; believe in hard work, family, the military and cops, and they know that abortion and socialism are evil.[16]

> Trump voters were asserting the importance of their culture and values and attempting to reclaim their dignity.

The two men wanted little to do with liberal America, and by extension the Democratic Party, which they saw as rewarding freeloaders. Like many others living in America's heartland, they voted for Trump because they were making a statement about the importance of their own culture and way of life. They were asserting their *dignity* and a right to be heard and counted. And they wanted something done about their economic circumstances. They were but one part of a *culture of defiance and resistance* that has spread across America. Trump, as the writer Chris Hedges has argued, came along promising revenge on college-educated elites and politicians who carried out the neoliberal assault on workers, and revenge on immigrants who were stealing their jobs.[17]

This populist revolt was a long time coming and it is important to trace its origins because it explains where we are today and how we ended up with a politics of resentment that combines cultural and class issues. There are two major factors that account for this: one is that both major political parties embrace the policies of neoliberalism;[18] second is the historic use of racial resentment to mobilize voters. Each has deep historic roots in the United States.

The Politics of Resentment

Our current economic system and ideas about how it works are rooted in the classical economic theories of Adam Smith and David Ricardo. Embedded in their theories are two fundamental notions: competition is *always* a good thing and individuals are responsible for their *own* fates. Classical economic theory further holds that employment is *voluntary*. If people wanted to work, they could. They just need to be willing to accept what the market offers in terms of wages. They don't need to make claims on the state or their fellow taxpayers. What we refer to today as neoliberal theory is grounded in these ideas and amplified in the work of contemporary authors like Milton Friedman. Friedman's classic *Capitalism and Freedom* (1962) lays out the argument that capitalism, as a competitive system, operating without governmental inference, will produce the necessary conditions for a prosperous and democratic society.[19] Neoliberal theory also attributes to the market an ethic of governance and behavior. We don't need people or governments to make decisions; the market will do that for us. Regulations, be they environmental or banking, are unnecessary and detrimental to the smooth functioning of the market. As the political theorist Paul Treanor has noted, neoliberalism is:

a philosophy in which the existence and operation of a market are valued in themselves, separately from any previous relationship with the production of goods and services, and without any attempt to justify them in terms of their effect on the production of goods and services; and where the operation of a market-like structure seen as an ethic in itself, capable of acting as a guide for all human action, and substituting for all previously existing ethical beliefs.[20]

The market, as neoliberal theory has it, takes on a quasi-religious character and becomes an ethical touchstone for how we live our lives. Contracts replace social bonds. As Karl Marx (1818–1883) long ago pointed out in *Economic and Philosophic Manuscripts of 1844*, when human relations are reduced to contract relations, and people's value is determined simply by their place in the marketplace, feelings of alienation automatically well up, because people no longer control their own fates.[21] Marx believed these feelings of alienation cut to the very heart of what it meant to be human and, because of that, people would ultimately rise up in protest demanding justice and recognition of their worth. We need to understand modern movements directed against neoliberal regimes as rooted in our desire to assert our humanness and to have our basic needs met. These needs extend beyond food and shelter; they extend to our need for respect, autonomy, and acceptance by others.

There is no firm date we can provide for the emergence of a neoliberal economic model and the politics of resentment that flowed from it, but opposition to the government stepping in to help people when the market failed them began with the administration of Franklin D. Roosevelt (1933–1945).[22] Many of us remember Roosevelt's policies favorably because they were an attempt to rescue the country from the Great Depression and achieve full employment by putting people to work building bridges and highways, dams, and public buildings. These actions and more were a boon to many Americans, though not all approved of Roosevelt's policies.

There were clergy who opposed government expansion for they feared it would undermine their own programs of relief.[23] The American Protestant Hospital Association mobilized to prevent what they saw as socialized medicine. Many condemned public welfare for they saw it as sapping independence and encouraging idleness. Industrialists were opposed to wage and price controls and the growing power of unions. Whites opposed relief to African-Americans and what they regarded as the dangerous underclasses in the cities. In short, New Deal policies exacerbated divisions between rural and urban Americans, the industrialized Northeast and the South, between races, and between those with economic means and those without. It laid the groundwork for the politics of resentment that first appeared in the 1960s, deepened during the 1970s, took firm hold on the nation's imagination by the time of Ronald Reagan's election in 1980, and reached its ascendancy during Bill Clinton's and Obama's time in office. Along the way, the economic interests of working Americans were lost.

Several trends developed side-by-side. As neoliberal economic policies took hold on the imaginations of political leaders in both parties, racial resentment and resentment of those whose *moral* values were different added to growing divisions within American society. Some of the discrete events that explain how we arrived at today include: the social and political chaos of the 1960s; the Great Society Programs of Lyndon Johnson that caused the loss of the Solid South to the Republicans; Roe vs. Wade; Nixon's Southern Strategy which played on racial resentment; Reagan's embrace of Evangelical Christians; the mobilization of the business community to fight for a neoliberal agenda; the embrace of neoliberalism by the Democratic Party under Bill Clinton; and the rise of the Tea Party. By the time Obama took office these factors, and the reality of a unified Republican Party determined to challenge his every action, meant that he could not move the Democratic Party to the left to embrace the needs of working men and women.

I have separated these trends for the sake of identifying their unique impacts, although they overlapped in time and melded together. For example, Evangelicals got involved in politics because of what they regarded as the moral chaos of the 1960s; and they were clearly on the pro-life side of debates over Roe vs. Wade. In the 2016 election, they cast 81% of their votes for Trump in the hope that he would appoint conservative Supreme Court justices.[24]

The 1960s

Optimism characterized the beginning of John F. Kennedy's administration (1961–1963). He promised a "new frontier." We would put a man on the moon and we would solve our collective problems of social and racial inequality. He signed legislation raising the minimum wage and increased Social Security benefits. However, he quickly ran into stiff opposition on his other initiatives, e.g., providing Medicare benefits to the elderly. The opposition came primarily from a bloc of conservative southern Democrats and Republicans who refused to expand on Roosevelt's New Deal. One of the flash points that riled southern Democrats was Kennedy's determination to provide Federal protection for those seeking to register African-Americans to vote in the South and to allow African-Americans to attend all-white schools. Symbolizing the South's growing discontent with Federal intervention, the Governor of Alabama, George Wallace, stood in the door of the University of Alabama on June 11, 1963, to block the entry of two Black students. He was acting on his campaign pledge of "segregation now, segregation tomorrow, segregation forever."

Racism wasn't just confined to the South. Riots broke out in Detroit, Los Angeles, and New York in response to segregation and violent and discriminatory policing. While Black leaders focused on poverty and oppression as being the cause of the riots, many whites saw the rioters as lawless thugs who did not want to work for a living.[25] Opposition to civil rights was couched in a *moral* language that underscored opposition to government interference in "private" life and opposition to those who relied on government help. A national opinion poll at the time revealed that a majority of southern whites believed they should not have to go to school with Blacks, live in the same neighborhoods as they did, or serve them in their places of business, if they did not want to.[26] Today, we have the same form of argument turned against the LBGT community. Bakers and florists should have the right to refuse to accommodate gay couples getting married if it is against their *moral* principles.

> Opposition to the Civil Rights Movement of the 1960s was couched in a moral language.

When Kennedy was assassinated in 1963, his Vice President Lyndon Johnson stepped into the Presidency. Using the considerable legislative skills he developed as former Majority Leader of the Senate, he pushed through Congress the Civil Rights Act of 1964 and the Voting Rights Act of 1965 which sought to end the discriminatory voting practices adopted in many southern states after the Civil War. As part of his Great Society efforts he signed the Medicare and Medicaid Acts, the Head Start program to help disadvantaged children prepare for success in school, a Job Corps program to retrain those displaced in a deindustrializing economy, and offered federal subsidies for urban redevelopment. While 48% of Americans approved of his anti-poverty efforts, a solid 31% disapproved and they were concentrated in the South.[27]

The growing ideological and religious divisions within the country, particularly between the South's Bible Belt and the two coasts, would come starkly into focus during Johnson's 1964 campaign for President against the conservative Arizona Senator, Barry Goldwater. Johnson called Goldwater's campaign disgusting.[28] His anger was piqued in part by the fact that in southern states outright racist flyers, newspaper advertisements, and radio announcements were warning African-Americans not to vote and whites to turn out to stop "them." Johnson won the 1964 contest in a landslide, carrying 44 states, by portraying Goldwater as a dangerous extremist who would usher in a nuclear holocaust. Nevertheless, Johnson lost what had been referred to as the solid South—Alabama, Georgia, Louisiana, Mississippi, and South Carolina—to Goldwater. Goldwater may have permanently alienated African-Americans from the Republican Party by his unequivocal rejection of Civil Rights, garnering only 6% of the votes of African-Americans nationwide. (Trump received 8% of African-American votes in 2016.) The campaign behind him, Johnson turned to his first full term as President. It was to be a tumultuous one. Ideological cracks deepened between geographic regions and cultural sectors of the population.

Johnson inherited from Kennedy the conflict in Vietnam but escalated it to a full-scale war in 1964. Soon after the draft began, protests against the war and the draft broke out across the country, primarily on college campuses. Students marched on local draft offices to burn their draft cards. Teach-ins were organized against the war, flags were burned, and classes cancelled. The protests expanded beyond the war to include multiple and overlapping themes. One was a challenge to authority in all of its forms—universities that sought to control student behavior, government institutions regarded as corrupt, an unpopular war, and the moral authority of previous generations. Second, there were demands for equal rights and social justice for women, minorities, and members of the LGBT community. The protests were also about freedom to choose—to drop out, to live in a commune, to reject conformity and consumer society, to choose what to do with your own body, and what to think. Much of this made no sense to working and middle-class citizens.

Backlash against what some regarded as moral chaos and the failure of government to protect the rights of whites was soon to come. And it came from several quarters. Evangelical and other conservative Christians stood in opposition to moral laxity, feminism, gay rights, and minority rights. It came from champions of states' rights, who opposed the growing power of the federal government. It came from southern whites who viewed Civil Rights legislation as a threat to their power. The Republican Party saw an opportunity to exploit the *moral* resentment that was growing in America.

Nixon's "Southern Strategy"

Lyndon Johnson shocked the country when he announced in a televised address to the nation (March 31, 1968) that he would not run for reelection. His reasons for doing so were growing opposition to the war in Vietnam and the fact that America's military strategy was not working. Johnson also faced opposition from within his own party; both Robert "Bobby" Kennedy and Eugene McCarthy intended to challenge him for the Democratic nomination. Hubert Humphrey, who had served as Johnson's Vice President, was eventually chosen as the Democratic standard bearer. The 1968 Democratic convention in Chicago proved to be a disaster. Radical counter-cultural protesters who came to oppose the war in Vietnam and advocate for various freedoms were beaten by baton-wielding Chicago police officers, as Civil Rights protesters had been beaten in the South. For some, the Democratic Party appeared to have lost control not only of their convention but of their ability to govern. Humphrey would emerge as the Party's choice, although one weakened by the legacy of the war and the backlash against the 1960s.

Richard M. Nixon was the Republican candidate but there was also a third-party candidate, George Wallace. Wallace, along with retired General Curtis LeMay, ran on the American Independent Party ticket and on an overtly racist states' rights platform. He dominated in the Deep South, winning the states of Arkansas, Louisiana, Mississippi, Alabama, and Georgia—the same states where Goldwater captured a majority in 1964. The Republican analyst and Nixon campaigner, Kevin Phillips, saw an opportunity. These rebellious southern voters could become Republican supporters if the Party appealed to the growing dissatisfaction of whites with liberal Democratic racial and welfare policies.[29]

Nixon and his lieutenants developed a playbook for his "Southern Strategy." In a confidential memo titled "Dividing the Democrats," they indicated they would work to capture those Democrats hostile to Eastern liberals, militant Blacks, and campus radicals. They planned to capture former southern Democrats as well as northern Catholic ethnics, blue-collar workers, and Evangelicals. They would nominate a strict southern constructionist to the Supreme Court and, although they failed to get their nominee from the Deep South appointed, Nixon was able to appoint four conservatives to the Court. Nixon's team intended to elicit white working-class support for Republicans by providing modest tax relief for middle-class voters and denouncing welfare.[30]

Nixon is credited with giving full throat to the *politics of resentment*, which the Pennsylvania State University professor of communication studies, Jeremy

Engels, has defined as a redefinition of normal, democratic political differences into differences in cultural and moral values.[31] The rhetoric of resentment was designed to destroy the New Deal coalition the Democrats had enjoyed. Phillips, referred to earlier, was Nixon's "ethnic" specialist and developed campaigns designed to stoke white fear of Blacks, and fear of social engineering that would open up the American Dream to other minorities, as well as women.

> Nixon's "Southern Strategy" was based on the politics of racial resentment.

Nixon's domestic policy chief, John Erlichman, later admitted that Nixon's "war on drugs" was, in fact, a thinly disguised assault on inner-city African-Americans and hippies designed to gain the support of white voters.[32] Nixon hammered on the theme of "law and order," first used in the Goldwater campaign.[33] Nixon claimed he was speaking for the *great silent majority*, who stood in opposition to a vocal minority who were trying to destroy the country. The real enemy was not the Viet Cong we were still fighting but our fellow Americans who were soft on crime, hated our troops, and hated capitalism. By 2016, the enemy would be those who supported diversity, welfare, and environmental regulations.

Nixon's rhetoric, which still resonates, reframed the great silent majority as the real victims. As Engels noted, Nixon:

> encouraged these victims to loathe their victimizers, the domestic enemies who were polluting the quiet of American public discourse. The problem with American society . . . was not war, racism, or economic injustice . . . The problem was that minorities had disregarded the democratic process and had begun yelling at the (silent) majority.[34]

President Trump used this theme in the 2016 elections, noting that good Americans were the victims of immigrants who were stealing their jobs, corporations that shipped jobs abroad, and trade deals that strengthened other countries at our expense.

A number of writers have argued that the rise of Donald Trump is a legacy of Nixon's Southern Strategy and long-standing appeals to racism.[35] One agency, Public Policy Polling, found in an analysis of the 2016 primary in South Carolina that Trump's support was "built on a base of voters among whom religious and racial intolerance pervades." Among his supporters, 70% wanted the Confederate flag to still be flying over the state capitol; 38% wished the South had won the Civil War; and not only would they support a ban on Muslims entering the country, 31% would support a similar ban on homosexuals.[36]

Business Fights Back

Nixon was also a champion of the kind of deregulation that characterizes neoliberalism. Nixon, unlike Johnson, did not believe it was the job of the government to provide full employment, or protect citizens from an unregulated market—but only to stimulate growth. One of Nixon's appointments to the Supreme Court was Lewis Powell, a corporate lawyer and member of 11 corporate boards. Shortly before his 1971 appointment, Powell wrote a confidential memo to the U.S. Chamber of Commerce outlining a strategy to counter the attack on the American free enterprise system.[37] He saw the attack as coming from "Communists, New Leftists and other revolutionaries who would destroy the entire system, both political and economic." What troubled him most was not this small minority but the "chorus of criticism coming from perfectly respectable elements of society: from the college campus, the pulpit, the media, the intellectual and literary journals, the arts and sciences, and from politicians." He foresaw liberals and social reformers as destroying or weakening the free enterprise system.

His solution was for businessmen to fight back, because the survival of their corporations and the "prosperity of America and the freedom of our people" were at stake. College campuses were suspect because scholarship and opinion were slanted toward criticism of capitalism. Balance needed to be provided by offering support for scholars who believed in free enterprise and the capitalist system. Books should be written; pamphlets published and distributed; and free enterprise courses embedded in the K-12 curriculum. The rise of conservative think tanks and advocacy groups such as the Heritage Foundation, Manhattan Institute, the Cato Institute, the American Enterprise Institute, and the Hoover Institute provided intellectual heft to the shift away from the government protecting its people to protecting and creating the conditions favorable to the growth of business and industry. Ideally, all regulations on the market would be eliminated. This idea seeped into policies embraced by both the Democratic and Republican Parties.

Jimmy Carter and the 1970s

When Jimmy Carter came into office (1977–1981) the economy was in a shambles. The costs of the Vietnam War, the social programs of Johnson's Great Society Programs, and growing foreign competition pushed inflation and unemployment to post World War II highs. Carter tried to solve the problem by increasing federal spending and the money supply, but inflation climbed

> In the 1970s business groups operated as a class seeking to substitute tax breaks and corporate welfare for social welfare.

to 13.3%. The Federal Reserve following "standard" policy cut the money supply to tamp down inflation but interest rates rose again, to 18%, the highest in the nation's history. Home buying plummeted and unemployment reached 11%.

The answer to this complex set of problems was to implement some of the policies being pushed by corporate and financial elites. Though reluctant at first, Carter embraced deregulation. He freed from government regulations the transportation industries—air and surface—and the savings and loan industries. Those who championed deregulation, and who continue to make the same arguments for it today, claimed it would increase competition, stimulate new investment, and force inefficient firms to become more efficient or close down.[38] Deregulation of the savings and loan industries would lead to their eventual collapse in the 1980s and a massive bailout at the expense of taxpayers.

Corporate and business leaders had become more active in politics. During the 1970s and beyond they began to act as a *class* rather than as disparate firms lobbying the government for special favors. They adopted a shared strategy of working to defeat consumer protection and the reform of labor laws. They sought tax breaks, worked against anti-trust legislation, and challenged regulations.[39] Corporate welfare was to be substituted for social welfare.

Another problem Carter inherited was the oil embargo imposed by the Organization of the Petroleum Exporting Countries (OPEC) in 1973. The OPEC embargo was intended to punish those nations that had supported Israel during the "Yom Kippur War" of 1973, a disaster for the Arab countries, principally Egypt and Syria, which had initiated it. The average price of a gallon of gas jumped from 38.5 cents to 55.1 cents. The era of cheap gas was over and it had a lasting effect on U.S. foreign policy. Oil was understood to be a weapon that could be deployed against the economic and military interests of our country.

Carter tried to rally Americans to work together. In a July 15, 1979, televised address he told the nation that he had brought people from all walks of life to a retreat and asked them what it would take to solve our collective problems. These problems, he said, were much "deeper than gasoline lines or energy shortages, deeper even than inflation or recession." We were, he emphasized, facing a "moral and spiritual crisis."[40] It was a crisis of confidence.

> . . . It is a crisis that strikes at the very heart and soul and spirit of our national will. We can see this crisis in the growing doubt about the meaning of our own lives and in the loss of a unity of purpose for our nation.

The erosion of our confidence in the future is threatening to destroy
the social and political fabric of our nation . . .

Instead of worshiping God, he intoned, "too many of us now tend to worship
self-indulgence and consumption." He claimed we were no longer defined by
hard work, close families and communities but "by what one owns."

Though his speech was well received at the time it would later be turned
against him in his debates with Ronald Reagan who would offer Americans a
more optimistic view—because we were, Regan said, the most powerful nation
on Earth.

Reagan and the Evangelicals

Whereas Carter had lectured America about what was wrong with us, Reagan
promised a rosy future. Reagan crushed Carter in the 1980 campaign taking
489 electoral votes to Carter's 49, and the Republicans captured the Senate for
the first time since 1954. Reagan had promised voters we would be stronger at
home and abroad; we would spend more on the military; control crime; slash
regulations so that businesses could grow; and we would assure prosperity
by cutting taxes. (This is in essence the platform of today's Republican Party.)
To do all of these things and balance the budget we would need to cut welfare
spending.[41] Those with reduced taxes would, theoretically, spend their new-
found cash on second homes, cars, other consumption goods, and invest it in
expanding their businesses. The results would, supposedly, trickle down to the
masses. There is little evidence that cutting taxes increases the prosperity of
working men and women.

Wealth did not trickle down; it became more concentrated. During the
Reagan era, wages became stuck in place, corporate profits increased, and
the wealth of the 1% began to expand. *This represented the major turning point in
American history—a division between the haves and have-nots.* The Republican Party
was emerging as the clear representative of corporate America while at the same
time capturing the votes of morally conservative white Americans.

Reagan built on and took full advantage of Nixon's politics of resentment
and his Southern Strategy to bring white working-class voters (later called
Reagan Democrats) over to the Republican Party. He told voters of an African-
American welfare queen (fictitious) who was taking advantage of the government at the expense of hard-working Americans. She wore furs, jewelry, drove
a Cadillac, and received welfare. He played on racial resentment stoked by the
Civil Rights Movement and the Great Society Programs. He upped the ante on
the war on drugs which devastated inner-city communities.[42] He used the same

argument for states' rights—meaning that states could continue to oppress minorities—which George Wallace had used in his 1964 presidential campaign and Nixon had likewise embraced.

One of Reagan's first campaign stops in the 1980 presidential contest was at the Neshoba County fairgrounds in Mississippi. The fairgrounds were close to Philadelphia, Mississippi where three civil rights activists—James Chaney, David Goodman, and Michael Schwerner—had been murdered by whites and then buried in an earthen-filled dam. Though the event occurred in 1964, it was not forgotten by those in Neshoba County.

Standing before a crowd of 10,000 people chanting, "We want Reagan. We want Reagan," Reagan made clear where he stood on the matter of civil rights. "I believe in states' rights . . . I promise to restore to states and local governments the power that properly belongs to them." As *The New York Times* opinion writer, Bob Herbert, has argued, Reagan knew exactly what he was doing. "He was tapping out the code." A code which said to whites, I am with you. That he had intended to oppose civil rights was evident in his presidency. He tried to weaken the Voting Rights Act of 1965, opposed a national holiday for Martin Luther King, Jr., and tried to get rid of the federal tax ban on exceptions for private schools that practiced segregation.[43]

The Christian Right so far had made modest forays into politics during the 1960s, but tended to warn parishioners about the dangers of creeping communism and moral laxity rather than urging them to support one party over the other.[44] That would change with the rise of the Moral Majority in 1979. Like Nixon's silent majority, they were standing against an immoral minority that was leading the country down a path to hell. The Moral Majority was founded by Jerry Falwell (1933–2007) and his associates to mobilize Christian conservatives to support the political campaigns of politicians who shared their values—pro-life, opposition to gay rights, pro-states' rights, and so forth. The Moral Majority was an early supporter of Reagan. Its strength lay primarily in the South among Evangelical Christians and at its height was estimated to have upwards of 4 million members whose votes could and did sway elections.[45]

> Nixon mastered the strategy of making one's political opponent one's moral opponent.

Texas, a center of this New Christian Right, warmly embraced Reagan. W.A. Criswell, pastor of the First Baptist Church in Dallas, had opened a two-day conference in 1980 to rally good Christians to fight against humanism and homosexuality. Reagan, invited to address the crowd, delivered a memorable line: "I know you can't endorse me. But I want you to know I endorse you."[46] Thunderous applause followed. In the 1980 election, 84% of Texas Protestants voted for Reagan.

Like Nixon, Reagan played on the fear of those with different values. Nixon had mastered the politics of resentment wherein one's political opponent became one's **moral opponent**. This, of course, makes political compromise difficult or impossible because to compromise would be to act against your *own moral* principles. This logic divides America today. Playing on the fears of those who were members of the silent and moral majority would propel the next Republican President into office.

Race and Crime

The issue of race and crime helped George H.W. Bush capture the White House in the 1988 election. Running to succeed Reagan, Bush was pitted against the governor of Massachusetts, Michael Dukakis. Though Dukakis was not the author of legislation that allowed convicted prisoners weekend furloughs, he was blamed for its consequences. William R. Horton, serving a life sentence for a brutal murder, was released for the weekend but never returned. He committed assault, armed robbery, and rape before he was captured. The Massachusetts legislature quickly passed a bill prohibiting furloughs for inmates like Horton but Dukakis vetoed it, reasoning that it would cut the heart out of rehabilitation efforts. The political action committee (PAC) supporting Bush jumped on the opportunity and developed an attack ad which suggested Dukakis was weak on crime. They branded William Horton "Willie," and ran a menacing mug shot of "Willie" Horton. Bush frequently referred to Horton throughout the campaign. The purpose, as Bush's campaign manager Lee Atwater said, was to get voters to "wonder whether Willie Horton is Dukakis' running mate."[47] Fear of crime, specifically fear of Black crime, helped push the elder Bush into the White House. The need to create high paying jobs was not on his agenda but continuing the Reagan legacy was.

During the 1970s and 80s, the Republican Party became the home of two very different *class groupings*—a corporate elite seeking to reduce taxes and regulations and a group of disaffected working-class whites, Nixon's Moral Majority. The values of the Moral Majority centered on cultural nationalism, moral righteousness, Evangelical Christianity, right-to-life issues, and opposition to environmentalism, feminism, and affirmative action.[48] This meant that the Party could advance a conservative economic and political agenda that favored corporate America by appealing to the prejudices of the white working class in the North and South that was contrary to their economic interests. This tactic is still being used. The Republican Party has maintained their hold on power across the South and Middle America by working to restrict the voting rights of minorities and the reproductive rights of women while advancing a corporate-friendly agenda.

The Clinton Presidency

Free trade is one of the keystones of neoliberalism. When Reagan declared his candidacy for President, he proposed a North American agreement to include Canada, Mexico, and the United States which would permit the goods and people of the three countries to cross borders more freely.[49] The North American Free Trade Agreement (NAFTA) was hammered out during the Presidency of George H.W. Bush and then signed into law by President Clinton in 1993. The Heritage Foundation, a conservative think tank which had been a strong advocate for the bill, proclaimed the realization of Reagan's vision, noting that the "politics of hope" had triumphed over the "politics of fear," meaning the fear of unions who believed the jobs of their members would be shipped south of the border. Writing for the Heritage Foundation in 1993, Michael Wilson proclaimed,

> The approval of NAFTA not only represents a victory for the U.S. economy and the American people, it also deals a blow to organized labor and other protectionist forces. The agreement reaffirms the American commitment to competition and free enterprise . . .[50]

What it presaged was the slow drain of jobs out of the country which then flowed back in as goods to the shelves of Wal-Mart, Target, and Costco. The left-leaning consumer rights organization, Public Citizen, estimates that NAFTA led to the loss of upwards of 1 million well-paying jobs.[51] Whatever the number may be, the reality is that free trade agreements have had a negative impact on the working class.

Some have seen Clinton's signing of the bill as a capitulation to the agenda of neoliberalism. As the economist Michael Meeropol has argued, Clinton came into office proclaiming, "People first," and left after abjectly surrendering to the politics of neoliberalism.[52] Clinton initially tried to roll back Reagan's neoliberal agenda. During the 1994 Congressional election campaign, the Republicans embraced a platform called a *Contract with America*: if they took the House of Representatives they would shrink the size of government, lower taxes, promote entrepreneurial activity, and institute both tort and welfare reform.

After the Republicans took back the House, Clinton decided he would have to "compromise" with them. He adopted populist positions such as a middle-class tax cut and used what was termed "triangulating," which involved pushing back against the Democratic Party's base on issues like welfare, crime, and trade. He signed the Welfare Reform Bill of 1996, or the Personal Responsibility and Work Opportunity Act of 1996, which the U.S. Chamber of Commerce celebrated as a return to the ethic of work. Welfare was ended as an entitlement program; benefits were restricted to two years; professional and occupational licenses were denied to illegal immigrants; and the funds were allocated to states as block grants.[53] States were permitted to place additional requirements on welfare recipients, and a number did. Clinton authorized $16 billion for new prisons and more police and his wife, Hillary Clinton, stumped for the bill, claiming there were "super predators" in the inner cities who needed to be "brought to heel."

Clinton adopted the pro-market orientation of the Republicans and wedded it with traditional Democratic concerns such as civil rights, protection for the environment, and higher taxes on the wealthiest Americans. Strategies for deregulation were begun under Carter, deepened under Reagan, and continued under Clinton. Free trade policies supported by Clinton opened up new markets and innovation in technology helped to create a surge in economic growth and the number of jobs.[54] But this growth was not evenly distributed and it disguised the fact that we were becoming a nation of debtors in hock to banks.

Credit card debt soared in the 1990s, as families were borrowing to make ends meet. During the 1990s the average American family's credit card debt rose by 53%. Americans were not using their cards for frivolous purposes. Their wages remained stagnant even as the economy boomed. Housing and health care costs increased. High rates and fees on cards meant that some "American families found themselves perpetually indebted to the credit card industry," one of the most profitable sectors of the banking industry.[55] This growing debt either deterred or delayed people's entry into the middle class, or their ability to hold on to their slippery position on the class ladder.

The Bank Bailout and the Housing Collapse of 2008

During Reagan's administration, the finance industry continued to grow at the expense of the rest of the economy and rules governing its management shrank.[56] By 2015 finance accounted for around 25% of GDP, while manufacturing continued its downward trend, dropping from 30% of GDP in 1950 to 12% by 2015.[57] This represented a massive shift in national wealth to bankers and hedge-fund managers ($280 billion by 2010) and away from working Americans.[58]

Banks and financial institutions became such an integral part of the economy that they were deemed "too big to fail." During the Great Depression of the 1930s, over 5,000 banks had gone under and many depositors lost all of their money. In response, government passed the Glass-Steagall Act as part of the Banking Act of 1933. The Act created the Federal Deposit Insurance Corporation to protect customers' deposits and, to keep the costs of insurance down, prohibited commercial banks from investing in anything other than government bonds and other low-risk ventures. High-risk ventures were left to investment banks, which issued stocks and bonds. This separation would change with repeal of the Glass-Steagall Act in 1999, the result of a $300 million lobbying effort by banking and financial services who wanted to break down the separation of commercial and investment banks.

As the Nobel-prize winning economist Joseph Stiglitz has explained, the financial crisis of 2008 and the collapse of the housing-market bubble was driven in part by the fact that banks and investment houses were now wedded.[59] To take just one example, Goldman-Sachs became an all-service firm brokering initial public offerings (IPOs), lending money for real estate, and selling stocks and bonds to investors. Risk and conflicts of interest multiplied. Banks were even making "mega-bets with one another through complicated instruments such as derivatives, credit-default swaps, and so forth."[60] They knowingly created risky home loans and rewarded agents who falsified credit applications. The Federal Securities and Exchange Commission (SEC) made things worse in 2004 when they allowed investment banks to increase their debt-to-capital ratio from 12:1 to 30:1, which meant that whatever real assets they had could be leveraged to take on even more risk. Ratings agencies like Moody's and Standard and Poor's, whose job it was to assure investors that all was well, were also part of the problem. Paid by the very firms whose products they were supposed to grade, they rated toxic mortgages as safe for pension funds and commercial banks. All of this ushered in the reign of casino capitalism, which enriched bankers and beggared the middle and working classes.[61] Many Americans were furious. It wasn't just, as the political writer Matt Taibbi declared, "because a tiny group of crooks on Wall Street built themselves beach houses in the Hamptons," or "caused property values in their neighborhoods to collapse"; it was that they were asked to pay for "this criminal responsibility with bailouts funded with their tax dollars."[62] Many voters had had enough.

> The origins of the Tea Party lay in Big Tobacco's fight against restrictions on smoking and tobacco taxes.

The Rise of the Tea Party

On February 18, 2009 the Obama administration announced a plan to aid 9 million homeowners facing foreclosure because of the financial collapse. The plan was to spend $275 billion to help people lower their mortgage payments so they could stay in their homes. The next day in a live broadcast from the floor of the Chicago Mercantile Exchange an editor for CNBC Business News, Rick Santelli, went on a rant. He shouted the government was rewarding bad behavior and that those people who had knowingly gotten high-risk mortgages were "losers" who deserved no support. He suggested holding a "Chicago Tea Party" where derivatives would be dumped in the river.[63] His remarks went viral and the notion of Tea Party patriots (modeled on the Sons of Liberty who dumped British tea into Boston Harbor on December 16, 1773) caught on with conservative voters who had long demanded a smaller government, less debt, and lower taxes. Tax revolts were nothing new, as Tax Day protests with reference to the Boston Tea Party had been around since the 1990s, but they had never gained sufficient attention to make them into a national movement. It took the financial collapse to create the conditions for the movement's growth.[64] Upwards of 1,000 chapters sprang up around the country. However, the Tea Party movement was anything but a grassroots effort.

A team of researchers at University of California, San Francisco traced the origins of the Tea Party movement to a 1980s effort by the tobacco industry to oppose restrictions on smoking and tobacco taxes. Tobacco lobbyists used rhetoric and images that evoked the 1773 Boston Tea Party as part of a "smokers' rights" campaign. If we infringed the rights of smokers, we would be infringing on freedom itself.[65] Before the Tea Party captured public attention, the Citizens for a Sound Economy (CSE) had already started what they called the US Tea Party Project. Partly funded by tobacco interests, its goals morphed to opposing *all* tax increases and to arguing relentlessly for an end to government regulations of *all* kinds.[66] CSE later split into Americans for Prosperity, a Koch-brothers funded effort, and Freedom Works. Billionaires put their money into strengthening the project because they hoped it would shrink the federal government and advance their interests.[67] The term *astroturfing* is used to refer to this kind of effort: elite support for what appears to be a spontaneous community effort but isn't.

Once the Tea Party attracted national attention, mainly as a result of Fox News giving its protests extensive coverage during the early years of the Obama administration, political operatives leapt at what they saw as an opportunity to advance their own interests. In Sacramento, California the GOP political consulting firm, Russo Marsh & Rogers, founded the Tea Party Express as a way of harnessing the energy of activists to elect conservative politicians and to oppose the agenda of the new President, Obama.[68] The movement comprised 1,000 different groups at its zenith and had a loose organizational structure. Local organizations exercised substantial influence in the election of legislators, who shared their views of the need for a less intrusive federal government and lower taxes, to local, state, and national offices. Tea Party activists, most of whom were Republicans, turned their anger against members of their own party—RINOs (Republican in Name Only)—who had failed after being elected to uphold a conservative political agenda and failed to do anything meaningful, such as creating well-paying jobs and blocking immigrants who they believed were taking away their jobs. They backed insurgent Tea Party candidates instead of Republican Party stalwarts. Michele Bachman (R Minnesota), Paul Ryan (R Wisconsin), Tex Cruz (R Texas), and Marco Rubio (R Florida) all benefitted from Tea Party support and enough Tea Party conservatives were elected to the House to form the conservative voting bloc, Freedom Caucus.[69]

Tea Party rhetoric combined two related themes. First, there were activists interested in shrinking the federal government and reducing taxes, especially those taxes that went to help people who weren't like them. Second, some simply hated Obama and what they imagined he stood for—someone willing to raise taxes, pass health care legislation they would have to pay for, as well as help immigrants and minorities at their expense. During their rallies they used coded language (dog whistles) to express their resentments.[70] So by the time of the 2016 elections, there were voters on both the left and right who felt they had been abandoned by professional politicians in both parties. Only one primary candidate, Bernie Sanders, spoke clearly to issues dealing with income inequality. Hillary Clinton, his Democratic competitor, focused on issues that had defined the party since the time of her husband's presidency—a nod to minority and women's rights, and the embrace of a neoliberal agenda. On the Republican side, we had Trump who stood outside the traditions of his adopted party and promised good jobs, while offering voters reasons why they found themselves in the circumstances they did; they had been cheated by crooked politicians and had their jobs taken away by immigrants. Trump's language closely paralleled that of Richard Nixon, as he appealed to the average American ignored by elites and government bureaucrats.

From the 1960s the Democratic Party has had a much more diverse coalition of women, African-Americans, Hispanics, union members, and urbanites, who are difficult to bring together on one or two major issues. However, advancing civil rights issues, LBGT rights, or protecting the welfare state are *not* unifying issues for working-class members. The writer and political analyst Thomas Frank has argued that the Democratic Party turned its back on the working class and now caters to the interests of a professional-managerial class, made up of doctors, lawyers, university professors, and Silicon Valley entrepreneurs. These "new" Democrats are urban dwellers who believe in meritocracy and individual opportunity, and thus shy away from policies that would lift the working class out of poverty.[71]

> The populist rebellion of 2016 was both a cultural and class rebellion.

Steve Fraser in *Limousine Liberal* also sees the Democratic Party as having abandoned the working class. He believes that both the Republicans and Democrats represent narrow elites, but two distinct groups of them. For Fraser, the Democrats represent a new cosmopolitan, managerial elite and the "techno frontiersmen" like Mark Zuckerman of Facebook and Bill Gates of Microsoft. The Republicans, on the other hand, represent "mom-and-pop" capitalism, those who own small businesses, also "entrepreneurial maestros" such as the Koch Brothers.[72] However these two writers characterize both parties, neither believes they now represent the needs of working-class voters. How can we best understand the kinds of rebellions taking place at the moment?

White Trash and Hillbillies

The populist rebellion of 2016 was as much a *cultural rebellion* as it was a *class rebellion*. Social class is a complex phenomenon composed of culture, consciousness, and economic position. Consciousness refers to how we perceive ourselves in relationship to others in society (and how they perceive us); culture refers to the range of practices and beliefs that shape our daily lives and our interaction with others. Economic position refers to the work we are paid to do. Social class is not a fixed category; it evolves over time in relationship to specific economic and historical circumstances. The working class of the 1950s is not the working class of today. Historically, we used to refer to *the* working class and assumed there was uniformity in how members of this class perceived and responded to the world. They were, as theory would have it, people who sold their labor power which meant they stood in opposition to those who pulled the levers of economic and political power. The union men and women of the 1950s who proclaimed, "Working class and proud of it!" are no longer with us. Today, we have a new designation for a portion of the working class, the *white* working class. The white working class takes on the character of a distinct ethnic group standing in opposition to those who are not white and those who do not share their cultural values.[73] It is a form of nationalism and can be infused with racism. Seeing class as multidimensional helps to answer the question: Why do some people, especially those stuck in place economically, vote against their own class or economic interests?[74]

To answer this question the sociologist Arlie Hochschild spent five years traveling from Berkeley, California to the bayous of Louisiana. She focused on an area where people were suffering from environmental crises caused by oil and chemical companies, where there were high rates of poverty, poor health, and low life expectancy. People had every reason to embrace the liberal welfare state, strong policies to protect the environment, and politicians who would help them, but they did not. Instead they voted for a conservative governor (Bobby Jindal) who slashed budgets for education and social welfare, gave tax breaks to companies, gutted state regulatory agencies, and embraced Tea Party politics. Hochschild met people who worked for chemical companies, truck drivers, mechanics, salesmen, and housewives. She attended church services, Trump rallies, and fish fries to better understand people's motivations. Eventually she constructed what she called a "deep story," one that she believed captured the "hopes, fears, pride, shame, resentment, and anxiety in the lives of those [she] talked with."[75]

The deep story she constructed was one grounded in the American Dream of progress and one widely shared by most Americans. It assumes that if you are a moral person, work hard, suffer through layoffs, put in long hours, and work in dangerous conditions you will have a good life and will do better than your parents. You are standing patiently in line waiting for your turn at the American Dream, but the line seems to no longer be moving. It might even be moving backwards. Your income and that of your friends has dropped over the last 20 years and good paying jobs are hard to find or nonexistent. You don't understand why this is happening, because you are a good person. You go to church, believe in monogamy, are patriotic, care about your family and your community. Yet you and your children are losing out, because *other people are cutting in line ahead of you*. Even worse, the federal government and the Democrats are helping them do so. Affirmative action, championed by educated elites, is allowing women, immigrants, refugees, and others to get in line ahead of you.

None of this is *fair* because it is "people like *you* who have made this country great." Furthermore, you are tired of being asked to sympathize with line cutters who may have it better than you do. You are tired of liberals suggesting you are ignorant, racist, or homophobic because you object to what is obviously unfair.[76] When Hochschild related this deep story to her Louisiana acquaintances and asked if it captured their lives, all of them agreed it did. They felt their culture, their way of life, was under assault. Like other Americans they wanted a good job and fair wages, but it was not just wages that had driven them to the right. They were shocked to find their values and way of life discredited by liberals. Their very dignity was being assaulted.

Related to and driven by class is the working man's concept of dignity. Michèle Lamont, Harvard professor of sociology, interviewed 150 blue-collar workers in France and the United States and compared their values with those of the middle class. What she found was that there is a set of distinct values and culture embraced by workers. It is a reverence for the work ethic and a disciplined self that causes them not to indulge, to save money, to live up to one's obligations, and to maintain close family ties. Given these values, it is not surprising that working men don't want handouts and they don't want others to receive them. They also have an interactive style that values straightforwardness, consistency, and integrity.[77] This is why some like Trump's "straight talk," speech not filtered for political correctness.

> Battles over economic issues have been transformed through the politics of resentment to battles over values.

The Battle over Values

Although many members of the American right suffer from low wages, poor health, and a lack of opportunity, the battle has been transformed from one focused on economic issues to one focused on *values*. It is seen by many on the right as a battle between those who ask for rights based on nothing more than their *individual identities*, and those who work hard, engage in righteous living, and *wait their turn*. This is one of the reasons why what is loosely termed *political correctness* is so galling to those who see themselves lacking opportunity. Political correctness seems to affirm the rights and suffering of those cutting in line while denying the rights and suffering of those who do not.[78] Those on the right believe that we have equality of opportunity and that failure to thrive and do well can only mean that people did not put forth sufficient effort to succeed. On the left, the perception is that people who do not share their values are ignorant white trash, clutching their Bibles and guns. These divisions of class and culture have deep roots in American history, dating to the founding of the American republic.

As the historian Nancy Isenberg observed in her provocatively titled *White Trash*, poor southern whites developed a culture that looks very similar to that described by Hochschild, where family, faith, patriotism, and a deep suspicion of the federal government are paramount.[79] This culture has been either denigrated or celebrated for its outlaw character by coastal elites and the mass media. But in either case, it is not a culture to be taken seriously.

There was, however, an ironic twist to the notion that in the valleys of Appalachia, in the bayous, in the small towns of the South and in the backwoods of the Carolinas and Georgia, there was a separate culture. Some of those on the downward rungs of the economic ladder fully embraced the culture. They were proud "rednecks." Rednecks were a class with their own ethnic heritage but a class that substituted its own culture for economic position.[80] Identifying also as members of a *white working class* they both celebrated their culture and distinguished themselves from those who were not white. This culture of a white working class "mixes race and class into a volatile compound, privilege and disadvantage crammed into a single phrase."[81] It generates a politics of resentment and has been easy to exploit by the alt-right and those politicians who play the race card.

Moral Shock and Moral Reasoning

In 2016 a number of Trump voters claimed they wanted to "Take Their Country Back." For some, that meant taking it back from a Black President. It also meant, as the conservative writer and essayist Joseph Epstein noted, taking it back from the cultural warriors who failed to recognize the values of their less fortunate compatriots. These warriors were the ones who pushed multiculturalism, identity politics, and political correctness. Epstein asked us to imagine a Trump supporter witnessing this fictitious montage on television or a right-wing website:

> Black Lives Matter protesters bullying the latest object of their ire; a lesbian couple kissing at their wedding ceremony; a mother in Chicago weeping over the death of her young daughter, struck by an errant bullet from a gang shootout; a panel earnestly discussing the need for men who "identify" as women to have access to the public lavatories of their choosing; college students . . . railing about the imagined psychic injuries caused by their professors or fellow students.[82]

The term **moral shock** was coined by the sociologist James M. Jasper to explain why people might join a social movement in the absence of previously existing social ties. They join because some events are so morally reprehensible to them that they must act. Not acting would be a betrayal of all they stand for. As Jasper says, "for a moral shock to lead to protest, it must have an explicit cognitive dimension as well as moral and emotional ones."[83]

Some pro-life advocates make use of graphic images to *shock people into supporting their cause*. People for the Ethical Treatment of Animals (PETA) have secretly videotaped disturbing scenes of cattle and poultry being slaughtered to make their case and mobilize people. I believe we can extend the concept of moral shock to include the shock that occurs when people feel their most important values are threatened and they must act. A neighbor of mine who voted for Donald Trump said after his election, "Now Life is safe." Trump, she believed, would appoint conservative, pro-life judges to the bench. People are fighting over what they regard as *morally* right and wrong. And in such fights facts can suffer or are simply irrelevant.

> The dual concepts of moral shock and moral reasoning explain why people mobilize and why "logic" alone is unlikely to change their positions.

Philosophers and psychologists use the concept of **moral reasoning** to explain the processes by which people try to distinguish between right and wrong before acting. Moral choices can be rational choices, as when one makes an economic choice that benefits either themselves or those close to them. But moral reasoning is primarily emotional.[84] Moral reasoning can be immune to hard facts.

The dual concepts of moral shock and moral reasoning can help to explain both why people mobilize—to protect their dignity and what they feel is sacred—and why "logic" alone is unlikely to cause people to change their positions.[85] In Chapter 5, where I discuss opposition to vaccinations from people who believe they cause autism, each new fact advanced by the scientific community to prove otherwise is swatted away. Deniers, who are seeking explanations for why a child is autistic and what might cure them, cannot accept the fact that no cure is available. Fear and uncertainty create the conditions for emotional appeals, and yield to denial. Value-based divisions driven by changes in our economy and our social relations are tenacious and difficult to change.

The German social theorist Jürgen Habermas argued that late capitalism is characterized by what he termed a *legitimation crisis*, or a decline in people's faith that the state has the administrative capacity to solve their problems.[86] If there is no legitimating ideology that helps with the integration of society, then people will create their own ideologies and seek to find meanings in groups that exist outside the bounds and control of the society.[87]

We hold tight to what we already know and seek out others who will reaffirm our cherished beliefs. No matter what we believe we can find others on social media sites who hold the same opinions. Or we will find the like-minded in our churches, voluntary associations, and neighborhoods. We do *not* seek out information that doesn't fit our ideas about how the world works, who is against us, and who we can count on. As we will see in a discussion of groups on the left and on the right, dense information and interaction networks form like black holes. Every idea and opinion is sucked into such a small dense space that no light can penetrate. Closed world views are the result. Belief that major institutions have failed us and that we can trust nobody outside of our immediate social circles erodes the very basis of a democratic society.

Cultures of Defiance

Social scientists use the term *culture* to refer to a group's particular way of life. A culture encompasses practices, beliefs, values, and symbols. As such the concept of culture embraces a wide range of groups: gang cultures, drug cultures, gun cultures, geek and nerds as well as the culture of the Appalachian coal miner or the Montana rancher. But not all cultures are oppositional. I am using the term *cultures of defiance and resistance* in this work to refer to cultures which stand in opposition to the dominant culture of neoliberal capitalism and the elites who support it. They seek to challenge and change it through some form of organized resistance. Cultures of defiance and resistance are:

- Driven by moral shock and outrage and anchored in fundamental values about right and wrong.

- Demands for justice.
- Characterized by moral reasoning which seldom yields to facts or scientific reasoning.
- Generated by fear and anger.
- Communities of meaning that seek to create and affirm a sense of dignity and self esteem.
- Tribal in nature, closed off from contradictions, and usually reinforced by social media, rather than face-to-face interaction.
- Opposed to elites: governmental, corporate, or social.
- Demands for freedom, which can be as personal as control over one's body and that of family members or freedom from economic, legal, and social oppression.

Cultures of defiance can be grounded in one's economic position or in values that stand in opposition to elites. Often, they combine both elements. The precarious economic position of the white working class, ignored by both parties, was an important reason for these voters casting their lot with Trump. Some, like those described by Hochschild, were also responding positively to Trump's cues that their fears (immigrants were taking their jobs or corporate and government elites had negotiated trade deals that caused the loss of manufacturing jobs) were recognized and that their *values* would be honored—values that placed faith, family, local community, and patriotism first. Moral outrage, driven by sexual, economic, and political discrimination, gives rise to movements that say, "Enough!" With the beginning of Trump's Presidency in 2017 we have seen a number of newly mobilized groups that closely fit my definition of cultures of defiance. The Women's March that occurred across the country immediately following his inauguration numbered in the millions. Environmental groups, immigrant groups, and social justice movements are working to defy and resist what they see as an assault on their dignity, their values, and the society.

Implications for Social Movement Theory: Social Class, Emotions, and Great Refusals

We underestimate the mobilizing power of fear and anger and a sense of violation of one's sense of dignity. Slave revolts, violent worker strikes and rebellions, and the Civil Rights Movement all serve as examples of people acting to take control of their lives. Mobilizing has driven our political processes since the founding of the Republic. Yet when we think of reasons why people mobilize, we often fail to give social class its due. Social class has a powerful explanatory value in understanding why people take some of the actions they do. Did working-class Americans vote against their *class interests* when they voted for a Republican outsider in 2016? I would argue the answer is "No." First, 62% of white women without college degrees voted for Trump over Clinton by a 28-point margin (62% to 34%). White women as a whole cast 53% of their votes for Trump. Only white women with college degrees cast a plurality (51%) of their votes for Clinton. If just 50% of all women had voted for Clinton she would have won the election hands down. But they did not, because class was more important than gender. One reason working-class women voted in such high numbers for Trump was that working-class women were worried about diminished opportunities for their husbands and sons.[88] Rural voters cast their votes for Trump and, as we noted above, these votes track closely to local economic conditions. While class matters it is not the whole story.

Joan C. Williams, a distinguished professor in law at the UC Hastings School of Law, suggests that workers supported Trump because of the issue of dignity:

> Manly dignity is a big deal for working-class men, and they're not feeling they have it. Trump promises a world free of political correctness and a return to an earlier era, when men were men and women knew their place . . . Many (men) still measure masculinity by the size of a paycheck.[89]

So when a politician promises a paycheck, or at least appears to recognize the suffering of working Americans, they pay attention. They don't want the mythical job that pays $15.00 an hour at McDonald's; they want, as Williams tells us, "steady, stable, full-time jobs that deliver a middle-class life" to the 63% of Americans who do not have a college degree and are in fact deeply suspicious of academia. Resentment of those who do not share these values, and elites who do not understand them, are also part of this mix.

> Contemporary social movements can be understood as active attempts by people to create the conditions of their own existence.

We need to understand movements of all types as active attempts by people to create the conditions for their own existence.[90] Human agency is primary; that is, *we* are driving history. Movements are an active testing of the borders of society as people attempt to not only understand their own experiences but to change them. Movements are attempts by us to realize our humanness and to meet basic human needs such as affection, understanding, autonomy, and respect.[91] Today's social movement can be understood against the historical background of neoliberalism and the politics of resentment it gives rise to, and the efforts of people to find meaning in their lives. Protests against a market economy are nothing new.

In the 1960s, the German-American social theorist Herbert Marcuse (1898–1979) argued in *One Dimensional Man* that in both capitalist societies and in the communist society of what was then the Soviet Union new forms of oppression had arisen that were not dependent on the use of force or violence.[92] Rather, we had been fooled into thinking that freedom and well being were to be achieved through consumption. Consumerism, driven by advertising, was a new form of social control. We had become cogs in an industrial machine, working to support needs defined by others and offered consumer products to satiate these new needs, instead of meeting our needs for acceptance and understanding.

One Dimensional Man was one of the most important books of the 1960s.[93] It offered its readers, particularly those involved in the student and protest movements of the time, an alternative to consumer-driven capitalism. It advocated a **Great Refusal**: a refusal to avoid unnecessary consumption and a refusal to engage in unnecessary work. It provided a way to stand in opposition to an over-rationalized, bureaucratic society. As we will see, many of the movements we will examine in the following chapters are still involved in this struggle: how to find meaning, dignity, freedom, and respect in modern society. One of the reasons oppositional behavior continues is that the conditions Marcuse described in the 1960s are still present. *Movements of resistance and defiance are best understood as a challenge to the dominant culture and as an attempt to take control of our lives.*

There is no inevitable outcome to social protests. They are constrained as well as shaped by specific social and economic conditions. Social history does not unfold in terms of some inevitable law. Rather, history evolves as people struggle to overcome oppression and run up against opposing forces and unanticipated barriers to change. Bursts of mobilization are followed by counter mobilization. It was not inevitable that neoliberalism would emerge as the dominant economic and "moral" force it is today. Each step, from Roosevelt to Nixon and on, was contested. It is still being fought against.

As we look back on the Trump phenomenon of 2016, it can be understood as a **social movement of the disconnected and disaffected** seeking to affirm their identities and to gain respect for their position, no matter what that position might be or how strange it must seem to those who do not share those beliefs. Like Howard Beale it was a shout of anger, amplified by Fox News and stoked by the flames of alt-right media sources such as Brietbart News. The presidential election provided an unusual opportunity for such a movement to gain both national and international attention as it challenged received wisdom about how political campaigns should be conducted and which topics were and were not taboo in a public forum. The movement disinterred issues thought to be long buried such as racism and resentment. It should not, however, overshadow the fact that other movements of defiance and resistance were present. And, if the beginning of 2017 serves as an example, there will be a wide range of both new and old groups that continue to organize to change our current political and economic system and to assert our basic human nature.

Notes

1 Douglas Kellner. 2017. *American Nightmare: Donald Trump, Media Spectacle, and Authoritarian Populism.* Boston: Sense Publishers, p.3.

2 Nick Corasaniti and Maggie Haberman. August 9, 2016. "Donald Trump Suggests 'Second Amendment People' Could Act Against Hilary Clinton." *The New York Times.* Retrieved on February 3, 2017 at: www.nytimes.com/2016/08/10/us/politics/donald-trump-hillary-clinton.html?_r=0.

3 The Civil Rights Movement of the 1960s was definitely greater, as was the Populist movement of the late 19th century.

4 *British Broadcasting System.* November 9, 2016. "Reality Check: Who Voted for Donald Trump?" Retrieved on January 12, 2017 at: www.bbc.com/news/election-us-2016-37922 587; *The Economist.* November 19, 2016. "Illness as an Indicator." Retrieved on January 12, 2017 at www.economist.com/news/united-states/21710265-local-health-outcomes-predict-trumpward-swings-illness-indicator. The Economist measured illness as the number with obesity, diabetes, heavy drinking, amount of physical exercise and life expectancy; Andrew Flowers. November 11, 2016. "Where Trump Got His Edge." *FiveThiryEight.* Retrieved on January 12, 2016 at: https://fivethirtyeight.com/features/where-trump-got-his-edge/; Alec Tyson. November 9, 2016. "Behind Trump's Victory: Divisions by Race, Gender, Education." *Pew Research Center.* Retrieved on January 12, 2017 at: www.pewresearch.org/fact-tank/2016/11/09/behind-trumps-victory-divisions-by-race-gender-education/.

5 Aaron Zitner. July 17, 2016. "U.S. Seen on Wrong Track by Nearly Three-Quarters of Voters." *Wall Street Journal.* Retrieved on January 13, 2017 at: www.wsj.com/articles/u-s-seen-on-wrong-track-by-nearly-three-quarters-of-voters-1468760580.

6 AFL/CIO. January, 2016. "Working America: Report from the Field." Retrieved on February 8, 2017 at: www.workingamerica.org/frontporchfocusgroup.

7 Gerald F. Seib. April 5, 2016. "Optimism is a Casualty in Campaign." *Wall Street Journal.* Retrieved on January 13, 2017 at: www.wsj.com/articles/optimism-is-a-casualty-in-campaign-2016-1459784331.

8 Steve Peoples and Emily Swanson. May 31, 2016. "AP-NORC Poll: Voters Feel Disconnected, Helpless during 2016 Campaign." *Associated Press, NORC.* Retrieved on January 13, 2017 at: http://bigstory.ap.org/article/c5e973e9c94748bb8cabedd2ce903321/ap-norc-poll-voters-feel-disconnected-helpless-2016.

9 The consequence of refilling it with billionaires has yet to be determined.

10 Peggy Noonan. May 7–8. "Trump Was a Spark, Not the Fire." *Wall Street Journal*, A11.

11 Drew Desilver. October 9, 2014. "For Most Workers, Real Wages Have Barely Budged for Decades." *Pew Research Center.* Retrieved on January 30, 2017 at: www.pewresearch.org/fact-tank/2014/10/09/for-most-workers-real-wages-have-barely-budged-for-decades/.

12 By working-class voter I am referring to those who engage in waged labor and whose household income puts them in the middle-third of the income distribution. This would be those households earning between $56,000 (the median household income) and $73,300 (the average household income).

13 Charles M. Blow. February 4, 2016. "White America's 'Broken Heart'." *The New York Times.* Retrieved on January 13, 2017 at: www.nytimes.com/2016/02/04/opinion/white-americas-broken-heart.html?_r=0.

14 Data from the political scientists Marc Hetherington and Drew Engelhardt reported by Thomas B. Edsall. May 11, 2016. "How Many People Support Trump but Don't Want to Admit It?" *The New York Times*. Retrieved on January 13, 2017 at: www.nytimes.com/ 2016/05/11/opinion/campaign-stops/how-many-people-support-trump-but-dont-want-to-admit-it.html.

15 Trip Gabriel. January 12, 2017. "In Iowa, Trump Voters are Unfazed by Controversies." *The New York Times*. Retrieved on January 13, 2017 at: www.nytimes.com/2017/01/12/us/ donald-trump-iowa-conservatives.html.

16 Robert Leonard. January 5, 2017. "Why Rural America Voted for Trump." *The New York Times*. Retrieved on January 13, 2017 at: www.nytimes.com/2017/01/05/opinion/why-rural-america-voted-for-trump.html.

17 Chris Hedges. March 2, 2016. "The Revenge of the Lower Classes and the Rise of American Facism." *Truthdig*. Retrieved on February 8, 2017 at: www.truthdig.com/report/item/ the_revenge_of_the_lower_classes_and_the_rise_of_american_fascism_20160302.

18 For an overview of the history of neoliberalism see: David Harvey. 2005. *A Brief History of Neoliberalism*. New York: Oxford University Press.

19 Milton Friedman. 1962. *Capitalism and Freedom*. Chicago: University of Chicago Press.

20 Paul Treanor. 2005. "Neoliberalism: The Economic Model: Origins, Theory, Definition." Accessed on May 11, 2016 at: http://web.inter.nl.net/users/Paul.Treanor/neoliberalism. html.

21 Karl Marx. [1844] 1959. *Economic and Philosophic Manuscripts of 1844*. Moscow: Progress Publishers.

22 Of course, during the post-Civil War period there was vehement opposition to helping African-Americans.

23 Robert Wuthnow. 2014. *Rough Country: How Texas became America's Most Powerful Bible-Belt State*. Princeton, New Jersey: Princeton University Press.

24 Lauren Markoe. November 9, 2016. "White Evangelicals, Catholics, and Mormons Carried Trump." *Religion News Service*. Retrieved on January 30, 2017 at: http://religionnews. com/2016/11/09/white-evangelicals-white-catholics-and-mormons-voted-decisively-for-trump/.

25 Scott Martelle. August 12, 2015. "Viewing the Watts Riots through Different Eyes." *Los Angeles Times*. Retrieved on June 6, 2016 at: www.latimes.com/opinion/opinion-la/la-ol-watts-reactions-kennedy-king-johnson-eisenhower-20150810-story.html.

26 Mildred A. Schwartz. 1967. *Trends in White Attitudes toward Negroes*. University of Chicago: National Opinion Research Center. Retrieved on June 6, 2016 at: www.norc.org/PDFs/ publications/NORCRpt_119.pdf.

27 Gallup Poll. 1999. "Timeline of Polling History: Events that Shaped the United States and History." Washington, D.C: Gallup. Retrieved on June 6, 2016 at: www.gallup.com/ poll/9967/timeline-polling-history-events-shaped-united-states-world.aspx.

28 From Lyndon Johnson, White House tapes, 1964. Cited in Robert Wuthnow. 2014. *Rough Country*. See Wuthnow for a detailed discussion of how the values of Evangelical Christians shaped politics in response to what they saw as the moral decay of the country. See, in particular, Chapters 8–10.

29 Kevin P. Phillips. 1969. *The Emerging Republican Majority*. New Rochelle, New York: Arlington.

30 The White House. October 5, 1971. "Confidential Memorandum to the Attorney General, H.R. Haldeman." Exhibit No. 179. Retrieved on June 7, 2016 at: http://thenewyorker. typepad.com/online__georgepacker/files/dividing_the_democrats1.pdf.

31 Jeremy Engels. 2015. *The Politics of Resentment: A Genealogy*. University Park, Pennsylvania: Penn State Press. See, in particular, Essay II, "The Rise of the Politics of Resentment."

32 Dan Baum. April, 2016. "Legalize It All: How to Win the War on Drugs." *Harper's Magazine*. Retrieved on May 25, 2017 at: https://harpers.org/archive/2016/04/legalize-it-all/.

33 President Trump during his inaugural address and during his campaign speeches promised to get tough on crime.

34 Jeremy Engels. 2015. *The Politics of Resentment*, p.89.

35 See for example, Jeet Heer. February 18, 2016. "How the Southern Strategy Made Donald Trump Possible." *The Nation*. Retrieved on June 7, 2016 at: https://newrepublic.com/article/130039/southern-strategy-made-donald-trump-possible.

36 Public Policy Polling. February 16, 2016. "Trump, Clinton Still Have Big SC Leads." Retrieved on June 7, 2016 at: www.publicpolicypolling.com/main/2016/02/trump-clinton-still-have-big-sc-leads.html.

37 Lewis F. Powell, Jr. August 23, 1971. "Confidential Memorandum: Attack of American Free Enterprise System." Retrieved on June 7, 2016 at the Reclaim Democracy site: http://reclaimdemocracy.org/powell_memo_lewis/. Greater causal value is given to the Powell memorandum than is sometimes warranted. It did not by itself cause corporate America to fight back. It does, however, capture the mood of the moment and lays out a pathway to the triumph of neoliberalism.

38 Digital History. 2016. "Whipping Stagflation." Retrieved on June 8, 2016 at: www.digitalhistory.uh.edu/disp_textbook.cfm?smtID=2&psid=3360.

39 Thomas Edsall. 1984. *The New Politics of Inequality*. New York: Norton, p.128.

40 James Earl "Jimmy Carter." July 15, 1979. *Crisis of Confidence Speech*. Public Broadcasting System. Accessed on June 8, 2016 at: www.pbs.org/wgbh/americanexperience/features/primary-resources/carter-crisis/.

41 Patric H. Hendershott and Joe Peek. 1989. "Interest Rates in the Reagan Years." Washington, D.C.: National Bureau of Economic Research, Working Paper No. 3037. Retrieved on June 10, 2016 at: www.nber.org/papers/w3037.

42 Kenneth B. Nunn. 2002. "Race, Crime and the Pool of Surplus Criminality: Or Why the 'War on Drugs' Was a 'War on Blacks.'" *Journal of Gender, Race and Justice*. Vol.6:381–445. Available at: www.antoniocasella.eu/archila/nunn_2002.pdf.

43 Many have tried to rewrite the meaning of Reagan's speech but the reality is made clear by Bob Herbert. November 13, 2007. "Righting Reagan's Wrongs?" *The New York Times*. Retrieved on June 8, 2016 at: www.nytimes.com/2007/11/13/opinion/13herbert.html?_r=0.

44 They did so because to advocate for one candidate or party over another was to risk losing their tax exempt status.

45 Patrick Allitt. 2003. *Religion in American Since 1945: A History*. New York: Columbia University Press; Robert Liebman and Robert Wuthnow. 1983. *The New Christian Right*. New York: Aldine Publishing.

46 Cited in Robert Wuthnow. 2014. *Rough Country*, p.325. See Chapter 10 in its entirety for a discussion of the growth and insertion of the Christian Right into politics in the 1980s.

47 Cited in Roger Simon. November 11, 1990. "How a Murderer and Rapist became the Bush Campaign's Most Valuable Player." *Baltimore Sun*. Retrieved on June 9, 2016 at: http://articles.baltimoresun.com/1990-11-11/features/1990315149_1_willie-horton-fournier-michael-dukakis. For a full discussion of the campaign see Roger Simon. 1990. *Road Show: In America, Anyone Can become President, It's One of the Risks We Take*. New York: Farrar, Straus, and Giroux.

48 David Harvey. 2005. *A Brief History of Neoliberalism*, p.84.

49 Ray. February 6, 2011. "How Ronald Reagan Gutted the Middle Class with Free Trade." *Politicus USA's Archives (2008–2011)*. Retrieved on June 10, 2016 at: http://archives.politicususa.com/2011/02/06/reagan-free-trade.html.

50 Michael G. Wilson. November 23, 1993. "The North American Free Trade Agreement: Ronald Reagan's Vision Realized." Washington, D.C.: The Heritage Foundation, Executive Memorandum 371. Retrieved on June 10, 2016 at: www.heritage.org/research/reports/1993/11/em371-the-north-american-free-trade-agreement.

51 For a summary of the effects of NAFTA see: Mohammed Aly Sergie. February 14, 2014. "NAFTA's Economic Impact." Washington, D.C.: Council on Foreign Relations. Retrieved on June 10, 2016 at: www.cfr.org/trade/naftas-economic-impact/p15790.

52 Michael Allen Meeropol. 2000. *Surrender: How the Clinton Administration Completed the Reagan Revolution.* Ann Arbor: University of Michigan Press.

53 U.S. Department of Health and Human Services. 1996. *Personal Responsibility and Work Opportunity Reconciliation Act of 1996.* Retrieved on June 15, 2016 at: https://aspe.hhs.gov/report/personal-responsibility-and-work-opportunity-reconciliation-act-1996.

54 An analysis of Clinton's economic policies and which led to growth is provided by the economists Jeffrey Frankel and Peter R. Orszag. November 2, 2001. "Retrospective on American Economic Policy in the 1990s." Washington, D.C.: The Brookings Institute. Retrieved on June 15, 2016 at: www.brookings.edu/research/papers/2001/11/02useconomics-orszag.

55 Tamara Draut and Javier Silva. 2003. *Borrowing to Make Ends Meet: The Growth of Credit Card Debt in the '90s.* New York: Demos: A Network for Action and Ideas. Retrieved on June 16, 2016 at: www.demos.org/publication/borrowing-make-ends-meet-rapid-growth-credit-card-debt-america.

56 Mike Collins. February 4, 2015. "Wall Street and the Financialization of the Economy." *Forbes.* Retrieved on June 16, 2016 at: www.demos.org/publication/borrowing-make-ends-meet-rapid-growth-credit-card-debt-america.

57 Federal Reserve Bank of St. Louis. "Manufacturing as a Percentage of GDP." Retrieved on June 16, 2016 at: https://research.stlouisfed.org/fred2/series/VAPGDPMA.

58 Thomas Philippon. 2012. "Finance versus Wal-Mart: Why Are Financial Services So Expensive?" in Alan S. Binder, Andrew W. Lo, and Robert M. Solow, eds. *Rethinking the Financial Crisis.* New York: Russell Sage Foundation, Chapter 9, pp.235–246.

59 Joseph E. Stiglitz. December 9, 2008. "Capitalist Fools." *Vanity Fair.* Retrieved on June 16, 2016 at: www.vanityfair.com/news/2009/01/stiglitz200901-2.

60 Stiglitz. 2008.

61 For a discussion of casino capitalism see: Henry A. Giroux. 2014. *Zombie Politics and Culture in the Age of Casino Capitalism,* 2nd ed. New York: Peter Lang; Susan Strange, who coined the term, 1986. *Casino Capitalism.* Manchester, England: Manchester University Press.

62 Matt Taibbi. 2017. *Insane Clown President: Dispatches from the 2016 Circus.* New York: Spiegel & Grau.

63 Cited in full in Eric Etheridge. February 20, 2009. "Rich Santelli: Tea Party Time." *The New York Times: Opinionator.* Retrieved on February 1, 2017 at: https://opinionator.blogs.nytimes.com/2009/02/20/rick-santelli-tea-party-time/?_r=0.

64 There is another argument which suggests the Tea Party's rise was largely due to the election of President Obama and was not just a reaction to the bank bailout. Interviews conducted by Venessa Williams and Theda Skocpol found Tea Party members used the term "hatred" of Obama to describe their reactions to his election and fears of a tax-and-spend liberal government asking hard-working Americans to pay for freeloaders and immigrants. Cited in Erin O'Donnell. January–February 2012. "Tea Party Passions." *Harvard Magazine.* Retrieved on February 6, 2017 at: http://harvardmagazine.com/2012/01/tea-party-passions.

65 Elizabeth Fernandez. February 8, 2013. "Study: Tea Party Organizations Have Ties to Tobacco Industry Dating Back to 1980s." *University of California, San Francisco.*

Retrieved on February 2, 2017 at: www.ucsf.edu/news/2013/02/13507/study-tea-party-organizations-have-ties-tobacco-industry-dating-back-1980s. See also: Brooke Jarvis. February 13, 2013. "Big Tobacco's Tea Party Ties Exposed." *Rolling Stone*. Retrieved on February 2, 2017 at: www.rollingstone.com/politics/news/big-tobaccos-tea-party-ties-exposed-20130213. The study on which these two reports were based is: Amanda Fallin, Rachel Grana, and Stanton A. Glantz. February 8, 2013. "'To Quarterback Behind the Scenes, Third-Party Efforts'; The Tobacco Industry and the Tea Party." *Tobacco Control*. Retrieved on February 2, 2017 at: http://tobaccocontrol.bmj.com/content/early/2013/02/07/tobaccocontrol-2012-050815.abstract.

66 When Trump was elected, the oil and gas lobby rolled out plans developed by Koch-funded organizations to remove all of the regulations imposed during the Obama administration. See Eric Lipton. February 5, 2017. "G.O.P. and Trump Hurry to Slash Oil and Gas Rules, Ending Industries' 8-Year Wait." *The New York Times*. A1,15.

67 Jane Mayer. August 30, 2010. "Covert Operations." *The New Yorker*. Retrieved on February 2, 2017 at: www.newyorker.com/magazine/2010/08/30/covert-operations.

68 Justin Elliott. September 9, 2010. "What You Need to Know about the Tea Party Express." *Salon*. Retrieved on February 2, 2017 at: www.salon.com/2010/09/15/tea_party_express_a_force/.

69 The Tea Party has not gone away. Local chapters rallied behind President Trump in the wake of protests against his election.

70 Meghan A. Burke. 2015. *Race, Gender, and Class in the Tea Party: What the Movement Reflects about Mainstream Ideologies*. Lanham, Maryland: Lexington Books. Burke, however, suggests that Tea Party racism is simply American racism and does not differ from that of the left. However, there is clear evidence that status anxiety drives resentment against minority groups making advancements at what Tea Party activists perceive to be their expense. See, for instance, Venessa Williamson, Theda Skocpol, and John Coggin. 2011. "The Tea Party and the Remaking of Republican Conservatism." *Perspectives on Politics*. Vol.9(1):25–43.

71 Thomas Frank. 2016. *Listen Liberal: Or, What Ever Happened to the Party of the People?* New York: Metropolitan Books/Henry Holt & Company.

72 Steve Fraser. 2016. *The Limousine Liberal: How an Incendiary Image United the Right and Fractured America*. New York: Basic Books.

73 George Packer. October 31, 2016. "The Unconnected." *The New Yorker*, pp.48–61. Packer notes that the meaning of working class has been degraded at the present time to include those who are downwardly mobile, poor, even pathological, p.50.

74 I am not arguing that we should no longer think of class in terms of one's relationship to the means of production because many modern movements, e.g., Occupy Wall Street, are directed against an elite that controls the means of production. I am noting that class needs to be understood as having a cultural dimension that influences social behavior. Conservative Catholics and Evangelical Christians are more likely to share the same beliefs and culture regardless of their economic positions. Race, in some instances, also shapes behavior in ways not predicted by economic position and the same is true of gender. Not all women are feminists and not all feminists support Roe vs. Wade. Values matter.

75 Arlie Russell Hochschild. 2016. *Strangers in Their Own Land: Anger and Mourning on the American Right*. New York: Perseus, p.135.

76 Hochschild. 2016. *Strangers in Their Own Land*, Chapter 9, "The Deep Story."

77 Michèle Lamont. 2002. *The Dignity of Working Men: Morality and the Boundaries of Race, Class, and Immigration*. Cambridge, Massachusetts: Harvard University Press.

78 Charles Murray in his 2012 book, *Coming Apart: The State of White America, 1960–2010* (New York: Crown), explains why the working class abandoned the Democratic Party.

The Democrat support for affirmative action undercut working-class values of equality and individualism. People should not be advanced on the basis of their race or gender; it isn't fair.

79 Nancy Isenberg. 2016. *White Trash: The 400 Year History of Class in America.* New York: Viking.

80 Isenberg. 2016, p.187ff.

81 George Packer. October 31, 2016. "'The Unconnected: The Democrats Lost the White Working Class. The Republicans Exploited Them. Can Hillary Win Them Back?" *The New Yorker*, pp.46–61.

82 Joseph Epstein. June 11–12, 2016. "Why Trumpkins Want Their Country Back." *The Wall Street Journal*. A13.

83 James M. Jasper. 1997. *The Art of Moral Protest.* Chicago: University of Chicago Press, p.180.

84 James Rest. 1983. "Morality," in John H. Flavell and Ellen M. Markman, eds. *Handbook of Child Psychology: Cognitive Development.* Vol.3. New York: Wiley, pp.556–629.

85 For a discussion of how the denial of dignity serves as the basis of class movements see Sam Friedman, Diana Rossi, and Gonzalo Ralón. January 7, 2015. "Dignity Denial and Social Conflicts." *Rethinking Marxism*. Vol.27(1):65–84. See also: Sam Friedman. 1991. "Alienated Labor and Dignity Denial in Capitalist Society," in Berch Berberoglu, ed. *Critical Perspectives in Sociology.* Dubuque, Iowa: Kendall/Hunt, pp.83–91.

86 Jürgen Habermas. 1975. *Legitimation Crisis.* Boston, Massachusetts: Beacon.

87 For an excellent discussion of how and why people mobilize under late capitalism see Lauren Langman. 2013. "Capitalism, Crises, and 'Great Refusals': Critical Theory, Social Movements, and Utopian Visions." *Radical Philosophy Review*. Vol.16(3):349–374.

88 Laura Morgan Roberts and Robin J. Ely. November 17, 2016. "Why Did So Many White Women Vote for Donald Trump?" *Fortune.* Retrieved on February 7, 2017 at: http:// fortune.com/author/robin-j-ely/.

89 Joan C. Williams. November 9, 2016. "What So Many People Don't Get about the U.S. Working Class." *Harvard Business Review.* Retrieved on February 7, 2017 at: https://hbr. org/2016/11/what-so-many-people-dont-get-about-the-u-s-working-class. See also: Joan C. Williams. 2017. *White Working Class: Overcoming Class Cluelessness in America.* Boston, Massachusetts: Harvard Business Review Press.

90 Many contemporary movements can be understood from a Marxist perspective which sees movements as a challenge to neoliberalism and austerity, both of which would deny our species being. See, for example, Colin Barker, Laurence Cox, John Krinsky, and Alf Gunvald Nilsen, eds. 2013. *Marxism and Social Movements.* Leiden, The Netherlands: Brill.

91 The list of human needs comes from Manfred Max-Neef. 1987. "Human Needs and Human Development." *Rainforest Information.* Retrieved on February 7, 2017 at: www. rainforestinfo.org.au/background/maxneef.htm. There is a similarity between Marx's concept of *species being* and Max-Neef's understanding of our basic nature. For an example of how Marx's concept of species being can be used to understand modern social movements see: Lawrence Cox and Alf Gunvald Nilsen. 2014. *We Make Our Own History: Marxism and Social Movements in the Twilight of Neoliberalism.* London: Pluto Press.

92 Herbert Marcuse. 1964. *One Dimensional Man.* Boston: Beacon Press.

93 Douglas Kellner. Nd. "From 1984 to One Dimensional Man: Critical Reflections on Orwell and Marcuse." Retrieved on May 16, 2016 at: https://pages.gseis.ucla.edu/faculty/ kellner/Illumina%20Folder/kell13.htm.

The Battle in Seattle   **2**
and Occupy Wall Street
Movement
The Meaning of Success and Failure

Consider:

- Over 50,000 protesters marched in Seattle in 1999 and successfully shut down the WTO ministerial in a protest against globalization.
- Few effective mass mobilizations are spontaneous.
- Mass movements, regardless of the numbers involved, may do little to alter existing political and economic power structures.
- The success of a mass movement may be delayed for several years.
- Just as movements learn from one another, so do security forces.
- There has been a militarization of the response to protests.
- Protests have become ritualized.

The Battle in Seattle

It was a captivating sight. Red-jacketed steelworkers (USW) marched alongside those wearing sea turtle costumes. One carried a sign, "Teamsters and Turtles: Together at Last." The Battle of Seattle (November 1999), as it would come to be known, brought together union workers, environmentalists, social justice activists, anarchists, as well as American, Korean, and Mexican farmers. Activists came from South Africa, Malaysia, Panama, India, the Philippines, and South America. All toll, there were 1,300 organizations from over 80 countries, represented in the Seattle protests.[1] Upwards of 50,000 people protested. What brought them all together? They were all there to protest against the World Trade Organization (WTO), to delay its meeting, and to bring public attention to issues of globalization and how it affected the lives of ordinary citizens.

Though the title of this book promises a look at 21st-century social movements, it is important to look back to the protests in Seattle because they have shaped the tactics and strategies of the movements that followed in their wake. A rich trove of materials about the Seattle protests was written in the aftermath by those who organized them and went on to mobilize protests elsewhere.[2] Looking at the Seattle WTO protest allows us to consider what is meant by movement success, and which factors contributed to it. Many movements fail to achieve their immediate goal. That doesn't necessarily signal failure. There is often a significant time lag between an action and its positive outcome. As I argued in Chapter 1, the election of Donald Trump in 2016 was in part the result of Americans waking up and acting on the full meaning of globalization in their lives. These feelings, first stirred in Seattle, were given voice by both Bernie Sanders and Donald Trump in the 2016 election.

> Effective mass mobilizations are seldom spontaneous; they take time and planning to carry off.

Organizing for Seattle

We sometimes imagine social movements are simply spontaneous uprisings of moral outrage and anger that cause people to take to the streets, but that is rarely the case. Clearly in Seattle, mass mobilization took time and planning to carry off. As David Solnit, one of the chief organizers of the protests, noted, the Seattle protests were effective because of "a common strategic framework and massive grassroots education, organizing, alliance building, and mobilizing."[3] Mobilizations also depend on there being a clear grievance or set of grievances. Seattle protesters had a basket full. The protests in Seattle would bring the issue of globalization and an obscure organization, the WTO, into American living rooms, but problems related to globalization were not new to those in the developing world.[4] Some believe the Seattle protests had their roots in the earlier Zapatista uprising in Chiapas, Mexico on January 1, 1994; the same day the North American Free Trade Agreement (NAFTA) was signed by President Bill Clinton.

The Zapatistas mobilized to oppose globalization and corporate incursions into Chiapas. They understood NAFTA would undermine peasant life and rural communities.[5] Opening up Mexican agricultural markets to the industrialized production of corn and wheat from Canada and the United States would drive small Mexican farmers out of business. If a single word summed up the

Zapatista's response to capitalism and globalism it was: Enough![6] The Zapatistas ideology demanded a form of participatory governance in which everyone had an equal voice, which meant consensus decision making was essential. This model of participatory democracy was adopted both by the Seattle protesters and by those involved in Occupy Wall Street (OWS).

One outcome of the Zapatista rebellion was the creation of the Peoples' Global Action (PGA) Network, which became an important worldwide network for social justice groups and those opposed to free trade and globalization. When the Zapatistas called for an organizing meeting in the jungle to discuss how groups could coordinate tactics and strategies, 6,000 people from 40 different countries answered the call. They agreed on a set of principles, the first of which was: "A very clear rejection of capitalism, imperialism, and feudalism; all trade agreements, institutions and government that promote destructive globalization." They also advocated for direct action and civil disobedience. Their belief in autonomy and independence meant that the PGA had, and has, no formal organization or leadership; it is a network of a wide variety of groups that subscribe to its principles and can rally to one another's causes.[7] This *spoke-and-hub model of organizing* in which there is a goal, but groups are free to pursue their own strategies to accomplish it, is extremely effective; and, as we will see in the case of the protests in Seattle and those that followed, worrisome to public officials.

Another factor influencing the Seattle protests was the action of international institutions like the World Bank and the International Monetary Fund (IMF). During the 1990s, both the World Bank and the IMF operated with what has been termed the "Washington consensus." Money would be provided to nations in crisis, provided they opened their markets to free trade, which usually meant implementing austerity programs to pay back the loans. The assumption was that free trade would create the conditions both for the development of democratic institutions and economic growth. Yet in many cases it had the opposite effect. It destabilized democratic governments and led to the rise of strong men, as happened in Venezuela when the sitting president had to cut government subsidies for food, gasoline, and other necessities, which led to riots and protests. Venezuelans turned to Hugo Chavez in 1998 to pull them out of that misery.

Growing out of both the Zapatista movement and the protests against the policies of the IMF and the World Bank was the notion that *direct action* was critical in exposing the illegitimate and undemocratic nature of existing global financial institutions and for creating a new vision for democracy.[8] Groups that speak of direct action intend that business as usual be disrupted by a variety of means: erecting blockades, closing down streets, sitting-in, squatting, and sometimes directly sabotaging corporate and government property. For those who advocate for direct action, the protests themselves and how they are organized are supposed to demonstrate what freedom and democracy actually look like. How, then, were the protests in Seattle organized and how and why did 50,000 people come together?

Organizing began as early as May of 1999, after the San Francisco group Art and Revolution put out a call for mass direct action and street theatre for November 30, 1999.[9] West Coast activists met up face-to-face and drafted a proposal asking for support from Global Exchange, another San Francisco-based organization that focuses on human rights, as well as economic, environmental, and social justice issues. Global Exchange picked the dates for the protests, beginning on November 30, and a new Seattle-based group, Direct Action Network (DAN), was created to work with Global Exchange on guidelines for the protests, jail solidarity, and organizational structure. Outreach efforts began to other organizations such as the Ruckus Society, which had experience in tree climbing, scaling buildings, and hanging banners to make pro-environmental protests more effective. The Rainforest Action Network (RAN), which works to protect rainforests, the climate, and human rights, signed on to the proposal, as did the radical environmental group EarthFirst!. Those involved in preparations for the Seattle protests had all been involved in other protest activities and most of them knew and had worked with one another. A high level of trust and cooperation between multiple groups contributed to the success of the protests in shutting down the WTO meetings.

> A group of professional social movement entrepreneurs helped to mobilize participants in Seattle and to frame the issues.

A call went out from DAN through mailings and social media sites to come to Seattle. Broadsheets with in-depth stories and postcards were sent out to over 50,000 people with the message:

> It is time to raise the social and political cost to those who aim to increase the destruction and misery caused by corporate globalization . . . There is an incredible opportunity to use street theatre—art, dance, music, giant puppets, graffiti art and theater—and nonviolent direct action to simplify and dramatize the issues of corporate globalization and to develop and spread new and creative forms of resistance. This will help catalyze desperately needed mass movements . . . capable of challenging global capital and making radical change and social revolution.[10]

Outreach efforts to local colleges—Central Seattle Community College, the University of Washington, and Evergreen State University—were initiated, and students from Oregon and California colleges also received news of the

November 30 event. Training camps were organized for protesters, where they learned, among other things, that two gallons of sugar-water mixed with a bottle of Johnson and Johnson's "No More Tears" could be used as an eye wash to neutralize the effects of both tear gas and pepper spray.[11] Workshops and centers were set up for making giant puppets, signs, and banners. Global Trade Watch, a group sponsored by Ralph Nader's organization Public Citizen, took responsibility for many of the activities planned for the week—lectures, NGO tribunals, debates, and protests.[12] Attended by hundreds, the lectures and seminars were designed to help people understand the impact of the WTO on jobs and the environment. Groups like the RAN and the Ruckus Society set up offices in Seattle weeks and months before November 30, which served as meeting halls and organizational hubs for individuals and groups pouring into Seattle.[13] Environmentalists, human rights activists, anarchists, union members, the curious, and those who simply wanted to participate in a carnivalesque atmosphere came to Seattle, as did those intent on shutting down the WTO meeting.

The Issues: Why Were Turtles Marching with Steelworkers?

The Earth Island Institute made 500 sea turtle costumes for marchers to wear. They were protesting a ruling by the WTO that the United States' Environmental Protection Act (EPA) was an unfair trade barrier. Under U.S. rules, shrimp trawlers needed to use extruders that would free sea turtles caught in their nets. Under WTO rules it did not matter that sea turtles were listed as an endangered species by the United States; these rules violated the fishing rights of countries like Malaysia.

As Jane Cover, a participant in the protests, said:

> [T]he WTO, is an undemocratic and secretive organization. The WTO can rule that a country's laws and regulations are barriers to free trade, regardless of the fact that those laws were passed by the people or in the public interest.

Further, she noted, corporations heavily influenced decisions made in secret with no chance for the public to have input, and the WTO violated human rights because it did not prohibit products produced by child or prison labor. Another objection of some protesters was that the WTO encouraged the consumption of hormone treated beef and genetically engineered foods.[14] Mac Lojowsky, another participant, noted, "Since its inception, the WTO has ruled every single public health, labor, and environmental law brought before them [as] illegal trade barriers."[15] National sovereignty, human rights, and democracy were subordinated to the rules of the WTO.

Teamsters, steelworkers, longshoremen, and other union members were marching because they were protesting the disappearance of manufacturing jobs to low-waged countries. In 1999, 135 countries already belonged to the WTO and China was seeking admittance as a favored nation, which would mean they would pay low tariffs on the goods exported to the United States. Unions envisioned more jobs disappearing to China. On the other hand, corporations and investors saw a significant opportunity in trade deals because China represented one of the largest untapped markets in the world. China, however, would be the main beneficiary. In 2016, Chinese exports accounted for 22% of all world exports to the United States for a total of $389 billion, while the U.S. exported only $80 billion worth of goods to China.[16] This imbalance has led to job layoffs in the United States primarily in manufacturing.[17] By one estimate, the U.S. has lost 5 million manufacturing jobs to trading partners since 2000.[18] Labor unions saw the WTO as pitting workers from one country against another. It wasn't just wages that were at risk, but hard-won concessions for worker safety, health benefits, and pensions; benefits that did not need to be provided by companies moving to China, Mexico, or Taiwan. As I noted in Chapter 1, these issues would be seized on by Trump and Sanders, and eventually Hillary Clinton, during the 2016 presidential race.

The AFL-CIO mobilized between 25,000–40,000 union members from all over the country to participate in an organized, non-violent, and *permitted* march. Their goal was not abolition of the WTO but rather to reform it, to assure that labor standards were the same for all WTO members, whether in advanced or developing countries.

The Protests: November 28–December 1

Between 50,000–60,000 protesters marched in Seattle including the AFL-CIO, Direct Action Network, Sierra Club, Earth First!, Greenpeace, War Resisters League, Radical Cheerleaders, Global Exchange, Ruckus Society, International Workers of the World, Rainforest Action Network, National Lawyers Guild, and the Raging Grannies. The turtles marched first on Sunday, November 28, to call attention to the link between WTO policies and threats to the environment; they were joined, as noted, by steelworkers and longshoremen. Numbering about 2,000 strong, they proceeded under police escort to a small stage set up close to the convention center. Brent Blackwelder, head of Friends of the Earth, informed the crowd that the WTO was simply a global security force for corporations that intended "to stuff unwanted products, like genetically engineered foods, down people's throats."[19] After the speeches, some of the marchers headed to a McDonald's where a group of French farmers were gathered to denounce bioengineered foods. One farmer pledged to start a worldwide campaign against "Frankenstein" foods, denounced Monsanto, its bovine-growth hormone, and its Roundup Ready soybeans. An enthusiastic crowd then stormed McDonald's smashing its windows and urging workers and customers to join the protests.[20] At this point in time, the police did not react to the property damage and the crowd dispersed.

The largest events were scheduled for Tuesday, November 30, the day the WTO ministers were to assemble at the Convention Center. A rally was to be held at Memorial Stadium, with speeches followed by a march downtown. The group that assembled numbered upwards of 40,000 people and was composed of members and supporters of the AFL-CIO, Sierra Club, the Washington Council of Churches, Ralph Nader's Public Citizen, as well as other groups committed to a non-violent demonstration. This group had a permit to march and it was assumed by the city that it would be easily controlled.

Tactics

The massive labor march was to start at the Space Needle and proceed down to the Convention Center, clogging the streets to prevent the opening of the WTO assembly. However, labor leaders accepted a Wednesday meeting with President Bill Clinton on the promise that the AFL-CIO would get a seat at the WTO table. As a result, when the labor march finally got underway at 1 pm it was directed *away* from the Convention Center, where more militant groups were attempting to shut down the WTO meeting.[21] Nevertheless, about 5,000 of those marching with labor split off and headed to join those at the Convention Center.

This faction was composed primarily of affinity groups made up of six to ten people, which in turn were organized into clusters charged with a specific task such as blocking a road or blocking one of the entrances to the Convention Center where the WTO ministers were to meet. These groups were extremely effective because once a task had been assigned, it was up to the cluster to carry out their charge without supervision. As a matter of principle, the clusters were organized democratically with decisions made collectively. The intent was to model what a democratic society could be.[22]

One cluster organized a "wrapping" of the local newspaper, *Seattle Post Intelligencer*, to inform readers about the WTO. A four-page replica of the newspaper's front page contained fake stories with headlines like, "Boeing (a major Seattle employer) to Move Overseas." A group of 75 people in 24 separate cars managed to distribute 15,000 copies of the phony paper. Bundles of newspapers dropped off for delivery were snatched up and rewrapped. As one of the participants, Elijah, explained the process:

> You grab your initial stack of papers in the very first one you go to, and then you take off in the car right away, and the person in the back, or the two other people, are disassembling the papers and then reassembling them. It takes a while to make them look nice. Then you build another stack, and then when you come to the next place, the person in the passenger seat takes the papers and they run out and they do a switch. So then it doesn't take that long; you just switch, and then you're off again.[23]

This snatching and rewrapping of papers, like many of the other activities on November 30, required significant advanced planning.

A map of the Convention Center and its entrances was divided into 13 different pieces of "pie" and clusters of affinity groups worked together to determine how they would shut down the WTO meeting. One cluster, assigned to the "F" section of the "pie," met and hammered out an agreement about who would do what. Half of the group would be locked down and the other half of the group would provide food, water, and Depends as bathroom breaks would not be possible. The lock-down tactic literally meant just that. Using u-shaped bicycle locks, demonstrators at one entrance placed locks around their own necks and then locked themselves to one another.

Another affinity group was given responsibility for blocking traffic on all four intersections of a street. The group "used chicken wire, duct tape, PVC piping, chains, and padlocks to secure themselves together by joining arms from shoulder to hands."[24] A group of students from Seattle Central Community College marched with an inflatable blue whale the size of a school bus, named "Moby One," to protest against whaling by blocking intersections. Another group held aloft a paper mâché cow, in protest of cattle being treated with growth hormones. The School of the Americas marched with a giant puppet with the face of the Aztec Sun God, demanding "Democracy not Empire."

The groups organized primarily by the Ruckus Society and the DAN formed a large and colorful parade. There were stilt-walkers waving poles with upside down American flags attached. Marchers from the Philippines held banners denouncing the WTO. Chinese activists demanded a free Tibet. EarthFirsters! from Eugene, Oregon built a 20-foot tall Trojan horse that held 14 people inside to be used to climb up and over buses that security forces had parked in front of the

Puppets represent tricksters in a society who can make fun of the elite, and therefore became a target of the police.

Convention Center to block protesters. Two women tasked with hanging anti-WTO banners from a large crane began their climb up to its top and then rappelled down after successfully completing their task. Banners were dropped over the freeway leading into downtown Seattle. Some marchers carried signs with pictures of dolphins and turtles saying, "I'm not a free trade barrier." Topless women from the Radical (aka Radikal) Cheerleaders danced in a form of performance art: "activism with pom-poms and middle finders extended."[25] Art, politics, and theatre were blended in a defiant statement intended to expose the illegitimate and ridiculous nature of existing political and economic institutions.

Masks and giant puppets—some effigies of political leaders like Bill Clinton and Al Gore, others that referenced indigenous movements and symbols from the global South—served important functions. Puppets and masks have historically been associated with carnivals, in which there is a role reversal between rulers and ruled, and the masks serve to protect the identity of those engaged in disrespectful behavior. Puppets are designed to mock rulers and point out their sins, foibles, and shortcomings. They represent the "tricksters" in a society who have permission for a short time, and in a restricted capacity, to break the rules of polite society.[26]

By the time 5,000 trade delegates from 134 countries and 3,000 journalists started for the Convention Center, streets were blocked and the Convention Center was surrounded by a human chain of protesters. Two U.S. officials, Madeline Albright, Secretary of State, and the U.S. Attorney General, Janet Reno, were barricaded in their hotel. According to a number of accounts, Albright, fuming in her hotel, called Seattle Mayor Paul Schell and demanded he take action to clear out the protesters so the convention could start.[27] The police swung into action.

Reaction of the Seattle Police and the Washington National Guard

On the first day of the protests, November 29, the police had arrived in black body armor, wearing their own masks—Darth Vader-like helmets—and carrying plastic shields. Some arrived on military personnel carriers but all of them stood down that day; they did not directly confront protesters. This would change dramatically on November 30, after they received orders to clear the streets.

A group of forest activists had blocked a downtown intersection and were told to clear out in five minutes or else they would be removed by force. Locked together they started a chant of "Non-vio-lence!" The response of the police was to fire tear-gas grenades into the tightly packed group of sitting demonstrators. Those who stood up, disoriented from the tear gas, were shot with rubber bullets.

Those foolish enough to respond by rushing toward the police were beaten to the ground with 4-foot-long clubs. Once subdued, they were cuffed and arrested. Those who tried to run away from the melee were shot in the back and head with rubber bullets. Those who endured the tear-gas attack were then sprayed directly in the face with pepper spray. Volunteer medics, who formed one of the many affinity groups, rushed to provide first aid, making use of the combination of sugar-water and baby soap to wash out people's eyes. The medics, in turn, were targeted by the police who beat them, shot rubber bullets at them, shot pepper spray into their eyes, and arrested them when they could.[28] By the time the police were done they had jailed upwards of 600 people, which overwhelmed the Seattle jail and the courts. (There are numerous postings of images on Facebook, Google, and YouTube that verify the stories of those involved.[29])

These encounters would be repeated all over downtown Seattle when police confronted protesters. Sometimes holiday shoppers were clubbed or found themselves victims of tear-gas attacks. Mounted police chased protesters down streets and alleys. Even Christmas carolers in one neighborhood were tear-gassed. As the Washington chapter of the American Civil Liberties Union (ACLU) reported:

> Police commanders authorized the use of force at inappropriate times and levels, and directed it against inappropriate targets. They approved the use of tear gas, pepper spray, rubber bullets and clubs against people who were demonstrating peaceably, against demonstrators who had not received or who were trying to obey police orders, against bystanders, and to quell disturbances the police themselves had provoked. The level of force simply was not proportionate to the threat.[30]

By late afternoon on November 30, the mayor declared a state of emergency, called in the National Guard, imposed a 7 pm to 7 am curfew and even banned the sale of gas masks.[31] The mayor also declared an illegal "no protest" area of five square blocks around the Convention Center so that the WTO meetings could move forward. These actions were all "legitimated" by the authorities as necessary to quell so-called riots. (These controversial decisions would result in the resignation of the chief of police, the defeat of the mayor in the next election, and a city payout of $250,000 in damages to 157 people whom the courts determined were arrested without cause.)

A small group of anarchists, or members of the black bloc, destroyed property and smashed the windows of a bank, the Gap, Nike, and other companies seen as representatives of

> The mass media simplifies the complex messages of mass protests into stories about violence and spectacle.

global capitalism. Their numbers were tiny, compared to the overall number of protesters; perhaps as few as a dozen, though their ranks may have been swelled by Seattle gang members who took an opportunity to engage in looting. Many of the non-violent protesters tried to stop them from committing property damage, though that would not be the focus of press reports. Instead of telling the larger story of why so many had come together to protest against WTO policies and their effects, the press focused on the handful of anarchists and imagined acts of violence by the demonstrators.[32]

The Media

The political scientist Jules Boykoff has identified five of the primary ways in which the mass media reports on global justice movements, like the WTO protests.[33] The media favor stories with controversy, novelty, and flair.[34] They frame stories for readers and viewers in such a way that complex issues become "understandable." *Frames*, as the social movement scholars Robert Benford and David Snow have noted, *are interpretive schemata that simplify the world for us*.[35] The frames that Boykoff identified are ones that reduce the complexity of a social movement to stories about violence, disruption, weirdness, ignorance, and an amalgamation of grievances. Sometimes these elements overlap, as is the case with the following story from the front page of *USA Today*, reporting on the Seattle protests. The headline alerted readers to "'This Weird Jamboree': Teamsters and Turtle Protectors on the Same Side." The lead which followed noted:

> President Clinton wants to put a "human face" on trade, but others want to give it a black eye. A bewildering spectrum of voices has converged on Seattle to disrupt the largest trade-meeting ever held in the USA. Their protests and arrests have exposed the huge chasm between those who want to harness globalization and those who intend to stop it.[36]

In one brief paragraph and headline we have a reference to weirdness, disruption, the black eye of violence, and the allegation that the disrupters are ignorant because they don't know whether to limit the harms of globalization or stop it altogether. The story also goes on to note the amalgamation or diversity of grievances—environmental, economic, and social—which subtly suggests that the protesters, rather than the "bewildered" writer, really did not know what they wanted.

The mass media is good at reporting on spectacles, because that makes the evening news cycle, but far less successful at communicating why people are protesting.[37] Though there were upwards of 50,000 peaceful protesters, media coverage focused on broken windows and burning dumpsters. *What this kind of reporting and reaction of the police does is to make lawful civil disobedience look like criminal behavior.*[38]

The New York Times later reported that demonstrators had "hurled Molotov cocktails, rocks, and excrement at delegates and police officers."[39] They had to retract that story, because not one word of it was true. Other newspapers reported widespread acts of arson but the only "arson" involved were fires in one or two dumpsters, which could well have been sparked by police gas grenades. (When city officials were interviewed before the protests, they had claimed they were "ready for violence" and had 400 emergency medical personnel on hand with 2,000–3,000 doses of medicine to deal with a biological or chemical attack.[40] The protesters were thus defined ahead of time as dangerous and violent, by both the mass media and city officials.)

In an attempt to counter misinformation, the DAN developed an independent media center (*Indymedia*) to cover the events. Journalists provided up-to-the-minute reports, photos, videos, and audio clips on its website, and produced five documentaries distributed to public access stations across the United States.[41] *Indymedia* provided an alternative way to tell the story of Seattle and the protests that would follow in its wake. It remains today an important source of independent news. But it was the story crafted by the mainstream media and the police that traveled and shaped government response to future protests.

To understand why demonstrators were able to shut down the WTO talks, the Pentagon commissioned the Rand Corporation to explain how it was done. Authors of the Rand report alerted the Pentagon to a new form of *warfare* "in which protagonists use network forms of organization . . . to communicate, coordinate, and conduct their campaigns via the Internet without a precise central command." They chose the metaphor of *"swarming"* to describe how a myriad of small, dispersed, networked units could converge and rapidly coalesce to achieve their goal. The future challenge, they warned, would be how to deal with a swarm that has no leadership and no head to decapitate.[42] Organizations with little bureaucracy and no hierarchy, which were focused on the same general goals, were seen by the Rand Corporation as their *strength*; they were like the internet on which they relied for communication.

Militarization of the Response to Protests

The **militarization** of the response of the police would become a common response to mass mobilizations that followed. A narrative of violent protesters and the need to limit their actions ahead of time was carried from one police department to another. Alerted to protests, police in other cities enforced large exclusion zones which limited where demonstrators could gather and where they could be more easily controlled. Police also arrested leaders ahead of time without cause and, following Seattle's lead, made liberal use of tear gas and pepper spray to control crowds.[43] More bizarrely, when they found puppet workshops they systematically smashed the puppets.[44] There would be no mockery of the elite or international institutions on their watch.

In March of 2000, Seattle police traveled to Boston to brief fellow officers in preparation for a biotech conference to be held in their city. The imagination of the Seattle police force had been stimulated. They warned Boston officers to be prepared for Seattle tactics. Demonstrators would supposedly use "chunks of concrete, BB guns, wrist rockets and large capacity squirt guns loaded with bleach and urine."[45] These stories traveled and caused police to assume the worst. Before demonstrations against the IMF took place in April 2000 in Washington D.C., the local police chief claimed to have discovered a workshop for making Molotov cocktails and homemade pepper spray. It was later admitted the peppers were for making gazpacho and the paint thinner was not for fire bombs but for art projects. The police seized and destroyed puppets made by the protesters.

Before the Republican Convention opened in Philadelphia in 2000, groups had been preparing to protest. Police, acting on a tip, raided a warehouse being used by demonstrators as a meeting place and as a workshop to make banners and puppets. The police destroyed all of the banners and art work, as well as all of the puppets. The police chief claimed to have discovered balloons filled with acid and C4 explosives in the warehouse, a claim later withdrawn. He also had to withdraw a claim that his forces had seized a van full of poison snakes and reptiles that demonstrators planned to release in the city. The van of snakes, as it turned out, was the existing property of a pet store owner.[46]

The strategy developed by security forces in response to mass mobilization was clear: claim that protesters were going to commit violent acts, accuse them of having explosives, poisons, and other "weapons of destruction," and move with full force to preemptively stop a protest. If they managed to assemble, the plan was to arrest as many as possible. Politicians and police thus worked to seize the narrative and reduce complicated issues to a story between the righteous (those trying to preserve public order) and those who would disrupt routine and challenge many norms of polite society. As a result, the story the protesters wished to tell was often lost in media headlines which focused on the preparation for "war" in a city and the alleged violence that might occur. The militarization of response to mass protests has today been aided by a federal program which allows for the transfer of surplus military equipment to local police and fire departments. The program (Federal 1033) has provided both rural and urban police forces with armored personnel carriers, mine-resistant vehicles, night-vision goggles, sniper scopes, assault rifles, and other weapons normally associated with a battlefield. Once such equipment is available, it will be deployed—for example, in response to current protests such as those of Black Lives Matter. (See Chapter 3.)

The Routinization of Global Summit Protests

As the police honed their response to demonstrators, so did social movement organizations protesting globalization develop a set of rules or lessons for future mobilization. However, the lessons protesters learned in Seattle depended on whether or not they thought they "won." David Solnit, a leader of the efforts, argued the WTO protests were a success because they prevented the WTO from taking action.[47] Paul de Armond, another leader, suggested it was a victory simply because people were able to continue protesting, defeating the police strategy of stopping them and, furthermore, it was a win because no meaningful agreements came out of the WTO meeting.[48] Others concluded the trade talks fell apart because the key players—the United States, Europe, and Japan—refused to budge from their position that agricultural subsidies which protected agricultural producers in developing nations should be eliminated.

When the Seattle protests occurred in 1999 the WTO had 135 members. By 2016, WTO membership had grown to encompass virtually all nation states which, combined, accounted for 97% of the world's GDP and 97% of all global trade. Though the protests were not effective in rolling back the growth and dominance of the WTO, some gains followed.

The Worker Rights Consortium, composed primarily of college students, moved from criticizing global corporations to developing specific policies. The international movement against GMOs got a push from the Seattle protests which then led to the banning of GMO foods from the grocery shelves of several European countries. Even the World Bank and the IMF refocused efforts away from the "Washington consensus" toward community-based development and debt relief for developing countries.[49] Given the varied success of the different groups involved in the Seattle protests, what lessons did people learn?

One of the lessons that future protesters learned from Seattle was the wrong one, argued David Solnit. They thought "Seattle was largely a spontaneous rebellion or that it depended mostly on the element of surprise, or even luck." As he noted, this "overlooks the massive amounts of grassroots organizing, mobilizing, networking, education, alliance building, media work, and the creation of a unifying strategic framework."[50]

There were a set of tactics that were on display in Seattle, a smorgasbord of choices from which future organizers could and did choose. They included:

- *Affinity groups* that are non-hierarchical and act autonomously in support of a general goal.
- *Black blocs* that engage in property destruction, as a means of calling attention to corporate and state power.
- *Blockading* streets to shut down an event.
- *Coalition building* in order to strengthen and diversify a base for continued effort.
- *Direct action* to challenge economic and political power. Direct actions can include property damage or actions that reveal what power looks like, as when police take action against non-violent demonstrators or when corporations hire scabs to break a strike.[51]
- *Lock boxes* so protesters cannot be separated for arrest.
- *Spokes counsels* to achieve consensus among members of a group.
- *Street theatre* and the use of masks and giant puppets designed to both call attention to one's cause, as well as ridicule elites.

Following the protests against the WTO in Seattle, activists decided to mobilize to shut down the spring 2000 meetings in Washington, D.C. of the IMF and the World Bank, two symbols of globalization and neoliberal capitalism. The major tactics they adopted from Seattle were the use of affinity groups, street theatre, and coalition building. They relied even more than the Seattle protesters on the internet. The organization Mobilization for Global Justice served to coordinate the actions of three groups: 50 Years Is Enough, Global Exchange, and the DAN. A website served as the home page for a diverse group of AIDS activists, environmentalists, peace activists, workers groups, and anarchists. (An important omission in this protest, and others like it, was the failure to include local organizations with interests rooted in their own community.) A consensus agenda was developed through online interaction, which meant that it was less focused than the one for Seattle. The website encouraged protesters to show up a week early to be trained on street tactics, first aid, what to do if arrested, and the construction of puppets. They were told to organize themselves by affinity groups, as in Seattle, and pick roles: who would stop traffic, stall the cops, or provide aid to others.[52] Affinity groups would operate democratically, deciding which actions to take and when.

As the demonstration began, they were told by the veteran activist, Kevin Danaher, that they could block an intersection and lock it down, or not. If people wanted to do something else, they could. Yet, as the journalist Naomi Klein

> Protests became a routine with scripted rules for both protesters and security forces.

explained, as a tactic this did not work. If the point was to block access and some protesters decided to leave their posts, then "delegates on their way out of the meeting could just hang a right instead of a left, and they would be home free. Which . . . is precisely what happened."[53] Democracy among the ranks led to chaos. Furthermore, the demonstration's stated goal—shut down the IMF and World Bank—was unobtainable.

The goal for some activists became keeping alive a culture of protest against capitalism and globalization. *Protesting itself, coming together, getting arrested, had an inherent value.* So did the process of making decisions democratically. A routine developed in which a call would go out over the internet alerting people to the next event. Social movement entrepreneurs did not want to be left out of the next "big" protest so they in turn would try to mobilize members of their organizations to commit to showing up, making puppets and banners, and getting arrested. Serial protesting or "summit hopping" became the norm. Summit protests against globalization were geared, as the Dutch activist Marco claimed, at generating spectacle, rather than at developing clear political and economic alternatives.[54] In 2000, the year following Seattle, there were, including the D.C. protests, nine major protests—at the Democratic and Republican nominating conventions, and at various economic summits held in Davos, Switzerland, Melbourne, Prague, Quebec, and Nice. Worldwide, anti-globalization protests would continue through the winter and spring of 2001, with little, if any, direct effect on the continued growth of global capitalism.

The strategies and tactics used by Seattle demonstrators would be debated by movement organizers in other locales. Some argued for stand-alone mass marches, while others wanted to engage in direct action and use black blocs to cause property damage and provoke local police. Which strategies and tactics were diffused from the Seattle protests to other organizations and cities depended on two primary factors. Had activists in a given city already been working with one another, or were they competing for resources and attention? Second, did they have some connection to Seattle?[55] Competition limited a group's willingness to consider new approaches and limited the nature of democratic decision making. Those who had been directly involved in the Seattle protests, or connected in some way, felt strongly about the importance of collaboration and democratic decision making, and were more willing to consider new ideas for mobilization.

One of the major critiques of the focus on global justice issues and summit protests was that they ignored local issues and sometimes drained financial, human, and organizational resources from groups in the cities that were targeted by protesters. Another criticism was that such protests privileged those few who could afford to go to the summits. The social movement theorist, Leslie J. Wood, participated in preparations for the G20 Summit (an inter-governmental forum of the world's major industrial democracies) to be held in Toronto in 2010. In this case, there was a conscientious effort to connect local grassroots organizing efforts to the summit campaign, so that after the major protests were over, local, long-term efforts would continue at the grassroots level. A Toronto Community Mobilization Network (TCMN) was formed with this goal.

Forty thousand people took to the streets, and in the words of the TCMN:

> . . . gathered in discussion, watched movies, set up a tent city, danced and fought . . . For the first time, an economic summit saw a march of thousands against colonization and for indigenous sovereignty . . . Instead of simplifying our diverse struggles in to one issue, we supported actions for queer and trans rights, environmental justice, income equity and community control over resources, gender justice and disability rights, migrant justice, and an end to war and occupation.[56]

This compilation of struggles was to persist in the following decades.

The events in Toronto were themselves shaped by a major historical event that derailed global justice movements. After the destruction of the World Trade Center buildings in New York, on September 11, 2001, mobilization slowed and people's energies shifted to organizing mass protests against war in the Middle East. Protests throughout the coming century would be played out against this background.

Governments Do Not Always Listen to Their People

There is no guarantee that in democratic societies a government will listen to the voices of the people. Congress authorized military action against Iraq in October of 2002, based on false intelligence that Saddam Hussein's regime possessed "weapons of mass destruction," and was harboring members of al-Qaeda linked to the destruction of the World Trade Center towers. Many believed there was still a chance to prevent war if their voices were heard. A series of worldwide protests were scheduled for the weekend of February 15–16, 2002. People marched and came together in 60 different countries and 600 cities with an estimated number of protesters ranging between 6 and 11 million people. It was declared the largest protest event in human history.[57] International coordination was facilitated by social movement organizations that had already been working with one another on social justice issues.[58] The anti-war protests were thus a mix of those against the war as well as those challenging the dominant economic framework of global capitalism. On March 20, bombs and missiles rained down on Bagdad and troops from the United States, Great Britain, Australia, Poland, and Denmark advanced. By April, the reign of Saddam Hussein had ended and civil war and economic chaos followed.

Why did mass protests not move the leaders of the United States and Great Britain to delay their plans? To take just the United States, almost three-fourths of the public supported the war.[59] The 9/11 attacks had contributed to a level of fear that created favorable conditions for Bush to act. Furthermore, a mass movement doesn't necessarily move a democratic government to act, because there are few counterweights to "legitimate" power.

War dampened mass protest activity in the United States and shifted the priorities and attention of the public. In 2002, 90% of Americans saw defending the country against terrorism as the top priority, with the need to strengthen the economy following at 70%.[60] Protests against globalization and the way in which they were framed by the mass media did not capture the imagination of the general public, though protest activity continued with organizations at the local, regional, and state level.

Environmental organizations continued their efforts, whether aimed at limiting global warming, protecting a local ecosystem, a species, or the release of toxic chemicals into the environment. In the California community in which I lived at the time, environmental activists continued to lobby in support of organic farming, renewable energy, public transportation, urban in-fill, and protection of endangered species. Across the country, gay rights activists continued their search for social justice, as did minority communities. Unions tried to fight back against jobs being outsourced to low-waged countries or a reduction in their benefits. In short, people did not stop protesting or mobilizing after 9/11; the protests simply failed to garner the attention of the national media. What did capture public attention was the financial crisis of 2008 that eventually gave rise to Occupy Wall Street (OWS). The OWS protests would take a very different form than the Seattle protests.

Occupy Wall Street

The economic crisis of 2008 was brought on by banks and other major financial institutions which had made substantial bets on the housing market, issuing bonds and securities made up of risky, subprime mortgages. The Emergency Economic Stabilization Act of 2008, signed by President George W. Bush, authorized the U.S. Treasury to spend up to $700 billion to prop up banks and insurance agencies. When President Obama took office, more government funds would be used to keep companies like Chrysler and General Motors afloat.

By 2009, unemployment topped 10% nationally and was even higher in some areas. People fell behind on mortgage payments, auto loans, credit cards, and student loans. Other people feared for their economic security, and were angered about the fact that the government gave banks and corporations a handout rather than helping ordinary citizens. It was a devastating crisis and one which took the country six years to overcome.

Origins and Background

In the time before OWS made its appearance there were several factors that served both to mobilize people and to give them hope. In January 2010, a decision by the U.S. Supreme Court (Citizens United) equated money with free speech, meaning that political action committees could give unlimited amounts of money to political candidates of their choosing. This mobilized people in opposition to the Court's decision. On the hopeful side of the equation were the beginnings of the Arab Spring, sparked in December 2010 by the immolation of a street vendor in Tunisia. Mass demonstrations in Tunisia led quickly to the resignation and flight of its president to Saudi Arabia. Protests then spread quickly to Algeria, Egypt, Libya, Syria, Tunisia, and Yemen. For a time, it appeared as though mass street demonstrations alone could provide a direct path to democracy. The two men whose brain child was OWS, Kalle Lasn and Micah White, were inspired by the Tahrir Square uprising in Egypt and hoped to create something similar in North America.

White, from Berkeley, California, had been an activist since his teens and had become an editor, along with Lasn, for the Canadian magazine, *Adbusters*, which advertised itself as a not-for-profit enterprise fighting against the commercialization of all aspects of our lives.[61] Lasn and White had previously worked together on a 2011 effort in Canada, Carnival Against Capitalism, encouraging people to buy nothing on Black Friday, the day after Thanksgiving. It was, according to White, a dismal failure, but one from which they learned. They concluded that people simply were not yet ready for an action that could be spread through a hashtag.[62] Trying again, and inspired by the Arab Spring, they decided to use the tactic of occupying public spaces to create change. They sent out a call to everyone on *Adbusters'* distribution list on February 2, 2011:

> All right, you ninety thousand redeemers, rebels and radicals out there
> . . . On September 17, we want to see twenty thousand people flood
> into Lower Manhattan, set up tents, kitchens, peaceful barricades and
> occupy Wall Street for a few months.[63]

White also created the hashtag #OCCUPYWALLSTREET, which he sent to every activist he knew. Another activist registered OccupyWallSt.org, which became the hub for the unfolding movement. The American rapper, Lupe Fiasco, took up the cause and promoted it to his 1 million followers. He created the movement's signature chant: "All Day, All Week, Occupy Wall Street!"[64] The idea for an occupation spread rapidly across activist websites. A Tumblr blog called "We Are The 99 Percent!" sprung up and went viral.

Many answered the charge to come to Manhattan; eventually there would be encampments in 951 cities across 82 countries. On Friday, September 17, 5,000 activists arrived at their chosen site, Zuccotti Park, at the heart of Wall Street. Zuccotti was chosen because it was a private park that, unlike city parks, could be occupied 24 hours a day. Three hundred set up camp the first night and vowed to hold the park until their *undetermined* demands were met.[65] White described the occupation as a total experience. Free kitchens provided daily meals to thousands, some of them homeless. One occupier, Amelia Byrne, recalled that she:

> A typical OWS protest was small, consisting of a handful of local social justice and environmental activists.

. . . was struck by the organization of the space: paths were clear, tents were neatly covered in tarps, folks were singing in one corner dedicated to song and spirit, delicious looking pizzas were being served for dinner, there were people staffing a media relations tent, and a library with books for loan and reference organized in rows inside waterproof containers.[66]

Yet OWS had no clear demands. They wanted a lot of different things: an end to the wars in Iraq and Afghanistan, an end to global warming, jobs for the unemployed, debt forgiveness for college students, help for homeowners in danger of losing their homes, an increase in the federal minimum wage, and so forth. With nobody in charge of the movement there were no means for speaking on behalf of everyone involved. A simple answer to the question, "What do they want?" could not be given.

When OWS began, it was ignored by major media outlets. It first gained public attention when, during a march on September 24, a woman was pepper-sprayed in the face. The image was captured on video and rebroadcast on the Daily Show with Jon Stewart. When 700 protesters were arrested on October 1 for blocking the Brooklyn Bridge, the story and tactic went global. The memes of OWS were appropriated by groups in other cities, sometimes with different issues. In Seattle, Portland, Los Angeles, Oakland, Philadelphia, and elsewhere people set up camps, marched and chanted, "We are the 99%!"

If there was such a thing as a typical Occupy encampment across country, it was small. It drew in people who had been previously active, either in environmental movements, social justice movements, or protests against rising college tuition. The few people who camped out in a city's park or plaza were often joined by the homeless, looking for food and company. On Saturdays, when people had time to spare, numbers increased substantially but only for the day. People carried signs expressing concerns about capitalism: "I am not a commodity." Some waved signs that complained about "Billions for Bankers," and others noted that "Foreclosure for citizens is not a democracy." Some demonstrators shifted their picketing to the sidewalks in front of banks.[67]

Is Consensus Decision Making a Problem?

There were numerous rules of conduct that evolved over the course of OWS New York, and in similar Occupy protests in other cities. General assemblies, where values and visions were discussed, operated on the basis of consensus. One rule was that nobody could be interrupted and nobody could clap to support an idea, because that was a form of interruption. To support an idea people waved fingers in the air. As a San Francisco member said, "Even though it's inefficient and can be frustrating, I love it."[68] OWS also made use of what was termed the "progressive stack." People lined up to speak but people could go to the front of the line if they were members of a minority community or a woman.[69] Demonstrations in other countries took the same form as those in New York, where achieving democratic consensus was a central value and there were no leaders outlining specific goals. A protest in Madrid drew 60,000 and consensus was achieved by people raising their hands in support of what a speaker said.[70]

If the protests and demonstrators made the evening news, the story was usually framed as one about a diverse group of people who made decisions in "funny" ways and who did not know what they wanted. It was easy to make fun of people wiggling their fingers to make decisions. Reporters were confused by such an approach because they did not recognize an attempt to model democracy in action. The protesters obviously had goals—challenging corporate influence on politics and inequality in the distribution of wealth and income—but they did not articulate how these goals were to be accomplished.

Who Came to Protest?

Who showed up to protest depended partly on which city was involved. When it was a college town, not surprisingly, a number of protesters were young students. In New York, however, the average age of a protester was 33 years. Participants did not fit neatly into the red and blue boxes we have come to associate with membership in one political party; most (71%) claimed to be independents. Sixty percent of them had voted for Obama in 2008 but 73% of them disapproved of how he was doing his job.[71] Most participants who were actively involved were white and a full 80% had a bachelor's degree or higher. The same percent (80%) had a job, but a third of them were worried about their precarious employment situation and their student debt.[72]

A core group of those who came and helped to organize the protests had previous experience in social justice efforts within New York, their home communities, and/or with national organizations. Participation in protests, whether for both veterans of these efforts or those who come for the first time, can serve to transform their understanding of power and politics. *The New York Times* photographer and reporter, Accra Shepp, followed a small group of people from the OWS protests and noted that although some had "returned to their former lives, all of them say they were transformed by the experience."[73] Shepp provided vignettes of several of them, who stand as examples of others who have a deep engagement with social justice issues.

Craig Bethel, an organizer of the protest, had just graduated from college and was working as a production assistant on documentary films. After seeing a woman pepper-sprayed during a march from Zuccotti Park, he offered his services to the movement to document what the police were doing and later went on to Washington D.C., Seattle, and Oakland to help organize protests in those cities. Udi Offer was a lawyer employed by the American Civil Liberties Union (ACLU) to monitor police activity and to provide help for those jailed. He went on to become head of the ACLU in New Jersey and led the successful fight to legalize same-sex marriage in that state. Alexandre Carvalho was a doctor and public health specialist who ministered to those in need of assistance, and went on to provide medical care for oil workers in Brazil. The couple had tried to get Trinity Church, where George was the Episcopal Bishop, to offer a small square of land owned by the church as a safe place for OWS, which the financiers on the board of the church refused to do. The Packards continued their activism, including fighting to stop a gas pipeline from being built next to the Indian Point nuclear power plant.

Corralling Protests

By the time OWS became a reality, there were already extensive efforts on the part of security forces to determine just how protests should be conducted: if protesters did not follow the model outlined by authorities, they could expect to be met with violent reactions. Demonstrators were required to get a permit to protest and encouraged to work with authorities on how voluntary arrests would be conducted. Activists were often confined to so-called free-speech areas where they could not be heard, and prohibited from blocking sidewalks.[74] Even the news media was corralled on occasion, to prevent them from photographing or interviewing demonstrators, especially confrontations between the police and protesters. The mobilization by security forces was highly organized.

As documents secured by Naomi Wolf of *The Guardian* revealed, when protesters were driven out of Occupy camps in major cities, it was a coordinated effort by the FBI, the Department of Homeland Security, local police, and the banks. Campus police on six campuses, without the knowledge of administrators, funneled information to the FBI about which students were involved with OWS. Banks used private security firms to gather data on protesters and provided it to the FBI. Documents obtained under the Freedom of Information Act and disclosures on Wikileaks made it clear that the FBI intended to treat OWS as a potential criminal and terrorist threat. Agency coordination took place wherever an OWS "branch" popped up, whether in Boulder, Colorado or Anchorage, Alaska.[75] As happened in Seattle, the police used the same militarized response: tear-gas canisters were lobbed at demonstrators, pepper spray was used, and people were beaten with batons. They also made use of a new sonic battlefield weapon, the sound cannon, which uses focused high-frequency sound waves that can cause extreme pain and even damage one's eardrums. These events raise a question about who, exactly, "owns" public space.

> Occupying a public space is a way of challenging the power of the state.

Who "Owns" Public Space?

Most of the OWS encampments were staged in public parks and plazas across the United States and internationally. In New York, Toronto, and elsewhere public officials claimed the right to clear demonstrators out based on the idea that OWS was privatizing public space, preventing the general public from using parks and plazas. In the case of Zuccotti Park and other public spaces around the country, encampments were defined as a public health hazard. Another way to understand the occupation of these spaces, as the political scientist Margaret Kohn has suggested, is to understand them as an assertion that a protest group has a right to occupy what rightfully *belongs* to the people. Demonstrators in Occupy Portland, Oregon, chanted when police tried to move them along, "Whose Street? Our Street!"[76] Occupying a public space is thus a way of challenging the power of the state.[77]

A Digital Revolution?

Much has been made of the potential of social media (Facebook, Tumblr, Twitter, and YouTube) as a means of mobilizing people for action. Benjamin Gleason, a professor of education with an interest in how young people learn, has argued that Twitter serves as an important learning platform for today's students. In the case of OWS, he found that Twitter, as opposed to reading newspaper accounts or even using Google to become informed, allowed people to become engaged in the OWS endeavor through creating, tagging, and sharing content.[78] Some were clearly motivated to join the protest by events they saw on YouTube, whether in New York or in one of the many small towns in America where parallel protests occurred.[79]

A more detailed study of the use of Twitter and its use by OWS participants was conducted by a group of scholars from the University of Indiana who were able to analyze 800 thousand tweets from 500 thousand separate accounts over a 15-month period, including three months prior to the beginning of the protests in New York. As often happens on Twitter, a few people posted most of the comments, which are then re-Tweeted to others. What the authors found was that the most vocal of the users were highly connected to one another *before the movement began*. However, in the months immediately following the birth of the movement, they appear to have lost interest as their communications with one another declined significantly.[80] The decline in the use of Twitter mirrored the decline in the movement itself as encampments were cleared out and people went back to their lives. This does not mean that social media was not important in OWS; it drew in people who might not have been attracted otherwise, and it helped with communications among participants who had to worry about the police and the details (e.g., getting food and medical care) of maintaining encampments. However, social media failed as a resource in building long-term commitments and developing a coherent set of plans and strategies for accomplishing a goal. (See Chapter 7 for an extension of this discussion.)

The Downside of Spontaneity

On November 15, 2011, almost two months after the beginning of the occupation, police notified those occupying Zuccotti Park that it had been declared a public health hazard and they would have to remove all tents, sleeping bags, and other equipment. Police in riot gear moved in and arrested a few of those who resisted destruction of their camp. Subsequent attempts to reoccupy Zuccotti would occur but all would prove unsuccessful. Some demonstrators then changed tactics and chose to occupy lobbies of banks and corporations, and staged sit-ins at homes marked for foreclosure. Others, who had grown weary of camping out in cold weather and battling the police, met in cafes to continue discussions about money, power, and politics. The police moved aggressively to close down Occupy camps across the country.

With no warning, they dismantled large camps in Philadelphia and Los Angeles.[81] Occupy Oakland did, however, record a success; a general strike in November managed to shut down the Port of Oakland and bring thousands of people into the streets carrying signs proclaiming they were part of the 99%. In Portland, Oregon, Occupy demonstrators claimed success because they did not leave the park blocks, where they were camped, until 8 am, after defying a midnight deadline to leave. Madison Dines told reporters that "We declared victory and went home."[82] The Seattle protests were highly organized and people planned for months ahead of time who would do what. The OWS priorities were not. Yet there appears to be a way to claim one was successful and the other not!

Movement Success

The issue of whether or not the Occupy protests were a success was squarely addressed by its co-founder, Micah White: "Occupy Wall Street failed to live up to its revolutionary potential: we did not bring an end to the influence of money on democracy, overthrow the corporatocracy of the 1 percent or solve income inequality."[83]

What Occupy did do, argued White, was to reveal the inadequacy of a model of change that relied solely on protests and mass marches. "Protests," he noted, "have become an accepted, and therefore ignored, by-product of politics-as-usual." What Occupy revealed for him was "that activists need to revolutionize their approach to revolution."[84] Instead of protesting against power, activists needed to work to *acquire* power. And to do that, they would need organizational strength and resources coupled with disruptive and at times violent acts.

> Focus on building a movement organization may make leaders more risk averse and less likely to bring about change.

White turned to the work of the social movement theorist William Gamson to understand what might work. Gamson had developed a database of 53 protest organizations in the United States between 1800 and 1945 and found that coalition building was not essential to a movement achieving its goals, since sometimes competition between organizations dissipated the energy and resources necessary to achieve a goal. The finding of Gamson's that most intrigued White was that contentious groups that used violence and strikes had a greater chance of success.[85] However, as Gamson cautioned, groups that had *already achieved visibility and strength* were more likely to use violence and disruptive tactics to force the hand of elites. Violence did not cause success; it was the result of it. Nevertheless, the conclusion White drew from Gamson's work was that street actions can bring about positive change. White could have found additional support for this idea in a work that followed Gamson's by two years.

In their book, *Poor People's Movements: Why They Succeed, How They Fail*,[86] Frances Fox Piven and Richard A. Cloward laid out what was a simple but controversial argument: because the poor have few resources their ability to create social change depends on the disruptive power of tactics such as "militant boycotts, sit-ins, traffic tie-ups, and rent strikes." If the poor wanted elites to pay attention to them, they needed to create excitement in the media and disrupt normal routines. Change did not occur, they argued, through slow, incremental action but through bursts of disruptive activity. Like Gamson, they argued that some historical moments were more advantageous for change than others, as when elites are in conflict. Their most controversial argument was that bureaucratic organizations would impede change because leaders would focus on trying to build the organization, becoming more risk averse, instead of devoting their energies to bringing about change.[87] These arguments were anathema to those scholars who had been involved in the Civil Rights Movement or protests against the war in Vietnam because they had experienced firsthand the importance of strong organizations in accomplishing their goals.[88] (See Chapter 7 for an extension of this discussion.)

Understanding the Battle in Seattle and Occupy Wall Street as Social Movement Organizations

All social movements and social movement organizations come into being and unfold within a specific historical context. As the sociologist and political scientist John Markoff put it: "Movement participants have unfolding lives, movement organizations evolve, and changing social, economic, and political circumstances provide new themes for contention and alter the possibilities for collective action."[89]

So it was with both the Battle for Seattle and OWS. When the events unfolded in Seattle the ostensible purpose of the protests was to call attention to the negative impacts of globalization and trade on the environment, indigenous rights, and the growing dominance of capitalism in our lives. The other purpose was to disrupt and shut down the WTO meetings, which protesters were successful in doing. However, as the protests were reported in the media, few of the public understood or learned what was at stake. Equally important was the fact that the protesters did not advance any specific policies for how things might be different. In short, nothing changed; WTO member states now account for almost all of the world's trade and GDP. One might argue that American citizens were not yet ready to embrace the idea that globalization and trade were problems that needed to be addressed.

The same argument could be made about OWS. It too was a massive social movement but failed to achieve its stated, but perhaps unobtainable, goal of changing the distribution of wealth and getting money out of politics. The political scientist, John Cioffi, writing about OWS at its inception, pointed out the difficulty of participatory, non-hierarchical organizations bringing about change from the bottom up:

> [OWS] does not articulate specific concrete political or policy demands; it is incapable of doing so. During their formation, movements have weak and unclear (if any) institutional structures and leadership. They are seldom, if ever, organized in ways that allow for effective deliberation or authoritative statements of goals. Participants in a social movement usually lack policy expertise, and as a group they have an array of potentially conflicting interests, priorities, and targets of protest.[90]

Cioffi predicted that OWS would likely follow in a long list of failed social movements. But did it fail?

In April of 2015, during her first campaign stop in Iowa, Hillary Clinton told voters that "the deck is still stacked in favor of those at the top." She also took a cue from her Democratic competitor, Bernie Sanders, and said she no longer supported the Trans-Pacific Partnership (TPP) because it would cost American workers jobs. Bernie Sanders drew large crowds while calling for the breakup of big banks, denouncing Wall Street greed, and the concentration of wealth among the 1%. Four years after OWS had splintered and disappeared into a number of causes, the framing of income inequality by OWS, "We are the 99%," had worked its way into the election cycle. Trump, the eventual winner of the presidency, campaigned on a platform of economic populism denouncing international trade and globalization, a position which could have been taken straight out of the playbooks of the Seattle and OWS protesters. As White later realized about the movement he co-founded, "most enduring victories . . . take generations to unfold."[91]

Piven and Cloward's strong argument that people's movements can be successful depends in large part not only on there being a grievance that resonates with large numbers but whether or not there is a *political opportunity*. The presidential election of 2016 allowed a range of issues to come to the fore because politicians were looking for votes. Building pressure from below, while bargaining at the top, requires both mass mobilization and an organization with resources to do the bargaining. *Movements are dynamic and ever changing*, adapting to both opportunities and challenges. (I will expand on Piven and Cloward's theory in Chapter 7.)

The sociologists David A. Snow and Dana M. Moss have pointed out that *spontaneity* is an often overlooked feature of social movements.[92] Spontaneous events tend to occur when there is a disruption in the script protesters were following. In the case of the non-violent protesters in Zuccotti Park, a break in the script occurred when a woman was pepper-sprayed in the face during a small march. When the image went viral on social media, it caused the numbers of demonstrators to swell. Police attempted to shut down the camp by making things uncomfortable for protesters by declaring gas-powered generators illegal. Protesters innovated. They hooked up bicycles to generators and took turns pedaling to produce power for their camp. When the camp was shut down, people altered their tactics and sat in the lobbies of banks and corporations. The police also innovated and tried to change the script by directing vagrants, drug users, and the homeless to Zuccotti Park, giving the demonstrators yet another set of problems to deal with, including maintaining security within the camp.

As we've seen, the police and other security forces have been adept at learning from one another. They have mounted effective **counter mobilizations** against protests by preemptively arresting ring leaders, destroying banners, art work, and puppets. They confine protesters to special "free" speech areas, and negotiate with organizers about how arrests will be conducted. They wall off public spaces from demonstrators, effectively making non-violent protests illegal. Yet protesters persist in demonstrating against a range of ills: global warming, low wages, money in politics, and environmental destruction. What do all of these protests have in common? They stem from two motivations: *moral shock* and the *desire to create community, not just as a concept but as a reality.*

Seattle and OWS were **class-based protests** that sought to "out" economic and political elites who had limited their life chances. Economic dislocation, brought on by the financial crisis that caused people to lose jobs and homes, was a moral shock. Banks, the government, and corporations seemed allied against the average person. Deeply troubling to many was the fact that not one banker *ever* served jail time for their actions. The two movements discussed in this chapter were both premised on the desire to create a democratic community. Though people protested against different things, they had to trust their fellow demonstrators to help and protect them if necessary. Some found community through adversity, coping together. The movements also stood for *freedom from* corrupt institutions, politicians, and the commercialization of our lives. They demanded justice not just for themselves but for all citizens of the planet. Though there was a joyous aspect to the protests, the coming together of people who shared common concerns, the protests represented a growing *culture of defiance and resistance*. Protesters were offering a vision of a different kind of world, and resisting the chains of consumerism and globalization which beggared families, students, and workers at the expense of the 1%. One of the major low-cost tools available to them for mobilizing people was the internet.

Social media played a variety of different roles in the two movements. In the case of Seattle, planning was done face-to-face and *within existing social movement organizations*. Most of the marchers in Seattle came from organized labor, others from well-established groups. The Seattle protests thus drew on previously existing *dense networks*, which allowed them to focus their actions on one goal— shut down the WTO. Social media was used during the demonstrations to communicate between protesters and to record acts of police violence.

On the other hand, OWS got started through the efforts of just two men, working for *Adbusters*. Social media served as their prime organizing force. People responded to the meme of the 1% vs. the 99% and the call to "Occupy Wall Street, All Day, All Night!" Facebook and YouTube videos served to communicate the festive atmosphere of the occupation, as well as record the destruction of the camps and incidents of police violence. Social media connected existing networks of protesters to one another. Twitter facilitated initial mobilization and communication but communication rapidly died away as the protests wound down. As noted, social policy is difficult to develop using just social media. This limits the ability of a group of protesters to affect change. In the case of OWS, with no structure, organization, or resources to continue the battle, the protests initially faded away.

There is what we might term a *culture of protest*. By this I mean that protests frequently follow a ritualized pattern.[93] A grievance is identified; a call goes out to mobilize; and people show up at an assigned time prepared to march or carry out some other specified action. Not infrequently, those who have organized a protest have secured a permit from authorities as to where the protest or march will take place, and have discussed with the police how arrests will be made. Of course there are spontaneous protests such as those that have erupted when a member of a minority community is shot and killed by the police. But even those demonstrations, as we will see in a discussion of Black Lives Matter in Chapter 3, have certain sameness to them. Demonstrators and police play out assigned roles. Police stand in battle lines, protesters stand shouting, property may be destroyed, and then some sort of settlement is negotiated, and the cycle repeats itself from city to city.

The Seattle protests also underscore the points made by the social movement theorists John D. McCarthy and Mayer N. Zald when they laid out the framework for *resource mobilization theory*.[94] They introduced the concept of *social movement entrepreneur* to describe movements that are professionalized and characterized by a full-time leadership. Membership is amorphous with members connected on social media. The movement entrepreneur is a professional organizer, who may identify the grievance, define how it should be addressed, and raise funds to stay employed. Most of those who spent time organizing against the WTO were experienced movement entrepreneurs, who helped define the grievance, develop the tactics, and raise funds. Some of them would continue "summit hopping," and some would go on to found new social justice organizations, such as those focused on the anti-GMO campaign. (See Chapter 6.)

The challenge for all movements that speak of community, justice, and freedom in today's world is to find opportunities and points of leverage to bring about actual change. The conditions are not constant, as they fluctuate with economic circumstances and with political opportunity, as may occur during an election cycle. A danger to be discussed in Chapter 7 is the need to avoid letting a movement, or a movement moment, be captured by an existing political party (as happened with the Tea Party being "captured" by the Republic Party) or some other large organization that may appropriate the rhetoric of change but do little to implement it.

If there are lessons to be learned from the Battle in Seattle and Occupy Wall Street, they might be:

- Mass movements unfold within a specific historical context. Timing or political opportunity, organizational strength, and strategy all determine success or failure.
- Spontaneity, while effective in bringing people into the streets, does not necessarily yield success.
- Planning matters. Organizational strength needs to be built and specific policy goals developed.
- Copying the organizational structure or tactics of another movement is not a guarantee of success.
- Ritualized protests will yield ritualized responses from law enforcement.
- To change social policy, a movement must focus on acquiring political power.
- To acquire power, something more than mass protest is necessary. Mobilization must be directed to electing public officials at all levels (school boards, city councils, state houses, and Congress) who share movement goals and values.
- A successful movement will have *specific* policy goals.
- As most movements unfold over time, it is essential to build *local* capacities to act and to sustain the movement.

Notes

1 George Katsiaficas. 2001. "Seattle Was Not the Beginning," in Eddie Yuen, George Katsiaficas, and Daniel Burton Rose, eds. *The Battle of Seattle: The New Challenge to Capitalist Globalization*. New York: Soft Skull Press, p.29.

2 The University of Washington interviewed participants and their responses and other materials from 1999 are archived at the University. *WTO History Project*. Some of the material is available online at: https://depts.washington.edu/wtohist/; a detailed account of the protest and its aftermath is provided in Eddie Yuen, George Katsiaficas, and Daniel Burton Rose, eds. 2001. *The Battle of Seattle: The New Challenge to Capitalist Globalization*. New York: Soft Skull Press; for the views of activists see David Solnit and Rebecca Solnit. 2009. *The Battle of the Story of the Battle of Seattle*. Oakland, California: AK Press; Lesley J. Wood. 2012. *Direct Action, Deliberation, and Diffusion: Collective Action after the WTO Protests in Seattle*. New York: Cambridge University Press.

3 David Solnit and Rebecca Solnit. 2009. *The Battle of the Story of the Battle of Seattle*, p.8.

4 I am using the term globalization to refer to the processes whereby international capital is no longer place bound but flows freely across international borders in search of cheap labor, energy, and raw materials. This process creates winners and losers and recently in the United States refers to the outsourcing of jobs to low-waged countries or countries with weaker environmental standards.

5 The Zapatistas, or the Army of National Liberation, fought for 12 days against the Mexican state before settlement talks began.

6 Manuel Callahan. 2001. "Zapatismo and the Politics of Solidarity," in Eddie Yuen, George Katsiaficas, and Daniel Burton Rose. *The Battle for Seattle: The New Challenge to Capitalist Globalization*. New York: Soft Skull Press, p.38.

7 Peoples' Global Action Network. *Organizational Principles*. Retrieved on November 18, 2016 at: www.nadir.org/nadir/initiativ/agp/cocha/principles.htm.

8 David Graeber. 2006. "On the Phenomenology of Giant Puppets: Broken Windows, Imaginary Jar of Urine, and the Cosmological Role of the Police in American Culture," p.3. Retrieved on November 18, 2016 at: https://libcom.org/files/puppets.pdf.

9 The history of organizing for the protests comes from David Solnit, who led the Direct Action Network. Interview with David Solnit by Jeremy Simer. March 23, 2000. Seattle: University of Washington History Project. Retrieved on November 18, 2016 at: http://depts.washington.edu/wtohist/interviews/Solnit.pdf. See also: David Solnit and Rebecca Solnit. 2009. *The Battle of the Story of the Battle of Seattle*. Oakland, California: AK Press; David Solnit. December 5, 2011. "Seattle WTO Shutdown '99 to Occupy: Organizing to Win 12 Years Later." *The Indypendent*. Retrieved on November 18, 2016 at: www.indypendent.org/2011/12/05/seattle-wto-shutdown-%E2%80%9999-occupy-organizing-win-12-years-later.

10 David Solnit and Rebecca Solnit. 2009. *The Battle of the Story of the Battle of Seattle*, pp.9–10.

11 Mac Lojowsky. 1999. "Comes a Time." *University of Washington WTO History Project*. Retrieved on November 28, 2016 at: https://depts.washington.edu/wtohist/testimonies/comesatime.htm.

12 Alexander Cockburn, Jeffrey St. Clair, and Allan Sekula. 2000. *Five Days that Shook the World*. New York: Verso, p.5.

13 Bill Aal. November 11, 2000. Interviewed by Michael Bocanegra. University of Washington History Project. Retrieved on November 22, 2016 at: http://depts.washington.edu/wtohist/.

14 Jane Cover. December 2–3, 1999. *The WTO History Project*. Retrieved on November 23, 2016 at: https://depts.washington.edu/wtohist/.

15 Mac Lojowsky. December 7, 1999. "Comes a Time." *The WTO History Project*. Retrieved on November 23, 2016 at: https://depts.washington.edu/wtohist/.

16 U.S. Bureau of Census. 2016. "Trade in Goods with China." Retrieved on November 26, 2016 at: www.census.gov/foreign-trade/balance/c5700.html.

17 David H. Autor, David Dorn, and Gordon H. Hanson. January, 2016. "The China Shock: Learning from Labor Market Adjustment to Large Changes in Trade." *National Bureau of Economic Research*. Working Paper No.21906. Retrieved on November 26, 2016 at: www.nber.org/papers/w21906.

18 Heather Long. March 29, 2016. "U.S. Has Lost 5 Million Manufacturing Jobs since 2000." *CNN Money*. Retrieved on November 26, 2016 at: http://money.cnn.com/2016/03/29/news/economy/us-manufacturing-jobs/.

19 Cited in Alexander Cockburn, Jeffrey St. Clair, and Allan Sekula. 2000. *Five Days that Shook the World*, p.19.

20 Cockburn, St. Clair, and Sekula. 2000, p.20.

21 Tico Almeida. 1999. *The University of Washington WTO History Project*. Retrieved on November 28, 2016 at: https://depts.washington.edu/wtohist/testimonies/TicoAlmeida.htm. See also: Cockburn, St. Clair, and Sekula. 2000. *Five Days that Shook the World*, pp.21–22.

22 Stephanie Guilloud. 1999. "Introduction to the WTO History Project." Retrieved on November 28, 2016 at: http://depts.washington.edu/wtohist/testimonies/introduction.htm.

23 Katie and Elijah. August 18, 2000. Interviewer Jeremy Simer. "Seattle Post Intelligencer." University of Washington WTO History Project. Retrieved on November 28, 2016 at: https://depts.washington.edu/wtohist/.

24 Janet Thomas. 2000. *The Battle in Seattle: The Story Behind and Beyond the WTO Demonstrations*. Golden, Colorado: Fulcrum, p.85.

25 Jeanne Vacccaro. August 2004. "Give Me An F: Radical Cheerleading and Feminist Performance." Retrieved on November 28, 2016 at: https://hemi.nyu.edu/journal/1_1/cheerleaders_print.pdf.

26 For a discussion of puppets in mass demonstrations see David Graeber 2007. "On the Phenomenology of Giant Puppets: Broken Windows, Imaginary Jars of Urine, and the Cosmological Role of the Police in American Culture." Retrieved on November 28, 2016 at: https://libcom.org/files/puppets.pdf.

27 Lynda V. Mapes. November 29, 2009. "Five Days that Jolted Seattle." *Seattle Times*. Retrieved on November 29, 2016 at: www.seattletimes.com/seattle-news/five-days-that-jolted-seattle/.

28 Two of the more detailed accounts of the early assaults by the police are: Mac Lojowsky. 1999. "Comes a Time," and Cockburn, St. Clair, and Sekula. 2000. *Five Days*, pp.21–32.

29 See for example the images available at: Lynsi Burton. November 29, 2014. "WTO Riots in Seattle: 15 Years Ago." *Seattle Post Intelligencer*. Retrieved on November 29, 2016 at: www.seattlepi.com/local/article/WTO-riots-in-Seattle-15-years-ago-5915088.php.

30 Washington Chapter of the American Civil Liberties Union. June 2000. *Out of Control: Seattle's Flawed Response to Protests Against the World Trade Organization*, p.9. Numerous explanations have been advanced for the response of the Seattle police, including lack of training, lack of sleep, lack of clear direction from commanders and so forth. See in particular: Patrick Gillham and Gary Marx. 2000. "Complexity and Irony in Policing and Protesting: The World Trade Organization in Seattle." *Social Justice*. Vol.7(2): 212–236.

31 Cockburn, St. Clair, and Sekula. 2000. *Five Days*, p.31. For greater detail about the imposition of a state of emergency see the ACLU report. 2000. *Out of Control*.

32 Black Bloc (anarchist) protesters have made their appearance at other protests garnering significant publicity. They forced the cancellation of a talk by the right-wing provocateur Milo Yiannopoulous at the Berkeley campus on February 1, 2017. The police did not prevent them from breaking windows and firing bottle rockets because the police had learned from other protests that it would result in negative publicity for law enforcement officers.

33 Jules Boykoff. June 2006. "Framing Dissent: Mass-Media Coverage of the Global Justice Movement." *New Political Science*. Vol.28(2):201–228.

34 Pierre Bourdieu. 1998. *On Television*. New York: New Press.

35 Robert D. Benford and David A. Snow. 2000. "Framing Processes and Social Movements: An Overview and Assessment." *Annual Review of Sociology*. Vol.26:611–639.

36 James Cox and Del Jones. December 1, 1999. "'This Weird Jamboree': Teamsters and Turtle Protectors on Same Side." *USA Today*. Cited in Jules Boykoff. June 2006. "Framing Mass Dissent," p.201.

37 For a detailed discussion of selection bias in stories about protests see: John D. McCarthy, Clark McPhail, and Jackie Smith. June, 1996. "Images of Protest: Dimensions of Selection Bias in Media Coverage of Washington Demonstrations, 1982 and 1991." *American Sociological Review*. Vol.61(3):478–499.

38 For a discussion of civil disobedience in modern society and the reaction of the media and police to it, see: Rebecca Solnit. 2004. "Jailbirds I Have Loved or 'No You Can't Have My Rights. I'm Still Using Them'." *TomDispatch*. Retrieved on December 19, 2016 at: www.tomdispatch.com/post/1857/rebecca_solnit_jailbirds_I_have_loved.

39 Rebecca Solnit, a participant in the Seattle movement, has written extensively on the false stories spread by the media. Rebecca Solnit. 2004. "Jailbirds I Have Loved or 'No You Can't Have My Rights. I'll Still Using Them'." David Solnit and Rebecca Solnit. 2009. "The Myth of Seattle Violence: My Battle with the New York Times" in *The Battle of the Story of the Battle of Seattle*, Chapter 2.

40 Cited in Boykoff. 2006, "Framing Dissent," pp.211–214.

41 Independent Media Center. 2016. "About Indymedia." Retrieved on November 30, 2016 at: www.indymedia.org/or/index.shtml.

42 John Arquilla and David Ronfeldt. 2001. *Networks and Netwars: The Future of Terror, Crime, and Militancy*. Santa Monica, California: Rand Corporation, pp.89–98.

43 Kit Oldham. October 13, 2009. "WTO Meeting and Protests in Seattle (1999), Part I and II." *History Link*. Retrieved on December 19, 2016 at: www.historylink.org/File/9183.

44 David Graeber. 2007. "On the Phenomenology of Giant Puppets."

45 Jose Martinez. March 4, 2000. "Police Prep for Protests over Biotech Conference at Hynes." *Boston Herald*. Cited in David Graeber. 2007. "On the Phenomenology of Giant Puppets." See also David Graeber. 2007. *Possibilities: Essays on Hierarchy, Rebellion and Desire*. Oakland, California: AK Press.

46 David Graeber gives a full accounting of the stories manufactured in support of the notion that protesters were prepared to engage in violent actions. David Graber. 2007. "On the Phenomenology of Giant Puppets," pp.14–17.

47 David Solnit and Rebecca Solnit. 2009. *The Battle of the Story of the Battle of Seattle*.

48 Paul de Armond. February 29, 2000. "Storming Seattle: Aftermath." *Albion Monitor*. Retrieved on December 19, 2016 at: www.albionmonitor.com/seattlewto/.

49 The successes of movements that grew out of the Seattle protests are discussed by Naomi Klein. June 22, 2000. "The Vision Thing: 'This Conference Is Not Like Other Conferences.'" *The Nation*. Retrieved on December 20, 2016 at: www.thenation.com/article/vision-thing/.

50 David Solnit in David Solnit and Rebecca Solnit. 2009. *The Battle of the Story of the Battle of Seattle*, p.18.
51 Joshua Kahn Russell. 2016. "Direct Action." *Beautiful Trouble*. Retrieved on December 21, 2016 at: http://beautifultrouble.org/tactic/direct-action/.
52 Chris Suellentrop. April 11, 2000. "The Battle of Washington.Com." *Slate*. Retrieved on December 20, 2016 at: www.slate.com/articles/news_and_politics/net_election/2000/04/the_battle_of_washingtoncom.html.
53 Naomi Klein. June 22, 2000. "The Vision Thing."
54 Cited in Lesley J. Wood. 2012. *Direct Action, Deliberation, and Diffusion*. New York: Cambridge University Press, p.85.
55 Wood. 2012. Wood systematically compares protests in New York and Toronto to explain what enhanced diffusion and what limited it. As she noted, social movement organizations are not static; they are shaped by local conditions and by historical circumstances. The World Trade Center attacks, for example, limited black bloc activities.
56 Lesley Wood. 2010. "Bringing Together the Grassroots: A Strategy and a Story from Toronto's G20 Protests." *Upping the Anti, Number 11*. Retrieved on December 21, 2016 at: http://uppingtheanti.org/journal/article/11-bringing-together-the-grassroots-a-strategy-and-a-story-from-torontos-g2/.
57 Stefan Walgrave and Dieter Rucht. 2010. *The World Says No to War: Demonstrations against the War on Iraq*. Social Movements, Protests, and Contention, Vol.33. Minneapolis: University of Minnesota Press. A pdf of the book is available at: http://uahost.uantwerpen.be/m2p/publications/1267098151.pdf#page=13.
58 Stephen Walgrave and Joris Verhulst. n.d. "The Worldwide February 15 Protests against the War in Iraq: An Empirical Test of Transnational Opportunities." Working Paper. Retrieved on November 17, 2016 at: http://citeseerx.ist.psu.edu/viewdoc/download?doi=10.1.1.571.4808&rep=rep1&type=pdf.
59 Gallup Poll. 2003. "Seventy-Two Percent of Americans Support War Against Iraq." Retrieved on November 17, 2016 at: www.gallup.com/poll/8038/seventytwo-percent-americans-support-war-against-iraq.aspx.
60 Pew National Research Center. January 27, 2014. "Thirteen Years of the Public's Top Priorities." Retrieved on December 20, 2016 at: www.people-press.org/interactive/top-priorities/.
61 *Adbusters.org*.
62 Micah White. 2016. *The End of Protest: A New Playbook for Revolution*. Toronto, Canada: Knopf Canada, p.13. White provides both a history of OWS, his reflections on why the movement failed, and his utopian ideas about what would be successful.
63 White. 2016, p.1.
64 Cited in White. 2016, p.18.
65 The estimates for those sleeping overnight in Zuccotti range from 100–300.
66 Cited in White. 2016. *The End of Protest*, p.10.
67 These observations by me are based on demonstrations that occurred in Chico, California and Ashland, Oregon.
68 Amy Westfeldt. December 15, 2011. "Occupy Wall Street's Center Shows Some Cracks." *Business Week*. Retrieved on December 23, 2016 at: https://web.archive.org/web/20130502045516/http://www.businessweek.com/ap/financialnews/D9RKV7H00.htm.
69 A. Barton Hinkle. November 4, 2011. "OWS Protesters Have Strange Ideas about Fairness." *Richmond Times Dispatch*. Retrieved on December 23, 2016 at: www.richmond.com/news/article_9aacde1b-931a-50a6-8471-d40ec1f78eff.html.
70 Laurie Penny. October 16, 2011. "Protest by Consensus: Laurie Penny on Madrid's Occupy." *New Statesman*. Retrieved on December 23, 2016 at: www.newstatesman.com/blogs/laurie-penny/2011/10/spain-movement-square-world.

71 Gloria Goodale. November 1, 2011. "Who Is Occupy Wall Street? After Six Weeks, a Profile Finally Emerges." *Christian Science Monitor*. Retrieved on December 22, 2016 at: www.csmonitor.com/USA/Politics/2011/1101/Who-is-Occupy-Wall-Street-After-six-weeks-a-profile-finally-emerges.

72 Jillian Berman. January 29, 2013. "Occupy Wall Street Not at All Representative of the 99 Percent, Report Finds." *Huffington Post*. Retrieved on December 22, 2016 at: www.huffingtonpost.com/2013/01/29/occupy-wall-street-report_n_2574788.html.

73 Accra Shepp. September 17, 2016. "Occupy Wall Street: Where Are They Now?" *The New York Times*. Retrieved on December 23, 2016 at: www.nytimes.com/interactive/2016/09/17/opinion/Occupy-Wall-Street.html?_r=0.

74 Micah White. 2016. *The End of Protest*, p.3.

75 Naomi Wolf. December 29, 2012. "Revealed: How the FBI Coordinated the Crackdown on Occupy." *The Guardian*. Retrieved on December 22, 2016 at: www.theguardian.com/commentisfree/2012/dec/29/fbi-coordinated-crackdown-occupy.

76 Katti Gray and Dean Schabner. November 13, 2011. "Occupy Portland Protesters Leave Park Peacefully." *ABC News*. Retrieved on December 23, 2016 at: http://abcnews.go.com/US/occupy-portland-leaves-parks-peacefully-police-order/story?id=14943270.

77 Margaret Kohn. March 1, 2013. "Privatization and Protest: Occupy Wall Street, Occupy Toronto, and the Occupation of Public Space in a Democracy." *Perspectives on Politics*. Vol.11(1):99–110.

78 Benjamin Gleason. July, 2013. "#Occupy Wall Street: Exploring Learning about a Social Movement on Twitter." *American Behavioral Scientist*. Vol.57(7):966–982.

79 Leslie Layton. October 15, 2011. "Unlikely Organizers Bring Occupy Movement to Chico." *New American Media*. Retrieved on December 23, 2016 at: http://newamericamedia.org/2011/10/unlikely-organizers-bring-occupy-movement-to-chico.php.

80 Michael D. Conover, Emilio Ferrara, Filippo Menczer, and Allessandro Flammini. May 29, 2013. "The Digital Evolution of Occupy Wall Street." *PLoS ONE*. Vol.8(5). Retrieved on December 22, 2016 at: http://journals.plos.org/plosone/article?id=10.1371/journal.pone.0064679.

81 Chris Hawley. December 1, 2011. "Occupy Protesters Shift Tactics after Raids in Philadelphia, Los Angeles." Boston.com. Retrieved on December 26, 2016 at: http://archive.boston.com/news/nation/articles/2011/11/30/after_raids_wall_street_protesters_shift_tactics/.

82 Katti Gray and Dean Schabner. November 13, 2011. "Occupy Portland Protesters Leave Park Peacefully." *ABC News*. Retrieved on December 26, 2016 at: http://abcnews.go.com/US/occupy-portland-leaves-parks-peacefully-police-order/story?id=14943270.

83 Micah White. 2016. *The End of Protest*, p.26.

84 White. 2016, p.27.

85 White. 2016, pp.77–79. See also: William Gamson. 1975. *The Strategy of Social Protest*. Homewood, Illinois: Dorsey Press.

86 Frances Fox Piven and Richard A. Cloward. 1977. *Poor People's Movements: Why They Succeed, How They Fail*. New York: Random House.

87 For an overview of Piven and Cloward's work and the controversies it generated see: Mark Engler and Paul Engler. May 24, 2014. "Can Frances Fox Piven's Theory of Disruptive Power Create the Next Occupy?" *Waging Nonviolence*. Retrieved on December 27, 2016 at: http://wagingnonviolence.org/feature/can-frances-fox-pivens-theory-disruptive-power-create-next-occupy/.

88 The strong argument about the importance of organizational strength gives rise to resource mobilization theory.

89 John Markoff. 2015. "Historical Analysis and Social Movement Research," in Donatella Della Porto and Mario Diani, eds. *The Oxford Handbook of Social Movements*. New York: Oxford University Press, pp.68–85.

90 Interview with John Cioffi. October 12, 2011. "'Occupy Wall Street' May Join Long List of Failed Social Movements." *University of California, Riverside, Newsroom.* Retrieved on December 27, 2016 at: https://ucrtoday.ucr.edu/896.
91 Micah White. 2016. *The End of Protest*, p.155.
92 David A. Snow and Dana M. Moss. 2014. "Protest on the Fly: Toward a Theory of Spontaneity in the Dynamics of Protest and Social Movements." *American Sociological Review.* Vol.79(6):1122–1143.
93 Chris Dixon. 2014. *Another Politics: Talking across Today's Transformative Movements.* Berkeley, California: University of California Press. Dixon writes about the tendency of modern movements to mimic one another in terms of organizational structure, rather than crafting strategies and policies that are appropriate for the circumstances.
94 John D. McCarthy and Mayer N. Zald. 1973. *The Trend of Social Movements in America: Professionalization and Resource Mobilization.* Morristown, New Jersey: General Learning Press; John D. McCarthy and Mayer N. Zald. May 1977. "Resource Mobilization and Social Movements: A Partial Theory." *The American Journal of Sociology.* Vol.82(6):1212–1241.

Black Lives Matter   **3**
The Evolution of a Social Movement

Consider:

- The shooting of Trayvon Martin and the acquittal of George Zimmerman gave rise to a national conversation about racial profiling and civil rights.
- Black Americans are more than 2.5 times as likely to be shot and killed than are whites.
- Minority communities are subject to policing for profit, when they are convicted for minor crimes as a way of boosting municipal budgets.
- Black Lives Matter represents a "movement moment," a time when mass protests from below can lead to significant social change.
- Blacks Lives Matter is simultaneously an organization, social movement, and ideology.
- The ideology of Black Lives Matter is sufficiently broad that many other organizations have adopted the name.

On the evening of February 26, 2012, Trayvon Martin, a 17-year-old African-American male, was returning to the house where he was a guest. He had gone out to a local convenience store for snacks, a bag of Skittles and a can of watermelon drink. Martin was wearing a grey hooded sweatshirt, walking along in the rain and talking with his girl friend on his cell phone. He was spotted by George Zimmerman, a volunteer watch coordinator for a gated neighborhood in Sanford, Florida.

Zimmerman, who made frequent calls to the police in his role as a watch coordinator, called in his sighting of Martin. He reported that he had seen a "real suspicious guy." During his call he referred to people like Martin as "punks" and "assholes [who] always get away." He then said, "He's running." In spite of the dispatcher's warning to Zimmerman that he was not to follow, Zimmerman got out of his car and chased Martin. What happened next was never clear but a fight ensued and Zimmerman shot the unarmed teenager in the heart.

Zimmerman was taken in by the police and questioned for five hours. He claimed that Martin had punched him and slammed his head repeatedly against the sidewalk. He was cut and bruised. The local police declined to prosecute Zimmerman for murder because under Florida's Stand Your Ground statute a person who feels their life is threatened has the right to use lethal force to protect themselves. This decision was widely challenged by civil rights advocates and protesters across the country who argued that Trayvon Martin was the victim of racial profiling. Even President Obama weighed in, urging a thorough investigation and adding, "If I had a son, he'd look like Trayvon." Florida's governor, Rick Scott, appointed a special prosecutor who charged Zimmerman with murder.

A year and a half later, on July 13, 2013, George Zimmerman was acquitted by a six-woman jury who rejected the prosecution's claim that Zimmerman had pursued Martin and killed him simply because he assumed a Black teenager wearing a hoodie must be a criminal. The reaction to the not guilty verdict was swift. That evening and on the following day demonstrators in New York, Boston, San Francisco, Chicago, Los Angeles, and Sanford, Florida took to the streets in support of Trayvon Martin's family and in condemnation of the Florida justice system. Some carried signs proclaiming: "We Are All Trayvon."[1] The President of the National Association for the Advancement of Colored People (NAACP), Benjamin Todd Jealous, issued a statement:

> We are outraged and heartbroken over today's verdict. We stand with Trayvon's family and are called to act. We will pursue civil rights charges with the Department of Justice . . . and we will not rest until racial profiling in all its forms is outlawed.[2]

A Florida-based group, Dream Defenders, sprang up and occupied Governor Rick Scott's office in a peaceful protest lasting 31 days. One of the other new groups that would soon capture the attention of the public and mainstream media was Black Lives Matter.

Founding

The day Zimmerman was acquitted an Oakland-based activist, Alicia Garza, took to Facebook and wrote: "Black people. I love you. I love us. Our lives matter, Black Lives Matter." Another activist and friend, Patrisse Cullors, turned it into a hashtag, #BlackLivesMatter, which went viral, and continues to be used to organize protests over the killing of Black men and women by the police. Cullors and Garza would be joined by Opal Tometi, a Nigerian-American who at the time was an immigration rights organizer in Phoenix. As the three women who created the movement explained, "It was a response to the anti-Black racism that permeates our society."[3] As the movement grew in prominence, variations on the theme of Black Lives Matter appeared: all lives matter, Black minds matter, Brown lives matter, migrant lives matter, our lives matter, and women's lives matter. But the name, Black Lives Matter, would become a *master frame* for embracing all efforts to achieve social justice for the Black community. This facilitated other groups "attaching" themselves to the larger movement.

As we noted in Chapter 2, a successful group will try to frame its concerns in a broad fashion so that it can connect ideologically to those with related issues.[4] In the case of Black Lives Matter, the national attention given to the organization meant that many other groups would try to link their message to the larger one of Black Lives Matter. Thus minority groups arguing for a $15 an hour minimum wage, those demanding the demilitarization of the police, or those in the Black Minds Matter organization could find a home under the broad umbrella of Black Lives Matter.

The founders, however, objected to the appropriation of this *framing device*, especially those who tried to turn it around and argue that "all lives matter." As they pointed out, doing so trivializes the experience of Black people and their unique struggle and oppression. "Please do not," they emphasized, "change the conversation by talking about how your life matters, too. It does . . . but we need a more active [solidarity] with us, Black people, unwaveringly, in defense of our humanity."[5] As it happens, these women also wanted to keep their focus on the larger queer community.

They wanted it made clear that the organization went beyond calling on "Black people to love Black, live Black and buy Black," while "keeping straight cis Black men in the front of the movement." Their stated purpose was to take up the cause of "our sisters, queer and trans and disabled folks, Black-undocumented folks, folks with records, women and all Black lives along the gender spectrum." It was a tactic designed to take those who had been marginalized in traditional Black liberation efforts and move them to the center of the discussion. Their intent was to take the spot-light off a few male charismatic leaders while allowing for full participation at the grassroots level.[6]

The movement would eventually rely on independent chapters from which the central organization would take its direction. Social media, principally Facebook and Twitter, would serve as the means to rally people to protest marches and to build a community. As we will see in the following, the initial focus on LBGT issues would cause some conflict with older established civil rights groups. Other groups, claiming a link to Black Lives Matter, would step forward with related agendas but ones more focused on accomplishing political and economic goals. Concerns about police violence would bring together

| Black Lives Matter began as a small organization but evolved to become an ideology and a social movement. |

many existing organizations as well as create new ones. While Black Lives Matter began as a small *organization* focused on a specific issue, it would grow to become both a *movement* and an *ideology*. The movement grew out of a social context that put Black lives at risk.

Social Context

Though the movement was precipitated by the acquittal of George Zimmerman, there were previously existing *structural factors* that contributed to its rise—endemic poverty, housing and job discrimination, and legitimate fear and distrust of police officers and local governments. These factors also meant that in many cities across the country, groups were already working to solve problems faced by minority communities. In spite of gains made during and after the civil rights era, a large part of the Black population remained stuck in place. Younger Blacks, in particular, were and are faced with a jobs crisis, a justice crisis, a health crisis, and an education crisis.

Economic Factors

Every year since 1976 the Urban League has published "The State of Black America."[7] In 2016, Black America was found to be just 72.2% equal to White America. To come up with this number the League looks at five categories: economics, education, health, social justice, and civic engagement. Blacks are compared to whites because the history of race in the country has conferred advantages to whites and disadvantages to Blacks that still persist. Blacks fall behind in all five categories.

Black households have traditionally suffered the most from economic downturns. During the crisis that began in 2008, unemployment rates for Blacks shot up to 16.8%, and foreclosures took their toll. According to the National Low Income Housing Coalition, Blacks lost *half* of all their wealth due to the combined housing and unemployment crises of 2008.[8] Unemployment rates for Blacks have improved since then to 8.3% in 2016, but this was still almost twice as high as the unemployment rate for whites (4.4%).[9]

Social policies such as redlining and the flight of whites to suburbs have meant that Blacks are concentrated in low-income urban areas where there are few jobs and if there are any, they don't pay much. Black children are three times more likely to live in poverty than white children. They are more likely to attend high-poverty schools and less likely to graduate from high school, limiting their future chance at educational and occupational success. They are more likely to suffer from low-birth weight and have less access to high-quality medical care.[10] They are also more likely to live in a household headed by a single woman and in families with less money, because Black men have been locked up.

The Criminal Justice System

One of the greatest differences found when comparing Blacks to other ethnic groups are the crimes they are charged with and the time they serve in jail. With 5% of the world's population, we have 25% (2.3 million) of all the world's prisoners behind bars. And Blacks constitute a disproportionate share of that number.[11] The overall numbers tell a discouraging story.

One in every ten Black men in his 30s is in prison at any given time. Blacks are six times more likely to be sent to prison than whites. But they are ten times more likely to serve time in jail for drug offenses than whites. As we saw in Chapter 1, the war on drugs under Nixon and Reagan was a conscious war on the African-American community. If current trends continue, 33% of all Black men born today will spend time in prison at some point in their life.[12] Some of these differences are due to economic disparities and the social and economic isolation of inner-city life, where jobs are few, the schools are poor, and social services are minimal. But they are also due to the differential application of the law and the deliberate targeting of Blacks and other minority populations.

> If current trends continue, 33% of all Black males born today will spend some time in prison.

This targeting stemmed in part from what is called "broken windows theory," a controversial idea advanced by the social scientists James Q. Wilson and George L. Kelling in 1982.[13] The theory, also referred to as zero tolerance, maintains that if police pursued all levels of crime, including broken windows, with equal vigor, then violent crimes would also decrease. But, as the Department of Justice pointed out, it resulted in minorities being differentially targeted. For example, from 2008–2011 New York officers issued eight citations for riding bicycles on the sidewalk in Park Slope, a well-to-do white neighborhood in Brooklyn. In nearby Bedford-Stuyvesant, a predominately Black and Latino neighborhood, 2,050 citations were issued.[14]

The issue of racial profiling has been the subject of a number of studies. As Floyd D. Weatherspoon, a professor of law, has said: "Every African-American male in this country who drives a vehicle . . . has been the victim of racial profiling by law enforcement officials."[15] As he noted, "the term 'driving-while black' has been used to describe the practice of law enforcement officials to stop African-American drivers without probable cause." According to Weatherspoon, "African-American males are not only singled out while driving, but also while schooling, eating, running for political office, walking, [or] banking . . ."[16]

Kelly Welch, a professor of sociology and criminal justice, has noted that the stereotyping of Blacks as criminals is so pervasive that the term "criminal predator" has become a euphemism for "young Black male."[17] President Bill Clinton's reference to "super predators" in signing a 1994 crime bill was later taken by many in the Black Lives Matter movement as a similar indictment. They assumed he was defining the Black body as a criminal body. Stopping and surveillance of African-Americans cannot be explained simply by reference to their criminality, because many innocent Blacks will be stopped simply for being in the wrong place.[18]

Roland Fryer, a Harvard professor of economics, looked at over 5 million cases in New York's Stop, Question, and Frisk Program from 2003–2013.[19] He found that Blacks and Hispanics were 50% more likely to encounter non-lethal police force—pushing, kicking, and baton wielding—than whites. In San Francisco, where it was revealed police officers had traded racist and homophobic text messages, a panel of retired federal and state judges found clear "racial disparities regarding S.F.P.D. stops, searches, and arrests, particularly for Black people." They also found that when stopped, Blacks were more likely to be the target of non-consensual searches of their vehicles and that "of all people searched without consent, Black and Hispanic people had the lowest 'hit rates' (i.e., the lowest rate of contraband recovered)." Whites who were searched without consent were found to have nearly two times more contraband than Blacks and Hispanics.[20]

In Ferguson, Missouri, the city that gave rise to the Black Lives Matter movement in 2014, the Department of Justice found that with only 21,000 residents, the police issued 9,000 arrest warrants for such minor violations as parking and traffic tickets or failing to mow one's lawn. Local police, politicians, judges, and prosecutors used the law to extract resources from its primarily Black population. A memo from the city finance director to the city manager made it clear that the police needed to increase revenue by 10% if the town was to meet its budget. Ferguson officers were evaluated and promoted based on their "citation productivity."[21] Not surprisingly, it was the minority community they "produced."

Policing for profit, which hits minorities hardest, is one way hundreds of millions of dollars are taken from people who are not even charged with a crime. On February 1, 2014, Drug Enforcement Officers at the Cincinnati/Northern Kentucky Airport seized $11,000 in savings from an African-American college student, Charles Clark. They reasoned that because he had bought a one-way ticket and his bag smelled of marijuana, the money must be from the sales of drugs. His money had actually come from his personal savings. He was arrested when he tried to prevent the agents from seizing his money. The charges were eventually dropped after a national organization took up his cause. Christopher Ingraham, the *Washington Post* reporter who covered the story, noted that the DEA intended to split the money they seized between 13 different police departments. Monies they claimed they needed to keep up their work.[22]

Cities and counties have even partnered with private "alternatives to incarceration" companies to boost their budgets by targeting poor whites and minorities. The reporter, Sarah Stillman, tells the story of Harriet Cleveland, an African-American woman living in Montgomery, Alabama, whose troubles began with a simple traffic ticket.[23] Cleveland was stopped at a police roadblock and charged with driving without a license and no insurance. As she was unable to pay her fine, the judge sentenced her to a two-year probation period with Judicial Correction Services (JCS). She was to pay JCS $200 a month, $40 of which was for a "supervision fee." She quickly fell behind on payments having lost her job as a full-time day-care worker. In 2012 she turned over most of her $2,000 tax rebate to JCS but court costs and fines, plus the amount she owed to JCS, had grown to $4,713.

She then received a letter from the District Attorney informing her that she owed the court $2,714 and would go to jail if she did not pay. She was jailed. Fortunately for Cleveland, her case was taken up by the Southern Poverty Law Center (SPLC). In the discovery process it was found that JCS had often placed her payments in their corporate accounts, rather than using them to reduce her court costs.

The indignities that low-income and minority Americans suffer on a daily basis—for profit policing, continued educational segregation, limited employment opportunities—are substantial, even without this added injustice. The shooting in Ferguson, Missouri (a suburb of St. Louis) would propel the growth of the Black Lives Matter movement and bring both it and discriminatory policing to national attention. As we will also see, additional shootings of unarmed African-Americans by the police would keep the movement in the news and lead to its growth.

Police Shootings

On the evening of August 9, 2014 in Ferguson, Missouri, a white police officer, Darren Wilson, shot and killed an unarmed teenager, Michael Brown. Brown was an 18-year-old Black male who had gone to a local liquor store, stole some cigarillos, and pushed a clerk on his way out the door. He and his friend, Dorian

Johnson, were strolling down the middle of the street when Officer Wilson pulled up beside them saying, "Get the [expletive] out of the street." He then started to drive away, changed his mind and backed up with tires squealing.[24] What happened next is not clear. An argument between Brown and Wilson broke out and Wilson claimed Brown tried to reach inside his car for his gun. What is clear is that two shots were fired, one grazing Brown's thumb. Brown ran. Wilson jumped out of his car following Brown, firing his weapon, missing several times. According to Johnson, who witnessed the shooting, Brown had stopped, turned around, raised his hands and said, "Don't shoot!"[25] That's when six bullets hit Brown's body, two into his head.

Brown's body lay in the street in plain view of neighbors and friends for four hours, surrounded by police who prevented Brown's parents from approaching his body. After the body was removed, a makeshift memorial was created with flowers and candles. The police returned, and according to Mark Follman reporting for *Mother Jones*, an officer on the scene with a dog he was controlling let the dog pee on the memorial. The flowers and candles were subsequently crushed as police drove over the memorial.[26]

The next day, August 10, began peacefully as people gathered for memorials to Brown and his family, but by the time of an evening candlelight vigil, things had changed. Some people had begun to loot and vandalize local businesses, and confronted the police who had blocked off certain areas of the city. Over 150 police officers responded and arrived in riot gear, dressed for battle. Photos taken by reporters and bystanders showed them with sniper rifles on tripods perched on top of armored vehicles, their guns pointed at the crowds of protesters. The Ferguson SWAT team arrived in body armor and armed with assault weapons.[27]

Protests continued from August 9 to August 25. Some protesters threw bottles, rocks, and Molotov cocktails at the police, while the officers responded with tear gas, smoke bombs, and rubber bullets. The Missouri National Guard was called out by the governor and they arrived in camouflage battle gear. U.S. Senator Claire McCaskill (D-MO) came to speak with the demonstrators. She said the "police were the problem, not the solution," and called for their demilitarization. The police, she claimed, were escalating the problems.[28] The Missouri Highway Patrol was ultimately assigned the responsibility for taking over all law enforcement in Ferguson. Its Captain, Ronald S. Johnson, walked at the head of a large peaceful protest on the evening of August 14.

Some of the marchers were chanting, "Hands Up Don't Shoot!" There were signs with the same message. Other, mostly homemade, signs said, "We Are Praying With Our Feet," "Freedom," "Black Power," "Police Should Not Look Like Soldiers," "We Are The Village," "We Will Not Be Silent," "Stop Police Killing of All Races." A large banner was carried at the front of the march by the "Urban League of Metropolitan St. Louis, Inc." Local and national civil rights

> In California, police shot and killed Blacks at almost five times the rate of whites.

leaders joined the ranks of the protesters. At this point there were no signs proclaiming "Black Lives Matter." They would come later.

The events in Ferguson attracted significant attention, both in the United States and abroad, because the matter of the shootings of unarmed Black Americans was a long-standing problem. The *Washington Post*, which has been tracking the death of unarmed Blacks by police officers, found that nationwide Black Americans are 2.5 times more likely to be shot than whites. In a study focusing on just California, it was found that police shot and killed Blacks at almost five times the rate of whites, and three times that for Latinos.[29]

Intimately related to the differential shootings of unarmed African-Americans by the police is the fact that the officers involved in the shootings are usually found blameless. Not just in Ferguson, but across the country people were waiting to see if the grand jury impaneled to review the shooting of Michael Brown would indict Wilson. In anticipation of the jury's results, the governor had declared a state of emergency. The grand jury's verdict was announced on November 24; they would not indict Wilson. Promptly, "Twitter users fired off 3.4 million tweets regarding the police killings of Black people."[30] Protests began immediately and galvanized scores of groups across the country. Some of the protests were spontaneous outpourings of anger, while others were organized by groups, like the Urban League, that had a long history of fighting for racial justice. Black Lives Matter would be a new actor in these efforts.

Dense Networks and the Strength of Weak Ties

Those involved in the early stages of the larger movement and the creation of Black Lives Matter were already experienced activists and many knew one another. They had a substantial well of knowledge and experiences on which they could draw. Alicia Garza was a labor organizer in Oakland and had deep ties to what she referred to as the queer community. She married Malachi Garza, a trans-male activist, who ran training sessions for community organizers. Malachi was director of the Bay Area group, Community Justice Network for Youth, and was actively involved in a campaign to assure justice for Oscar Grant, an unarmed African-American male who had been shot and killed by a transit officer.

Garza met Patrisse Cullors in 2005 in Providence, Rhode Island, where they were attending a conference. Cullors had been organizing in the LGBT community since she was a teenager and at the time of the founding of Black Lives Matter was director of a center for human rights in Oakland. She was attending a meeting of young Black activists in Chicago when news came that

Zimmerman had been found not guilty. She and others experienced what we referred to in Chapter 1 as *moral shock*, the profound feeling that one's culture is under siege. She would eventually move back to Chicago as the national director of the Black Young Project 100, and is active in a movement (Black Work Matters) to raise the minimum wage to $15 an hour.

Garza met Opal Tometi at the Black Organizing for Leadership and Dignity conference in 2012. When she and Cullors began promoting Black Lives Matter, Tometi, who was an immigration rights organizer in Brooklyn, offered to build a social media platform on Facebook and Twitter.[31]

The social movement that came to be identified as Black Lives Matter would extend far beyond these three women. Their original vision would be transformed by others seeking to create new organizations or seeking to connect what they were already doing to the larger goals of this new movement, especially the focus on racial profiling and civil rights. Membership was a fluid, dynamic concept. Scores of organizations would seek to frame their message as being compatible with that of Black Lives Matter.

DeRay Mckesson would become one of the most visible and active members of Black Lives Matter and came to national attention when *The New York Times* did a profile of him.[32] When he heard about the shooting in Ferguson, he quit his job in the Minneapolis public school system and spent months in Ferguson documenting the protests, partly to counter the mainstream media's sensationalist focus on the rioting. The day after he arrived he was tear-gassed. His photographs and tweets documented daily events in Ferguson. "Y'all, tons of police." "Tear gas. It has begun #Ferguson."

Mckesson soon teamed up with a local protester, Johnette ("Netta") Elzie. Like Mckesson, Elzie developed a large following on Twitter and both of them became widely recognized spokespersons for events unfolding in Ferguson. As *The New York Times* reporter, Jay Caspian Kang, described them, they "were developing a model of the modern protester: part organizer, part citizen journalist who marches through American cities while texting."[33]

Others joined their efforts in Ferguson—high school students, a local rapper, and an activist who created political t-shirts and hoodies. Brittany Packnett, the executive director of St. Louis's Teach for American Program, and Justin Hanford, a law professor, published a newsletter, *This is the Movement*, which chronicled daily events in Ferguson and was widely read by reporters, protesters, and officials within the Department of Justice.[34]

Many others who had experience in organizing came to Ferguson in 2014. Ashley Yates of Oakland was chairwoman of the University of Missouri's Legion of Black Collegians. With other activists, she created Millennial Activists United and was one of several who would later be invited in December 2014 to meet with President Obama to discuss issues of police violence and racial profiling.

Erika Totten came to head the Virginia and Maryland chapter of Black Lives Matter; she had previously shutdown a highway in Washington D.C. to protest Ridley Scott's movie, *Exodus: Gods and Kings*, which she deemed a piece of "white supremacist propaganda." Michelle Taylor (who goes by the name Feminista Jones) is a New York social worker who started the hashtag #NMOS14 (National Moment of Silence) to honor Brown's memory. She is now a weekly columnist for *Ebony.com* and hosts her own podcast.[35]

The number of activists who became involved in the larger movement and the groups and hashtags they created (#WeTheProtesters, #SayHerName, #IfWeAintSafeInChurch, #YouOKSis, #MikeBrown, #MappingPoliceViolence, #JusticeTogether, #Ferguson) were many. It meant that the movement, Black Lives Matter, did not have just one meaning, for those seeking to understand its goals or for those who identified with it. It was at its inception an inclusive movement. It embraced and was often affiliated with groups focused on increasing the minimum wage, of spot-lighting the murders of Black transgendered women, of addressing housing, and protesting all forms of violence practiced against the Black community.

The loose structure of the movement and the creation of individual chapters meant that participants could respond quickly to events in their own communities and to issues that resonated with local populations. This combination of a core group with weak ties to diverse organizations allowed for the rapid and widespread diffusion of information to like-minded activists.[36]

National Black leaders also entered the conversation and spoke about the significance of the Ferguson protests to their own communities. Rev. Jesse L. Jackson, Sr. of the Rainbow Push Coalition in Chicago in an open letter said, "There is a Ferguson near you." The Ferguson troubles, he noted, were telling Blacks what they already knew: race determines how you and your children will be treated by the police. "They are more likely to be picked up, more likely to be arrested if stopped, more likely to be jailed if arrested, more likely to jailed if charged."[37]

Continued Resistance

As the protests evolved in Ferguson and nationally, activists called for Officer Darren Wilson to be indicted for murder. At the request of President Obama, U.S. Attorney General, Eric Holder, traveled to Ferguson to meet with residents and Brown's parents. Amnesty International sent a 13-member team to Ferguson to train activists in non-violent protest methods. They would ultimately release a report condemning the Ferguson police for the abuse of human rights.[38]

Black Lives Matter organized a high profile activity for the Labor Day weekend of August 30, 2014 which garnered national attention. Freedom riders from across the country, in the spirit of the 1960s Freedom Rides to register African-American voters in the South, convened at St. John United Church of Christ in St. Louis. Upwards of 500 participants came; many of the young attendees had raised money for their trip on Go Fund Me. The idea for the rides came from Black Lives Matter founder Patrisse Cullors, and support came from Darnell Moore, a Brooklyn-based activist, as well as other organizations. Moore, who describes herself as a queer, feminist organizer, picked up on the theme originally emphasized by Black Lives Matter. Black women, and especially members of the LBGT community, needed to be central in the effort to achieve justice and equity for African-Americans. As she said in reference to the rides, "If the mantra of this trip is 'Black life matters,' it is important to us to emphasize that *all* Black lives matter." It was an opportunity to be truly inclusive.[39]

> The success of a mass movement depends on being able to turn anger and frustration into legislation.

A "Weekend of Resistance" was called for Saturday, October 10; approximately 1,000 protesters streamed through downtown St. Louis. Many were chanting, "Don't Shoot!" "Hands Up!" Small groups representing very diverse constituencies met to plan a protest march against police brutality. By the time the march began it included members of the clergy, unions, LBGT organizations, law students, families, and community organizers from around the country. Even the climate organization, 350.org, offered its support with the reasoning that the death of the planet and the death of Blacks at the hands of white policemen were both forms of genocide. Planned Parenthood offered its support.[40] It may be fair to say that no national organization focused on issues of social justice wanted to be seen as sitting on the sidelines of what could be a new and potentially dominant movement.

The protests wound down the day (November 25, 2014) of Michael Brown's funeral at the request of his parents. His father said, "Tomorrow all I want is peace. That's all I ask." National media reported that upwards of 4,500 mourners attended the funeral.[41] The Rev. Al Sharpton spoke reflecting on the frustration that many felt over Brown's death, and argued that it was time to move beyond demonstrations and turn anger and frustration into legislation.

An issue that would divide organizations was the question: Who was in charge or who "owned" the movement? National groups such as the NAACP and Rev. Al Sharpton's National Action Network were on the scene as well as the New Black Panther Party and the Nation of Islam. Local political leaders and civil rights activists and church leaders helped to organize protests. The Black Lawyers for Justice turned out wearing "Peacekeeper" t-shirts to provide a barrier between the police and protesters.[42] In the early Ferguson protests, local groups such as the Organization for Black Struggle, Hands Up, Don't Shoot, Missourians Organizing for Reform and Empowerment, and the Justice for Michael Brown Leadership Coalition took the lead. For every group, different goals and policies materialized. All, however, would embrace the larger issue of racial profiling and civil rights.

The issue of police violence against members of the Black community continued to be stirred by new events. Shortly after Michael Brown was shot, Eric Garner was approached by two officers on July 17, 2014 in New York City. Garner was one of a group of men, mostly Black and Hispanic, who routinely sold untaxed cigarettes for $1 each and other cheap goods near the Staten Island Ferry Terminal. Two officers confronted Garner and, anticipating his arrest, called for backup. Four more officers arrived. One officer, Daniel Pantaleo, put Garner in a chokehold while others wrestled him to the ground where his head was pushed to the sidewalk. As he was being handcuffed, Garner said, "I can't breathe." He repeated these words, his last, 11 times. No aid was provided to him at the scene, either by the police or the emergency medical technicians (EMTs) who finally arrived.[43]

The initial police account of Garner's death made no mention of his being held in a chokehold. The rationale for not performing CPR at the scene was that the EMTs believed he was breathing. The medical examiner, however, made it clear Garner died from an illegal chokehold and compressions of his chest. His death was ruled a homicide by the examiner and the case was sent to the grand jury.

The entire incident might have been handled internally if Garner's friend, Ramsey Orta, had not recorded everything that happened on his cell phone. The images went viral and there was no doubt about what had really happened— Garner was choked to death. The first protest occurred two days after Garner died, led by Rev. Al Sharpton. When the grand jury decided on December 3, 2014 not to indict Pantaleo, in spite of what the video clearly showed, protests broke out across the country in Atlanta, Baltimore, Berkeley, Chicago, Minneapolis, and New York. Marchers held signs saying, "I Can't Breathe," "Demilitarize the Police," "Justice for Eric Garner," and "Black Lives Matter." Over a period of seven days, 4.4 million Tweets kept the focus on the issue of the fight for police accountability.[44] Garner's family sued the city and eventually received $5.9 million.

The December protests would be fueled by the video recording of yet another death. On November 22, 2014 two Cleveland police officers responded to a call that there was a "Black male sitting on a swing and pointing a gun at people." Tamir Rice, a 12-year-old African-American boy, had been playing in a snowy city park with a toy gun. Within seconds of the officers' arrival, one fired two shots, killing Rice. Neither officer at the scene administered any first aid.[45] Evidence of the shooting was given to a grand jury, which failed to indict either of the officers. Rice's family sued and, eventually, the City of Cleveland settled the case for $6 million without admitting any guilt.

The tactics of the movement, which initially involved blocking streets and sitting in front of court houses, were a low-cost effort to magnify individual protests and a key way to draw national attention to the movement. On Black Friday, November 28, 2014, Black Lives Matter activists in league with Oakland's BlackOutCollective decided to disrupt the holiday shopping season in San Francisco malls. They used the busiest shopping day of the year to call attention to issues commonly ignored by non-Blacks.[46] Similar disruptions, facilitated by social media, occurred in Boston, Chicago, New York, and Seattle.

The Role of Social Media and Cell Phone Cameras

Black Lives Matter was unique in its use of social media. It was extremely effective in alerting people to mass protests in the aftermath of George Zimmerman going free and the failure to find police guilty in the death of Eric Garner. It was able to bypass the mainstream media and call directly on people to act.[47] The ability to document police and civilian interactions on a cell phone video or camera can offer incontrovertible evidence of what actually happened at a scene.

In side-stepping the national media, social media also prevents the shaping of a narrative where Seattle protesters are defined as looters and rioters, rather than as people with legitimate grievances. It is, however, hard to develop solutions or policy based on Tweets. The limit of 280 characters automatically reduces the complexity of the communication and rather than encouraging people to change their opinions, it rallies those of like minds. I want to emphasize, as have others, that social media is extremely effective in getting people to turn out for an event but it is not necessarily effective in building organizational strength.[48]

> Social media propelled the growth of Black Lives Matter and allowed a narrative to be created by the movement rather than by the national media.

Social media also exacerbates the problem of who is in charge of a movement or organization, because anybody can fire off Tweets or comment on Facebook. Many of those involved in the overall social movement, Black Lives Matter, created their own hashtags and websites. The result was that some of their activities appeared episodic and unfocused to outside observers.[49] The deaths of Freddie Gray in New York, Alton Sterling in Baton Rouge, and Philando Castile in a Minneapolis suburb in 2015–2016 were all caught on videos and gave rise to both local and national protests.[50]

Who Leads?

One of the questions raised about the burgeoning movement was "What do they want and who is in charge?" Oprah Winfrey, in an interview with *People* magazine, said, "I think it's wonderful to march and protest and it's wonderful to see all across the country, people doing it." But it's not enough to march. "What I'm looking for is some kind of leadership to come out of this to say, 'This is what we want. This is what has to change, and these are the steps that we need to take to make these changes, and this is what we're willing to do to get it.'" Ferguson protesters fired back, telling Oprah that if she were in Ferguson, she would see that the movement was a collective effort and that a "messiah style of leadership" was not them.[51] The Black Lives Matter website characterizes the movement as not being leaderless but "leaderfull."[52] But many leaders do not make for uniform efforts and Ferguson was not the only place protests were being held.

The Dream Defenders occupied the Florida statehouse for four weeks to get the governor to call a special session to review the racist policies they claimed led to Trayvon Martin's death.[53] The co-founder of Dream Defenders, Umi Selma (then known as Phillip Agnew), became the voice of Dream Defenders but was also seen by the national media as a leading voice for Black Lives Matter. *Ebony* magazine dubbed him "one of this generation's leading voices." Some saw in Selma the embodiment of Nelson Mandela.[54] CNN identified him as one of a group of key "disrupters" who were calling attention to the issues faced by the Black community. By the summer of 2016, Dream Defenders had grown into a substantial organization with a staff of seven and a $500,000 a year budget, which made them unique among the many other groups affiliated with Black Lives Matter. They had resources, a plan, and an organization to carry out their goals.

At the December 2014 "Justice for All" protest in Washington, D.C., organized by the Rev. Al Sharpton's organization, National Action Network, tens of thousands came and listened to Michael Brown's mother, as well as family members of Tamir Rice, speak. The rally was interrupted by a dozen protesters who announced they were from St. Louis and Ferguson and demanded the right to speak. Johnetta ("Netta") Eliza took the stage and told the crowd that this movement was started by young people who wanted action, not just a show like the one being put on by Rev. Sharpton. It was not clear just what kind of action she proposed. Sharpton told the crowd before they began marching, "Don't let no provocateurs get you out of line . . . We are not here to play big shot. We are here to win."[55] Sharpton was emphasizing the need to focus on social policy.

Disorder, competition, and dissidence among groups seeking change and competing for public attention and resources is not new. During the 1960s Civil Rights Movement there were a number of groups, both ad hoc and formal, that worked to achieve equality for African-Americans: the National Association for the Advancement of Colored People (NAACP), the Congress of Racial Equality (CORE), the Southern Christian Leadership Conference (SCLC), the Student Nonviolent Coordinating Committee (SNCC), the Nation of Islam, and the Black Panthers. These groups were not united around strategy or tactics but they were all focused on the issue of social justice, equality before the law, and the elimination of racism. So it is with Black Lives Matter and current organizations that seek to deal with police violence.

When Black Lives Matter first arose, it was in response to the death of Trayvon Martin—a local event and a specific injustice. By December 2014, when the Justice for All march took place in Washington, D.C., and the accompanying Millions March NYC happened in New York, it became a movement about Black lives in general—no longer a Ferguson problem but a national problem.

As Alisa Robinson, the founder of *Elephrame*, explains the evolution of the Black Lives Matter movement:

> [T]he movement entered another state of evolution: discussion and education. In 2015, classes, forums and similar community operations have proliferated. The movement was still taking its message to the streets, but it began to infiltrate universities, churches and other institutions as well.[56]

However, what got done in the *name* of Black Lives Matter, as opposed to what got done by the original *organization*, wasn't always the same.

The Black Lives Matter website notes it is "an online forum intended to build connections between Black people and our allies to fight anti-Black racism, to spark dialogue among Black people, and to facilitate the types of connections necessary to encourage social action and engagement."[57] As Herbert Ruffin, a Syracuse University professor of African-American studies, noted, their goal was to include those who had been on the margins of traditional Black freedom movements—women, the working poor, the disabled, undocumented immigrants, and those who identified as queer or transgendered.[58]

Individual chapters, of which there were 37 in the United States and one in Toronto as of July 2017, have the autonomy to respond to local events and to craft responses that the membership of the chapter deemed appropriate, including protest marches. This generates a variety of activities and it generates a cadre of leaders with loose ties to the organization of Black Lives Matter.

DeRay Mckesson, "Netta" Elzie, and others created Campaign Zero to focus on specific policy changes. Among their demands were: end broken windows policing, create community oversight boards, require body cameras for all officers, end for-profit policing, and demilitarize police forces.[59] The *Washington Post* was quick to commend Black Lives Matter for developing a practical, thoughtful, and urgent agenda.[60] However, the Black Lives Matter organization did not create this campaign, as those from Campaign Zero quickly pointed out. This fissioning of efforts meant that slowly the core group of organizers was losing control over the larger agenda and in some cases directly opposing what others were doing in the name of Black Lives Matter.

One of the divisive issues was DeRay Mckesson's (of We the Protesters and Campaign Zero) willingness to meet with political candidates when the intent of some of the local Black Lives Matter chapters and individuals was simply to confront those candidates. During the 2016 campaign, Black Lives Matter activists challenged both Hillary Clinton and Bernie Sanders at different times. After activists disrupted a Sanders' rally in Seattle, he offered to meet with them but they said they had no interest in doing so. Campaign Zero, on the other hand, responded to an overture from the Sanders campaign and scheduled a meeting. Criticism from those identified with the Black Lives Organization was quick in coming. Mckesson was accused of perpetuating an Al Sharpton style of leadership, offering up reformist rather than radical ideas, stepping on their toes, and duplicating their efforts. According to a BuzzFeed reporter, activists with Black Lives Matter indicated they were going to develop their own blueprint for action, similar to that of Campaign Zero, and it would include a proposal for reform centered on correcting the plight of transgender women.[61]

In July of 2016, the Toronto chapter of Black Lives Matter shut down a gay rights parade. They had been given the honor of marching at the head of the Pride parade in Toronto. The Black Lives Matter float stopped and its marchers sat down. They refused to move until the organizers of the parade agreed to a set of demands which included funding for Black Queer Youth, a prioritizing of black trans women in hiring, and the creation of community spaces for South Asian, indigenous, and people living with disabilities. Toronto Police, who had a history of participating in the Pride Parade, were to be banned in the future, as they were seen as symbols of repression.[62]

Conflict about tactics and goals cropped up with other groups, which spurred Black Lives Matter in the summer of 2016 to protect its "brand" and what it meant. Readers of their website were cautioned not to support an event in Pittsburgh:

> You may have received an email from a man named Todd Elliott Kroger, the person putting this event together. Todd is not affiliated with the BLM Network and is using the Black Lives Matter banner to raise money for an event that is antithetical to our work.

It was antithetical because he was, in their words, using women's work to raise money for regressive activities.[63]

The group in question, Black Life Matter PGH, argued that Black Lives Matter was at fault for focusing on just the issue of police shootings and that the movement had to be more than just an online forum aimed at creating mass protests. As Kroger explained about the group in Pittsburgh,

> Our strategy is to do more than agitate antagonistically and ineffectively. We're not going to hide cowardly without "central leadership" behind a veneer of collective action. If we want to be taken seriously we must lead with a national headquarters and day-to-day operations.[64]

This idea, that for the movement to be successful it must develop a national headquarters with funding, has been a normal strategy for other groups seeking to change social policy. It continues to be a challenge for the organization as others seek to capitalize on a movement that has captured national attention.

In December of 2014, President Obama, along with Vice President Joe Biden and Attorney General Eric Holder, invited seven young activists who served as representatives of this new emerging leadership to the White House. Ashley Yates represented Millennial Activists United, a collective of "queer black women." T-Dubb-O, a St. Louis hip-hop artist and self-proclaimed revolutionary who had Tweeted and rapped about Ferguson, was there. Two students were represented, one from the Ohio Student Association (James Hayes) and the other from Young Activists United of St. Louis (Rasheen Aldridge). Philip Lopez represented the Latino group, Make the Road New York. Brittany Packnett, another St. Louis activist who had deep roots in St. Louis and was the Executive Director of Teach for America, attended. Finally, Umi Selma (formerly Phillip Agnew), Executive Director of the Dream Defenders, was there.

The demands of this diverse group included demilitarization of the police, the defunding of police departments that used excessive force, using the power of the federal government to prosecute police officers who kill or abuse people, and investing in community-led programs that would serve as alternatives to being locked up.[65] How to achieve all of these goals was a vexing question, even with the moral support of the U.S. Attorney General and President Obama.

Some of the young movement leaders had thought carefully about whether or not to draw on the tradition of the Civil Rights Movement to legitimate their efforts. One reason for not doing so was that a comparison to what happened 50 years ago might "dilute the immediacy of the today's protests."[66] Traditional civil rights leaders criticized Black Lives Matter protests for being too aggressive, as opposed to the Martin Luther King, Jr. model of non-violent resistance. The response of this new generation was that with the rollback of voting rights, deepening economic inequality, and violence directed at the Black community, new forms of action are now required.

Evolution of the Movement

Black elites have argued for top-down mobilization rather than mobilization from the bottom up in part because they do not know how to respond to the efforts of grassroots organizers. Black youth organizers, as the sociologist Sekou M. Franklin notes, also must solve the problem of how to sustain their movements over the long term, which requires developing a hierarchical structure and a resource base. They need also to move beyond high-risk strategies such as protests that may turn violent and develop policies that can address the conditions that gave rise to the movements. All of these issues would arise as the movement evolved.[67]

Charlene Carruthers, the national director of the Black Youth Project 100 (BLP100), and Janaé Bonsu, its national chair of public policy, explained what the Movement for Black Lives (M4BL) wanted to do:

> To fill this void in leadership and intervene in this current political moment (the national elections), dozens of local and national organizations have come together for over a year to build our own platform to repair the harm caused by centuries of racial and economic oppression of black people. We know that no political party or candidate will save us, and it is time for us to articulate our ambitions and vision on our own terms.[68]

Michaela Brown, communications director of Baltimore Bloc, one of the groups involved, said the purpose of M4BL was to seek radical transformation. They demanded an end to bail bonds, voter suppression, privatized prisons, militarization of the police, solitary confinement, the death penalty, charter schools, and the criminalization of drugs and prostitution.[69] They also wanted reparations paid to Black Americans for "past and continuous harms."

> Tensions would develop within the movement in terms of strategy and tactics and the wisdom of aligning efforts with traditional political parties.

Montague Simmons of the Organization for Black Struggle said that the demands extended beyond the issue of policing to all forms of state violence that include "failing schools that criminalize our children, dwindling earning opportunities, wars on our trans and queer family that deny their humanity, and so much more."[70] The expansion of issues outlined by M4BL mirrored those raised on college campuses during 2015 and 2016. A critical difference and tension between M4BL and DeRay Mckesson's organization, Campaign Zero, is that M4BL made it clear they wanted to operate outside of traditional political parties, while Mckesson believed in working within the system.[71] So, while all groups were focused on trying to alleviate structural problems in minority communities, they differed in terms of the tactics and issues they believed were most important.

Timing and Political Opportunity

The question of when or whether a social movement is successful in implementing or changing social policy has a lot to do with *timing*. Two related factors—the continued death of unarmed African-Americans at the hands of the police and the run-up to the presidential election of 2016—were factors in the continued evolution and success of the Black Lives Matter *social movement*, as opposed to the organization.

On October 20, 2014 in Chicago, Laquan McDonald was shot 16 times by an officer standing 10 feet away from him. McDonald had been carrying a knife and, when police approached, he began to walk away. Officer Jason Van Dyke arrived at the scene and began shooting at McDonald six seconds after he exited his car. McDonald fell to the ground after the first shot. Van Dyke then unloaded the entire clip of his 9mm while McDonald lay on the ground. The dash-cam from the police was not released until 15 months after the shooting. It completely contradicted the police reports of what happened. As a result, Chicago's police chief, Garry McCarthy, was fired and the U.S. Department of Justice opened a review of the conduct of the entire Chicago force.

Walter Scott, another unarmed African-American, was stopped for a non-functioning brake light in North Charleston, South Carolina on April 4, 2015. Whatever his reasons were, Scott decided to flee the scene. A video surfaced which showed Officer Michael Slager shooting Scott in the back as he ran, contrary to the official police report. The Department of Justice intervened and Slager was indicted on federal charges of violating Scott's civil rights.

In Baltimore, Freddie Gray, a 25-year-old African-American, was arrested for possessing what the police termed an illegal switchblade. Witnesses to the April 12, 2015 arrest claimed that excessive force had been used. Gray's feet and hands were shackled and he was placed in a police van with no seat belt to hold him in place. On his way to the station he suffered spinal cord injuries that led to his eventual death on April 19. All six officers who were involved in the arrest were charged with murder, because they failed to properly secure Gray in the van. Yet the Baltimore County Attorney was unsuccessful in her attempt to convict the officers because it was determined that the officers were simply following standard procedure. The U.S. Department of Justice opened an investigation into departmental practices and, eventually, the City entered into an agreement to reform police practices.

On July 5, 2016, Alton Sterling was selling CDs outside of a convenience store in Baton Rouge, Louisiana. The 37-year-old Black man was held to the ground by two white police officers, one of whom fired several shots into his chest. Two videos recorded by bystanders of the shooting appeared online. One showed Sterling on his back and on the ground with one officer kneeling next to him and another holding his legs down. After the shots are fired one officer is seen reaching in to Sterling's pocket to remove what was reported to be a gun. Both officers were placed on administrative leave and the U.S. Department of Justice took over investigation of the shooting.[72]

On the same day that Sterling died, another shooting occurred that attracted national attention. Philando Castile was pulled over during a traffic stop in a St. Paul, Minnesota suburb on July 6, 2016. Castile was returning from the grocery store with his girlfriend, Diamond (Lavish) Reynolds, and her 4-year-old daughter. The officer, Jeronimo Yanez, told the dispatcher he was going to stop them because they looked like people who had been involved in a robbery. "The driver looks more like one of our suspects, just because of his wide-set nose."[73] At the stop, Castile explained to the officer that he had a concealed weapon and a permit and told Yanez he was going to reach into his pants pocket to get out his billfold. As he reached for his billfold, Yanze fired into Castile's chest, killing him. Castile's girlfriend, Diamond Reynolds, then filmed and live-streamed the aftermath, including Castile's last breath. She can be heard telling the officer, "Please don't tell me my boyfriend's dead." Her daughter in the backseat says, "It's alright mommy; I'm here."[74] Minnesota's governor, Mark Dayton (D), questioned whether Castile would have been shot if he was white. He responded to his own question by saying, "I don't think it would have . . . I think all of us in Minnesota are forced to confront this kind of racism."[75]

Police shootings of unarmed African-Americans would continue into the summer of 2016 and on into 2017. On August 9, 2016, 18-year-old Paul O'Neal was shot after he crashed a stolen Jaguar into one of the police cars pursuing him. A series of video clips released by the Chicago Independent Police Review Authority, which was created in the aftermath of the death of Laquan McDonald, showed officers giving one another high fives, after turning off their body cameras.[76] Black Lives Matter activists spoke out against this violence, as well as other violent acts.

At a gay night club, Pulse, in Orlando, Florida in June of 2016, Omar Mateen, a 29-year-old security guard who pledged allegiance to Islamic terrorists, killed 49 people and wounded 53 others. In response, Black Lives Matter extended "love, light, protection, and abundance" to the gay community. They emphasized they would continue to fight for a "movement that celebrates Black and Brown Trans women," and not let the movement be appropriated by white progressives who wanted to focus on gun control or Islamic terrorism.[77]

They spoke out when a lone gunman attacked 11 officers in Dallas, killing five; and when three officers were killed in Baton Rouge. They warned that the attacks on police should not be linked to the movement as they were opposed to violence in all of its forms.[78]

The result of this continued violence against unarmed Blacks, as well as police officers, kept the movement in the news. It prompted the U.S. Department of Justice to open investigations into the shootings as well as individual police departments. And it brought about real changes.

Movement Success

Political candidates were paying close attention to the movement. During the Republican presidential primary, candidate Chris Christie, the Republican governor of New Jersey, labeled Black Lives Matter protesters as thugs. New York's former mayor, Rudolph Giuliani (R), decried Black lives Matter as an inherently racist organization. At the Republican National convention in July, Giuliani and Milwaukee's African-American Police Chief, David Clark, argued in support of the police, "Blue Lives Matter." (This was in response to the deaths of three police officers in Baton Rouge and five in Dallas who had been shot in separate incidents by two Black men.) Not to be outdone, the a.m. radio host Rush Limbaugh labeled the movement as "Black Lives Murder" and termed it a hate group. The right-wing website of David Horowitz rushed to judgment by proclaiming that it was Black Lives Matter terrorists who murdered the Dallas police.[79]

The Democratic candidates Sanders and Clinton both reached out to the leadership of the Black Lives Matter movement. Clinton called for police to wear body cameras, asked for a renewed focus on preventing crime, and called for an end to mass incarceration. She and Sanders both called for police reform. Not all Black Lives Matter activists supported Clinton and a number showed up to protest her nomination at the Democratic convention, chanting outside the hall, "Hell no, DNC! We won't vote for Hillary!"[80] The Black Lives Matter organization did not want their movement co-opted by the Democratic Party or by other groups whose aims they claimed were reformist rather than revolutionary.

How can one evaluate the success of the movement? *Time* magazine declared Black Lives Matter the runner-up for the 2015 Person of the Year Award and christened it a new civil rights movement. They had, the magazine argued, forced politicians to grapple with questions of race and justice. They saw it as a genuine political force that had "hounded police chiefs from their jobs, [and] won landmark prosecutions."[81] How successful was it?

> *Time* magazine declared Black Lives Matter the runner-up for the 2015 Person of the Year Award.

It received a great deal of publicity, not always critical, and kick-started a national discussion about policing and race. It has been successful in getting the U.S. Department of Justice to investigate shootings of unarmed Blacks and getting the Department to demand and implement changes in police practices. In Ferguson, the Department of Justice successfully sued the city to force them to adopt a framework to institute "constitutional policing." The 127-page agreement required new guidelines for police training, including de-escalation and the use of force. The agreement also required police to wear body cameras and the overhaul of the municipal court system, which had been run for profit at the expense of minorities.[82]

In Baltimore, the U.S. Department of Justice investigated police practices and found that the civil rights of Blacks were routinely violated. Overall, African-Americans accounted for 95% of individuals stopped by Baltimore police, while making up only 65% of the population. One mid-50-year-old Black man had been stopped 30 times in less than four years. Each time police had to let him go because he had done nothing wrong.[83] The City agreed to change how their officers were trained, to require the use of technology (body and dash-cameras) to ensure officer behavior was monitored, and to develop strategies to regain the trust of the communities the police serve.[84] The path forward is not smooth, however, as the powerful police union of Baltimore has pushed back against some of the recommendations, as have police unions in other cities that entered into consent decrees.[85]

This pattern—the U.S. Department of Justice investigating and cities consenting to change police practices—played out in other cities across the country. The Department of Justice, in their report on policing in Baltimore, also took aim at the "broken-windows" policy used in many cities, which encouraged zero-tolerance policing. The demand to end "broken-windows" policing is a specific goal of those organizations associated with Black Lives Matter, along with a call to demilitarize the police, a sentiment echoed by Clinton and Sanders, as well as President Obama and the U.S. Attorney General,

Loretta Lynch. However, the goals of the movement extended well beyond minority communities.

Campus Movements

In 2015–2016 there was an explosion of activity on college campuses associated with the ideas of Black Lives Matter. Black students have often had to overcome substantial financial and social obstacles to get into college, and to succeed they must sometimes adjust to a different culture than the one from which they came. Depending on the college they attend, they can experience forms of discrimination and racism they thought they had left behind. They do not want to deny their heritage and they want to see equality on campus practiced not just in words but in deeds. Activism among off-campus groups like Black Lives Matter and its allied organizations were a call to many students to get involved.

The African-American scholar and Harvard University professor, Henry Louis Gates, Jr., has written about the desire and the pressure for minority students to rise and to help others rise with them.[86] Storm Ervin, a University of Missouri student majoring in sociology and Black Studies, said that one of the things she wanted to do was "give back to black people." Some students wanted to transform their campuses. Amanda Bennett, majoring in English and African-American studies at the University of Alabama, grew up in Atlanta among middle-class Blacks and was stunned to find segregation alive and well on her new campus.[87]

Student demands took many forms. At the University of Missouri's Columbus campus, the football team went on strike in support of student demands. They refused to play unless the president of the University System, Tim Wolfe, resigned, acknowledging his white privilege. They also wanted Chancellor R. Bowen Loftin, who oversaw the Columbus, Missouri campus, to quit. Both were forced out by student complaints that they had done too little to address racism on campus.[88] Students seeking reform on campuses across the country took this as a sign of what they might accomplish on their own campuses, if they mobilized.

Students on different campuses learned from one another, and their demands, though rooted in specific issues, took on common themes. Amherst College students wanted the president to issue a statement that the College would not tolerate students who pinned up "All Lives Matter" posters. He was also to issue a press release denouncing the inherent racist nature of the unofficial mascot, Lord Jeff. Babson College students wanted the curriculum redesigned, and faculty hired to teach a curriculum that focused on diversity and inclusion. Bard College students and those at Brown demanded the hiring of more people of color as faculty, counselors, and administrative staff. At Oberlin, students spelled out which faculty members should be given immediate tenure, in which departments new hires should occur, and how the curriculum should be revamped.[89]

Many colleges agreed to improve diversity training, hire more minority faculty, and devote increased resources to both recruiting and retaining minority students. Some campuses also responded to requests to develop degree programs focused on the LBGT community and, if they already had such programs, to enhance them. It is unlikely that such sweeping changes would have occurred without pressure from minority students. Another reason for the success of the students was that universities are by their nature supposed to be able to deal with issues of race, gender, and class.

Understanding Black Lives Matter as a Social Movement

Social movement theorists have long sought answers to questions about what leads to the rise of a mass democratic movement and what leads to its success.[90] They focus on four primary factors: *grievances*, *organizational strength*, *timing*, and *political opportunity*. Frances Fox Piven and Richard Cloward argue in their classic, *Poor People's Movements*, that social change occurs *outside* the bounds of formal organizations like political parties. It does so because poor people have few resources with which to affect political elites or organizations. Thus, instead of proceeding incrementally, the dispossessed must turn to disruptive actions such as boycotts, sit-ins, traffic tie-ups, and rent strikes to achieve their goals. In addition, they argue that the *timing* of mass demonstrations is important. To be successful they need to coincide with a *political crisis*. In Piven and Cloward's argument, organizational strength is discounted because movement organizers will often waste their time trying to maintain the organization itself instead of focusing their energies on bringing about social change.[91] *Resource mobilization* theorists argue a contrary position. Movement success depends on a strong *organizational structure* and on human and material resources to affect meaningful political change.[92]

Sidney Tarrow adds that protests arise when *the political opportunity structure* expands in the presence of *deep grievances*.[93] Charles Tilly has suggested that both political opportunities and timing are keys to mobilization as well as to success.[94] Timing and political opportunity are sometimes treated as the same thing in the literature but there is a meaningful distinction to be made.[95] In the case of Black Lives Matter and related groups, protests arose immediately after the acquittal of George Zimmerman. Other mass demonstrations across the country followed when other unarmed Black men were killed. The immediacy or timing of the protests made it clear there was a direct link between these deaths and the larger issue of structural discrimination.

The 2016 presidential campaign provided a clear *political opportunity* to challenge candidates on their commitment to the reform of police practices and their commitment to social justice issues. A conflict between political elites within each major party and between the parties provided an opportunity for a challenge from Bernie Sanders on the left and Donald Trump on the right.

Black Lives Matter was also provided with a *political opportunity* when President Obama spoke out, saying that if he had a son, he would look a lot like Trayvon Martin. Equally important were the decisions by his Attorneys General, Eric Holder and Loretta Lynch, to pursue cases against police departments. How important this was in terms of context and timing became starkly clear when President Trump appointed Jeff Sessions (R-Senator from Alabama) to be his Attorney General. One of Sessions first orders of business was to fire Sally Yates, a veteran of the Obama administration, because she refused to defend Trump's ban on immigration from seven (later modified to six) Muslim countries. Shortly thereafter, Sessions tried to intervene in the decision made by the City of Baltimore to enter into a consent decree to reform police practices. Sessions made it be known that he would be supporting police officers, not Black protesters.[96] The political opportunity provided by the Obama administration may have vanished as police advocacy groups pushed back. Some writers are now referring to a "Ferguson Effect," claiming that increased scrutiny of police practices has led to an increase in crime rates in major U.S. cities; others dispute this.[97]

The *dense ties* between organizers and the many networks to which they had loose connections allowed them to mobilize quickly and to address both local and national concerns using *social media*. Tweets could quickly mobilize people and images captured on cell phone and camera videos served to undercut official explanations of the shooting of an unarmed person. The *resources* they were able to bring to bear were primarily human resources, the collective of thousands who showed up to protest, to demand justice and the transformation of police departments and college campuses. With one or two exceptions, the organizers had full-time jobs or were full-time students. Neither the organization of Black Lives Matter nor the groups associated with them attracted substantial funding. The disruptive *tactics* they adopted—shutting down highways, disrupting shopping, sitting in statehouses, and protesting in front of court houses and police stations—brought the movement to national light and kept it there but it did not lead to organizational strength.

As for the deep grievances referred to by Sidney Tarrow, African-American communities have suffered from years of structural discrimination. Government policy has treated the poverty of Black and minority communities as a crime, locking people up for being poor. Black Lives Matter began as a group of three women but grew rapidly into a national movement with an ideology focused not just on police violence but one that focused on all forms of violence and discrimination suffered by minority communities. The felicitous choice of the phrase, Black Lives Matter, created a ***master frame*** that made it possible for disparate groups, whether local or national, to mobilize under its banner. The movement grew without a strong organizational structure. Those who embraced the ideology wanted to move beyond protests and bring about real political change. Some groups spun off and created organizational structures to pursue electoral politics. Also, because they did not have a strong organizational structure, the movement was vulnerable to being absorbed by other groups, such as the Rev. Al Sharpton's National Action Network or the NAACP. Numbers do not always translate into success.

Can we label Black Lives Matter as a ***culture of defiance***? My argument would be that it is. It is grounded in the larger culture of dispossessed urban Blacks and campus cultures that focus on issues of gender and equity. Certainly those who went to Ferguson, who founded the movement, and those who created related organizations, all indicated that when Michael Brown was shot, their reaction was: "I have had enough!" They experienced ***moral shock***. Further shootings only reaffirmed and deepened feelings of outrage. The organization itself has also taken a radical and courageous stand in supporting the Black and Latino LBGT community and speaking out when states like Louisiana and North Carolina passed laws restricting bathroom use to the gender cited on one's birth certificate.

Black Lives Matter has moved on from a narrow focus—police violence—to all forms of structural violence, including poverty, attacks on labor unions, unemployment, discrimination, and low wages.[98] It is an attempt to (re)build a Black liberation movement. In the words of Peniel E. Joseph:

> Black Lives Matter has moved beyond many of the blind spots and shortcomings of its predecessors, embracing the full complexity of black identity and forging a movement that is far more inclusive and democratic than . . . civil rights activists envisioned.[99]

As Black Lives Matter is focused on including *every one of us* in the American family, it is important that it succeeds.

Notes

1 Lizette Alvarez and Cara Buckley. July 13, 2013. "Zimmerman is Acquitted in Trayvon Martin Killing." *The New York Times.* Retrieved on July 18, 2016 at: www.nytimes.com/2013/07/14/us/george-zimmerman-verdict-trayvon-martin.html; Richard Luscombe and Haroon Siddique. July 15, 2013. "George Zimmerman Acquittal Leads to Protests across US Cities." *The Guardian.* Retrieved on July 18, 2016 at: www.theguardian.com/world/2013/jul/15/trayvon-martin-protests-streets-acquitta.   For   a

detailed overview of the shooting of Trayvon Martin see: "Shooting of Trayvon Martin." Wikipedia. Retrieved on July 18, 2016 at: https://en.wikipedia.org/wiki/Shooting_of_Trayvon_Martin.

2 NAACP. July 13, 2013. "NAACP Statement in the Acquittal of George Zimmerman in the Killing of Trayvon Martin." Retrieved on July 18, 2016 at: www.naacp.org/press/entry/naacp-statement-in-the-acquittal-of-george-zimmerman-in-the-killing-of-tray.

3 All comments about the founding of the organization come from the Black Lives Matter Home Page. Retrieved on July 18, 2016 at: www.blacklivesmatter.com/her/story.

4 Robert D. Benford and David A. Snow. 2000. "Framing Processes and Social Movements: An Overview and Assessment." *Annual Review of Sociology*. Vol.26:611–639.

5 Black Lives Matter Home Page. Retrieved on August 28, 2016 at: www.blacklivesmatter.com.

6 This point was made by Patrisse Cullors in an interview conducted by Jelani Cobb. March 14, 2016. *The New Yorker*, pp.34–40.

7 National Urban League. 2016. State of Black America. *Locked Out: Education, Jobs, Justice*. Washington, D.C.: National Urban League. Retrieved on July 19, 2016 at: https://app.box.com/s/21ur87auumzr6630rlps0czoae3iv03g.

8 National Low Income Housing Coalition. August 30, 2013. "Report Shows African Americans Lost Half Their Wealth Due to Housing Crisis and Unemployment." Retrieved on July 19, 2016 at: http://nlihc.org/article/report-shows-african-americans-lost-half-their-wealth-due-housing-crisis-and-unemployment.

9 U.S. Department of Labor. "Bureau of Labor Statistics." Retrieved on July 19, 2016 at: www.bls.gov/news.release/empsit.t02.htm.

10 American Psychological Association. 2016. "Ethnic and Racial Minorities & Socioeconomic Status." Retrieved on July 19, 2016 at: www.apa.org/pi/ses/resources/publications/minorities.aspx.

11 Many discussions of crime statistics combine Black and Latino numbers because both groups are subject to "unequal" policing. As this discussion focuses on Black Lives Matter, so too will the data reported.

12 NAACP. 2016. "Criminal Justice Fact Sheet." Retrieved on July 19, 2016 at: www.naacp.org/pages/criminal-justice-fact-sheet. See also: Nazgol Ghandnoosh. February 23, 2015. "Black Lives Matter: Eliminating Racial Inequity in the Criminal Justice System." The Sentencing Project. Retrieved on July 19, 2016 at: www.sentencingproject.org/issues/racial-disparity/.

13 James Q. Wilson and George L. Kelling. March, 1982. "Broken Windows: The Police and Neighborhood Safety." *The Atlantic*. Retrieved on August 28, 2016 at: www.theatlantic.com/magazine/archive/1982/03/broken-windows/304465/.

14 Timothy Williams and Joseph Goldstein. August 10, 2011. "In Baltimore Report, Justice Dept. Revives Doubts about Zero-Tolerance Policing." *The New York Times*. Retrieved on August 11, 2011 at: www.nytimes.com/2016/08/11/us/baltimore-police-zero-tolerance-justice-department.html?emc=edit_th_20160811&nl=todaysheadlines&nlid=73002002&_r=0.

15 Floyd D. Weatherspoon. 2004. "Racial Profiling of African-American Males: Stopped, Searched, and Stripped of Constitutional Protection." *John Marshall Law Review*. Vol.38:439.

16 Weatherspoon. 2004, p.440.

17 Kelly Welch. 2007. "Black Criminal Stereotypes and Racial Profiling." *Journal of Contemporary Criminal Justice*. Vol.23(3):276–288.

18 Albert J. Meehan and Michael C. Ponder. 2002. "Race and Place: The Ecology of Racial Profiling African American Motorists." *Justice Quarterly*. Vol.19(3):399–400. See Ghandnoosh. 2015. "Black Lives Matter" for a detailed breakdown of differential rates of traffic stops.

19 Roland G. Fryer, Jr. July, 2016. "An Empirical Analysis of Racial Differences in Police Use of Force." *The National Bureau of Economic Research*, NBER Working Paper No. 22399. Fryer also found that Blacks were no more likely to be shot by the police than whites, a finding that has been widely challenged.

20 Cited in Kia Makarechi. July 14, 2016, "What the Data Really Say about Police and Racial Bias." *Vanity Fair*. Retrieved on July 20, 2016 at: www.vanityfair.com/news/2016/07/data-police-racial-bias.

21 Edward P. Stringham. July 30–31, 2016. "Is America Facing a Police Crisis?" *Wall Street Journal*. C5–6.

22 Christopher Ingraham. June 20, 2015. "Drug Cops Took a College Kid's Savings and Now 13 Police Departments Want a Cut." *Washington Post*. Retrieved on August 1, 2016 at: www.washingtonpost.com/news/wonk/wp/2015/06/30/drug-cops-took-a-college-kids-life-savings-and-now-13-police-departments-want-a-cut/?utm_term=.2f02fbc13300.

23 Sarah Stillman. June 23, 2014. "Get Out of Jail, Inc." *The New Yorker*, pp.48–61.

24 Eyder Peralta. November 26, 2014. "Ferguson Documents: What Michael Brown's Friend Saw." *National Public Radio*. Retrieved on July 20, 2016 at: www.npr.org/sections/thetwo-way/2014/11/26/366827836/ferguson-documents-what-michael-browns-friend-saw.

25 This account of Brown raising his hands was disputed by others. See, for example, Jonathan Capehart. March 16, 2015. "'Hands Up, Don't Shoot' Was Built on a Lie." *Washington Post*. Retrieved on June 15, 2017 at: www.washingtonpost.com/blogs/post-partisan/wp/2015/03/16/lesson-learned-from-the-shooting-of-michael-brown/?utm_term=.ad5a625d64b8.

26 Mark Follman. August 27, 2014. "Michael Brown's Mom Laid Flowers Where He Was Shot—and Police Crushed Them." *Mother Jones*. Retrieved on July 20, 2016 at: www.motherjones.com/politics/2014/08/ferguson-st-louis-police-tactics-dogs-michael-brown.

27 See for example, Jon Bremosch. November 25, 2014. "Photos of Ferguson." *Buzzfeed*. Retrieved on July 21, 2016 at: www.buzzfeed.com/jonpremosch/ferguson-michael-brown-darren-wilson-protests-photos-grand-j?utm_term=.qyla10RAE#.beQjN23gG.

28 Jacqueline Klimas. April 2, 2014. "Sen. Claire McCaskill: Police Are the Problem, Not the Solution, in Ferguson, Missouri." *Washington Times*. Retrieved on July 21, 2016 at: www.washingtontimes.com/news/2014/aug/14/sen-claire-mccaskill-police-are-problem-not-soluti/.

29 Philip Reese. July 12, 2016. "The Facts about Police Shootings in California: Black, White, and Latino." *Sacramento Bee*. Retrieved on July 21, 2016 at: www.sacbee.com/site-services/databases/article89089872.html.

30 Dani McClain. April 19, 2016. "The Black Lives Matter Movement is Most Visible on Twitter: Its True Home is Elsewhere." *The Nation*. Retrieved on July 27, 2016 at: www.thenation.com/article/black-lives-matter-was-born-on-twitter-will-it-die-there/.

31 Biographical details come from a number of sources but three of the primary ones which featured the leaders are: Jelani Cobb. March 14, 2016. "The Matter of Black Lives." *The New Yorker*, pp.34–40; Brandon Griggs, Emanuella Grinberg, Katia Hetter, Wyatt Massey, Melonyce McAfee, David Shortell, Tanzina Vega, and Eli Wakins. August, 2015. *CNN*. Retrieved on August 11, 2016 at: www.cnn.com/interactive/2015/08/us/disruptors/; Jay Caspian Kang. May 4, 2015. "'Our Demand Is Simple: Stop Killing Us'." *The New York Times*. Retrieved on August 11, 2016 at: www.nytimes.com/2015/05/10/magazine/our-demand-is-simple-stop-killing-us.html?_r=0.

32 Jay Caspian Kang. May 4, 2015. "Our Demand Is Simple: Stop Killing Us."

33 Jay Caspian Kang. May 4, 2015. "Our Demand Is Simple: Stop Killing Us."

34 Jay Caspian Kang. May 4, 2015. "Our Demand Is Simple: Stop Killing Us."

35 The biographical information comes from: CNN. August 2015. "The Disruptors." Retrieved on August 12, 2016 at: www.cnn.com/interactive/2015/08/us/disruptors/.

36 It also serves as a demonstration of the points made by Mark Granovetter. 1973. "The Strength of Weak Ties." *American Journal of Sociology.* Vol.78(6):1360–1380; and Mark Granovetter. 1983. "The Strength of Weak Ties: A Network Theory Revisited." *Sociological Theory.* Vol.1:201–233.

37 Rev. Jesse L. Jackson, Sr. August 18, 2014. "There Is a Ferguson Near You." Rainbow Push Coalition. Retrieved on July 22, 2016 at: www.rainbowpush.org/commentaries/single/there_is_a_ferguson_near_you.

38 Amnesty International. October 24, 2014. "Amnesty International Releases New Ferguson Report Documenting Human Rights Abuses." Retrieved on July 21, 2016 at: www.amnestyusa.org/news/press-releases/amnesty-international-releases-new-ferguson-report-documenting-human-rights-abuses.

39 Akiba Solomon. September 5, 2014. "Get on the Bus; Inside the Black Lives Matters 'Freedom Ride' to Ferguson." *Color Lines.* Retrieved on July 26, 2916 at: www.colorlines.com/articles/get-bus-inside-black-life-matters-freedom-ride-ferguson.

40 Deidre Smith. August 20, 2014. "Why the Climate Movement Must Stand with Ferguson." 350.org. Retrieved on July 21, 2016 at: http://350.org/how-racial-justice-is-integral-to-confronting-climate-crisis/.

41 CBS/AP. August 25, 2014. "Ferguson, Missouri Shooting: Michael Brown's Funeral Draws Thousands in St. Louis." Retrieved on July 21, 2016 at: www.washingtonpost.com/news/morning-mix/wp/2014/08/22/thousands-donated-to-crowdfunding-campaign-for-darren-wilson-the-officer-who-shot-michael-brown/.

42 Monica Davey and Tanzina Vega. August 20, 2014. "Chaos in Ferguson Is Fueled by Tangle of Leadership." *The New York Times.* Retrieved on July 25, 2016 at: www.nytimes.com/2014/08/21/us/chaos-in-ferguson-is-fueled-by-tangle-of-leadership.html?_r=0.

43 One of the more complete accounts of what happened was provided by *The New York Times'* reporters Al Baker, J. David Goodman, and Benjamin Mueller. June 13, 2015. "Beyond the Chokehold: The Path of Eric Garner's Death." *The New York Times.* Retrieved on July 26, 2016 at: www.nytimes.com/2015/06/14/nyregion/eric-garner-police-chokehold-staten-island.html?_r=0.

44 Dani McClain. April 19, 2016. "The Black Lives Matter Movement is Most Visible on Twitter."

45 Elahe Izadi and Peter Holley. November 26, 2014. "Video Shows Cleveland Officer Shooting 12-Year Old Tamir Rice within Seconds." *Washington Post.* Retrieved on July 26, 2016 at: www.washingtonpost.com/news/post-nation/wp/2014/11/26/officials-release-video-names-in-fatal-police-shooting-of-12-year-old-cleveland-boy/?utm_term=.f72a19bb41f1.

46 Herbert Ruffin. 2015. "Black Lives Matter: The Growth of a New Social Justice Movement." *Black Past.* Retrieved on August 12, 2016 at: www.blackpast.org/perspectives/black-lives-matter-growth-new-social-justice-movement.

47 Bijan Stephen. October, 2015. "Social Media Helps Black Lives Matter Fight the Power." *Wired.* Retrieved on July 27, 2016 at: www.wired.com/2015/10/how-black-lives-matter-uses-social-media-to-fight-the-power/.

48 See, for example, Malcolm Gladwell. October 4, 2016, "Small Change: Why the Revolution Will Not Be Tweeted." *The New Yorker.* Retrieved on September 1, 2016 at: www.newyorker.com/magazine/2010/10/04/small-change-malcolm-gladwell.

49 For a discussion of Black youth movements and their fragmented and episodic nature see Sekou M. Franklin. 2014. *After the Rebellion: Black Youth, Social Movement Activism, and the Post-Civil Rights Generation.* New York: New York University Press.

50 As Robin Miller pointed out to me in reading this chapter, it is difficult to attribute all of these protests or the success that followed to Black Lives Matter. As any movement grows and others embrace its causes, it is difficult to trace change to any particular group of actors.

51 Mary Green. January 3, 2014. "Oprah Winfrey's Comments about Recent Protests and Ferguson Spark Controversy." *People*. Retrieved on July 29, 2016 at: www.people.com/article/oprah-winfrey-david-oyelowo-selma-protests-ferguson.

52 Black Lives Matter. July, 2016. "11 Major Misconceptions about the Black Lives Matter Movement." Retrieved on August 17, 2016 at: http://blacklivesmatter.com/11-major-misconceptions-about-the-black-lives-matter-movement/.

53 Dani McClain. April 19, 2016. "The Black Lives Matter Movement is Most Visible on Twitter."

54 Independent Sector National Conference. 2015. "Umi Selah (formerly Phillip Agnew)." Biography retrieved on July 29, 2016 at: http://isembarks2015.com/Speaker/phillip-agnew/.

55 CBS News Report. December 13, 2014. "'Enough Is Enough': Tens of Thousands March to Protest Police Violence." Retrieved on July 26, 2016 at: www.cbsnews.com/news/eric-garner-ferguson-missouri-protesters-converge-on-washington/.

56 Alisa Robinson. March 16, 2015. "Black Lives Matter: The Evolution of a Movement." *Occupy.com*. Retrieved on July 27, 2016 at: www.occupy.com/article/black-lives-matter-evolution-movement#sthash.07Y4exqW.dpbs.

57 Black Lives Matter. Retrieved on July 27, 2016 at: http://blacklivesmatter.com/find-chapters/.

58 Herbert Ruffin. 2015. "Black Lives Matter: The Growth of a New Social Justice Movement." *BlackPast.Org*. Retrieved on August 24, 2016 at: www.blackpast.org/perspectives/black-lives-matter-growth-new-social-justice-movement.

59 Campaign Zero. 2016. "Policy Solutions." Retrieved on July 29, 2016 at: www.joincampaignzero.org/#vision.

60 Radley Balko. August 25, 2015. "The Black Lives Matter Policy Agenda Is Practical, Thoughtful—and Urgent." *Washington Post*. Retrieved on July 29, 2016 at: www.joincampaignzero.org/#vision.

61 Daren Sands. September 13, 2015. "The Success and Controversy of #CampaignZero and Its Successful, Controversial Leader, DeRay Mckesson." *BuzzFeed*. Retrieved on August 2, 2016 at: www.buzzfeed.com/darrensands/the-success-and-controversy-of-campaignzero-and-its-successf.

62 Peter Edwards. July 7, 2016. "Black Lives Matter 'Will Not Stand Down' on Police Ban from Pride Parade." *The Toronto Star*. Retrieved on August 18, 2016 at: www.thestar.com/news/gta/2016/07/07/pride-toronto-volunteer-team-lead-resigns-in-protest.html; James Kirchick. July 6, 2016. "Politics on Parade: How Black Lives Matter Halted a Gay Pride Parade in Toronto." *Los Angeles Times*. Retrieved on August 18, 2016 at: www.latimes.com/opinion/op-ed/la-oe-kirchick-gay-pride-black-lives-matter-20160705-snap-story.html. See also the posting of activists involved in the controversy: Jackie Lucas. July 6, 2016. "Resignation Letter." *Facebook*. Retrieved on August 18, 2016 at: www.facebook.com/jacqie.jaguar/posts/10153902809127054.

63 Black Lives Matter. July, 2016. "Pittsburgh Convening Regresses Efforts for Black Liberation, Unaffiliated with BLM Network." Retrieved on August 18, 2016 at: http://blacklivesmatter.com/pittsburgh-convening-regresses-efforts-for-black-liberation-unaffiliated-with-blm-network-3/.

64 Todd Eliott Kroger. July, 2016. "Black Life Matter PGH." Retrieved on August 18, 2016 at: www.blacklifematterpgh.org/.

65 Ferguson Action. December 1, 2014. "Breaking: Ferguson Activists Meet with President Obama to Demand an End to Police Brutality Nationwide." Retrieved on July 25, 2016 at: http://fergusonaction.com/white-house-meeting/.

66 Jay Caspian Kang. May 4, 2015. "Our Demand Is Simple: Stop Killing Us."

67 Sekou M. Franklin. 2014. *After the Rebellion: Black Youth, Social Movement Activism, and the Post-Civil Rights Generation*. New York: New York University Pres.

68 Charlene Carruthers and Janaé Bonsu. August 1, 2016. "#M4BL: New Policy Agenda Centers Black Demands as Presidential Campaign Hits Full Stride." *The Root*. Retrieved on August 2, 2016 at: www.theroot.com/articles/news/2016/08/movement-4-black-lives-black-youth-project/.

69 Jamiles Laretey. August 1, 2016. "Coalition of Activists Affiliated with Black Lives Matter Outline Policy Agenda." *The Guardian*. Retrieved on August 2, 2016 at: www.theguardian.com/us-news/2016/aug/01/black-lives-matter-release-policy-statement. See also: M4BL.org, "A Vision for Black Lives: Policy Demands for Black Power, Freedom and Justice." Retrieved on May 30, 2017 at: https://policy.m4bl.org/.

70 Cited in James Lartey. August 1, 2016. "Coalition of Activists Affiliated with Black Lives Matter Outline Policy Agenda." *The Guardian*. Retrieved on August 15, 2016 at: www.theguardian.com/us-news/2016/aug/01/black-lives-matter-release-policy-statement.

71 Collier Meyerson. August 1, 2016. "Black Lives Matter Did Something Huge Today." *Fusion*. Retrieved on August 2, 2016 at: http://fusion.net/story/332164/black-lives-matter-policy-demands-m4bl/.

72 Catherine E. Shoichet, Joshua Berlinger, and Steve Almasy. July 6, 2016. "Alton Sterling Shooting: Second Video of Deadly Encounter Emerges." *CNN*. Retrieved on August 9, 2016 at: www.cnn.com/2016/07/06/us/baton-rouge-shooting-alton-sterling/.

73 Andy Mannix. July 12, 2016. "Police Audio: Officer Stopped Philando Castile on Robbery Suspicion." *Star Tribune*. Retrieved on August 8, 2016 at: www.startribune.com/police-audio-officer-stopped-philando-castile-on-robbery-suspicion/386344001/#1.

74 Diamond Reynold's video tape. July 6, 2016. CNN, "Woman Streams Graphic Video of Boyfriend Shot by Police." Retrieved on August 8, 2016 at: www.cnn.com/videos/us/2016/07/07/graphic-video-minnesota-police-shooting-philando-castile-ryan-young-pkg-nd.cnn/video/playlists/philando-castile-shot-in-minnesota/.

75 Cited by T. Rees Shapiro, Lindsey Bever, Wesley Lowery, and Michael E. Miller. July 9, 2016. *Washington Post*. Retrieved on August 8, 2016 at: www.washingtonpost.com/news/morning-mix/wp/2016/07/07/minn-cop-fatally-shoots-man-during-traffic-stop-aftermath-broadcast-on-facebook/.

76 Dan Hinkel. July 28, 2016. "City Declines to Identify Cops in O'Neal Fatal Shooting, Cites Their Safety." *Chicago Tribune*. Retrieved on August 10, 2016 at: www.chicagotribune.com/news/local/breaking/ct-chicago-police-shooting-paul-oneal-cop-names-met-20160809-story.html.

77 Black Lives Matter. 2016. "In Honor of Our Dead: Latinx, Queer, Trans, Muslim, Black—We Will Be Free." Retrieved on August 11, 2016 at: http://blacklivesmatter.com/in-honor-of-our-dead-queer-trans-muslim-black-we-will-be-free/.

78 Black Lives Matter. 2016. "The Black Lives Matter Network Advocates for Dignity, Justice, and Respect." Retrieved on August 11, 2016 at: http://blacklivesmatter.com/the-black-lives-matter-network-advocates-for-dignity-justice-and-respect/.

79 Matthew Vadum. July 8, 2016. "Black Lives Matter Terrorists Murder Dallas Cops." *Front Page*. Retrieved on August 17, 2016 at: www.frontpagemag.com/fpm/263443/black-lives-matter-terrorists-murder-dallas-cops-matthew-vadum.

80 S.A. Miller. July 26, 2016. "Black Lives Matter Supporters March Against Hillary Clinton: 'Hard to Trust.'" *Washington Times*. Retrieved on August 10, 2016 at: www.washingtontimes.com/news/2016/jul/26/hillary-clinton-loses-black-lives-matter-supporter/.

81 Alex Altman. 2015 Cover Issue. *Time* Person of the Year 2015 Runner-Up: Black Lives Matter. Retrieved on August 11, 2016 at: http://time.com/time-person-of-the-year-2015-runner-up-black-lives-matter/.

82 Laura Wagner. March 15, 2016. "Ferguson City Council Accepts Consent Decree Worked Out with Justice Department." *National Public Radio*. Retrieved on August 11, 2016 at: www.npr.org/sections/thetwo-way/2016/03/15/470598733/ferguson-city-council-accepts-deal-with-justice-department.

83 Ian Duncan. August 10, 2016. "DOJ Report Starts Years of Costly Reform Efforts in Baltimore." *The Baltimore Sun*. Retrieved on August 11, 2016 at: www.baltimoresun.com/news/maryland/baltimore-city/bs-md-doj-report-whats-next-20160810-story.html.

84 U.S. Department of Justice. August 10, 2016. "Justice Department Announces Findings of Investigation into Baltimore Police Department." Retrieved on September 1, 2016 at: www.justice.gov/opa/pr/justice-department-announces-findings-investigation-baltimore-police-department.

85 Kevin Rector. August 30, 2016. "Heading Toward a Consent Decree on Policing, Baltimore Activists Prepare for Opposition from Officers' Union." *The Baltimore Sun*. Retrieved on September 1, 2016 at: www.baltimoresun.com/news/maryland/baltimore-city/doj-report/bs-md-ci-doj-fop-role-20160830-story.html.

86 Henry Louis Gates, Jr., February 7, 2016. "Black America and the Class Divide." *The New York Times, Education Life*, pp.10–11.

87 Abby Ellin. February 7, 2016. "The New Activists." *The New York Times, Education Life*, pp.12–15. The quotations come from interviews Ellin did with students from different campuses.

88 Susan Svriuga. November 9, 2015. "U. Missouri President, Chancellor Resign over Handling of Racial Incidents." *Washington Post*. Retrieved on August 18, 2016 at: www.washingtonpost.com/news/grade-point/wp/2015/11/09/missouris-student-government-calls-for-university-presidents-removal/.

89 Black Liberation Collective. March, 2016. "Our Demands." Retrieved on August 18, 2016 at: www.blackliberationcollective.org/our-demands/.

90 Doug McAdam, Sidney Tarrow, and Charles Tilly. 2001. *Dynamics of Contention*. Cambridge, UK: Cambridge University Press. There are scores of social movement theorists who have addressed this set of questions. The bibliography of the McAdam, Tarrow, and Tilly book provides a resource for exploring these ideas.

91 Frances Fox Piven and Richard Cloward. 1977. *Poor People's Movements: Why They Succeed, How They Fail*. New York: Vintage.

92 John D. MCarthy and Mayer N. Zald. 1977. "Resource Mobilization and Social Movements: A Partial Theory." *American Journal of Sociology*. Vol.82:1212–1241.

93 Sidney Tarrow. 1989. *Democracy and Disorder: Protests and Politics in Italy, 1965–1974*. Oxford, UK: Oxford University Press.

94 Charles Tilly. 1978. *From Mobilization to Revolution*. Reading, Massachusetts: Addison-Wesley.

95 David S. Mayer. 2004. "Protest and Political Opportunities." *American Review of Sociology*. Vol.30:125–145. Mayer argues that the notion of what constitutes a political opportunity varies greatly in the literature. I am using it to refer to the specific social and economic factors that gave rise to Black Lives Matter, the crises that developed with the continued shooting of unarmed Black men and women, as well as the timing of the 2016 presidential campaign.

96 Sheryl Gay Stolberg and Eric Lichtblau. April 3, 2017. "Sweeping Federal Review Could Affect Consent Decrees Nationwide." *The New York Times*. Retrieved on May 30, 2017 at: www.nytimes.com/2017/04/03/us/justice-department-jeff-sessions-baltimore-police.html?_r=0.

97 Heather Mac Donald has made the strongest argument for the so-called Ferguson Effect claiming there is a war on police. Heather Mac Donald. 2016. *The War on Cops*. New York: Encounter Books. For an analysis of what the data show see Shaila Dewan. March 29, 2017. "Deconstructing the 'Ferguson Effect.'" *The New York Times*. Retrieved on May 30, 2017 at: www.nytimes.com/interactive/2017/us/politics/ferguson-effect.html?_r=0. See also: Neil Gross. October 2, 2016. "Is There a 'Ferguson Effect'?" *The New York Times*. SR9.

98 In May of 2017, Black Lives Matter had begun to build a stronger organizational structure into which other groups could "plug into BLM's emerging ecosystem." Retrieved on May 30, 2017 at: www.facebook.com/events/744803755695494/.

99 Peniel E. Joseph. April 6, 2017. "Why Black Lives Matter Still Matters." *The New Republic*. Retrieved on May 30, 2017 at: https://newrepublic.com/article/141700/black-lives-matter-still-matters-new-form-civil-rights-activism.

Cultures of Hyper-Masculinity

4

Guns, the NRA, and Militias

Consider:

- Forty-five percent of American households have guns.
- 14.5 million Americans have permits to carry concealed weapons.
- The National Rifle Association has 5 million members.
- The number of militias grew rapidly after the election of Obama and surged again after he was elected for the second time. So did gun sales.
- If you join a patriot militia, you can become a sovereign citizen, set up your own government, and no longer have to pay taxes; or so certain militias claim.

On January 2, 2016, a small group of armed men, led by Ammon Bundy, announced that they would take over the federal Malheur National Wildlife Refuge in eastern Oregon and occupy buildings used by staff. They settled in, blocked the roads, and took up defensive positions. They had audacious plans. They were there to protest the plight of local ranchers Dwight and Steven Hammond, father and son, who had been sentenced to prison for setting brush fires on the Refuge. They wanted them freed immediately. Their second goal was a demand that the federal government turn over the entire Refuge to locals. In western states such as Arizona, Montana, Oregon, and Utah, where much of the land is locked up in national forests and other protected areas, there is an effort to transfer public land to the management of the states in anticipation that these lands would be opened up for mining, ranching, and logging. Bundy and his followers acted in response to this effort.

The Refuge is located in a sparsely settled area of eastern Oregon, about 30 miles from the town of Burns, Oregon. It now encompasses 187,757 acres and was established in 1908 by Theodore Roosevelt as a preserve and breeding grounds for over 300 species of birds. Birders come from surrounding states and across the nation for a chance to see migrating Sandhill Cranes, phalaropes, snowy plovers, grebes, ruddy ducks, herons, and egrets to name but a few. The terrain of the Refuge is as diverse as the species that call it home. It comprises sage brush and high desert, as well as thousands of acres of meadows and marshlands. There are deer and numerous small animals like jack rabbits, as well as rattlesnakes.

An iron grey cold settles over the land in the winter where highs in January and February average around 35–39⁰F with lows of 15–18 degrees.[1] Though the occupiers picked a time when few birders would be there, they chose a time when it was difficult to stay warm, especially after power to the buildings was cut by law enforcement. Some supporters left, not willing to endure hardship conditions.

By the time the occupation ended on February 11, 2016, when the last four remaining holdouts surrendered, one man had been killed and the group that led the takeover was in jail. The story of the occupation, those who rallied to its cause and those who opposed it, offers an insight into the motivations of those who believed they might spark a national uprising. It also provides us with a better understanding of why efforts by sincere actors sometimes fail. Those who staged the rebellion, as they termed it, were armed with assault rifles, hunting rifles, and numerous handguns. The guns were not just about the ability to ward off police officers; they stood as symbols of patriotism, manliness, and honor.

Our Gun Culture

Guns are now ubiquitous in American society; 45% of American households have them and 14.5 million of us have concealed weapons permits.[2] And those who have them don't want them taken away. Sixty-five percent of American adults believe the 2nd Amendment guarantees the right to own a gun and that this right should never be infringed.[3] On the other hand, a 2016 poll revealed the general public supports curbs on both who should have guns and what kind they should be. The public strongly favors background checks (83%) at gun shows and for private sales. Most people (81%), but not all, want to keep guns out of the hands of the mentally ill and prevent those on do-not-fly lists from getting them (74%). There are significant variations between people in terms of their willingness to impose controls based on their political leanings, age, and education.

Polls showed in 2016 that Trump supporters, many of whom were white males without a college degree, were much more likely (54%) than Clinton supporters (15%) to oppose the creation of a federal database to track gun sales. Trump supporters were also more likely to oppose bans on high-capacity magazines (66%) and bans on assault rifles (64%), compared to Clinton supporters (25% and 24%, respectively). Young white men with a high school education were also more likely to oppose expanded background checks, compared to those with a college degree.[4]

We have not always been a nation well armed, especially with assault rifles. Colonial militiamen had their trusty flintlocks and 19th-century frontiersmen had their rifles but we thought of these primarily as "tools of civilization" to shoot outlaws, Indians, and predators. In spite of movies like *Gunfight at the O.K. Corral*, *High Plains Drifter*, or *The Magnificent Seven*, historically American citizens were not allowed to carry guns wherever they went. As the political scientist Robert Spitzer notes in his *Guns Across America*, for the first 150 years of the country's existence, gun laws were extensive: "They spanned every conceivable category of regulation, from gun acquisition, sale, possession, transport, and use, including . . . outright confiscation, to hunting and recreational regulations, to registration and express gun bans."[5]

After the Civil War, six states banned all pistols and the state of Wyoming banned all firearms from any city, town, or village.[6] Why, then, did we end up with so many guns in the hands of citizens?

The historian Pamela Haag argues in *The Gunning of America* that an increase in gun ownership was driven by manufacturers like the Winchester Repeating Arms Company. Having provided guns for Union soldiers, after the Civil War, the Remington Arms company needed to develop new markets. They pushed the sale of guns by drawing on legends of the Wild West which were enshrined in dime novels where the "heroes" shot buffalo and Indians and "tamed" the frontier. The gun was linked to romantic notions of individualism, conquering of the frontier, and masculinity. In short, we have been invited to "love" guns by their modern-day manufacturers.[7]

Gun ownership says something important about a citizen's relationship with the government. We may fear the government and, thus, like the men who occupied the Malheur Refuge, we want to protect ourselves from that government. Or we believe the government cannot protect us in all circumstances and therefore we have the right to arm ourselves to protect ourselves and others. Here I want to tell a real story.

At the end of each semester my wife and I would invite the students from the senior honors class we co-taught to our home for a barbecue. We provided beer and wine for them and most behaved responsibly. One year, however, a male student drank far too much. We refused to let him drive home. He called his girlfriend, and while we waited for her to arrive he asked us if we wanted to see his gun. "Sure," we said. He pulled out of his pants pocket what we learned was a Beretta 9mm handgun. He then unloaded the magazine to show us the kind of bullets he used. They were hollow-core bullets designed to do maximum damage to the human body. I asked him why on earth he was carrying a gun to our home. Did he expect to shoot somebody? He told us he carried the gun every day, including when he was on campus, and had a concealed weapons permit. He explained that if a shooter broke into our classroom he would be able to "take them down," thus protecting us.

The notion that people carry concealed weapons because they see themselves as citizen protectors was a theme identified by the sociologist Jennifer Carlson in her study of gun owners, *Citizen-Protectors*. Carlson interviewed 60 predominately white males in Michigan about gun ownership, and also engaged in activities with them—shooting at gun ranges and taking gun-training classes. She got a concealed weapons permit and became a National Rifle Association (NRA) certified firearms instructor. She concluded that carrying a gun is less about the gun than it is about what the gun signifies. A gun "says" that the person carrying the gun is a law-abiding citizen who deserves to be treated with dignity. Dignity was in short supply among those she interviewed, who were suffering from the economic decline that wracked the economy of Michigan, 2008–2014. She reasoned that those carrying guns acquire from them, out of a heightened sense of responsibility, a moral duty to protect others. Some gun owners have fantasies of being the hero when they come to the aid of others who are threatened.[8] For those on the margins of society, or those who feel left behind by economic forces over which they have little control, the gun can be a symbol of righteous power.

> A gun "says" that the person carrying the gun is a law-abiding citizen who deserves to be treated with dignity.

Another sociology professor, Angela Stroud, interviewed men in Texas who had concealed weapons permits. Like Carlson, she found that their primary reason for having a weapons permit was to protect their wives and children; they also wanted to compensate for the loss of strength that comes with growing age, and they wanted to defend themselves against dangerous people, especially minority men. A gun allowed them to identify with a male-dominated culture with its fantasies of threats and self-defense.[9] However, that is not the whole story.

The shooting at the Sandy Hook Elementary School in Newtown, Connecticut in December of 2012 took the lives of 20 school children and six teachers. This mass killing was preceded and would be followed by more shootings on college campuses and high schools. A husband-and-wife team of homegrown terrorists, claiming alliance to ISIS, killed 14 people and wounded 22 at a training center in San Bernardino, California in December, 2015. In June of 2016, 49 were killed and 53 wounded at a gay nightclub in Orlando by a man declaring allegiance to

ISIS. Then in October of 2017, a lone gunman, firing into a crowd of 22,000 concert-goers from the window of his luxury hotel room in Las Vegas, killed 58 people and wounded close to 500 more. It was the deadliest mass killing in American history. Given the number of mass shootings in the United States, why don't we limit people's access to guns? The answer is a bit surprising.[10]

After the Sandy Hook shooting, 11 states passed stricter gun control laws but at least 24 loosened theirs.[11] During the Obama administration (2008–2016), after each mass killing the President spoke out demanding stricter gun laws. The results were the opposite of what he intended. Obama's calls and that of other leaders went unheeded and sales of guns and ammunition shot up. One reason for an increase in gun sales is that mass shootings heighten people's fears and they want a gun to protect themselves and others.[12] The second reason relates to the 2nd Amendment and the NRA.

The National Rifle Association (NRA)

The NRA may be one of the most effective *social movement organizations* of our time. It describes itself as the oldest civil rights organization in the United States and has a laser-like focus on upholding the right and the *need* of Americans to own guns. Relying on the 2nd Amendment, which guarantees the right to own any number of guns, they have managed to block any meaningful gun control legislation. After school shootings, the NRA has taken the position that if teachers were armed, students would have been saved. The problem with 49 gays being killed and 53 wounded at the Orlando nightclub was not the crazy person with the assault rifle; it was that none of the victims could defend themselves because they were not armed. Strange as this reasoning may seem, it provides an effective *framing* of the issue, where the gun is never the problem; it's always the solution. Guns are associated with personal safety, the main reason an increasing number of citizens are armed.

Another way in which the NRA frames opposition to gun control is that guns and freedom are equated; therefore, restrictions on guns limit our freedom. The NRA is also indirectly involved in a larger cultural war; one closely linked with ideas of masculinity. As the author of *Gun Crusaders* has argued, "the NRA is not just fighting for guns. Committed NRA members' support for gun rights is about freedom, independence, self-reliance, and the American Way of Life."[13] Edward Leddy in *Magnum Force Lobby* has suggested we think of the NRA as a person:

> The NRA is one of America's most successful social movement organizations with strong grassroots support in every state.

[H]e would be a pioneer heading west with a rifle. He is self-reliant, morally strong, and competent. He is also peaceful by preference, but ready to defend himself from attack. He believes in personal honor rather than collective responsibility . . . He opposes the arbitrary abuse of government power but is openly patriotic.[14]

Our pioneer is male. Men, as a Gallup Poll survey revealed, are five times more likely than women to own a gun; they are also more likely to be married and live in the South.[15] Women, unlike men, do not associate guns with safety.[16]

Mass shootings are often committed by men who are unpopular loners attempting to demonstrate their masculinity. (A notable exception would be the December 2, 2015 mass shooting in San Bernardino, California carried out by a husband-and-wife team committed to the goals of ISIS. That shooting was politically and religiously motivated.) One example would be Elliott Rogers, who killed six people and injured 14 others in Isla Vista, California, which is near the campus of the University of California, Santa Barbara. Rogers began his spree on May 23, 2014; he stabbed three men to death in his apartment then drove to a sorority house where he shot three women, two of whom died. He continued on to a local deli where he killed a male student and then sped through the town of Isla Vista shooting at pedestrians and hitting others with his car. With police in pursuit he crashed into a parked car and then shot himself in the head. Before driving to the sorority house he uploaded a YouTube video outlining his plans and giving his reasons for the attacks. In the video he calmly describes his frustrations over not having a girlfriend, his hatred of women in general, as well as his contempt for minorities. The shootings were, he said, "retribution."[17]

Chris Harper-Mercer, 26 years old, offered similar reasons for his murder of eight students and one professor at Umpqua Community College in Oregon on October 1, 2015. Harper-Mercer was a regular on an obscure website (4chan) where one can post anonymously. He told fellow bloggers the day before the shooting that he intended to shoot up a school in the Northwest, without specifying where. Some bloggers urged him on. "I suggest you enter a classroom and tell people that you will take them as hostages. Make everyone get in one corner and then open fire." Another person told him to "spare the fools, humdrum druggies and churchies and go for he whom really terrorizes the populous. Chads and Stacies who have scorned many and yourself."[18] He was seen by some as part of a "Beta Rebellion"; a beta being a weak male who couldn't get a girlfriend. Others saw him as a class warrior for targeting the "Chads and Stacies" of the world.[19] For men like Rogers and Harper-Mercer, power was just a trigger pull away.

Those who own guns, and are not mass murderers, are primarily white, middle-aged men, living in rural areas. They see themselves as a new minority community, being plotted against by urban liberals and Democrats to take away their gun rights.[20] The NRA plays on these fears and does not allow for a middle ground. In their view you are either a "gun grabber" or a "gun supporter." Gun control is portrayed by the NRA as the first step toward seizure of all arms. At the NRA's national convention in 2000, the actor and president of the NRA at the time, Charlton Heston, ended his speech by noting that Al Gore (who was running for president at the time against George W. Bush) was going to smear gun owners as the enemy:

> [Gore] will slander you as gun-toting, knuckle-dragging bloodthirsty maniacs who stand in the way of a safer America. Will you remain silent? I will not remain silent. If we are going to stop this, then it is vital to every law-abiding gun owner in America to vote and show up at the polls on Election Day.

Heston paused, picked up the replica of a Revolutionary-era flintlock rifle, and continued:

> So, as we set out this year to defeat the divisive forces that would take freedom away, I want to say those fighting words for everyone within the sound of my voice to hear and heed, and especially for you, Mr. Gore, "From my cold, dead hands!"[21]

"From my cold, dead hands," became a rallying cry and bumper sticker for gun rights.

The NRA claims it has close to 5 million members and its annual convention draws prominent Republican governors and senators as speakers. The NRA was founded in 1871 and originally focused on training and marksmanship. It was started by a Union general who had been dismayed by the inability of Union soldiers to shoot straight.[22] It has an annual budget of over $300 million but spends only a modest amount of this ($3 million) on direct lobbying.[23] Most of the money, which comes from membership dues and the firearm's industry, goes for local newsletters, sporting evenings, gun safety education, and training.

More importantly, the NRA grades candidates for elected state and federal offices in terms of their commitment to gun rights, supports those with the best grades, and punishes those with poor grades by campaigning aggressively against them. The NRA focuses primarily on election to state legislatures because that is where gun laws are made. It has broad-based support from active chapters in every state, giving it a broad reach.[24] The general public is divided on whether or not they think the NRA has too much influence. White, conservative, Republicans are more likely to believe it has the right amount of influence while women, minorities, and liberal Democrats see it as having too much.[25]

The NRA derives its strength from the fact that gun supporters are more politically engaged than gun opponents. As Adam Winkler, the UCLA law professor and author of *Gunfight*, has noted, "NRA members are politically engaged and politically active. They call and write elected officials, they show up to vote, and they vote based on the gun issue."[26] By focusing on just one issue and connecting it to core values like individualism, freedom, and patriotism, they are able to advance their case at the grassroots and national level. Concealed carry is now legal in all 50 states. The NRA has thus been more effective than gun control advocates in marshalling its cultural, political, social, and economic resources. It has managed to convince a significant number of people that one can become an "authentic" American by owning a gun. But this is changing.

In the aftermath of the Newtown (Sandy Hook Elementary School) shooting, there was a major push to expand background checks on gun buyers. A bipartisan bill (Machin-Toomey) advanced to the senate which was supported by 90% of the public. Obama lobbied for it, and a group backed by New York's Mayor, Michael Bloomberg, spent $12 million to convince senators to vote for it; it failed on April 17, 2013 by *just five votes*. It failed in part because many senators feared they would be "punished" by the NRA if they supported the bill. A similar bill advanced in 2015 after the shootings in San Bernardino, California also failed. But gun control forces have by no means given up.

Gun control advocates have now adopted the strategies of the NRA. Bloomberg created a Super Pac, Independence USA, to pour money into campaigns supporting those who are pro-gun control. Efforts are in place to ban assault rifles, high-capacity magazines, and the sale of guns to those on do-not-fly lists and those who are mentally disturbed.[27] They are also pushing those things that responsible gun owners favor such as gun safety—keeping guns locked up and putting safety devices on the triggers so that they can't be fired by anybody but the gun owners. The Million Moms for Gun Control was started after the Sandy Hook shootings and later merged with Bloomberg's group to form Moms Demand Action, which in 2016 had 3.5 million members. Like the NRA they have chapters in every state to mobilize voters in support of their goals.[28] While there is significant support for gun control, there is little support among the larger public for any attacks on the 2nd Amendment. And guns still have an allure rooted in our cultural history. They stand for toughness.

Hyper-Masculinity

Hyper-masculinity refers to the belief that to be a man you must in no way resemble a woman, because to do so would be to strip him of his masculinity.

Typical male stereotypical behavior such as strength, aggression, and sexuality are emphasized.[29] The hyper-masculine male also believes that women need to fulfill what men regard as traditional roles. The Public Religion Research Institute (PRRI), which tracks public opinion on a number of issues, asked people in 2016 whether or not they thought American society had become too soft and feminine. Not surprisingly, there were significant differences between the answers given by men and women. Fifty percent of the men felt society was becoming too soft and feminine, while just 34% of women agreed with the statement. When responses were categorized by support for a particular political candidate, almost 70% of Trump supporters felt society was too feminine; the opposite was true for supporters of Sanders (28%) and Clinton (31%). Trump supporters were also most likely (65%) to say that what the country needed was a leader who would break the rules.[30] In our mythology of the American West it was men with guns who made and enforced the rules, especially upon people of color. Women were to be a civilizing and softening force.

As a presidential candidate, Trump was described in many ways but one of the things he clearly represented was somebody who could and would, if elected, break the rules of civilized society. He told his Republican colleagues, who were panicked about some of his incendiary comments to "Man Up!," that politicians had become "so politically correct anymore that they can't breathe." Saying whatever was on his mind was "totally fine."[31] In spite of degrading comments about the handicapped, women, and minorities, his base of support among white men with less than a college education remained strong. There are many ways to read this but my interpretation is that Trump represented "whiteness" for his supporters, a backlash against feminism and the so-called softening of American society. We were not winning wars anymore; we had not defeated ISIS; we had not stood up to China; and we were letting Mexico send rapists and criminals over the border. We had an African-American in the White House for eight years, and the danger of a woman becoming President. We were being kicked around. What was a man to do? Fight back, resist any efforts to take away his guns, and make women, along with minorities, scapegoats. Trump even suggested that 2nd Amendment supporters take care of Hillary Clinton if she got elected.[32]

> Gun owners and white males without a college education believe they are being discriminated against.

The 2016 campaign, and Donald Trump's crude and dismissive comments about women, brought to light divisions that might have remained obscure without them. A PEW Research poll prior to the election asked whether or not women still faced significant obstacles toward progress in American society. Not surprisingly gender made a difference in people's answers. Women reported (56%) they still faced significant obstacles while only 41% of men felt women did. Party alliance revealed even greater differences. Seventy-five percent of Republican men felt that barriers had been removed for women, while only 39% of male Democrats expressed a similar opinion.[33]

Dan Cassino, a political scientist writing in the *Harvard Business Review*, noted that in spite of the fact that males earn more than women, hold more CEO positions, and constitute more than 80% of the House and Senate, *men feel discriminated against*, especially if they are Republicans. If we add up all of the men who say they face a great deal of discrimination—a lot, or a moderate amount—we end up with a total of 41% of Republican males who feel discriminated against. In the 2016 election, one of the strongest correlates of the belief that men are being discriminated against was support for Donald Trump. And the more marginalized a man felt, the more likely he was to oppose Hillary Clinton. As Cassino argued, feeling you are discriminated against increases identification with your gender group, lowers your self esteem, increases anger, and causes men to "lash out at the group they see as doing the oppressing."[34] These are men who clearly fear women in power.

Many men, as the reporter Olga Khazan argued, saw Trump as the candidate who would restore men's status in society.[35] A headline on the opinion page of the conservative *Wall Street Journal* explained support for Trump under the heading of "Trump and the Emasculated Voter."[36] Much of the anger toward women has been latent and stems in part from reactions to affirmative action and the women's movement. Men who have lost jobs or seen their prospects decline over past decades have targeted women with their anger. The Southern Poverty Law Center (SPLC), which tracks extremist groups in the United States, has seen an uptick in the number of groups that exist to express animosity and sometimes violence toward women. One blog, *Boycott American Women*, denigrates women:

> In a nutshell, American women are the most likely to cheat on you, to divorce you, to get fat, to steal half of your money in the divorce courts, don't know how to cook or clean, don't want to have children, etc. Therefore, what intelligent man would want to get involved with American women?[37]

One of the most vicious and misogynistic of the sites tracked by the SPLC is *The Philosophy of Rape* which promotes "corrective" rape of sluts and harlots to humble them.[38]

There is a great deal of anger loose in American society, and much of this anger is also directed against the government. As recent polls show, trust in the government to always do what is right or most of the time has declined from a high of 73% in 1958 to only 19% in 2015.[39] Michael Needham of the conservative policy group Heritage Action for America, in explaining the Trump phenomena, said voters wanted to simply "punch Washington in the face!"[40] The desire for radical political and economic change is manifest in the actions of the diverse groups that constitute American militias and the hate groups which seek to establish white supremacy.

Growth of the Militias and Right-Wing Movements

The militia movement here refers to those armed far-right patriot groups that refer to themselves as militias or constitutional militias. Militias come in all forms and virtually all are anti-government, but their ideologies vary widely. Some are part of the "Christian Identity" movement which argues that Aryans are God's chosen people and that the Jews are the offspring of the Devil and Eve.[41] Some groups are made up of white supremacists, while others are anti-immigrant, opposed to abortion, and opposed to the LBGT community. Many supremacist groups believe we are in the end of days and need to stockpile food and weapons. There is, however, no fast line between such groups; rather there is an overlap in many of their ideas and what they stand for. For example, white supremacist groups also embrace anti-immigrant ideas and are opposed to rights for the LBGT community. Some are violent; some are not, but hate crimes are on the rise.

Mark Potok of the SPLC dubbed 2015 as a "year of hate and extremism . . . [Domestic extremists] laid plans to attack courthouses, banks, festivals, funerals, schools, mosques, churches, synagogues, clinics, water treatment plants and power grids. They used firearms, bombs, C-4 plastic explosives, knives and grenades."[42]

Those on the far right, who are almost exclusively white, are angry at many things: the legalization of abortion, gay marriage, feminists, affirmative action, immigrants, the economy, their diminishing fortunes, and the fact that they may soon be a minority in their own country. They feel betrayed and furious at a government they believe has aided and abetted, at their expense, those who are *not like them.*

Most such groups have an online presence, where they sell gear, subscriptions to magazines, peddle conspiracy theories, and offer an opportunity to donate. One of the first to realize the potential of the internet in building support for white power groups was Don Black, a former Alabama Klan leader, who spent three years in prison for plotting to overthrow a Caribbean island government.[43] He set up *Stormfront* in 1995, which has become the most popular site for white nationalists to post comments and get the "news." *Stormfront* asserts: "We are the voice of the new, embattled *White minority.*"[44] *Stormfront* now has 300,000+

registered members but most of these members, as is the case for membership in other militant groups, are inactive. High online numbers can create an illusion among both followers and their leaders that they have greater influence than they do and, as we will see later, can cause them to engage in risky and ineffective actions.

Much of the ire of militias is directed at educated elites, Washington, and Wall Street. (Those who comprise the membership of far-right groups and militias, unsurprisingly, tend to be lower-middle and working-class men.[45]) For some, Obama—smart, educated, well spoken, and the first African-American president of the most powerful nation on earth—was their worst nightmare come true. After Obama took office in 2008, the FBI reported that in the months following, 7 million people had applied for criminal background checks so they could buy a weapon.[46] The U.S. Department of Homeland Security worried that the ensuing economic downturn in 2008 and Obama's election could be "significant drivers for rightwing radicalization and recruitment."[47] They issued a report expressing concern that disgruntled military veterans coming home from Iraq and Afghanistan could be prime targets for extremists who "will attempt to recruit and radicalize returning veterans in order to exploit their skills and knowledge derived from military training and combat."[48] The document, which was intended only for use by law enforcement officials, was leaked to the press; the blowback was immediate and intense. Conservative groups and politicians decried the notion that any returning veteran would commit violent acts. The Veterans of Foreign Wars also lodged protests against the notion that soldiers could become domestic terrorists. The report was withdrawn.[49] The reality, as we will see, is that militias do have military veterans, as well as law enforcement officers, in their ranks.

> The election of Obama was a driver in the rapid growth of extremist groups in the United States.

"Patriot" groups or militias, among the panoply of rightist organizations, have experienced the most rapid growth; they now number over 1,000.[50] Their recent growth was fueled by the success of a Nevada cattle rancher, Cliven Bundy, who stopped federal officials at gunpoint from seizing his cattle, because of his non-payment of grazing fees. We will return to the Bundys later.

Roots of Modern Militias

The modern militia began in the 1960s with the *Posse Comitatus*. The Posse claimed their legitimacy was grounded in the common-law authority that a sheriff had in the 19th and early 20th century to conscript men for a posse to pursue outlaws like Butch Cassidy and the Sundance Kid. The Posse believed this meant that a sheriff was the highest legal authority in a county and there was *no legitimate form of government above the county level*. Thus, the federal government had no authority at the county level and the Posse Comitatus law, enacted in 1878, explicitly forbid the use of federal troops to enforce order in a state, unless authorized by Congress to do so. (This idea would be one on which the Malheur occupiers relied in claiming the sheriff was the highest legal authority, not the federal government, in Malheur county.[51])

The Posse was known for its conspiracy theories, its anti-government agenda, and its anti-Semitism. They had ties to the white Christian Identity movement which, among other things, portrayed Jews as seeking to destroy civilization and undermine the rights of whites by means of the Federal Reserve and the Internal Revenue Service.[52] The Posse, like other militias, claims an adherence to what they call "common law." Common law in the handbooks they distribute is a mishmash of ideas from the Bible, the Magna Carta, and the U.S. Constitution.[53] The upshot is the federal government is illegitimate and militias are free to create their own courts and government. Based on their reading of Article 1, Section 8, of the U.S. Constitution they claim the government has no right to control vast tracts of the West. As the Constitution states, Congress shall have the power:

> To exercise exclusive Legislation in all Cases whatsoever, over such District (not exceeding ten Miles square) as may, by Cession of particular States, and the Acceptance of Congress, become the Seat of Government of the United States, and to exercise like Authority over all Places purchased by the Consent of the Legislature of the State in which the Same shall be, for the Erection of Forts, Magazines, Arsenals, dock-Yards and other needful Buildings.[54]

The Posse and militia members read this literally, meaning that the federal government can only control land for the purposes listed. The Supreme Court has, however, ruled on several occasions that Article 4, Section 3, Clause 2 of the Constitution gives the federal government the right to own land and to regulate grazing, mining, and logging on those lands.[55]

Nevertheless, the Posse argued that anybody could become a *sovereign citizen*, subject only to common law, meaning, among other things, that one did not have to pay taxes or get a driver's license. To accomplish this you would buy a piece of property, set up a compound, and declare yourself a new, sovereign nation and, of course, defend it with your own militia. Some groups argued that if Native Americans could have sovereign lands on which federal law did not apply, so could they. The SPLC, which tracks sovereign citizen extremists, estimated that in 2010 there were 100,000 hard-core believers and another 200,000 sympathizers testing sovereign techniques of resisting the government.[56]

Interest and support for far-right patriot and sovereign citizen movements died down but surged again in the 1990s after two events that "martyred" militia leaders. In August of 1992 federal agents from the FBI, the U.S. Marshalls Office, and Alcohol, Tobacco, and Firearms (ATF) surrounded the cabin of Randy Weaver at Ruby Ridge, Idaho. AFT agents developed trumped-up weapons charges against Weaver because they wanted him to serve as an informant for them with an Aryan nations group in northern Idaho. By the time the siege was over, federal law enforcement officers had shot and killed Weaver's wife, his son, and the family dog. After an investigation, the federal government reached an out-of-court settlement that awarded Weaver $100,000 and his three daughters $1 million each. (There was no admission of guilt on the part of the government.[57])

Twelve months later in 1993 a new disaster occurred at a compound outside of Waco, Texas. The Branch Davidians, a religious cult under the leadership of David Koresh, were thought to have illegal firearms. There were other more serious charges. The local *Waco Tribune-Herald* began publishing a series of articles titled "The Sinful Messiah" which claimed Koresh had abused children and committed statutory rape by taking underage girls as brides who were as young as 12 and 13. As a polygamist, Koresh believed he was entitled to at least 140 wives and the right to claim any woman in the compound as his.[58] The ATF attempted to serve a search and arrest warrant and were met with armed resistance; four ATF agents and six Branch Davidians were killed. The FBI then initiated a 51-day siege (February 28–April 19, 1993) of the compound and on the 51st day began a tear-gas attack. During the attack a fire broke out in the compound and 76 people died, including David Koresh. Eleven others who had fled the compound were arrested.

The long siege and the fact that many died at the hands of the federal government "proved" to some that the federal government was corrupt and determined to stamp out patriotism and religious freedom. Ruby Ridge and Waco stimulated the growth of militias across the country. In April 1995, Timothy McVeigh bombed the federal building in Oklahoma City killing 168 and wounding another 600 in revenge for the Waco siege. Another standoff occurred in 1996 in the eastern Montana town of Jordan, where a group of Freemen claimed sovereignty over a 960-acre compound. A local attorney described the Freemen as a "bunch of sad, middle-aged men who had lost their homes, who had not paid loans back or taxes, and wanted someone to blame."[59] Militias around the country were alerted to the standoff and took what were sometimes diametrically opposed positions. Some argued that the Freemen did not represent the patriot movement, as they were simply criminals. A Kansas militia member sent a fax to other militias titled "Operation Worst Nightmare," in which he urged patriots to raid armories, gun stores, and jails to get guns and head to Montana because he feared another Waco or Ruby Ridge. Another militant vowed to show up and unleash the "dogs of war" against the FBI, if they did not stand down.

An Idaho militia leader and former Green Beret, James "Bo" Gritz, was brought in by the FBI to try and negotiate an end to the standoff but gave up in frustration after listening to rants about the "Zionist Occupational Government," and vows to God not to surrender. His conclusion was that the Freemen represented a "potpourri circus of over-the-hill outlaws, people with no past or future." After 81 days, the Freemen finally surrendered.[60]

One reason the Montana Freemen had difficulty in rallying people to their cause is that there was strong disagreement about their strategy among members of other militia groups. The Freemen's claim that they were sovereign citizens and not subject to the law of the land was rejected, not only by law enforcement officials, but by those in the larger community. Their attempt to create a movement was undermined by the fact that neither the individuals themselves nor their cause were seen as worthy. In addition, communication between militias was not then facilitated by social media which limited their ability to connect and generate support for their efforts. There was no Facebook or Twitter to spread the word. (There are literally hundreds of militias in the country, but the reality is that most are small and widely dispersed organizations, which still limits their ability to rally people for a specific event or to get people to commit to a long, drawn-out event.)

> Just as militias learn from their past actions, so does the FBI.

The standoff in Montana also demonstrated that the FBI had learned from their encounters at Ruby Ridge and Waco. They needed to settle armed conflicts through negotiation if there was no imminent danger to life, no matter how long it took. Whatever the Freemen might have learned was irrelevant, as they went to jail. Others might have learned that trying to set up a sovereign state to avoid paying one's debts wasn't going to work. We provided examples in Chapter 2 of cases when protesters did learn from one another. In the aftermath of the protests against the World Trade Organization (WTO) in Seattle, it was found that the spoke-and-hub or "leaderless" model allowed for a greater diversity of action among participants and an increase in the numbers who turned out for demonstrations. Those who initiated and were involved in the Occupy Wall Street (OWS) movement took this lesson to mean that mass democratic action was to be favored over centralization and a unified message. But groups seeking social and political change can sometimes learn the *wrong* lesson about what will be effective, as in the case of those who occupied the Malheur National Wildlife Refuge in 2016. They took as a lesson the successful standoff between the Bureau of Land Management (BLM) and armed supporters of the Nevada rancher, Cliven Bundy.

The Bundy Ranch Standoff

Cliven Bundy (April 1946), a Mormon cattle rancher with a wife and 14 children, lives outside of Bunkerville, Nevada. The surrounding area gets little rain and the land is sparsely covered with sage brush, yucca, rabbit brush, Mormon tea (ephedra), cheat grass, and the occasional juniper. It is a barren land and easily damaged by grazing cattle. Bundy had been involved in a long-standing dispute with the BLM dating back to 1993 when he refused to pay for grazing his cattle on public land. Like others before him, he claimed that under Article 1, Section 8 of the U.S. Constitution, the land was his to use. Federal court rulings in 1998 and 2013 prohibited him from continuing to graze his cattle and trespass on public land. By 2014, Bundy owed the government more than $1 million for unpaid grazing fees.

Bundy's refusal to pay was loosely grounded in the ideology of the Sagebrush rebellion of the 1970s and the 1980s, when it was determined that the BLM needed to better manage public lands to protect the environment, cultural resources, and opportunities for recreation, rather than simply opening them up for logging, mining, or ranching. Proponents of the Sagebrush rebellion saw the federal government as grabbing "their" land and demanded that *all* public lands within the domain of a state be transferred to that state to be managed at the county level. Rural poverty, they claimed, was entirely the fault of the federal government. This idea, which is today pushed by conservative Western politicians and advocates of ranching, mining, and logging, is sometimes referred to as the "Wise Use" movement.[61]

On April 4, 2014, Shawna Cox, a friend of Cliven Bundy and his wife Carol, received a message on her answering machine from Cliven letting her know that the government was going to confiscate his cows and he needed her help. Cox was in the middle of a Tea Party meeting when she got Bundy's message telling her he would do "whatever it took" to stop them. He needed her to bring friends and cowboys.[62] The government was proposing to seize 1,100 head of his cattle and sell them at auction for the sum of $996,000. Bundy told Cox that he only had 500 head of cattle and maybe 100 new-born calves that had not yet been branded. Calls went out to friends, neighbors, and militia members, the Constitutional Sheriffs and Peace Officers Association (CSPOA), the Oath Keepers, and other patriot organizations to come to the ranch and bring guns.[63]

Bundy used his family's blog (#BundyRanch) to post a YouTube video that showed a scuffle between Bundy's sons and BLM officials who had arrived to supervise the roundup. Bundy proclaimed it the first step in a real war, "Range War begins tomorrow at Bundy Ranch." It went viral on anti-government websites. Ryan Payne, 650 miles away in Anaconda, Montana, heard the call.

Payne, a former soldier and a member of a small militia organization, West Mountain Rangers, got in touch with Bundy, promising he would bring militia and patriot groups from all over the country. He jumped in his truck and drove through the night with a friend to reach Bundy's ranch. During the long drive he reached out to his connections with other militias and the news quickly spread. Hundreds responded.[64]

Bundy was a force in mobilizing resistance. He went on Glenn Beck's right-wing online network, "The Blaze," to outline his case against the government. He claimed to have the right to run cattle on public land, because he had done it all his life and, besides, the land belonged to the people of Clark County, not the federal government. Media from around the country descended on the ranch seeking interviews with Bundy.

Bundy made for good press. On camera he appeared as an archetypal cowboy with his big white hat, blue jeans, large brass buckle, and snap button western shirt. His face was deeply lined and tanned from a life outdoors. From his shirt pocket a copy of the U.S. Constitution peeked out. The Constitution that he and his followers carried is referred to as the Skousen Constitution. W. Cleon Skousen (1913–2006) was an active anti-communist, writer, and a popularizer of Mormon theology. His version of the Constitution is the same as the original, except for a six-page preface of selected quotations from the founders which seeks to demonstrate that the Constitution is a God-given document.[65] Bundy himself asked, rhetorically, "If our Constitution is an inspired document by our Lord Jesus Christ, then isn't it scripture?" As a devout Mormon, Bundy believed his resistance to federal agencies had the blessings of the Lord.[66]

> Many militias believe the Constitution is a divinely inspired document.

Militias frequently cite the Book of Mormon or the Bible along with the U.S. Constitution as justifying their actions. The reliance on them and the belief that they are divinely inspired gives focus and purpose to their lives in a world of uncertainty and misfortune. The militias are not just fighting the federal government, they are, as Cox said, fighting *evil* itself.[67] Cox, citing the conservative Harold B. Lee, noted that the Mormons "devoutly believe that if the Constitution should be in danger of being over thrown, their lives, if need be, are to be offered in defense of its principles."[68] At the Bundy ranch, the end of days was at hand and only good patriots were standing between the rest of us and Armageddon. Many who came to Bundy's aid saw themselves as patriotic Americans protecting their country.

The BLM began to round up and corral Bundy's cattle on April 5 and over the next several days Bundy, always surrounded by his personal bodyguard, would attempt to "negotiate" with various officials. Over time his demands escalated. Bundy did not just want his cows back, he wanted the Park Service officers to be disarmed, the government to relinquish claims over all national parks, and all federal lands turned over to the management of states.[69] The showdown came on April 12, when Bundy rallied about 20 armed men on horseback to take back his cattle. His snipers were also positioned on a bridge overlooking the wash where the BLM was attempting to load cattle on to trucks. The BLM stood down because their officers were at a serious disadvantage and feared they would be killed. Shortly thereafter a banner was unfurled declaring "The West Has Now Been Won." This was an emotional victory for those who came to stand with the Bundy family.

One of the founders of sociology, Émile Durkheim, described a phenomena he called *collective effervescence*. It was the extraordinary degree of exaltation that occurred when people came together to affirm their unity and, united, felt secure.[70] The standoff had brought people close together and, after the BLM withdrew, Bundy reported that he saw a light shining above the heads of those heading back to the ranch house. He believed their victory was divinely inspired.[71]

As I noted earlier, social movement organizations try to draw on cultural symbols that resonate with potential followers. The iconic cowboy on a horse with a gun strapped to his thigh is a potent, though mythical, reminder of the lone cowboy who rides into town dispensing justice. The character Clint Eastwood plays in *High Plains Drifter* exemplifies this type. He acts on behalf of spineless, citified townspeople and then rides off again, leaving the girl and civilization behind, saved. The cowboys were also fighting environmentalists who, they imagined, came from places like California and urban areas where they cared more for protecting endangered species than they did for people trying to make a living.

Cowboys, however, were not just gunmen; they exemplified an ethic in American culture that valued courage, optimism, and hard work. They do dangerous work; are tough but fair; and keep the promises they make.[72] They are honorable men. Honor is something that societies had before regulations and contracts and modern-day capitalism. Cowboys do what Cliven Bundy said he would do: "Whatever it takes!" A cowboy rides tall in the saddle. Ranchers draw on a romantic past where they see themselves as rugged and honorable individualists, in spite of the fact that they are heavily subsidized. The fees they pay for grazing on public land are about one-tenth of what it would cost them on private land.

The cowboys and militia members carried flags: the American flag, the Gadsden Flag ("Don't Tread on Me"), and the Liberty Flag from the Revolutionary War. Those men not on horseback wore the gear of a modern-day warrior: camouflage, combat boots, flak jackets, rifles and side arms. Bundy's Praetorian Guard wore dark sunglasses, carried guns, and had ear buds and walkie-talkies. They mimicked the look of FBI agents ready for a firefight. Many carried in their shirt pockets copies of the Skousen Constitution. All of this made for great news and photo opportunities.

Conservative media and politicians rushed to embrace Bundy's stand and his victory in the desert. Sean Hannity of Fox News reported effusively on Bundy's standing up to an "out-of-control federal government." The Nevada Assemblywoman, Michele Fiore, also inserted herself into the unfolding drama and would later reappear during the Malheur occupation. Fiore is a 2nd Amendment supporter and her 2015 Christmas card showed her and her entire family armed with handguns and assault rifles wishing us all "Merry Christmas!"[73] (Many of the politicians and conservative news commentators who were quick to embrace Bundy and his cause were, however, quick to flee after he offered up racist comments.)

Bundy, speaking to his supporters in the afterglow of his victory, began to muse during his daily news conferences about a number of subjects including abuses of welfare, abortion, and race. He offered his thoughts on race based on his observations as a young man in North Las Vegas:

> I want to tell you one more thing about the Negro. [They sit on the steps of public housing] because they don't have anything to do. They didn't have nothing for their kids to do. They didn't have nothing for their young girls to do. And because they were basically on government subsidy, so now what do they do? They abort their young children, they put their young men in jail, because they never learned how to pick cotton. And, I've often wondered, are they better off as slaves . . .?[74]

Bundy was no longer a newsworthy subject, except on the blogs of militias. Bundy's sons, however, would play a leading role in occupation of the Malheur Wildlife Refuge.

Occupation of the Malheur National Wildlife Refuge

Their victory in Bunkerville convinced a core group of Bundy's supporters that they could expand their efforts to open up federal lands in the West for mining, ranching, and logging. They believed they could rally people to their cause, as Bundy had done, and assumed they would have the support of western communities. They discounted the fact that the vast majority of those who swelled the crowds at the Bundy ranch and arrived for the picnic were neighboring ranchers, friends, and members of the same church (Latter Day Saints) as the Bundys. Only a small number of the protesters, perhaps 100, were armed militia members. The lessons they seem to have learned, because they later relied on them in Oregon, were: they had a righteous cause; ranchers would support them; politicians would step up in support of their efforts; they could call on and get the support of militias throughout the country; and, they could secure federal land for local use. None of these would translate into success in a new setting and the 41-day siege (January 2–February 11, 2016) would end with one man dead and others facing prison terms. In short, they learned the *wrong* lessons from their short-lived victory in Nevada. Conditions can change significantly from the time of one mobilization to the other and *failure to account for changed conditions can lead to movement failure*.

The Back Story, December 2015

Before the takeover of the remote Malheur National Wildlife Refuge, Ryan Payne, who had been in charge of security at the Bundy ranch, and Ammon Bundy, Cliven's son, approached Harney county sheriff, Dave Ward. They explained to the sheriff that he was the highest law in the county and they expected him to protect two local ranchers facing prison time. If he did not, they promised his county would be invaded by armed citizens who would.[75] The father-and-son ranchers, Dwight and Steven Hammond, were facing close to four years in federal prison for lighting fires on the refuge to cover up their poaching. Ward pointed out to Bundy and Payne that he had no authority to defy the courts. They advised him of another demand; they wanted the federal government to turn over the Wildlife Refuge to Harney county.

Bundy and Payne, calling themselves Citizens for Constitutional Freedom, laid the groundwork for the eventual occupation and took up residence in Burns, Oregon, a small town of 2,700 occupants about 30 miles from the Refuge. They called a December meeting at the Harney County fairgrounds to rally support for the Hammonds. A Committee of Safety was formed, modeled on those formed during the American Revolution which provided for the safety and protection of people in the absence of government protection.[76] If Sheriff Ward would not protect the Hammonds, the Committee would.

Four days after Christmas, December 29, 2015, Ammon Bundy sent out a video on Facebook titled, "BREAKING ALERT! URGENT CALL TO ACTION! ALL CALL FOR PATRIOTS! MILITIAS! OATH-KEEPERS! FROM AMMON BUNDY RANCH!"[77] In the video Bundy is seated on a couch, wearing his black cowboy hat and a plaid shirt. He has a neatly trimmed full beard and a copy of the Skousen Constitution is sticking out of his left pocket. Speaking calmly and softly he urges viewers to come to Burns, make a stand, and protect the Hammonds. "I'm asking you," he continues, "and you know who you are, you that came, and you that felt to come to the Bundy Ranch." He needed them to come on January 2.

There was one major flaw in this plan. The Hammonds did not want Bundy's help. Their lawyer made it clear that "Neither Ammon Bundy nor anyone in his group/organization speaks for the Hammond Family. . . . Dwight Hammond and Steven Hammond intend to voluntarily report to the designated federal facility on January 4, 2016, as required."[78]

In addition, the Hammonds may not have been the most worthy citizens for which to mount a rebellion. The fires they set on the Refuge threatened the lives of professionals fighting a series of lightening-strike fires on the Refuge. The Hammonds were well known to federal officials; they had threatened to kill them when they fenced off a canal the Hammonds were using to water their cows, and threatened to wrap the child of one of the officials in barbed wire and drop him down a well.[79]

On December 30, U.S. Fish and Wildlife Service (USFWS) officials aware of Bundy's call for militias to come to Burns, protect the Hammonds, and seize the Refuge, told those working at the Refuge to go home and stay there until they were called back. Militia men with out-of-state license plates began to follow the spouses and children of federal employees to their homes and school.[80] The town was on edge and fears of violence grew as armed men began to walk the streets of Burns.

January 1, 2016[81]

Seeking a way to defuse growing tensions in Burns, citizens held a public forum at the county fairgrounds, attended by around 60 people. Burns residents confronted militia members about their fears of violence and by the end of a sometimes profanity-filled meeting it was agreed that maybe the Hammonds were being treated too harshly and a peaceful rally might help call attention to their plight. A rally was called for the next day.[82]

The Occupation Begins, January 2, 2016

About 300 protesters gathered in the parking lot of the local Safeway and marched to the home of Dwight and Steven Hammond. The rally had been organized by the Pacific Patriots Network (PPN), an umbrella organization that also includes the III%ers. They call themselves the III%ers because that is the percentage of the population they believe stood up to the British at the beginning of the Revolutionary War of

> There is intense competition between militias for members and public attention.

1776.[83] They left at the end of the day but would return later, armed with semi-automatic rifles, to "diffuse" the situation, claiming they wanted to prevent another Waco.[84]

At the end of the march, Ammon Bundy announced that he and a few others in the group were going to occupy the Refuge. Ammon and his two brothers, Mel and Ryan, along with 16 others, including Ryan Payne and Jon Ritzheimer—who had stood with the Bundys at Bunkerville—accompanied him to the Refuge where they set up road blocks, occupied empty buildings, and settled in. This group formed the core of the protesters but more were needed. Ammon Bundy posted another video on his Facebook page asking fellow patriots to come and stand against tyranny, protest in support of the Hammonds, and demand the federal government relinquish control of the Refuge. Bundy claimed to have 150 armed personnel backing him up but reporters, who had been allowed in to speak with the occupiers, suggested that initially there were no more than a dozen, and perhaps as few as six.[85] More would come but not in the numbers Bundy hoped.

One reason is that another western militia organization, The Oath Keepers, warned their members away from any involvement. The Oath Keepers was founded by Stuart Rhodes, a former Army paratrooper and graduate of Yale Law School. The Oath Keepers membership is made up of former and current military, police, and first responders who took an oath to defend the Constitution and to defy unconstitutional orders to disarm the American people. Their motto is "Not on our watch!"[86]

Even before the occupation began, Rhodes posted extensive comments on the home page of Oath Keepers in response to Bundy's December 29 request for people to come to Burns. As Rhodes explained, "We cannot force ourselves or our protection on people who do not want it . . . No patriot group or individual has the right or the authority to force an armed standoff on this family." This was neither the time nor the place, he said, to take a hard stand. Instead he wanted to wait for "Obama and his fellow traveler Marxist buddies [to] 'step on the dicks' on the gun issue, and make a hard stand to resist that." He urged his readers to "get organized, get trained, and get equipped."[87]

Not all of those who read Rhode's message agreed with him. Some "keyboard warriors" saw the Bundy stand as critical in preventing a one-world order. D. Bertrand felt we had to resist a rogue president (Obama) from handing the country over to the United Nations and establishing Sharia law. PeaceSouljer urged the Oath Keepers to build up their armories to prevent a socialist cabal led by Obama from establishing martial law and targeting law-abiding citizens. Liberty Shirl told Rhodes, "you either stand up against injustices, or you don't." Bill Hickey relied upon Ecclesiastes, which he said predicted a perfect storm coming when we will have to take up arms to turn out the bankers and money lenders. Others weighed in about government corruption, Waco and Ruby Ridge, the 2nd Amendment, and the need to create a base where patriots could make a stand.[88] Rhodes would eventually relent and send a small group of unarmed Oath Keepers to Burns but not to the Refuge.

The trouble with inviting everybody to your protest is that others may come with a different agenda and, as a result, those standing with you may not be the best representatives of your cause. As the social movement theorists Charles Tilly and Lesley Wood have suggested, a successful movement needs to operate with idioms recognized by others. Others must see leaders and the cause as *worthy*; the group needs to be *unified*; there must be sufficient *numbers* that people pay attention to the cause; and followers must have *commitment*, e.g., a willingness to show up in difficult circumstances, in bad weather, and make visible sacrifices.[89]

> For a movement to succeed it needs to be seen as worthy, have sufficient numbers of committed members, and be able to change social and political policies.

Clearly there was a unified core group who demonstrated their commitment by settling in for an extended siege under difficult circumstances. The number of armed militia members Bundy hoped for never materialized. On the issue of worthiness, reporters for *The Oregonian*, a Portland-based paper, sought to account for who, exactly, was at the Refuge. They relied on news reports, photographs, social media posts, and YouTube videos to identify all of the 108 adults and 20 children who passed through the Refuge at some point during the 41-day occupation. Some of those who came were simply curious and turnover among participants was high, because many needed to get back to their jobs and families and others did not want to commit to the hardships of winter. Men made up the majority (77%) of those who were at or visited the site, and the women who were there filled traditional gendered roles—cooking and tidying up. Among the occupiers were several ranchers, others were retirees, and there was a mix of occupations: barber, lawyer, marketing director, roofer, and truck driver. Sixteen had formerly served in the military; seven had felony convictions, including one for murder; and 31 had a past bankruptcy, lien, or judgment against them. In general most of the participants lived their lives on the economic margins of society.[90]

Jon Ritzheimer, a Marine veteran from Arizona, was known nationally for organizing a protest against a mosque in Phoenix and selling anti-Islamic t-shirts. He was seen by Rhodes, of the Oath Keepers, as having the potential to create a firefight with law enforcement officers. On December 31, Ritzheimer created a video for his family saying he was willing to fight to the death in support of the Hammonds. "We need real men here . . . Americans who have the intestinal fortitude to come . . . and take a stand and say enough is enough." He told his family he loved them and to know that he stood for something.[91] David Fry, a 27-year-old Ohioan, who would be one of the last four holdouts at the Refuge, was known for his regular postings of homophobic and anti-Semitic messages on social media. He took over the computers at the Refuge to create a website for the protest, *Defend Your Base*. He would later explain he was "just kidding" when he posted comments suggesting he was favorably disposed to Hitler and ISIS.

There was a mix of ideologies among the diverse group who came to the Refuge. In addition to expressions of wide-ranging anti-government sentiment, there were expressions of anti-Semitism, homophobia, Islamophobia, a celebration of the culture of the gun, and an ethos of hyper-masculinity. These ideas were, for many members of the larger public, repugnant and a reason not to support Bundy's efforts.

January 3, 2016

The day after the occupation began, the media showed up in force. Television trucks from regional stations were parked on the road leading into the Refuge. Reporters came from Idaho, Montana, Oregon, and Washington, and coverage was provided in virtually all regional newspapers. National newspapers (*The Los Angeles Times*, *The New York Times*, the *Washington Post*, and the *Wall Street Journal*) followed unfolding events. International newspapers like UK's *The Guardian* and *The Independent* had stringers on the scene. In what would become a routine event, Ammon Bundy held a news conference and explained his intentions, one of which was to revive the economy of the region for logging and outdoor recreation.[92] LaVoy Finicum, a ranching neighbor of Cliven Bundy, also addressed the press, while standing in front of a professionally made sign: "BLM Another Intrusive Tyrannical Government Entity Doing What They Do Best. Abusing Power & Oppressing the Backbone of America."[93] Finicum, with his cowboy hat and earmuffs underneath, became a frequent spokesman for their efforts. He would explain, in length, the group's unique interpretation of the Constitution. But, as happened in the case of the Seattle and Occupy Wall Street protests described in Chapter 2, the media portrayed this attempted takeover of federal land and the message of the protesters as bizarre.

The county sheriff, David Ward, contributed to these perceptions by holding his own press conference, telling television reporters that the militants intended to overthrow the government and spark a nationwide movement. He asked deputies from surrounding counties to come and help him.[94] Ward pleaded with the occupiers: "It's time to go home, be with your own families and end this peacefully." At his press conference he spoke directly to those at the Refuge:

You said you were here to help the citizens of Harney County. That help ended when a peaceful protest became an armed and unlawful protest. The Hammonds have turned themselves in. It is time for you to leave our community. Go home . . .[95]

January 4–25, 2016

By the next day, the FBI had taken the lead in responding to the occupation. In short order they placed an informant among the protesters, who would later testify at the trial of the occupiers. The town of Burns took on a circus atmosphere, filling restaurants, bars, and motels with a mix of reporters, FBI agents, police, and gun-toting militants quoting the Constitution to whomever would listen. There wasn't a motel room to be found within 70 miles.[96]

While some residents were sympathetic to the message of the militants, not everyone was happy that the militants had come to their town. On the second day of the occupation schools were closed and a community meeting was scheduled to discuss safety concerns. At that meeting Sheriff Ward asked people if they wanted the militants to leave and *everybody* raised their hands, indicating "Yes."[97] In spite of Ryan Bundy's statement that they would leave if the community did not want them, they stayed.

Power and telephone lines were cut to the Refuge and it became freezing cold. The militants built a fire outdoors and sat around it bundled up in outdoor gear. Depending on the day, Bundy, Payne, or Finicum would meet with law enforcement officials who offered safe passage out of the county, if the occupiers would just leave. These offers were rejected by Bundy who repeated the ultimatum that they were not leaving until the federal government surrendered all of its holdings to the people of the county. People came and went from the Refuge with armed groups rotating in and out of Burns. Conservative politicians who were supporters of the movement to return federal lands to the states would also show up and meet with the militants for what they termed a "fact-finding" mission.[98]

> In the face of continued opposition and failure to secure initial demands, protesters will frequently expand their demands and change their tactics.

As a stalemate developed, the occupiers tried different tactics to mobilize support for their cause. They started by expanding their demands. Not only did they want the Hammonds freed and federal lands turned over to private ownership, they wanted all federal grazing permits voided, and the county to manage the Refuge, rather than the U.S. Fish and Wildlife Service. LaVoy Finicum and some of the militants started up a Caterpillar tractor and tore down a barbed-wire fence between the Refuge and an adjacent ranch. The idea was to provide the ranchers with free access to the Refuge. The ranchers put the fence back up.[99] A self-proclaimed "judge" who arrived from Colorado served the sheriff, county judge, and other officials, charging them with a variety of nonsensical crimes. Kenneth Medenbach from Crescent, Oregon was arrested in the lot of the local Safeway for driving a vehicle he stole from the Refuge. He told reporters, "I feel the Lord's telling me to possess the land, and I can legally do it, because the U.S. Constitution says the government does not own the land."[100]

Counter-protests

Opposition to the Bundy occupation began to build and came from a diverse number of groups outside the community. The Northern Paiute petitioned President Obama to return the land to them, as it had been taken away from them to form the Refuge. The Paiute also noted the occupiers were desecrating sites and objects sacred to them.[101] The Paiute considered the Refuge to be part of their reservation and they had legal access to it for cultural purposes.[102] The National Center for Biological Diversity, a Tucson, Arizona-based group with 633,000 members, sent a representative to point out that the Refuge belonged to all Americans, not just the people of Oregon or Harney County. Hunters who were shut out of the reserve registered their protests. The Portland Audubon Society wanted the occupiers gone. Two brothers, Zach and Jake Klonoski of Eugene, Oregon, launched a fund-raising campaign, G.O.H.O.M.E., to pressure the occupiers out of the Refuge. After a few hours of going live they had raised $4,000 to be distributed to gun control advocates, wildlife organizations, and the Paiute.[103] Environmentalists petitioned President Obama to end the occupation of the Malheur Refuge and some gathered near the Refuge with signs saying, "Bundy Gang Get Off the Refuge!," and "Keep Public Lands Public." A man with a "Go Home Bundy" sign walked the streets of Burns.[104]

Others suggested more provocative actions. The internet lit up with claims that the occupiers were domestic terrorists who needed to be put down by the National Guard, using shoot to kill orders. Some thought using drones with Hellfire missiles was the solution and others called for SWAT teams.[105] Law enforcement had, however, learned from other standoffs and decided that simply waiting was the best strategy. Nevertheless, the longer the occupation went on, the greater was the demand that action be taken. Oregon's governor, Kate Brown, complained to the Department of Justice and the White House that the citizens of Harney County were being overlooked and underserved by federal officials' lack of response to the occupation. She demanded a quick end to the occupation, all wrongdoers held accountable, and for the federal government to reimburse the expenses for additional law enforcement.[106]

The End Game

The militants continued throughout January to try and build support for their movement. A petition posted on the Bundy Ranch website demanding relinquishment of federal land to the states was signed by such groups as the Pacific Patriot Network, Liberty Watch of Washington, the Oregon Oath Keepers, the Idaho III%, the Central Oregon Constitutional Guard, and the Bearded Bastards of Oregon.[107] Ammon continued to call press conferences at the Refuge to discuss the Constitution and hopefully to build support among sympathetic listeners. The militants promised a coming event at which an Oregon rancher and one from New Mexico would give up their federal grazing rights and stop paying grazing fees, but only one, a convicted felon from New Mexico, showed up to do so.[108]

The sheriff from another eastern Oregon county, Glenn Palmer, expressed support for the occupation and suggested that one way to defuse the situation at the Refuge would be to free the Hammonds.[109] Palmer was aligned with the Constitutional Sheriffs and Peace Officers Association, a national organization that seeks to limit federal powers. With Palmer's support and that of some locals, a community meeting had been arranged in the town of John Day so that Bundy and his supporters could explain their goals and actions.

On January 26, a small group including the Bundy brothers, Ryan Payne, and Finicum set off in two vehicles for a long winter drive to John Day, Oregon, 100 miles from the Refuge. Finicum was driving the lead vehicle with Ryan Payne in the front seat. The following vehicle was driven by Mark McConnell with Ammon Bundy as a passenger. About 20 miles into their trip, police vehicles with flashing lights pulled up behind Finicum. He stopped and hesitated, while staying inside the car. He then told his passengers he was going to see Sheriff Palmer and sped off. One of his passengers, Shawna Cox, yelled "gun it, gun it." Shortly after, he saw a roadblock that had been set up by the FBI and the Oregon State Police to take them into custody. He headed toward the roadblock at a high rate of speed and at the last second veered to his left into a deep snow bank. Payne quickly rolled down his window and stuck his hands out. Finicum got out of his SUV and charged officers screaming, "Shoot me, shoot me, shoot me!" He repeatedly raised and lowered his arms. Stumbling around in the snow he appeared to reach for a gun on the inside of his jacket. He was shot and killed.[110]

The movement had its martyr. Cliven Bundy, speaking from his Nevada Ranch, said Finicum was "sacrificed for a good purpose," protecting our liberties.[111] The Finicum family posted a statement on the Oath Keepers' website saying an innocent man was gunned down.[112] As the controversy spread across numerous radical sites claiming Finicum was assassinated, the FBI took the unusual step of releasing video footage of the entire incident taken from a police helicopter.[113] It is hard to tell from the video whether or not Finicum was reaching for his weapon. The FBI said he was.

After Ammon Bundy learned that LaVoy Finicum had been killed, he told those at the Refuge: "I love you . . . Please stand down. Go home and hug your families. This fight is ours for now in the courts. Please go home."[114] The day after Finicum's death, law enforcement officials closed all entrances to the Refuge, prohibited reporters from mingling with the occupiers, and told those still inside that they could leave peacefully if they wanted to; most fled. The FBI arrested and charged 20 for their actions at the Refuge including the Bundy brothers, Shawna Cox, and Ryan Payne. The few of those remaining at the Refuge decided to dig in.

The FBI continued to negotiate with the occupiers and by February 10, there were only four remaining holdouts, all of who had been indicted on conspiracy charges. Cliven Bundy, contradicting his son Ammon, urged those remaining not to give up. He got on a plane to Portland, Oregon with the intention of driving to the compound and standing with those who remained. When he got off the plane in Portland, he was arrested by federal officers and charged in the U.S. District Court of Nevada with a variety of crimes relating to the standoff at his ranch in 2014.[115]

Fearing they would be shot like Finicum, the remaining holdouts agreed they would turn themselves in if Michele Fiore, a Nevada state Assemblywoman, would meet them at the gates to guarantee their safety. Fiore had developed a relationship with the Bundy family and was an advocate for returning federal lands to the management of the states. The evening before the surrender was to take place, the occupiers placed a call to Gavin Seim, a self-proclaimed liberty speaker and supporter of the occupation. Seim streamed the call live online, so that we could all listen.

The remaining occupiers included a husband-and-wife team Sean (48) and Sandy (47) Anderson of Riggins, Idaho; Jeff Banta (46) of Elko Nevada; and David Fry (27) of Blanchester, Ohio. During Wednesday night's call the four worried out loud that they would be killed. David Fry yelled at an FBI negotiator, "You're going to hell. Kill me. Get it over with." Fry claimed they were innocent people simply camping at a public facility. Sandy Anderson prayed that there would be a revolution "if we die here."[116] They also ranted about a number of subjects including Obamacare (Affordable Care Act) and wanted to be guaranteed a pardon for their actions, arguing that it was not fair that other people were allowed to leave peacefully.

I began listening on Thursday morning. Sandy Anderson had more to say about Obamacare. "It is forcing you to take out insurance on your own life." She argued the government did not have a right to own land; we needed to strengthen state's rights; Saudi Arabia was corrupt; and she was standing up for liberty and freedom. Others joined the telephone conversation, including an FBI negotiator. Michele Fiore was on the line as was Kris Anne Hall, a constitutional speaker. Everyone on the line was trying to calm down David Fry, who was threatening to kill himself.

Fry expressed a range of opinions and concerns. He was opposed to abortion, against paying taxes that were used to commit atrocities by bombing civilians and killing children in the Middle East and wondered who was going to pay for destroying these countries. He offered his opinions about energy policy: "We should be on solar, not oil," and claimed "nuclear plants are leaking." He feared that if he went to prison he would be raped and if he had to go to prison he "should be given special protection, like rich people." He wanted to take a stand "like a man," and begged them to let him take a stand. He complained about the things that had been taken away from him, including his marijuana. He criticized those listening for not stepping up; if they had, "this would not have happened." Fiore continued to reassure him that he would be safe, his message was getting out, and he needed to stay alive. Fry said, "I had better get a pizza if I come out." The surrender ended peacefully. Ammon Bundy would later say without apparent irony that David Fry was not a member of the core group.

A total of 26 were charged in Federal District Court with conspiracy and with preventing federal officials at the Refuge from doing their jobs. Some pleaded guilty, and seven professing their innocence were held for trial in Portland, Oregon, including Ammon and Ryan Bundy and Shawna Cox. The defendants tried to use the trial to explain their interpretation of the Constitution but were repeatedly prevented from doing so by the judge. Ammon Bundy wanted to provide scriptural justification for the takeover saying he had been called by God to take action and was also prevented from doing so. He explained that the only reason people were heavily armed was because they wanted to be taken seriously. Attorneys for the defense argued that nobody but the federal government had prevented Refuge employees from going to work. The occupiers would have welcomed them. The defendants and their lawyers all expected a guilty verdict but on October 27, 2016 the jury acquitted all of them, although the Bundy brothers and their father would still face a trial in Nevada for the 2014 armed standoff.

The overwhelming reaction to the not guilty verdict was shock. Matthew Schindler, a lawyer for one of the men, said, "You don't walk into a federal court and win a case like this." The verdict was "off the charts unbelievable."[117] Oregon's governor, Kate Brown, expressed disappointment, and federal officials worried that the acquittals might encourage similar confrontations and the occupation of federal lands and facilities. Readers of *The New York Times* were dumbfounded by the verdict. There were close to 3,000 postings in which people agreed with sentiments like those posted by Ravenwing:

> I have absolutely no clue how any jury could have acquitted this lot . . . This is a classic case of jury nullification where the jurors basically ignore the laws in question and vote to acquit because they harbor sympathies for the defendants.[118]

On the other hand, Bundy supporters were ecstatic. Supporters outside the courthouse waved flags and blew a horn. Those posting on the Bundy Ranch Facebook page said, "Our prayers have been answered. It's a miracle!"[119] The occupation has been pegged as a social movement but did the acquittal mean they had achieved their goals and sown the seeds for a new Sagebrush Rebellion?

Understanding Cultures of Hyper-Masculinity, Guns, and Militias as Social Movement Organizations

Movements that seek to transform society and change policies need to be seen as *worthy* by the larger public, and their aspirations need to align with the interests of political actors. The militants who occupied the Malheur National Wildlife Refuge were ridiculed by the larger public, and their goals were contrary to the interests of other stakeholders such as Native Americans, bird watchers, hunters, and environmentalists. The protesters also contained within their ranks the un-employed, people with felony convictions, and debtors. The few politicians drawn to their cause, like Michele Fiore, were conservatives who saw an opportunity to solidify support among gun owners and those who demanded the federal government turn over lands to the states. In short, there were not many among the ranks of the protesters and their sympathizers who were seen by the larger public as worthy of support. The larger public—environmentalists, Oregon politicians, and law enforcement officers—became a ***counter mobilization*** force determined to discredit the efforts of the occupiers and to drive them from the Refuge.

Tactics and strategies adopted to accomplish the goal of freeing the Hammonds from jail, and assuring the citizens of Harney County had control of federal land, were destined to fail. A high-risk strategy made it difficult to mobilize other militias to come to their defense. They could lose jobs, if they had them; they would suffer from inadequate facilities at the Refuge; and there was the likelihood they would be arrested or shot. The armed occupation brought local, state, and federal law enforcement officers into the mix and the governor of Oregon demanded quick action to remove the occupiers and open

> The occupiers of the Refuge tried to argue that their protests were no different than those of civil rights protesters.

up the Refuge to others. The majority of the citizens of Burns, Oregon saw armed protesters as a threat and wanted them to leave. Some militia members vowed to stay until their demands were met, which led to the eventual arrest of key organizers and Finicum's death.

The occupiers *framed* their demands in a unique reading of the Constitution which, contrary to established law, led them to believe the federal government was not authorized to own land. Framing, as I noted earlier, is important because it guides action, communicates what a group is about, and hopefully draws in others by making the issues relevant to them. The framing offered by the occupiers—the federal government cannot own land—was self-limiting. It did not resonate with urban populations and it was directly contrary to the interests of birders, sportsmen, recreationalists, and environmentalists, among others. Despite attempts to get ranchers to back them by refusing to pay for grazing sheep and cattle on federal land, only one stepped forward.

They tried to *bridge* their efforts to other groups by labeling themselves as Christians, Patriots, and Constitutionalists. They tried to claim their efforts were no different than those of civil rights activists in the 1960s and 1970s, arguing that they were not engaged in an armed takeover but simply exercising their constitutional right to assembly and free speech. They also adopted the rhetoric of conservative groups claiming the government was involved in overreach and attempts to control the lives of American citizens. They blamed the poverty of rural ranchers, miners, and loggers on the federal government and its "locking up" of resources.

Their *social capital*, a critical resource for mobilization, was limited. The core group of occupiers, which ranged between 10–20 people at most, did not have widely *distributed networks* they could tap into. The group that first took over the Refuge was composed primarily of those who had defied the government in 2014 at Cliven Bundy's ranch in Bunkerville, Nevada. They tried to build local support in Burns, Oregon by organizing a demonstration in support of the Hammonds. However, at the end of the protest Bundy and his followers announced they intended to take over the Refuge. Some of those in attendance expressed dismay, feeling they had been tricked, and walked away. Calls were sent out to militias across the country but few responded.

There was contention among *social movement entrepreneurs* which limited the likelihood of success. Other groups, such as the Oath Keepers, claimed *they* represented the patriot movement and were adamant that the occupation was a mistake, and feared that some of the participants might engage in violent actions which would only set the patriot movement back. Those politicians who were lobbying for the return of federal lands to the states also came to believe that the occupation was a mistake.

The occupiers adopted familiar *cultural symbols* like the American flag and the "Don't Tread on Me" flag from the Revolutionary War. A lone cowboy on horseback patrolled the grounds, holding the American flag aloft. The occupiers also embraced the culture of the gun. Calls went out to other militias to come and stand by their side and to bring guns, preferably rifles. Everywhere they went—into town, driving around, talking with law enforcement officials, or walking around the Refuge—they were armed. This mass arming was designed, Ammon Bundy later claimed in his trial, to make sure that government officials took them seriously. Guns served not just for protection but as a powerful symbol that these were serious men, armed like their revolutionary forefathers to whom they claimed a link. They were the new patriots.

They clearly represented a *culture of defiance and resistance*. They used these terms themselves, telling people to embrace defiance and rebellion against a tyrannical and overreaching government. They drew on the culture of the gun, the rancher, and the cowboy to craft an image of the last honorable man standing against the forces of civilization and urban America, against those who wanted to protect the environment at the expense of those who wanted to make an honorable living. A *culture of hyper-masculinity*, where a man stands tall, keeps his word, and shows up and does the job, characterized the actions and beliefs of the core group of militants.

Social media served an important role in communicating with potential sympathizers and probably extended the length of the occupation. The website for the Bundy Ranch, *#BundyRanch*, had thousands of followers, as did the websites for the Pacific Patriots, and the Oath Keepers. Reports from the standoff were passed along to networks of patriots and militias, which gave the occupiers the illusion that they had a groundswell of support and that if they held out long enough, hundreds would rally in support of their issues. In fact, they claimed that a national uprising was in the making. "Keyboard warriors" vowed that it was now or never and that an armed confrontation was inevitable and desirable. The occupation also attracted considerable national and international media attention. Reporters from western states, as well as those from major media outlets like *The New York Times* and the *Washington Post*, covered the events as did reporters from international papers. Ammon Bundy and LaVoy Finicum gave frequent interviews to the media. However, the effect of all this publicity was that counter-protests evolved and public opinion shifted away from curiosity to opposition.

The armed occupation at the Wildlife Refuge required constant negotiation, as the key organizers tried to determine what to do next. Circumstances kept changing. Supporters came and then, worried about the FBI presence, left. Others left because it was cold and they had jobs and families waiting for them. Ammon Bundy and his supporters knew public opinion in Burns was fast eroding and that demands for their removal had been made by the governor of Oregon. They tried to broaden their appeal to surrounding counties. They decided to travel to John Day, Oregon where they anticipated a sympathetic sheriff would protect and welcome them. On that trip to seek help, LaVoy Finicum was shot and killed. At that point, Ammon Bundy told the remaining holdouts at the reserve to return to their families. Like other militia activities aimed at defying the federal government, their effort had failed.

The Logic of Social Movements

Social movements do not unfold according to some logical principle and certainly not all of them succeed.[120] In fact, failure is common. The outcome of the Malheur Refuge occupation may seem inevitable to those of us looking back at it. What else was going to happen, other than the fact that the federal government was *not* going to turn the Refuge over to the county? It seemed *inevitable* that those occupying a federal facility and carrying weapons would be arrested; after all, that's what the law required. Yet Bundy and his supporters drew a false sense of success from the standoff at the Bundy ranch in Nevada. They took off for Oregon expecting that ranchers would rally to the cause they espoused. Bundy had little direct control over who showed up for the protest. Some of those who did managed to discredit the effort in the eyes of the larger public. But that was *not* inevitable. The Hammonds who Bundy showed up to help wanted nothing to do with the protest organized on their behalf. Gun-toting supporters walking the streets of Burns turned the vast majority of the community against the occupiers. LaVoy Finicum's death was *not* inevitable; he made a bad decision, although one regarded as courageous by his compatriots. His death ended the occupation, led to the arrest of the occupiers and the eventual surrender of the four holdouts at the Refuge.

Every day the occupiers made decisions that led to this outcome. Different decisions could have been made and different strategies and tactics could have been pursued. Imagine they had taken the opportunity to explain the depths of rural poverty and what might be done to overcome it. The point is that *all movements evolve along their own paths and their outcomes depend on a mix of factors*: the political and economic context, who shows up to support the effort, the resources the group has at its disposal, and the actions others take in response to the mobilization. We are now seeing a surge of populist movements on both the left and right because of a changing economic and political context. As I argued in Chapter 1, many of the populist movements on the right are directed at the Washington consensus, which prioritizes neoliberal policies of globalization and free trade, because they have washed the sand out from underneath the feet of

American working men and women. Men like Bundy and those who stood with him were trying in their own way to uphold the values of hard work, family, and community. These are all good things, but they were mixed with a toxic brew of guns and masculinity. Their commitment to do "whatever it takes" to make things right drove the "inevitable" outcome. We should understand that movements on both the left and right are gaining strength grounded in some of the same values, although absent the guns and the focus on masculinity. The guns meant, as Bundy claimed, that they wanted to be taken seriously and their commitment to an armed occupation was a way of asserting their dignity. It should come as no surprise that when people feel cut out of their own society and their values are denigrated, they will sometimes find extreme and undemocratic ways to maintain their dignity. Extremist movements need to be understood within this context.

Notes

1 U.S. Fish and Wildlife Service. January 5, 2016. "Malheur National Wildlife Refuge, Oregon." Accessed on October 11, 2016 at: www.fws.gov/refuge/malheur/.
2 The Gallup Poll indicates 45% of households own guns; the General Social Survey indicates the figure is closer to 33%, down from a high of 50% in 1970. See Alec MacGillis. May 27, 2013. "This Is How the NRA Ends." *The New Republic*. Retrieved on October 17, 2016 at: https://newrepublic.com/article/113292/nras-end-real-gun-control-movement-has-arrived.
3 Rassmussen Reports. January 18, 2013. "65% See Gun Rights as Protection against Tyranny." Retrieved on October 12, 2016 at: www.rasmussenreports.com/public_content/politics/current_events/gun_control/65_see_gun_rights_as_protection_against_tyranny.
4 Pew Research Center. August 26, 2016. "Opinions on Gun Policy and the 2016 Election." Retrieved on October 13, 2016 at: www.people-press.org/2016/08/26/opinions-on-gun-policy-and-the-2016-campaign/. See also: Hannah Fingerhut. January 5, 2016. "5 Facts about Guns in the United States." Pew Research Center. Retrieved on October 14, 2016 at: www.pewresearch.org/fact-tank/2016/01/05/5-facts-about-guns-in-the-united-states/.
5 Robert J. Spitzer. 2015. *Guns Across America: Reconciling Gun Rules and Rights*. New York: Oxford University Press. See also: Adam Winkler. 2013. *Gunfight: The Battle Over the Right to Bear Arms in America*. New York: W.W. Norton & Co.
6 Spitzer, 2015.
7 Pamela Haag. 2016. *The Gunning of America: Business and the Making of a Gun Culture*. New York: Basic Books. See also David Cole's review of her book as well as that of Spitzer's. David Cole. July 14, 2016. "The Terror of Our Guns." *The New York Review of Books*, pp.28–30.
8 Jennifer Carlson. 2015. *Citizen-Protectors: The Everyday Politics of Guns in an Age of Decline*. New York: Oxford University Press.
9 Angela Stroud. February 21, 2012. "Good Guys with Guns: Hegemonic Masculinity and Concealed Handguns." *Gender and Society*. Vol.26(2):216–238. See also: Angela Stroud. 2016. *Good Guys with Guns: The Appeal and Consequences of Concealed Carry*. Chapel Hill: University of North Carolina Press.

10 Ben Agger and Timothy W. Luke argue that gun ownership and violence are linked to a decrease in public civility in the United States. They also provide comparative data to demonstrate how far outside international norms gun ownership and gun legislation are in the United States. Ben Agger and Timothy W. Luke. 2014. *Gun Violence and Public Life*. New York: Routledge.

11 David Cole. 2016. "The Terror of Our Guns," p.28.

12 Firmin DeBrabander. 2015. *Do Guns Make Us Free? Democracy and the Armed Society*. New Haven: Yale University Press.

13 Scott Melzer. 2009. *Gun Crusaders: The NRA's Culture War*. New York: NYU University Press, p.5.

14 Edward Leddy. 1987. *Magnum Force Lobby: National Rifle Association Fights Gun Control*. New York: Rowman & Littlefield, p.32.

15 Jeffrey M. Jones. February 1, 2013. "Men, Married, Southerners Most Likely to Be Gun Owners." *Gallup*. Retrieved on October 14, 2016 at: www.gallup.com/poll/160223/men-married-southerners-likely-gun-owners.aspx.

16 Joan Burbick. 2006. *Gun Show Nation: Gun Culture and American Democracy*. New York: The New Press.

17 Elliot Roger. May 23, 2014. "Elliot Roger's Retribution." YouTube. Accessed on October 15, 2016 at: www.youtube.com/watch?v=mu6NKHtLzks.

18 Comments posted on We Hunted the Mammoth. October 1, 2015. Retrieved on October 16, 2016 at: www.wehuntedthemammoth.com/2015/10/01/umpqua-community-college-shooter-apparently-announced-his-plans-on-4chan-yesterday/. I have not changed the grammar from the post.

19 Soraya Chemaly. October 5, 2015. "Mass Killings in the U.S.: Masculinity, Masculinity, Masculinity." *The Huffington Post*. Retrieved on October 16, 2016 at: www.huffingtonpost.com/soraya-chemaly/mass-killings-in-the-us-w_b_8234322.html.

20 Scott Melzer. 2009. *Gun Crusaders*, p.11.

21 James Dao. May 21, 2000. "N.R.A. Leaders Cast Gore as Archenemy." *The New York Times*. Retrieved on October 15, 2016 at: https://partners.nytimes.com/library/national/052100 nra-gore.html.

22 National Rifle Association. "Brief History of the NRA." Retrieved on October 15, 2016 at: https://home.nra.org/about-the-nra/.

23 Open Secrets. 2016. "National Rifle Association." Retrieved on October 15, 2016 at: www.opensecrets.org/lobby/clientsum.php?id=d000000082.

24 David Cole. 2016. "The Terror of Our Guns," p.29.

25 Bruce Drake. April 24, 2014. "5 Facts about the NRA and Guns in America." Pew Research Center. Retrieved on October 15, 2016 at: https://partners.nytimes.com/library/national/052100nra-gore.html.

26 Adam Winkler cited in James Surowiecki. October 19, 2015. "Taking on the NRA." *The New Yorker*. Retrieved on October 15, 2016 at: www.newyorker.com/magazine/2015/10/19/taking-on-the-n-r-a. See also: Adam Winkler. 2011. *Gunfight: The Battle Over the Right to Bear Arms in America*. New York: W.W. Norton & Co.

27 Alec MacGillis. 2013. "This Is How the NRA Ends."

28 Chris Arnold. June 17, 2016. "A Million Mom Army and a Billionaire Take on the NRA." *National Public Radio*. Retrieved on October 17, 2016 at: www.npr.org/2016/06/17/482343185/a-million-mom-army-and-a-billionaire-take-on-the-nra.

29 The "bathroom wars," which would restrict the use of bathrooms to one's gender at birth, are driven in part by the fear of feminization. Hyper-masculine males do not want there to be confusion about gender roles.

30 Donald Cox and Robert P. Jones. April 7, 2016. "Two-Thirds of Trump Supporters Say Nation Needs a Leader Willing to Break the Rules." Public Religion Research Institute.

Retrieved on October 13, 2016 at: www.prri.org/research/prrithe-atlantic-survey-two-thirds-trump-supporters-say-nation-needs-leader-willing-break-rules/#.VwfLdxIrLak.

31 Cited by Carl Hulse. June 8, 2016. "Donald Trump's Advice to Panicked Republicans: Man Up." *The New York Times.* Retrieved on October 13, 2016 at: www.nytimes.com/2016/06/09/us/politics/donald-trump-republicans.html?_r=0.

32 Nick Corasaniti and Maggie Haberman. August 9, 2016. "Donald Trump Suggests 'Second Amendment People' Could Act Against Hillary Clinton." *The New York Times.* Retrieved on October 13, 2016 at: www.nytimes.com/2016/08/10/us/politics/donald-trump-hillary-clinton.html?_r=0.

33 Hannah Fingerhut. August 16, 2016. "In both Parties, Men and Women Differ over Whether Women Still Face Obstacles to Progress." *Pew Research Center.* Retrieved on October 17, 2016 at: www.pewresearch.org/fact-tank/2016/08/16/in-both-parties-men-and-women-differ-over-whether-women-still-face-obstacles-to-progress/.

34 Dan Cassino. September 29, 2016. "Why More American Men Feel Discriminated Against." *Harvard Business Review.* Retrieved on October 17, 2016 at: https://hbr.org/2016/09/why-more-american-men-feel-discriminated-against.

35 Olga Khazan. October 12, 2016. "The Precarious Masculinity of 2016 Voters." *The Atlantic.* Retrieved on October 17, 2016 at: www.theatlantic.com/politics/archive/2016/10/male-trump-voters-masculinity/503741/.

36 David Gelernter. October 15/16, 2016. "Trump and the Emasculated Voter." *The Wall Street Journal*, p.A9.

37 Boycott American Women. June 29, 2012. Retrieved on October 17, 2016 at: http://boycottamericanwomen.blogspot.com/.

38 Mark Potok. March 20, 2015. "The 'Philosophy' of Rape." *Southern Poverty Law Center.* Retrieved on October 17, 2016 at: www.splcenter.org/fighting-hate/intelligence-report/2015/'philosophy'-rape; Gina Bellafante. October 16, 2016. "This Election, Misogyny Is Back. Did It Ever Go Away?" *The New York Times*, p.28.

39 Pew Research Center. November 23, 2015. "Trust in Government, 1958–2015." Retrieved on October 17, 2016 at: www.people-press.org/2015/11/23/public-trust-in-government-1958-2015/.

40 Robert Draper. October 2, 2016. "How Donald Trump's Candidacy Set Off a Civil War within the Right Wing Media." *The New York Times* Magazine, pp. 36–41, 54–55.

41 Timothy G. Baysinger. 2016. "Right-Wing Characteristics and Ideology." *Homeland Security Affairs.* Vol.12. Retrieved on October 19, 2016 at: www.hsaj.org/articles/166.

42 Mark Potok. February 17, 2016. "The Year in Hate and Extremism." *Southern Poverty Law Center.* Retrieved on October 19, 2016 at: www.splcenter.org/fighting-hate/intelligence-report/2016/year-hate-and-extremism.

43 Southern Poverty Law Center. 2016. "Don Black." Retrieved on October 19, 2016 at: www.splcenter.org/fighting-hate/extremist-files/individual/don-black.

44 Stormfront. 2016. Retrieved on October 19, 2016 at: www.stormfront.org/forum/. Emphases added.

45 Carolyn Gallaher. 2002. *Fault Line: Race, Class, and the American Patriot Movement.* New York: Rowman and Littlefield.

46 Eli Lake and Audrey Hudson. April 14, 2019. "Federal Agency Warns of Radical on Right." *The Washington Times.* Retrieved on October 19, 2016 at: www.washingtontimes.com/news/2009/apr/14/federal-agency-warns-of-radicals-on-right/.

47 U.S. Department of Homeland Security. Office of Intelligence and Analysis. 2009. *Rightwing Extremism: Current Political Climate Fueling Resurgence in Radicalization and Recruitment*, p.2.

48 U.S. Department of Homeland Security. 2009, p.7.

49 Heidi Beirich. June 17, 2011. "Inside the DHS: Former Top Analyst Says Agency Bowed to Political Pressure." Southern Poverty Law Center. Retrieved on October 19, 2016 at: www. splcenter.org/fighting-hate/intelligence-report/2011/inside-dhs-former-top-analyst-says-agency-bowed-political-pressure.

50 Mark Potok. February 17, 2016. "The Year in Hate and Extremism."

51 Stephen Atkins. 2011. *Encyclopedia of Right-Wing Extremism in Modern American History.* New York: ABC-CLIO.

52 Peter Knight. 2003. Editor. *Conspiracy Theories in American History: An Encyclopedia.* New York: ABC-CLIO.

53 Anti-Defamation League. 2016. "Militias and 'Common Law Courts': Patriots of the Web." Retrieved on October 19, 2016 at: http://archive.adl.org/poisoning_web/militias. html.

54 U.S. Government. Constitution. Retrieved on October 21, 2016 at: www.whitehouse. gov/1600/constitution.

55 Carol Hardy Vincent, Laura A. Hanson, and Jerome P. Bjelopera. December 29, 2014. *Federal Land Ownership: Overview and Data.* Congressional Research Service. Retrieved on October 21, 2016 at: http://fas.org/sgp/crs/misc/R42346.pdf.

56 James Timothy Turner. 2010. "Sovereign Citizens Movement." Southern Poverty Law Center. Retrieved on October 18, 2016 at: www.splcenter.org/fighting-hate/extremist-files/ideology/sovereign-citizens-movement.

57 *Wikipedia.* 2016. "Ruby Ridge." Retrieved on October 18, 2016 at: https://en.wikipedia. org/wiki/Ruby_Ridge.

58 Mark England and Darlene McCormick. February 27, 1993. "The Sinful Messiah." *Waco Tribune-Herald*, A1. Retrieved on October 18, 2016 at: www.wacotrib.com/news/branch_davidians/sinful-messiah---part-feb---page-a/image_3ed4d566-a90a-11e2-b3ed-0019bb2963f4.html.

59 Nick Murnion. March 25, 1996. "U.S. Domestic Terrorism: Montana Freemen Standoff with FBI." *History Commons.* Retrieved on November 5, 2016 at: www.historycommons. org/timeline.jsp?timeline=us_domestic_terrorism_tmln&us_domestic_terrorism_tmln_specific_events=us_domestic_terrorism_tmln_freemen_fbi_standoff.

60 A detailed day-by-day account of the events is available at the Center for Grassroots Oversight, The History Commons, March 25–November 8, 1996. "U.S. Domestic Terrorism." Retrieved on October 18, 2016 at: www.historycommons.org/timeline. jsp?timeline=us_domestic_terrorism_tmln&us_domestic_terrorism_tmln_specific_events=us_domestic_terrorism_tmln_freemen_fbi_standoff.

61 The idea that federal land should be returned to the states is pushed by the American Legislative Exchange Council (ALEC), a conservative group that develops boiler-plate legislation for use by members of state legislators. ALEC. 2016. "Resolution Demanding that Congress Convey Title of Federal Public Land to the States." Retrieved on October 21, 2016 at: www.alec.org/model-policy/resolution-demanding-that-congress-convey-title-of-federal-public-lands-to-the-states/.

62 The story about the attempts to take Bundy's cows and the resistance from friends and militia members was chronicled by Shawna Cox. 2014. *Last Rancher Standing: The Cliven Bundy Saga, a Close-Up View.* New York: Legends Library.

63 Cox. 2014, p.97.

64 There are different estimates of how many militia members showed up. At a picnic that would later celebrate Bundy's victory, Shawna Cox reported 1,500 celebrants, many of whom were friends and neighbors. My own estimates from counting the number of people in photos posted online are that at most there were about 100 militants, 40–50 who were carrying guns, that were engaged in the actual standoff. Ryan Palmer told Bundy that

he had 150 militia members responding to the call but many simply did not show. See Southern Poverty Law Center. July 9, 2014. "War in the West: The Bundy Ranch Standoff and the American Radical Right." Retrieved on October 9, 2017 at: www.splcenter. org/20140709/war-west-bundy-ranch-standoff-and-american-radical-right. The Bureau of Land Management estimated there were 100 people who confronted them.

65 *The Constitution of the United States.* 2009. Malta, Idaho. The National Center for Constitutional Studies. Available at: https://nccs.net/.

66 The Bundy quotation is cited in John Sepulvado. January 4, 2016. "Why the Bundy Militia Mixes Mormon Symbolism with Anti-Government Sentiment." *Oregon Public Broadcasting Station.* Retrieved on October 24, 2016 at: www.pbs.org/newshour/updates/why-the-bundy-militia-mixes-mormon-symbolism-with-anti-government-sentiment/. See also: Carli Brosseau. February 16, 2016. "Oregon Standoff: What Does Mormonism Have to Do with the U.S. Constitution?" *The Oregonian.* Retrieved on October 24, 2016 at: www. oregonlive.com/oregon-standoff/2016/02/oregon_standoff_what_does_morm.html. The Mormon Church issued a statement on its website rejecting the idea that there was any scriptural basis for armed resistance to federal authority.

67 Shawna Cox. 2014. *Last Rancher Standing*, p.53.

68 Harold B. Cox. April 14, 1941. *An Expression of Faith.* Cited in Shawna Cox. 2014. *Last Rancher Standing*, p.83.

69 Shawna Cox. 2014. *Last Rancher Standing*, p.73.

70 Émile Durkheim. 1912/2008. *The Elementary Forms of Religious Life.* Mark S. Cladis, ed. New York: Oxford University Press, p.162. This point has also been made by Arlie R. Hochschild. 2016. *Strangers in Their Land: Anger and Mourning on the American Right.* New York: The New Press.

71 Shawna Cox. 2014. *Last Rancher Standing*, p.89.

72 For an expansion of the code of the West see: James P. Owen. 2005/2015. *Cowboy Ethics: What Wall Street Can Learn from the Code of the West.* New York: Skyhorse Publishing.

73 Michele Fiore. 2016. "Merry Christmas." Retrieved on October 24, 2016 at: www.google. com/search?q=michele+fiore,+christmas+card&espv=2&biw=1280&bih=918& tbm=isch&imgil=sZ5W35Qv946F4M%253A%253BuDe_trWASmP5YM%253Bhttp% 25253A%25252F%25252Fwww.cnn.com%25252F2015%25252F12%25252F05%25252Fus %25252Fmichele-fiore-gun-holiday-card-feat%25252F&source=iu&pf=m&fir=sZ5W35 Qv946F4M%253A%252CuDe_trWASmP5YM%252C_&usg=__1kJQThdI5gOf4ISUhmJI-ff61xw%3D&ved=0ahUKEwip3Knk-fPPAhVCS7wKHVuaAIMQyjcIQQ&ei=6kIO WKm_DcKW8QXbtIKYCA#imgrc=sZ5W35Qv946F4M%3A. Her attempts to capitalize on her anti-government, pro-militia, and pro-gun stands backfired when she came in a distant third in a race to fill a House seat for Nevada.

74 Adam Nagourney. April 13, 2014. "A Defiant Rancher Savors the Audience that Rallied to His Side." *The New York Times.* Retrieved on October 24, 2016 at: www.nytimes. com/2014/04/24/us/politics/rancher-proudly-breaks-the-law-becoming-a-hero-in-the-west.html?_r=0.

75 Steven Dubois. September 15, 2016. "Sheriff: Occupiers Warned of Invasion." *Missoulian/ Associated Press*, A8.

76 Harney County Committee of Safety. Retrieved on October 25, 2016 at: www. hccommitteeofsafety.org/.

77 Ammon Bundy. December 29, 2015. "Breaking Alert!" *YouTube.* Retrieved on October 24, 2016 at: www.youtube.com/watch?v=PEvbIbxrj3Y.

78 Cited in the story posted by The Oath Keepers. January 1, 2016. "The Hammond Family Does NOT Want an Armed Stand Off, and Nobody Has a Right to Force One on Them." Retrieved on October 24, 2016 at: www.oathkeepers.org/the-hammond-family-does/.

79 Denis C. Theriault. January 6, 2016. "Oregon Militants: Death Threats from Radicals Reports Years before Standoff." *The Oregonian*. Retrieved on October 25, 2016 at: www. oregonlive.com/politics/index.ssf/2016/01/oregon_militants_years_before.html.

80 Les Zaitz. February 22, 2016. "Every Gun in House Is Loaded: Scare Tactics Rattle Oregon Residents near Oregon Occupation." *The Oregonian*. Retrieved on October 25, 2016 at: www.oregonlive.com/oregon-standoff/2016/01/residents_near_oregon_occupati.html.

81 A day-by-day account of the major events that occurred during the 41-day standoff is available at: Wikipedia. Retrieved on October 26, 2016 at: https://en.wikipedia.org/wiki/Timeline_of_the_occupation_of_the_Malheur_National_Wildlife_Refuge.

82 Les Zaitz. January 2, 2016. "Burns Residents Confront the Militia over Fears of Violence." *The Oregonian*. Retrieved on October 25, 2016 at: www.oregonlive.com/pacific-northwest-news/index.ssf/2016/01/burns_residents_confront_milit.html.

83 The III% Club. 2016. "Who Are the III%ers." Retrieved on October 26, 2016 at: www. threepercentersclub.org/index.php/pages/education.

84 Oregon Public Broadcasting Staff. January 3, 2016. "New Armed Group Enters Harney County, Meets with Sheriff." Retrieved on October 26, 2016 at: www.threepercentersclub. org/index.php/pages/education.

85 Adam Whitnall. January 3, 2016. "'Oregon under Attack': Anger over Limited Response to Hostile Militia Takeover of US Government Building." *The Independent*. Retrieved on October 26, 2016 at: www.independent.co.uk/news/world/americas/oregon-under-attack-anger-as-armed-white-militia-takes-control-of-a-us-government-building-to-a6794421.html.

86 The Oath Keepers. 2016. "About Oath Keepers." Retrieved on October 26, 2016 at: www. oathkeepers.org/about/.

87 Stuart Rhodes. January 1, 2016. "'The Hammond Family Does NOT Want an Armed Stand Off, and Nobody has a Right to Force One on Them." *The Oath Keepers*. Retrieved on October 26, 2016 at: www.oathkeepers.org/the-hammond-family-does/.

88 Posting on the Oath Keepers website. Stuart Rhodes. January 1, 2016. "The Hammond Family." Note: None of these comments are archived on the homepage. They were originally downloaded on January 3, 2016 at: www.oathkeepers.org/the-hammond-family-does/.

89 Charles Tilly and Lesley J. Wood. 2013. *Social Movements, 1768–2012*. Boulder, Colorado: Paradigm, p.5.

90 Lynne Palombo. March 26, 2016. "Oregon Standoff: Occupiers and Sympathizers Revealed." *The Oregonian*. Retrieved on October 26, 2016 at: www.oregonlive.com/oregon-standoff/2016/03/oregon_standoff_a_snapshot_of.html.

91 Jon Ritzheimer. December 31, 2015. "Breaking Message from Marine Jon Ritzheimer! BLM Alert!" *YouTube*. Retrieved on October 26, 2016 at: www.youtube.com/watch?v=sbGdMKpHDDE.

92 Ammon Bundy, January 3, 2016. "Militant Leader Explains Intentions on Oregon Refuge Takeover." *YouTube*. Retrieved on October 27, 2016 at: www.youtube.com/watch?v=eb8Oq83Uzb0.

93 LaVoy Finicum. January 3, 2016. "LaVoy Finicium, Neighboring Rancher of Cliven Bundy, Explains Oregon Refuge Takeover." *YouTube*. Retrieved on October 27, 2016 at: www. youtube.com/watch?v=yX6icu72bRg.

94 KTVZ Bend Oregon. "Sheriff Claims Refuge Occupiers Seek to Overthrow Government." Retrieved on October 27, 2016 at: www.ktvz.com/news/Sheriff-Refuge-occupiers-seek-to-overthrow-government/37245518.

95 Nigel Duara and Molly Hennessey-Fiske. January 4, 2016. "Oregon Refuge Occupation: 'It's Getting Dark, and It Is Freezing'." *Los Angeles Times*. Retrieved on October 27, 2016 at: www.latimes.com/nation/la-na-ff-militia-oregon-20160103-story.html.

96 Kirk Johnson. January 31, 2016. "An Unwanted Circus Descends, and An Oregon Town Strives to Stay Kind." *The New York Times*. Retrieved on October 27, 2016 at: www. nytimes.com/2016/02/01/us/an-unwanted-circus-descends-and-an-oregon-town-strives-to-stay-kind.html?_r=0.

97 Conrad Wilson and Ryan Hass. January 8, 2016. "Harney County Sheriff: Who Wants the Bundy's to Go?" *Oregon Public Broadcasting*. Retrieved on October 27, 2016 at: www.opb. org/news/series/burns-oregon-standoff-bundy-militia-news-updates/harney-county-residents-speak-out-on-occupation/.

98 Luke Hammill. February 22, 2016. "Oregon Standoff: Unsolicited Help Flocks to Burns to 'Assist' Law Enforcement." *The Oregonian*. Retrieved on October 27, 2016 at: www. oregonlive.com/pacific-northwest-news/index.ssf/2016/01/oregon_standoff_unsolicited_he.html.

99 Julie Terkewitz. January 11, 2016. "Protesters Rip Out Fence at Refuge in Oregon." *The New York Times*. Retrieved on October 28, 2016 at: www.nytimes.com/2016/01/12/us/protesters-rip-out-fence-at-refuge-in-oregon.html?_r=0.

100 Sam Levin and Nicky Woolf. January 15, 2016. "Oregon Militia Standoff: Man Arrested Driving Stolen Government Vehicle." *The Guardian*. Retrieved on October 28, 2016 at: www.theguardian.com/us-news/2016/jan/15/oregon-militia-standoff-arrest-stolen-government-vehicle-burns-oregon-police-kenneth-medenbach. Wanda Moore, January 17, 2016. "Takeover Day 15: Clash with Environmentalists, Arrest Update." Bend, Oregon: KTVZ. Retrieved on October 28, 2016 at: www.ktvz.com/news/politics/takeover-day-15-clash-with-environmentalists-arrest-update/69142163.

101 Change.org petition, "Return Bundy-Occupied Federal Land to the Northern Paiute." Retrieved on October 27, 2016 at: www.change.org/p/barack-obama-return-bundy-occupied-federal-land-to-the-northern-paiute.

102 Terrence Petty and Manuel Valdes. January 7, 2016. "Oregon Tribe: Armed Group 'Desecrating' Their Land." *Missoulian*, A4.

103 Jess McHugh. January 17, 2016. "Oregon Standoff Update: Local Brothers Launch Anti-Bundy Campaign Against Armed Ranchers." *International Business Times*. Retrieved on October 28, 2016 at: www.ibtimes.com/oregon-standoff-update-local-brothers-launch-anti-bundy-campaign-against-armed-2268758.

104 KOIN 6 News Staff. January 23, 2016. "'We the People' Petition White House to Arrest Bundy." Retrieved on October 26, 2016 at: http://koin.com/2016/01/23/we-the-people-petition-white-house-to-arrest-bundy/.

105 Jesse Walker. January 8, 2016. "Are the Oregon Occupiers 'Terrorists?'" *Missoulian*, B4.

106 Kristena Hansen and Terrence Petty. January 21, 2016. "Oregon Governor Calls on Feds to Act Against Armed Group." *Missoulian*, A4.

107 Bundy Ranch. 2016. "We the People." Retrieved on October 28, 2016 at: http://bundyranch.blogspot.com/2015/12/notice-redress-of-grievance-action.html.

108 Les Zaitz. February 2, 2016. "Oregon Standoff: Ranchers, Including Ex-Con, Renounce Grazing Permits." *The Oregonian*. Retrieved on October 28, 2016 at: www.oregonlive.com/oregon-standoff/2016/01/post_1.html.

109 Les Zaitz. January 24, 2016. "Oregon Standoff: Grant County Sheriff Urges Release of Hammonds." *The Oregonian*. Retrieved on October 31, 2016 at: www.oregonlive.com/oregon-standoff/2016/01/post_2.html.

110 Les Zaitz. February 6, 2016. "30 Minutes of Chaos: Witness Details Events of Finicum Shooting." *The Oregonian*. Retrieved on October 31, 2016 at: www.oregonlive.com/oregon-standoff/2016/02/30_minutes_of_chaos_witness_de.html.

111 Cited in Heavy News. January 26, 2016. "LaVoy Finicum Dead: 5 Fast Facts You Need to Know." Retrieved on October 31, 2016 at: http://heavy.com/news/2016/01/lavoy-

finicum-dead-dies-rip-funeral-youtube-school-family-ammon-bundy-arrested-malheur-standoff-wife-jeanette/.

112 Finicum Family. January 29, 2016. "Statement from the LaVoy Finicum Family." Oath Keepers Site, February 1, 2016. Retrieved on October 31, 2016 at: www.oathkeepers.org/statement-from-the-lavoy-finicum-family-1-29-2016/.

113 FBI Video. January 26, 2016. "Complete, Unedited Video of Joint FBI and OSP Operation." *YouTube.* Retrieved on October 31, 2016 at: www.youtube.com/watch?v=aAGxDWKrjPQ.

114 Cited in Julie Turkewitz, Dave Seminara, and Kirk Johnson. January 27, 2016. "3 More Arrests in Oregon as Protest Leader Says 'Go Home.'" *The New York Times.* Retrieved on October 31, 2016 at: www.nytimes.com/2016/01/28/us/oregon-standoff.html?_r=0.

115 Daniel G. Bogden, U.S. Attorney, United States District Court, District of Nevada. February 11, 2016. Case No. 2:16-mj-00127-PAL.

116 Terrence Petty. February 11, 2016. "FBI Says It Has Surrounded Last Occupiers at Oregon Refuge." *Missoulian*, A4.

117 Fred Barbash. October 28, 2016. "Off the Charts Unbelievable." *Washington Post.* Retrieved on November 1, 2016 at: www.washingtonpost.com/news/morning-mix/wp/2016/10/28/off-the-charts-unbelievable-will-acquittal-of-oregon-refuge-occupiers-embolden-extremists-militias/.

118 Courtney Sherwood and Kirk Johnson. October 27, 2016. "Bundy Brothers Acquitted in Takeover of Oregon Wildlife Refuge." *The New York Times.* Retrieved on November 1, 2016 at: www.nytimes.com/2016/10/28/us/bundy-brothers-acquitted-in-takeover-of-oregon-wildlife-refuge.html.

119 Bundy Ranch. Facebook. Retrieved on November 1, 2016 at: www.facebook.com/bundyranch/.

120 This point is made by Kathleen M. Blee. 2012. *Democracy in the Making: How Activist Groups Form.* New York: Oxford University Press. Blee followed 60 activist groups in Pittsburg and traces in detail how simple things such as who shows up for the first meeting can determine a group's success or failure.

The Anti-Vaccine Movement

5

Bounded Rationality

Consider:

- Vaccination for measles, mumps, and rubella (MMR) can cause autism.
- The Center for Disease Control (CDC) is suppressing information on the devastating health effects of vaccinations.
- Big Pharma makes money from forcing vaccines on the American population.
- There are no Amish who are autistic, because they don't vaccinate.
- We can reverse the effects of autism through a healthy diet and detoxification.
- The "chem." trails that are emitted from high altitude jets are aerosol vaccinations.
- None of these statements are true.

The novelist and children's writer, Roald Dahl, perhaps best known for *Charlie and the Chocolate Factory* and *James and the Giant Peach*, suffered the tragic death of his 7-year-old daughter, Olivia. She died suddenly after catching measles in 1962, a year before a reliable vaccine for measles was introduced. Dahl took hurried notes about his daughter's trip to the hospital after she collapsed at home:

> Awful drive. Lorries kept holding us up on narrow roads. Got to hospital. Ambulance went to wrong entrance. Young doctor . . . gave her 3mg sodium amatol. Sat in hall . . . Felt frozen. (Another doctor arrived. Said she had an even chance.) Not meningitis. It's encephalitis. (His wife arrived and went in to see Olivia.) Still unconscious . . . We drank whiskey. Told doctor to consult experts. Call anyone. (Dahl went

home with his wife; got a call from the hospital and headed back.) Two doctors advanced on me from the waiting room. How is she? I'm afraid it's too late.[1]

Dahl became a vocal advocate for parents getting their children vaccinated, because measles is a dangerous disease. Often a child simply experiences a cough, runny nose, diarrhea, and red spots over their body. But in some cases measles can cause lifelong brain damage from encephalitis, deafness, pneumonia, or, as it did in the case of Olivia, death.[2]

There is, fortunately, a safe vaccine for measles combined with one that also protects against mumps and rubella (the MMR shot), which should be given to children aged 12–15 months and again when they are between 4–6 years. Yet a significant number of parents refuse to allow their children to be vaccinated. Why? Because they believe the MMR shot causes, among other things, autism. The refusal of upwards of 10% of the American population to vaccinate either themselves or their children puts others at risk and is a public health challenge. Resistance to vaccines is not a new phenomenon and some of the historical reasons resonate with today's resisters.

A Brief History of Resistance to Vaccinations

Edward Jenner (1749–1823) is generally credited with modern immunization and the ultimate eradication of smallpox. Smallpox is not a new disease. It first appeared around 10,000 years ago, about the same time humans settled into agricultural villages. While now in check, it remains a deadly disease and has been identified as a possible agent of bioterrorism.[3] The symptoms of smallpox include fever, extreme fatigue, back pain, and vomiting, as well as skin lesions that develop into blisters filled with pus. People who survive the disease develop lifelong immunity. If you lanced the blister of a sick person and introduced the pus under the skin (usually on the arm or leg) of a healthy person, they would develop immunity, after a rash or blister formed and after suffering flu-like symptoms for a short period of time.

In 18th-century Europe, 400,000 people died annually of smallpox; one-third of the survivors were left blind; and most who survived were left with disfiguring scars. Catching it was close to a death sentence since 60% or more of adults died and 80–98% of infants succumbed to the disease. The practice of taking pus from an infected person and transmitting it to a healthy person (variolation or inoculation) took hold throughout the medical profession, even making its way to the American colonies. The Reverend Cotton Mather (1663–1728) wanted everyone inoculated after an epidemic of smallpox broke out in Boston. When

General George Washington failed to take Quebec from the British because of an outbreak of smallpox among his troops, he insisted that all of them be inoculated before any new expeditions were launched.[4]

The first major step in finding a cure for smallpox came with Edward Jenner's observation that dairymaids who suffered from cowpox were protected from contracting smallpox. The symptoms associated with cowpox—fever, muscle pain, and a rash or skin blisters at the point of contact—were not nearly as severe as smallpox and usually passed without incident. Jenner decided to experiment. He found a dairymaid with fresh lesions and transmitted the material from them to an 8-year-old boy. Two months later he gave the boy an injection from a fresh smallpox lesion and, when no disease developed, believed he had found a cure. He set out to test his theory but had little luck in securing volunteers. Nevertheless, he had good connections with other physicians and shared his ideas and methods which were soon widely adopted. It was possible to bring the scourge of smallpox under control, if everyone cooperated.

> Working-class opposition to vaccination in 19th-century England was driven in large part by a desire to resist the intrusion of the state into their private lives.

The British government, recognizing the opportunity, passed the 1853 Compulsory Vaccination Act which ordered vaccinations for infants up to 3 months old, and the Act of 1867 extended this age requirement to 14 years, adding fines for those who refused.[5] But, rather than welcoming legislation that would protect children and the general population, the public reacted fiercely against compulsory vaccination, opposing it on sanitary, religious, scientific, and political grounds.

Some of the clergy in Victorian England had doubts about vaccination because the vaccine came from an infected animal; members of the public had reasonable fears about the results of being inoculated with ooze from lesions on another person's arm. But the greatest resistance to vaccination came from members of the working class and others who believed it was their right, not the government's, to decide what to do with their bodies and how best to protect their children. This argument is still used today, as we will see, by those in the anti-vaccination movement.

In the Leicester Demonstration March of 1885, thousands of anti-vaccinators marched to protest compulsory vaccinations, carrying a child's coffin and an effigy of Jenner. A young mother who refused to have her children vaccinated was accompanied by a cheering crowd as she marched into the police station to be arrested, as the law demanded.[6] The University of Utah history professor, Nadja Durbach, has argued that this largest of all medical resistance campaigns ever mounted in Europe was about working-class resistance to the intrusion of the modern state into one's private life.[7]

Part of the resistance to vaccination was that it was seen as but one more in a long line of attempts to control the lower orders of British society and wall them off from their "betters." The notorious Poor Laws, amended a number of times, placed paupers in workhouses where they were subjected to grossly inhumane treatment and in some cases literally starved. These miserable conditions were driven by the desire of the upper and middle classes to control "dangerous" populations and to lower the taxes they were required to pay to support workhouses. The poor and members of the working classes had every reason to believe they were treated differently than others. Vaccination was just one more form of political tyranny.

Vivid posters were created warning of the need to protect innocent children from vaccines. One poster portrayed a coiled snake labeled "vaccination" poised to bury its fangs in a plump baby being held out of harm's way by its mother. An 1881 handbill, *The Vaccination Vampire*, warned of the universal *pollution* of *pure* babies by the vaccinator.[8] Among the many claims driving fear in the 19th century was that the vaccination would cause smallpox, as well as tuberculosis and syphilis. Cases of suicide and murder were also attributed to vaccination. The "best" strategy, then, was to avoid vaccination; a claim made by today's anti-vaxxers.

As one flyer proclaimed: "Any idiot could tell that cutting septic pus, called Vaccine 'Lymph,' into babies' arms would only kill and spread diseases such as leprosy."[9] Medicine was, quite simply, not to be trusted. Commonsense and the natural were. *The natural was elevated above the unnatural* and natural healers using herbs and other potions found in nature could, supposedly, cure people with success rates of 98–100%. The magnitude of the protests were so successful that the British government was pressured in 1898 to introduce a "conscientious objector" clause that allowed parents to opt out of compulsory vaccination, if they acknowledged they understood the implications of their choice.[10]

The anti-vaccination movement made its way to the United States when outbreaks of smallpox spurred local governments to pass or enforce laws requiring vaccination. Anti-vaccination societies formed; the first in 1879 after the British anti-vaccinationist William Tebb came to the United States on a speaking tour; the second in 1882, with another popping up in New York City in 1885. The main goal of these societies was to try and repeal mandatory vaccination laws in several states and the reasons—vaccinations were harmful, individuals knew best how to take care of themselves—were the same. Further, vaccinations were for others, the stranger, and the immigrant. When the last smallpox epidemic broke out in 1898 in the United States it was believed that whites were not susceptible to the disease but Blacks, Italians, Irish, and Mexicans were. The middle classes needed to be protected against those without power and those living in urban tenements.[11] Then, as now, it was the upper levels of society who saw themselves as best qualified to make decisions about their own health and that of their children. The claims of 19th- and early 20th-century anti-vaccine advocates seem unfounded. But these ideas continue to live today, primarily on the internet, and are presented in arguments remarkably similar to those of the 19th century.[12]

The case for mandatory vaccination came to a head following a 1902 outbreak of smallpox in Cambridge, Massachusetts. The board of health had decreed that everyone was to be vaccinated. A resister, Henning Jacobson, refused, claiming it violated his right to care for his own body. The case eventually made its way to the U.S. Supreme Court in 1905 where it was decided that states could, indeed, enforce mandatory vaccination laws. This should have ended the matter but it did not.

In the 1970s an international controversy over another vaccine broke out. A report from a London hospital for sick children reported that the vaccine DTP (diphtheria, tetanus, and pertussis or whooping cough) was responsible for the neurological disorders of 36 children. Television and newspaper coverage and the work of the Associated Parents of Vaccine Damaged Children (APVDC) led to a steep drop in vaccinations and to three major epidemics of whooping cough.[13] Confusion about whether or not to vaccinate was fueled by the fact that an expert committee deemed the DTP vaccine safe while some medical doctors expressed reluctance to give it to their patients. One physician, Gordon Stewart, published a series of reports claiming that neurological disorders could be linked to DTP. Parents from the APVDC attempted to use Stewart's findings to seek financial compensation in the courts but were denied because they could provide no evidence that DTP caused any harm.[14]

The controversy over DTP was, like the one over smallpox, exported to the United States. Parents were alerted to the alleged risks of DTP in a 1982 documentary, *DTP: Vaccination Routlette*.[15] Numerous anti-vaccine websites attribute this film to giving rise to today's anti-vaccine movement.[16] Lea Thompson, the reporter who developed the Emmy-winning documentary, echoed the claims made by British parents: DTP causes brain damage. The *Journal of the American Medical Association* called her report "biased, histrionic, inaccurate, amoral, and psychopathic."[17] Regardless of the mainstream medical community's assurances that the vaccine was safe, those who were opposed to vaccinations pointed to other "evidence." It was claimed that doctors "had expressed concern, agreed that there was a cause for alarm, and confirmed that they believed the pertussis vaccine did indeed cause

The British Dr. Andrew Wakefield sparked the current anti-vaccine movement when he claimed, incorrectly, that the vaccine for measles, mumps, and whooping cough caused autism.

injury, including SIDS" (sudden infant death syndrome).[18] This was enough to cause some parents to avoid vaccinations.

A book by Harris L. Coulter in 1991, *A Shot in the Dark*, deepened the controversy.[19] Coulter focused strictly on DTaP (which is a form of DTP with a reduced dose of the diphtheria and pertussis vaccines) and offered case histories of children who were supposedly brain damaged and killed by the vaccine. Coulter told stories of families who had gone to court to prevent their children from being vaccinated, and claimed that drug companies were making millions from the forced vaccination of children. One mother, who sought an explanation from her child's pediatrician as to why her child "had inconsolable high pitched screaming for 6 hours straight after her 4 mo. shots," and had "stopped cooing and making eye contact for nearly four weeks," was told it could not be from the vaccine. But on reading Coulter's book, she believed she had found confirmation that she was right: her child's distress had been caused by the vaccine.[20] The overall result of campaigns against the DTP (and DTaP) were a raft of lawsuits filed against the manufacturers of vaccines, which caused some companies to stop making the vaccine entirely. They were not making enough money from them to make it worth fighting lawsuits.

The next great controversy, and one that still animates the anti-vaxxers, began in 1998 when a British gastroenterologist, Andrew Wakefield, published an article claiming he had found a link between the vaccine for MMR and autism, as well as "leaky bowel" syndrome that caused toxins to be sent into the bloodstream. His findings, published in the prestigious medical journal, *The Lancet*, sparked a media storm and general public confusion. It took 12 years (2010) before the paper was formally retracted when it was found that Wakefield had a serious conflict of interest and moreover had faked his data. He was being paid by a group of lawyers to support a case brought by parents who claimed that the MMR vaccine had caused their children's autism. He was ultimately barred from practicing medicine.[21] (We will return to Wakefield later to find him directing a film claiming there is a link between the MMR vaccine and autism in spite of what the scientific evidence shows.)

Prior to 2001 a few vaccines contained thimerosal, which was used to prevent the growth of bacteria and fungi. Thimersol contains ethylmercury which passes quickly from the body, unlike methylmercury which can accumulate in the body from eating certain kinds of fish. Government agencies contributed to confusion and fear when they said that three childhood vaccines *might* expose children to more mercury than recommended because they contained thimerosal. Anti-vaxxers also choose to ignore the fact that many of the common vaccinations for MMR, or those for chickenpox, polio, or pneumonia, had *never* contained it.[22] Yet with public uncertainty about the safety of vaccinations growing, the American Academy of Pediatrics and the Public Health Service recommended that children's exposure to thimerosal should be limited. Seeking to calm the fears of parents, they only made things worse with their statement, saying "current levels of thimerosal will not hurt children, but reducing those levels will make safe vaccines even safer."[23] What many heard was the opposite of what was intended—vaccines contained unsafe levels of mercury. Thimerosal was finally taken out of childhood vaccines in the United States in 2001. Why would people continue to reject findings from numerous scientists and public agencies that vaccines were harmful?

Bounded Rationality

We seek out information to confirm what we already know and believe. We go to websites of like-minded people to avoid confusion; we read books and articles that confirm what we think we know. We develop narratives that explain away contradictory information. We claim that those who advocate for vaccination are shills for the drug industry and that doctors are getting rich by prescribing harmful medications. We embrace the brave few who argue otherwise, such "experts" as Dr. Gerhard Buchwald, who warns us against putting ourselves and our children at risk. "Consider carefully whether you want to let yourself or your children undergo the dangerous, controversial, ineffective and no longer necessary procedure called vaccination, because the claim that vaccinations are the cause for the decline of infectious diseases is nonsense."[24] The world of medicine, disease, vaccinations, and how to maintain our health is a confusing one. So we look for certainty.

The polymath Herbert Simon is credited with developing the **theory of bounded rationality**. He was one of the first to recognize that we humans are only partly rational. Much of the time we act irrationally. We use heuristics, or rules of thumb, to make quick decisions in a complex world. These decisions are not the result of a complicated process of weighing the pros and cons of each decision. We make decisions on the basis of the information we have on hand. As a result, the decisions we make are often not the best ones in the long run.[25]

> Closed systems of beliefs are characteristic of cults.

Simon's ideas were expanded by a number of scholars, particularly the two psychologists Daniel Kahneman and Amos Taversky, who sought to understand why we make suboptimal decisions.[26] We do so when we are faced with uncertainty. If we think of rules of thumb as hypotheses about how the world works, then we can better understand the anti-vaxxers who demonstrate what is termed **confirmation bias**. Confirmation bias, as the term is used in the psychological literature, refers to seeking or interpreting evidence in ways that are partial to existing beliefs, expectations, and how we think the world works.[27] Elaborate narratives are developed as a way to process inconvenient realities. When the CDC and the Institute of Medicine released reports in 2003 and 2004 stating unequivocally that there was *no* evidence that thimerosal or the MMR vaccine caused autism, anti-vaxxers relied on websites that told them these very agencies were involved in a gigantic cover-up. *Natural News*, an anti-vaxxer's website, took aim at Dr. David Gorski, an oncology surgeon at the Wayne State School of Medicine. His alleged crime was that he writes a pro-science blog attacking the ideas of those who oppose vaccinations. The headline blared, "Pro-vaccine shill Dr. David Gorski, linked to cancer fraudster, in cahoots with pharma to develop lucrative autism drug."[28] The reality is that Wayne State received funding from the vaccine maker Sanofi-Aventis to test a new drug, Riluzole, for dementia.

Our deeply held beliefs are resistant to change and in their most extreme form limit the choices available to us. Turning inward to groups that never challenge one's understanding of the world can take on the characteristics of a cult. The sociologist Janja Lalich expanded Simon's concept of bounded rationally in her *True Believers and Charismatic Cults*. There she develops a new concept, **bounded choice**, to recognize that cults make it seem to their members that there is only one way to do or think about things.[29] Those who challenge received wisdom are quickly banished from the group.

Megan Sandlin had a number of Facebook friends on groups such as *Great Mothers Questioning Vaccines*. She was told by group members that she was an awesome mother and an inspiration for others, because she wasn't vaccinating. She changed her mind. When she "came out" as pro-vaccine she was "removed from groups, blocked by strangers, accused of being brainwashed and warned that her daughters would get autism now that they've been vaccinated."[30] At one time Juniper Russo believed without question Wakefield's claims that vaccines cause autism. Then, her non-vaccinated child developed autism. Realizing her mistake she challenged the wisdom of the anti-vaxxers and found that she was "subject to relentless abuse, emails telling me . . . how can I sleep at night because of what I've done and that I'm working for the drug industry and that I'm somehow involved in some sort of global conspiracy to cause harm."[31]

The feeling of being duped has been reported by a number of those who have left the anti-vaccine movement. Maranda Dynda wrote about her searching for a home-birth midwife, who asked her if she was going to vaccinate her newborn. The midwife explained that she had a son who regressed and became autistic after being vaccinated. Maranda then began her own online exploration:

> It was like I stepped into another universe. The stories, the blogs, the information. There were mothers who said their children became autistic, developed epilepsy, or even died after receiving a vaccine . . . I heard tall tales about how doctors got paid premiums to vaccinate our

children, and that the medical community is purposely poisoning everyone . . . under the sun . . . Horror stories about ingredient lists, toxins, and mercury were spread around like candy.[32]

Asking herself why she wanted to believe those who also believed in essential oils, chemtrails (the vapor trails behind jets, which some believe are really aerosol vaccinations), FEMA death camps, and even denied the existence of AIDS, caused her to reconsider. Her ultimate conclusion, "I had been duped." She lost friends and gained enemies, as had others who left the movement.

The war between pro- and anti-vaccine forces is waged primarily over the internet and insults are freely exchanged. Sometimes family members are directly attacked. An 11-year-old girl received a posting on Facebook that she thought was from her aunt. It read:

Your mother is a fat ugly lazy piece of shit who tried to kill you. She is a bully and suffers from mental problems. She is under investigation for the hate groups and illegal computer hacking crimes she is committing.[33]

The reason the young girl received the email? She had been vaccinated and her mother posted that news on the Facebook page, *Anti-Vax Wall of Shame*, the purpose of which is to mock and ridicule the anti-vaxxers. The posting to the child was traced back to a pro-vaxxer site, *Anti-Vax Wall of Shame—Fall of the Wall*. Demonizing those who do not share your perspective is common among such groups. An anti-vaccine website has a "WANTED FOR GENOCIDE" poster of Dr. Paul Offit. His crime? He is a pediatrician and head of the vaccine education center at the Children's Hospital in Philadelphia.[34]

> Anti-vaccine advocates bridge to the ideas offered by sites advocating holistic health, organic foods, and natural remedies.

An increasing number of people get information to support their positions from the internet. Anti-vaxxers can collect and develop an elaborate set of "reasons" for not vaccinating their children from numerous blogs and websites. There are at least 1,000 such blogs. A detailed content analysis of 480 of these sites by Professor Megan Moran of the Johns Hopkins School of Public Health and her colleagues coded for vaccine misinformation, the types of persuasive tactics used, and the values promoted on the sites.[35] The study found a great deal of misinformation. Specifically, the majority of the sites claimed that:

- Vaccines were dangerous (65.6%).
- Vaccines caused autism (62.2%), and brain injury (41.1%).

Furthermore, the sites used discredited "scientific" evidence (64.7%) and personal stories (30%) to support their claims. In terms of the values expressed on the website they emphasized:

- Freedom of choice (41%).
- Individuality (17.4%).

> Attempts to break through the wall of anti-vaxxer sentiment are difficult because decisions not to vaccinate are based on a set of values about what is pure, natural, and what a parent's rights are.

Many sites for the anti-vaxxers co-promote other websites, and other websites promote them. There is an attempt, to use a term from social movement theory, to **bridge** between similar ideas from another group in order to grow the movement. The most common co-promotions found by Morgan and others were for alternative medicine (18%), homeopathy (10.2%), and eating a healthy and organic diet (18.5%). There were also promotions for cleansing one's body of toxins and the virtues of breastfeeding.

The website for *National Vaccine Information Center* provides one example of the alarms raised by the anti-vaxxers and the interconnections with other groups. On the Center's website they warn of the government and the CDC trying to expand their police powers.

Many of the anti-vaccine sites connect with that of Dr. Mercola, who will be discussed in Chapter 6 on the anti-GMO movement. Mercola has been branded a fraud by the business, regulatory, medical, and scientific communities. He was ordered by the Food and Drug Administration to stop making false claims about his products' ability to prevent or cure such diseases as cancer. Nevertheless, the links for co-promotion are substantial. As of this writing, there were 13 groups ranging from those opposed to vaccinating animals (*Rabies Challenge Fund*), homeopathy (*Grassroots Health Organization, Alliance for Natural Health, the Vitamin Council*), anti-GMO groups (*Institute for Responsible Technology*), the *Fluoride Alert Organization*, and one for *Mercury Free Dentistry*.[36] These sites peddle scientifically discredited information, raise alarms about the hazards of modern medicine, and promise natural cures for a variety of ailments.

Attempts to break through the wall of anti-vaxxer sentiment are difficult because *decisions not to vaccinate are driven by emotion and based on a set of values about what is pure, natural, and what a parent's rights are.*[37] A survey conducted with 1,759 parents in the United States sought to change behavior so that parents would be more likely to vaccinate. They provided parents with data from the CDC demonstrating that the MMR vaccine was safe and did not cause autism. They gave them information about the nature of the diseases that can be prevented by the MMR vaccine; showed them images of children who have diseases that could be prevented; and provided a dramatic story about an infant who almost died from measles. The unexpected result was that those who were most opposed to vaccination became even *more* convinced they should not vaccinate. The images of sick children reinforced their belief that vaccines were harmful and caused autism.[38]

Google has recently entered the fray and tweaked its algorithm so that those searching for words like "vaccination" and "fluoridation" are taken, first, to vetted medical information.[39] While this step is intriguing it is unlikely to change opinions because the position of anti-vaxxers isn't just about the science. It is also about the right to control one's own body and to decide what is best for one's family and children. Not vaccinating is about freedom from coercion and stems in part from a distrust of big—Big Pharma and big government. And it is also about fear.

Who Doesn't Vaccinate and Why?

The 19th- and early 20th-century anti-vaccine movement was driven in England by members of the working class, who saw themselves as the equivalent of slaves at the mercy of the regulatory state. Mandatory vaccinations meant their bodies were not their own and their fight against vaccines was a fight for control of their own bodies. Today, the class basis of the anti-vaxxers movement has shifted. Many of those who question the safety of vaccines are wealthier, better-educated parents as well as those who resist government intrusion into our private lives.[40]

Most (83%), but by no means all, Americans view vaccines as safe. Nine percent think they are unsafe, and 7% aren't sure.[41] Forty-one percent of younger Americans (18–29 years of age) believe parents should have the right to decide whether or not to vaccinate their children. The suspected reason for this finding is that people in this age category have not witnessed firsthand friends or neighbors who contracted polio or went deaf because they caught the measles. At the other extreme, only 20% of those 65 and older believe parents should have the right to choose, because they have experience with diseases that can be controlled by vaccines.[42] As one person noted in advocating for vaccination asked rhetorically, "Know anyone who has died from small pox, any children paralyzed from polio or any kids who have gone deaf from measles? No." As the writer wanted us to understand, we need to vaccinate so these diseases do not reestablish themselves.[43]

There are also important differences by race. Blacks (26%) and Hispanics (15%) are more likely than whites (6%) to view vaccines as unsafe. Members of minority communities generally have had limited access to medical care and negative experiences with medicine in general. A 2016 outbreak of tuberculosis in the rural Alabama community of Marion hit the Black community hard. The incident rate was 100 times greater than that for Alabama as a whole and higher than that of some developing countries. Many had not been immunized because they did not trust health officials and did not want them poking into their private lives. But many had not been vaccinated and did not respond to the cash offers to be tested for tuberculosis because they remembered the Tuskegee experiments.[44]

> Political conservatives are more likely to oppose vaccinations.

The notorious Tuskegee experiment lasted 40 years, 1932–1972. It was decided that it would be a good idea to study the natural development of syphilis. A group of impoverished sharecroppers, some of whom had syphilis (399) and some who did not (201), were enrolled in a study jointly conducted by Tuskegee University and the Public Health Service. All were told they were being treated for "bad blood." Given room and board and medical care, they were well taken care of, except *none* of the 399 who had syphilis were told they had the disease nor were they treated for it even after penicillin had become available. The scandal came to light in 1972 and led to new laws protecting human subjects, but the experiment was not forgotten among members of the African-American community.

Those with a high school education or less are also more likely (14%) to believe vaccines are unsafe, compared to just 6% of those with a college education.[45] There are also important regional variations in terms of vaccination rates. Overall, 91.8% of all U.S. teenagers 13–17 have been vaccinated. In the Deep South, the figure drops to 89.0%, while in northeastern states like New Jersey and New York it is 93.8%. The national outliers in terms of rates tend to be politically conservative states: Arizona (85.5%), Idaho (85.2%), Kansas (86.9%), Mississippi (88.3%), Texas (87.3%), Utah (87.5%), and West Virginia (83.2%).[46] There is also a growing gap between people based on their political affiliation. Republicans (34%) are significantly more likely than Democrats (22%) to oppose mandatory vaccinations.[47]

Virtually all mainline religious denominations in the United States support vaccination but see it as a parental choice, not one based on doctrine. The Jehovah's Witnesses, which reject some forms of medical intervention, are clear that it is the parents' choice as to whether or not to vaccinate but parents need to live with the consequences of their choices and not blame outcomes on God.[48]

The Old Order Amish are frequently offered as "proof" by the anti-vaxxers that vaccines cause autism because they believe the Amish don't vaccinate. They do, at rates of about 85%, and some children do develop autism, but not because of vaccines. The Amish are pretty much like the rest of the population; Amish parents resist immunizations for the same reasons non-Amish do. They are worried about the effects of vaccines. The pro-vaccine article that reported these facts was followed by 70 pages of comments, most of which questioned these findings. Clearly many wanted and needed to believe the myth that the Amish don't vaccinate.[49]

Some use religious beliefs as a reason to try and opt out of state vaccination requirements. In Texas, 45,000 students received a non-medical exemption from vaccinations.[50] When the State of Montana determined in 2015 that all school children would be vaccinated against chickenpox, tetanus, diphtheria, and pertussis and given appropriate booster shots, unless parents had a religious objection, the number of religious objections jumped up. In one religious school, Pines Academy, 82.1% of students had an exemption. In the conservative Bitterroot Valley county of Ravalli, south of the university town of Missoula, a massive advertising blitz by school officials failed, because of an increase in religious exemptions, to achieve *herd immunity*.[51]

The term herd immunity is based on the idea that by immunizing a critical portion of the population, the whole community can be safe:

> Just as a herd of cattle or sheep uses sheer numbers to protect its members from predators, herd immunity protects a community from infectious diseases by virtue of the sheer number of people immune to such diseases. The more members of a human "herd" who are immune to a given disease, the better protected the whole population will be from an outbreak of that disease.[52]

The perhaps unfortunate use of the word "herd" suggested to many anti-vaxxers that their children would be led like sheep and cattle to slaughter. Public health departments recommend aiming for 100% immunization rates, recognizing that some children can't be immunized because they may have a compromised immune system, may have had a transplant, or are undergoing radiation or chemotherapy treatment. They need other children to be vaccinated so they are safe.

The rates vary for what is needed to achieve herd immunity because some diseases are more difficult to catch than others. A vaccination rate of 75–86% is needed to check outbreaks of mumps but 92–94% is required for a non-vaccinated child to avoid whooping cough.[53] For the clever anti-vax parent, it means they can avoid having their child vaccinated, if everyone else has had their child vaccinated.[54] *Free riders*, who benefit from public immunization programs, but don't vaccinate their own children because they'll be protected by those who have, are a source of conflict and a public health challenge. Many of today's anti-vaxxers, unlike those of the 19th century, are affluent people concentrated in communities where there are other like-minded parents. As the sociologist

Jennifer Reich found in her 10-year study of parents who do not vaccinate, they tend to be supermoms who favor organic foods and gluten-free products. They believe their job is to protect *their* children.[55] These issues crystallized with California's decision (SB 227) to eliminate free riders from the system by eliminating *all* religious exemptions and allowing exemptions only when they were based on the recommendation of a licensed physician.

California and Senate Bill 227

In the spring of 2015, somebody brought measles to Disneyland and it quickly spread. The low rate of vaccination among the children and some of their parents visiting the park meant that just one person was ultimately responsible for the spread of the disease to 145 people in the United States, as well as several more from Mexico and Canada.[56] The CDC believed that an overseas' visitor, probably from the Philippines, was responsible for the outbreak, yet what happened was a clear example of what could happen because of a non-immunized U.S. child.[57]

The California Legislature decided to act and push back against the growing number of Californians, particularly the affluent, who were choosing not to vaccinate their children.[58] The bill mandated that the only way to avoid having your child vaccinated was for a doctor to provide a *medical* reason for the exemption. Any child attending school had to be vaccinated against such diseases as measles, mumps, and whooping cough. The measure attracted vocal crowds as the bill worked its way through the legislature, challenged at every step by those opposed to vaccines.

Senator Richard Pan, a pediatrician and original co-sponsor of the bill, was attacked for being in the pocket of the pharmaceutical industry. Kent Heckenlively, who has an autistic son, writing for the anti-vaccine website, *The Age of Autism*, compared SB 227 to the Fugitive Slave Act of 1850 and the anti-vaccine forces to runaway slaves:

> Consider the slave-owning South prior to the American Civil War. A trickle of slaves, perhaps 1,000–5,000 were escaping each year . . . beginning their lives in the North, and speaking freely of what they endured under the lash of their slave masters.
>
> The escaped slaves presented no existential threat to slavery . . . But that wasn't enough for the South. The escaped slaves drove them crazy. Just like the 1.5% of California . . . parents with philosophical or religious exemptions drive people like Senator Richard Pan . . . absolutely nuts, just like escaped slaves drove their Southern masters crazy.[59]

Some anti-vaxxers compared themselves and their children to Jews and the Holocaust. Others argued their children would be like those in Flint, Michigan, poisoned, in their case by lead, because of a gigantic government cover-up. Lobbyists in favor of the bill, like Jodi Hicks, were stalked and photographed by anti-vaxxers. Hicks' photo later appeared on Twitter under the caption, *#DevilWithTheBlueDress*. Other posts claimed there was a special place in hell waiting for her. Brian Stenzler, president of the California Chiropractic Association, produced a video urging people to stalk lobbyists all day long, for which he was rebuked by the California Medical Association.[60] Leah Russin, founder of *Vaccinate California*, testified before the Senate committee considering the bill. She said she founded the group because, like many mothers, she was afraid to take her son to school, because other children were not vaccinated. Her home address was provided on *The Age of Autism* website and opponents of vaccines were urged to gather there for a protest:

> If you think that peacefully marching around a person's neighborhood is going too far, remember that this person has succeeded in forcing many of us out of the state . . . This person has been the leading voice to bring FORCED and COERCED insertion of unethically derived vaccines (many of which are produced from the cells of aborted fetuses . . .) into every child who seeks a public education.[61]

Hundreds came to the state capitol, Sacramento, to protest against the bill. The groups opposed were, to put it mildly, diverse. The Nation of Islam was opposed, claiming mandatory vaccination was equivalent to the Tuskegee experiments. Save California, an anti-abortion and anti-gay group, claimed the bill was tyrannical and anti-family. The Tea Party joined forces with the Canary Party to stand up for victims of medical injury, and to oppose environmental toxins, as well as an industrial food system.[62] Prominent Scientologists Kirstie Alley, Danny Masterson, and Jenna Elfman added their voices to the opposition because vaccines were seen by them as toxins, contrary to the "purification" cleansing program advocated by Scientologists to treat drug abuse and exposure to toxins.[63] Vaccines were for them a form of pollution of naturally pure bodies.

The comedian and actor, Jim Carrey, known for such films as *Ace Ventura: Pet Detective* and *Dumb and Dumber*, used Twitter to express his outrage at the legislation. According to Carrey, Governor Brown was saying yes to poisoning children with mercury and aluminum in vaccines laden with neurotoxins. "This form of corporate fascism" had to be stopped he Tweeted. He was not, Carrey claimed, anti-vaccine, he was really just anti-neurotoxin, like Robert Kennedy Jr.[64]

Kennedy had been recruited by anti-vaxxers to come to California to try and stem the tide against the passage of SB 227. He told a galvanized audience in Sacramento: "They can put anything they want in that vaccine and they have no accountability."[65] He promoted, as he had previously, the false claim that there was a link between thimerosal, a vaccine preservative, and autism.[66] He failed to tell his audience that thimerosal (in harmless trace amounts) had been removed from childhood vaccines in 2001. In spite of the support from celebrities, politicians, and a mélange of other groups, SB 227 was signed into law by Governor Jerry Brown in 2015. The anti-vaxxers were furious and looked for the guilty parties.

> Celebrities and politicians have been responsible for spreading misinformation about the dangers of vaccination.

Writing for the anti-vaccine website, *National Vaccine Information Center*, Dawn Richardson reported:

> Despite some of the most articulate, accurate, passionate and vocal opposition the legislature has seen from citizens spanning all political, socioeconomic, ethnic, religious, and medical backgrounds, a pro-mandatory vaccination lobby backed by the pharmaceutical, medical trade and public health industries prevailed.[67]

Lisa McLaughlin, posting to Richardson's story, blamed the media. "The media was SHAMEFUL on this one!! On the take from big pharma, they rarely gave the other side of the story." She wondered why no informed anti-vax voices had been on Fox News.[68]

The anti-vaxxers mobilized to repeal the law with a ballot referendum. They gained about 200,000 signatures, far short of the 365,880 required under California law to put the question before the voters. The leader of the referendum, Tim Connelly, asserted the campaign failed because it "was sabotaged from without and within by powerful forces from its inception."[69]

The attempts to reverse the bill were also fueled in part by Andrew Wakefield's return to the scene in the spring of 2015. He claimed he had finally found the smoking gun which would prove him right and demonstrate once and for all that the MMR vaccine caused autism. It was his chance at redemption. He directed the film *Vaxxed: From Cover-up to Catastrophe*, in which the voice of William Thompson, a CDC scientist, is heard, although Thompson never appears. The movie reveals that Thompson was secretly recorded when he talked to Brian Hooker, an anti-vaccine advocate with an autistic child. In the film Thompson is heard saying to Hooker, "Oh my god. I cannot believe what we did." What Thompson claims he and his colleagues at the CDC did was toss in a trashcan evidence demonstrating that Black children in Atlanta who had been vaccinated demonstrated high rates of autism.[70]

The film portrays Thompson and his colleagues working secretly to hide this information. But this was unlikely. Thompson was listed as the co-author on the paper based on the very data which concluded there was no link between the MMR vaccine and autism.[71] Even more interesting, the data still existed; it was never thrown out with the trash. Jim Frost, the statistician who analyzed the original data, went back and reanalyzed the data and got the same results. "The criticism that the study discarded data from African American subjects just doesn't hold water. No data were discarded," he stated.[72] Nevertheless, John F. Kennedy, Jr. likened the supposed withholding of information about African-American rates of autism to another Tuskegee experiment.[73]

The film *Vaxxed* was supposed to be premiered at the Tribeca Film Festival in New York in March 2015 but support was withdrawn for its screening. Robert De Niro, founder of the film festival and father of an autistic child, told the press:

> My intent in screening this film was to provide an opportunity for conversation around an issue that is deeply personal to me and my family. But after reviewing it over the past few days with the Tribeca Film Festival team and others from the scientific community, we do not believe it contributes to or furthers the discussion I had hoped for.[74]

The promotional materials for the film had been intended to revive a controversy many believed settled. In addition to promising testimonials from physicians and parents, viewers were also promised high drama:

> The most vitriolic debate in medical history takes a dramatic turn when senior-scientist-turned-whistleblower Dr. William Thompson of the Centers for Disease Control turns over secret documents, data and internal emails confirming what millions of devastated parents and "discredited" doctors have long suspected.[75]

Because the onset of autism occurs after a child is vaccinated, this has led a number of parents to conclude that vaccination causes autism.

The film was, however, discredited by the medical community. Nevertheless, what some viewers of the film found compelling and convincing were the statements given by parents of autistic children.

The Power of Narrative

Imagine for a moment that you have a child who is diagnosed with a severe form of autism and you are told by your doctor, as was an acquaintance of mine, that she should be prepared for her child "never saying I love you, never making eye contact, and never talking." You would be devastated and you would most likely look for an answer to the question "Why?"

The TV and film actress and 1994 Playmate of the Year, Jenny McCarthy, has become for many anti-vaxxers the face of the movement. McCarthy became an activist after her son, Evan, was diagnosed with autism, when he was 2½. One morning when he was sleeping late she looked in on him and found him "struggling to breathe, and pasty white, blue lips, and shaking." After rushing Evan to the hospital the doctors told her that he might be having an epileptic seizure. But she rejected that diagnosis; it had to be something else. "And then I knew—that mommy instinct—there was something more to the story." She went over in her mind what might have caused Evan's reactions and realized that his development was perfectly normal until he got the MMR vaccine. That's when Evan started regressing.[76]

One of the coincidences that cause parents like McCarthy to link vaccines and autism is that autism typically manifests itself between 18 months and three years, about the same time a child is receiving vaccines to boost their immunities to potentially crippling diseases. After a neurosurgeon told her that Evan was autistic, she went home crying. That night she went on Google and typed in "autism." Then she went to a link sponsored by *Generation Rescue* and found that "autism is reversible." Skeptical, she continued her search: "and I found not just a guy who made the Web site, but this whole *community of thousands of parents that were actually healing their child, recovering them from autism.*"[77] Based on the advice she found, she eliminated wheat and dairy from Evan's diet, gave him vitamins and cod liver oil. According to McCarthy, Evan made better eye contact, started saying two-word sentences, and his stimming (flapping of hands) got better. She became a spokeswoman "for a dizzying variety of autism nostrums—special diets, supplements, detox, chelation, hyperbaric chambers, etc., none of which has been shown to have any scientific validity."[78] Yet numerous sites offer parents both false science and false hope and some are simply fraudulent.[79]

The desire to cure one's child is an understandable one; and one which may cause them to search for any possible remedy. Like McCarthy, they frequently seek out other parents of autistic children to create, even if online, a community. With like-minded others they share stories about how they are coping, about new dangers and new "cures" they discover on the web. Many are convinced we are in the midst of a health epidemic—autism, attention deficit disorder (ADHD), asthma, and children with rheumatoid arthritis—and it's all due, as *Mothering Magazine* asserts, to vaccines.[80]

The Movement to Understand Autism

We now know that autism occurs along a spectrum, referred to as autism spectrum disorders (ASD). At one end of the extreme, children will not be able to use spoken language, will engage in aggressive behaviors (hitting and biting), engage in self-injuries (head banging), and will take no notice of others. They may also have gastrointestinal issues and some will require 24/7 care and institutionalization. At the other end, ASD manifests itself as having poor and inappropriate social skills, an ability to tune others out, and a preference to play or work alone.

> Autism is not just one thing or symptom; it occurs along a spectrum.

It took a long time for the medical profession to recognize that autism was not just one thing. The breakthrough in understanding came with the work of the psychiatrist Lorna Wing, whose daughter, Susie, was severely disabled by autism and required care in a residential home. However, she understood that Susie represented just one point on the scale of autism and there were others who were less afflicted. She coined the term *Asperger's syndrome* after a pediatrician of the same name, who had worked with a group of oddly precocious children, who he referred to as his "little professors."[81] Wing developed a scale for a triad of impairments (social interaction, social communication, and social imagination) that fit all forms of autism. It was quickly adopted by pediatricians and clinicians because it matched behaviors they were already observing. As the television journalists John Donavan and Caren Zucker—both of whom have autistic family members—wrote, this had the effect of driving the number of those diagnosed with autism higher. And, because there was a range of behaviors, it made some forms of autism, such as Asperger's, less frightening and made more people willing to talk about it.[82]

Another factor driving rates higher occurred when Wing convinced the American Psychiatric Association to add a definition of autism to the all-important *Diagnostic and Statistical Manual* (DSM) and convinced the World Health Organization to add it to their classification of diseases. The rising numbers of diagnoses made it appear that the country was in the midst of an autistic "epidemic."[83] But as Donovan and Zucker have pointed out, *there isn't an autism epidemic and there never has been one.*[84] We are simply better at diagnosing autism and more parents are aware of the behaviors associated with it.

Public interest in autism and a better understanding of its nature spiked with the 1988 movie, *The Rain Man*. Dustin Hoffman played an autistic adult spirited away on a road trip to Las Vegas by his younger brother, played by Tom Cruise. In the movie, Hoffman displays some of the behaviors typical of autism. His need for sameness and routine is disrupted on the road trip; he echoes back phrases or questions from his brother; he exhibits sensitivity to loud and unexpected noises; and he rocks back and forth and occasionally flaps his hands. The movie played an important role in driving funding and treatment for autistic children. Parents who had children enrolled in school, who might not be doing well because of behavior problems, sought a diagnosis of autism so their child could receive appropriate resources. As Daniel Smith has pointed out, the problem in declaring and identifying an "epidemic," is that people feel threatened by an epidemic and "they're going to wonder what caused it. And, in the absence of a clear answer, distrust and fear rush in."[85]

Parents of autistic children had long sought a diagnosis and understanding of what caused autism. One of the first and most damaging ideas was advanced by Bruno Bettelheim, an art historian who had managed to convince the University of Chicago to let him set up shop as a child psychologist. Bettelheim concluded, in an article in the *Scientific American*, that autism was a perfectly rational response to a **deficit of maternal emotion**. The boy he described, Joey, had become a "mechanical boy," and it was his mother's fault.[86] The idea that "bad" mothers or fathers were to blame only increased pressures on families to find solutions and explanations. Some tried Applied Behavioral Analysis (ABA), a program of behavior modification pioneered by the psychologist Ivar Lovaas. Lovaas claimed to be able to restore 47% of autistic patients to normality.[87] One problem for parents is that in the 1980s it cost up to $50,000 a year for a home-based program.[88] That made it even more imperative that public resources be found to treat autistic children in the classroom and successful political campaigns were mounted to do so.

The same year that *Rain Man* came out, Andrew Wakefield published his claims, later discredited, that the MMR vaccine caused autism. But parents embraced his ideas because it meant there was "scientific" proof they were not to blame. "Mercury moms" and other advocacy groups formed to get the mercury out of vaccines and when the counterargument was made that the MMR vaccine did not cause autism, and that autism was probably due to genetic factors, the response was to claim a cover-up.

The 2015 release of Wakefield's movie only seemed to harden the belief of anti-vaxxers that the "truth" was being hidden. The search for the cause of autism remains undiminished. One study suggests that fine particulate matter in the air is linked with an increased risk for autism.[89] Another claim is that ultrasounds in the first trimester of pregnancy might be linked to autism.[90] The report on this possible link came with several caveats, among the most important was that this link had been based on parental reports; parents *thought* their child was autistic because the mother had an ultrasound. The report went on to note that autism is most likely the result of genetics and as yet undetermined environmental stressors, but parents were looking beyond genetic explanations. "Some medical leaders worry that these studies could produce an unwarranted backlash of the sort that occurred when now-debunked research allegedly tied childhood vaccines to autism."[91]

It is understandable that parents would want to find an explanation, and possible cure, for autism. The "solutions" people try vary greatly from changing a child's diet, to chelation therapy which involves injecting a solution that binds to the toxins in the blood and washes away harmful chemicals. There are campaigns to "green" vaccines to assure nothing harmful is in them. Some anti-vaxxers argue that children are getting "too many vaccines too soon," or advocate that children get vaccinated for only one disease at a time to lower the risk of autism.

Autism is real and a desire to find an explanation and a cure for it revolves around what it means to be a good parent and to protect one's child from unknown dangers. It is assumed that the body, especially a baby's, is pure, as is the womb and mother's milk. Any harm to the child must, therefore, come from other sources—vaccines or environmental toxins. Vaccines are seen as a form of poison, injected into an unwitting and unwilling population. Genetics, which may be the scientific answer, is for many parents not an answer because it means that nothing can be done to help the most severely affected children. It also suggests that there was something wrong with the parent—their sperm, eggs, and genetic makeup. The anti-vaxxer movement is above all an attempt to shift the blame from the parent to the pharmaceutical industry and doctors. Science and arguments about the common good are not sufficient to overcome conspiracy theories or escape the trap of bounded rationality.

Understanding the Anti-Vaxxers as a Social Movement

There are really two social movement *campaigns* involved in the autism movement. The first began with efforts to understand its nature and range. That campaign, aided by the work of Lorna Wing and the popular portrayal of an autistic man in *Rain Man*, was successful in getting the issue before the public. And it was successful in getting an official diagnosis, which garnered public resources to help autistic children and their families. But this successful campaign also alerted people to the possibility of an autism epidemic.

The second campaign is exemplified by the efforts of anti-vaxxers in California to defeat SB 227. The *master frame* used by the anti-vaxxers focused on the larger issues of personal freedom. "Your health, your family, your choice!" They argued for the purity of the body. They drew on "science" which they believed clearly demonstrated the harmful effects of vaccines. When their efforts to prevent the passage of SB 227 failed, they claimed their defeat was caused by the pharmaceutical industry and by medical doctors who were supposedly getting rich from vaccinations.

Another *framing device*, not just for the California campaign but nationwide, drew on the assumption that healthy mothers had given birth to healthy children and that if something had gone wrong, it was *not* the mother's fault. "Cures" thus involved purifying a child by changing its diet, as recommended by a number of those peddling false hope, vitamins, and other "natural" nostrums.

The *social context* which gave rise to the movement and still sustains it is the uncertainty surrounding any disease, its causes, and possible cures. We read daily about superbugs, about new and frightening diseases like the Zika and Ebola viruses. We read about drug companies gouging patients with ever higher prices and find that lobbying groups have derailed efforts to curb U.S. consumption of drugs like OxyContin, Vicodin, and Percocet.[92] If we follow news about the environment, we are privy to stories about toxic chemical spills, oil pipelines leaking, and the devastation of wildlife. To be worried is rational. It is not rational to reject the science that supports vaccinations.

The anti-vaxxers, because of *closed and dense networks* which exist on the web, find only reinforcement for their theories. *Great Mothers Questioning Vaccines* post similar concerns from other websites. Some of the sites attempt to *bridge* to those sites like Dr. Mercola's which provide stories, like Jenny McCarthy's, of how they cured their child by changing its diet. There is thus a tight link of like-minded people who advocate for natural cures, organic foods, and those concerned about autism.

The **resources** that anti-vaxxers bring to the table are limited. That is partly because they exist in the realm of the internet and there are many (perhaps a 1,000) competing for attention and resources. Virtually every site has a button you can click: "Donate." There is no national organization setting an agenda or funding the wide range of activity in which anti-vaxxers engage. The larger collective, however, sustains the conversation online about the dangers of vaccines and sustains the efforts of those who profit from the fears and anxieties of the group.

There is clearly a *culture of defiance and resistance* driven by fear and a lack of trust. Blame is attributed to others and demands for justice are loud. Arguments are rejected that challenge the wisdom of internet forums and a form of *bounded rationality* takes over, where new contrary information cannot penetrate. New ideas about the causes and the development of autism keep the movement alive. My intention is not to argue that having an autistic child can be argued away or that the concerns of parents aren't real. They are. But by rejecting medical opinion the anti-vaxxers put larger populations at risk by insisting on protecting the purity of their own children. As we will see in the next chapter, anti-vaxxers are not the only group rejecting scientific consensus.

Notes

1 Quoted in Sarah Loving, March 27, 2013. "How Dangerous Is Measles?" Oxford Vaccine Group. University of Oxford. Retrieved on September 9, 2016 at: http://vk.ovg.ox.ac.uk/blogs/ojohn/how-dangerous-measles.
2 Centers for Disease Control and Prevention. "Measles and the Vaccine (Shot) to Prevent It." Retrieved on September 9, 2016 at: www.cdc.gov/vaccines/parents/diseases/child/measles.html.
3 Stefan Riedel. January 18, 2005. "Edward Jenner and the History of Smallpox Vaccination." Proceedings of the Baylor University Medical Center. Vol.18(1):21–25.
4 Riedel. January 18, 2005.
5 College of Physicians, Philadelphia, Pennsylvania. April 12, 2010. "History of Anti-Vaccination Movements—History of Vaccines." Retrieved on September 12, 2016 at: www.historyofvaccines.org/content/articles/history-anti-vaccination-movements.
6 Nadja Durbach. 2000. "They Might as Well Brand Us: Working Class Resistance to Compulsory Vaccination in Victorian England." *The Society for the Social History of Medicine*. Vol.13(1):45–62.
7 Nadja Durbach. 2004. *Bodily Matters: The Anti-Vaccination Movement in England, 1853–1907 (Radical Perspectives)*. Durham, North Carolina: Duke University Press.
8 Cited in Eula Biss. 2014. *On Immunity and Inoculation*. Minneapolis, Minnesota: Greywolf Press.
9 "The Vaccine Poisoning Racket." See the website: http://whale.to/vaccines/smallpox.html, as well as the site Vaccine Liberation, "20 and 1 Reasons to Avoid Smallpox Vaccine": www.vaclib.org/news/smallpoxalert.htm.
10 Elizabeth Earl. July 15, 2015. "The Victorian Anti-Vaccination Movement." *The Atlantic*. Retrieved on September 12, 2016 at: www.theatlantic.com/health/archive/2015/07/victorian-anti-vaccinators-personal-belief-exemption/398321/.
11 Eula Biss. 2014. *On Immunity and Inoculation*.
12 Robert M. Wolfe and Lisa K. Sharp. January 9, 2002. "Anti-Vaccinationists Past and Present." *British Medical Journal*. Vol.325(7361):430–432. Available at: www.ncbi.nlm.nih.gov/pmc/articles/PMC1123944/.
13 J.P. Baker. September 8, 2003. "The Pertussis Controversy in Great Britain, 1974–1986." *Vaccine*. Vol.21:4003–4010. Available at: www.ncbi.nlm.nih.gov/pubmed/12922137.
14 College of Physicians, Philadelphia. April 12, 2010. "History of Anti-Vaccination Movements—History of Vaccines."
15 WRC-TV. 1982. *Vaccination Roulette*. Washington, D.C.
16 See for example, The Thinking Moms' Revolution. "From 'Vaccine Roulette' to 'Vaxxed': The Importance of Documentaries." Retrieved on September 14, 2016 at: http://thinkingmomsrevolution.com/vaccine-roulette-vaxxed-importance-documentaries/.
17 Cited in The Thinking Moms' Revolution. April 19, 2016. Retrieved on September 13, 2016 at: http://thinkingmomsrevolution.com/vaccine-roulette-vaxxed-importance-documentaries/. See also: Gary L. Freed, Samuel L. Katz, and Sarah J. Clark. 1996. "Safety

of Vaccinations: Miss America, the Media, and Public Health." *Journal of the American Medical Association*. Vol.276(23):1869–1872.

18 Thinking Moms' Revolution, April 19, 2016.

19 Harris L. Coulter. 1991. *A Shot in the Dark*. New York: Penguin.

20 Comments posted to the Amazon webpage for Coulter's book. Retrieved on September 13, 2016 at: www.amazon.com/Shot-Dark-H-Coulter/dp/089529463X.

21 The British reporter, Brian Deer, conducted an award-winning and detailed study of Wakefield's fraud. See for example: Brian Deer. 2003–2011. "Exposed: Andrew Wakefield and the MMR-Autism Fraud." Retrieved on September 13, 2016 at: http://briandeer.com/mmr/lancet-summary.htm; Brian Deer. January 6, 2011. "How the Case against the MMR Vaccine Was Fixed." *British Medical Journal*. Vol.342:c5347. Retrieved on September 13, 2016 at: www.bmj.com/content/342/bmj.c5347.

22 Centers for Disease Control and Prevention. 2016. "Thimerosal in Vaccines." Retrieved on September 14, 2016 at: www.cdc.gov/vaccinesafety/concerns/thimerosal/.

23 Cited in Amy Wallace. October 23, 2009. "A Short History of Vaccine Panic." *Wired*. Retrieved on September 14, 2016 at: www.wired.com/2009/10/a-short-history-of-vaccine-panic/.

24 Cited on the website of Whale.to. Retrieved on September 14, 2016 at: http://whale.to/.

25 Herbert Simon. 1957. *Models of Man, Social and Rational: Mathematical Essays on Rational Human Behavior in Social Setting*. New York: Wiley.

26 Amos Taversky and Daniel Kahneman. 1973. "Availability: A Heuristic for Judging Frequency and Probability." *Cognitive Psychology*. Vol.5(2):207–232; Amos Taversky and Daniel Kahneman. 1974. "Judgment Under Uncertainty: Heuristics and Biases." *Science*. Vol.185(4157):1124–1131. For a summary of Taversky and Kahneman's work see Kahneman. 2011. *Thinking Fast and Slow*. New York: Farrar, Straus, and Giroux.

27 For a detailed summary of the literature on confirmation bias see: Raymond S. Nickerson. 1998. "Confirmation Bias: A Ubiquitous Phenomena in Many Guises." *Review of General Psychology*. Vol.2(2):175–220.

28 Julie Wilson. April 18, 2016. "Pro-Vaccine Shill Dr. David Gorski, Linked to Cancer Fraudster, in Cahoots with Pharma to Develop Lucrative Autism Drug." Retrieved on September 14, 2016 at: www.naturalnews.com/053706_David_Gorski_autism_drug_Karmanos_Cancer_Center.html.

29 Janja Lalich. 2004. *True Believers and Charismatic Cults*. Berkeley, California: University of California Press.

30 Cited in Cosima Marriner. June 14, 2016. "I Now View Anti-Vaxxers as a Sort of Cult." *Daily Life*. Retrieved on September 15, 2016 at: www.dailylife.com.au/life-and-love/parenting-and-families/i-now-view-antivaxxers-as-sort-of-a-cult-20160613-gpi0rh.html.

31 Cited in BBC News. August 5, 2015. "What's Behind the 'Anti-Vax' Movement?" Retrieved on September 15, 2016 at: www.bbc.com/news/health-33774181.

32 Maranda Dynda. Nd. "I Was Duped by the Anti-Vaccine Movement." *Voices for Vaccine*. Retrieved on September 15, 2016 at: www.voicesforvaccines.org/i-was-duped-by-the-anti-vaccine-movement/.

33 Cited in Anna Merlan. June 29, 2015. "Meet the New, Dangerous Fringe of the Anti-Vaccination Movement." *Jezebel*. Retrieved on September 15, 2016 at: http://jezebel.com/meet-the-new-dangerous-fringe-of-the-anti-vaccination-1713438567.

34 We Are the People. "Dr. Paul Offit." Retrieved on June 12, 2017 at: www.waronwethepeople.com/paul-offit-2/. The wanted poster is included in the post.

35 Megan Moran, Kristen Everhart, Melissa Lucas, Erin Pricket, and Ashley Morgan. November 4, 2015. "Why Are Anti-Vaccine Messages So Persuasive? A Content Analysis of Anti-Vaccine Websites to Inform the Development of Vaccine Promotion Strategies."

American Public Health Association. Retrieved on September 16, 2016 at: https://apha. confex.com/apha/143am/webprogram/Paper329083.html.

36 Dr. Mercola. "Vaccines and Autism." Retrieved on September 16, 2016 at: http://autism. mercola.com/.

37 Meredith Wadman and Jia You. April 28, 2017. "The Vaccine Wars: Debunking Myths, Owning Real Risks, and Courting Doubters." *Science.* Vol.356(6336):364–366.

38 Brendan Nyham, Jason Reifler, Sean Richey, and Gary L. Freed. February, 2014. "Effective Messages in Vaccine Promotion: A Randomized Trial." *Pediatrics.* DOI: 10.1542/ peds.2013-2365.

39 George Johnson. August 25, 2015. "The Gradual Extinction of Accepted Truths." *The New York Times,* D6.

40 S. Leib, P. Liberatos, and K. Edwards. July–August, 2011. "Pediatricians' Experience with and Response to Parental Vaccine Safety Concerns and Vaccine Refusals: A Survey of Connecticut Pediatricians." *Public Health Reports.* Vol.126(Supplement 2):13–23. Retrieved on September 16, 2016 at: www.ncbi.nlm.nih.gov/pubmed/21812165.

41 Rounding errors mean these figures add up to 99%, not 100%.

42 Monica Anderson. July 17, 2015. "5 Facts about Vaccines in the U.S." *PEW Research Center.* Retrieved on September 15, 2016 at: www.pewresearch.org/fact-tank/2015/07/17/5-facts-about-vaccines-in-the-u-s/.

43 Comment posted to a website in response to the article by Manny Schewitz. January 21, 2014. "The Anti-Vaccine Movement is the Left's Intellectual Problem with Science." *Forward Progressives.* Retrieved on September 16, 2016 at: www.forwardprogressives.com/ the-anti-vaccine-movement-is-the-lefts-intellectual-problem-with-science/.

44 Alan Binder. January 17, 2016. "In Rural Alabama, a Longtime Mistrust of Medicine Fuels a Tuberculosis Outbreak." *The New York Times.* Retrieved on September 16, 2016 at: www. nytimes.com/2016/01/18/us/in-rural-alabama-a-longtime-mistrust-of-medicine-fuels-a-tuberculosis-outbreak.html?_r=0.

45 Monica Anderson. July 17, 2015. "5 Facts about Vaccines in the U.S."

46 Centers for Disease Control and Prevention. July 25, 2014. "National, Regional, State, and Selected Local Area Vaccination Coverage among Adolescents Aged 13–17—United States, 2013." Retrieved on September 15, 2016 at: www.cdc.gov/mmwr/preview/mmwrhtml/ mm6329a4.htm.

47 Monica Anderson. July 17, 2015. "5 Facts about Vaccines in the U.S."

48 Ontario Consultants on Religious Tolerance. April 20, 2014. "About the Jehovah's Witnesses Christian Denomination—Past Opposition to Vaccinations." Retrieved on September 15, 2016 at: www.religioustolerance.org/witness6.htm.

49 Seth Mnookin. June 28, 2011. "Anecdotal Amish-Don't-Vaccinate Claims Disproved by Fact-Based Study." *PLOS BLOGS.* Retrieved on September 15, 2016 at: http://blogs.plos. org/thepanicvirus/2011/06/28/anecdotal-amish-dont-vaccinate-claims-disproved-by-fact-based-study/; J.S. Yoder and M.S. Dworkin. December, 2006. "Vaccination Usage among an Old-Order Amish Community in Illinois." *Pediatrics Infectious Diseases Journal.* Vol.25(12):1182–1183. Retrieved on 14 September, 2016 at: www.ncbi.nlm.nih.gov/ pubmed/17133167.

50 Peter J. Hotez. February 8, 2017. "How the Anti-Vaxxers Are Winning." *The New York Times.* Retrieved on June 12, 2017 at: www.nytimes.com/2017/02/08/opinion/how-the-anti-vaxxers-are-winning.html.

51 Derek Brouwer. July 14–21, 2016. "Shot Down: New Vaccine Requirements Prompt Parents to Find Religion." *Missoula Independent,* p.9.

52 Emily Willingham and Laura Helft. September 9, 2014. "What Is Herd Immunity?" *NOVA.* Retrieved on September 15, 2016 at: www.pbs.org/wgbh/nova/body/herd-immunity. html.

53 Paul Fine, Ken Eames, and David L. Heymann. 2011. "'Herd Immunity': A Rough Guide." *Clinical Infectious Diseases.* Vol.52(7):911–916.
54 Melissa Davey. January 23, 2016. "Researchers Study Motivations of Parents Who Refuse to Vaccinate Children." *The Guardian.* Retrieved on September 15, 2015 at: www.theguardian.com/society/2016/jan/24/parents-who-keep-anti-vaccination-stance-a-secret-put-others-at-risk.
55 Jennifer Reich. 2016. *Calling the Shots: Why Parents Reject Vaccines.* New York: New York University Press.
56 Maimuna S. Majumder, Emily L. Cohn, Sumiko R. Mekanu, Jane E. Huston, and John S. Brownstein. May, 2015. "Substandard Vaccination Compliance and the 2015 Measles Outbreak." *Journal of the American Medical Association.* Vol.169(5):494–495.
57 Karen Kaplan. March 16, 2015. "Vaccine Refusal Helped Fuel Disneyland Measles Outbreak, Study Says." *The Los Angeles Times.* Retrieved on September 19, 2016 at: www.latimes.com/science/sciencenow/la-sci-sn-disneyland-measles-under-vaccination-20150316-story.html.
58 Soumya Karlamangla. August 28, 2015. "California Lags in Vaccinating Children, CDC Says." *The Los Angeles Times.* Retrieved on September 19, 2016 at: www.latimes.com/science/la-me-california-vaccinations-20150828-story.html.
59 Cited in Orac, June 30, 2015. "Revealing the True Face of the Antivaccine Movement." Retrieved on September 19 at: http://scienceblogs.com/insolence/2015/06/30/revealing-the-true-face-of-the-antivaccine-movement/.
60 Anna Merlan. June 29, 2015. "Meet the New, Dangerous Fringe of the Anti-Vaccination Movement." *Jezebel.*
61 Age of Autism. April 28, 2015. "Who Should Make Vaccine Decisions for Your Children." Retrieved on September 19, 2016 at: www.ageofautism.com/2015/04/who-should-make-vaccine-decisions-for-your-child.html. As for the claim that vaccines were derived from the cells of aborted fetuses, there is a small grain of truth. The cells used in the MMR vaccine were obtained originally from an electively aborted fetus to start a cell line which was multiplied over and over so that there would be consistent genetic makeup for the cells in the vaccine.
62 The Canary Party. 2017. "What Is the Canary Party." Retrieved on June 12, 2017 at: http://canaryparty.org/.
63 Travis Gettys. August 31, 2016. "Scientology's Anti-Vaxxer Celebrities Are Responsible for Making America Sick." *Raw Story.* Retrieved on September 19, 2016 at: www.rawstory.com/2016/08/scientologys-anti-vaxxer-celebrities-are-responsible-for-making-america-sick-report/.
64 Staff for the *Hollywood Reporter.* June 30, 2015. "Jim Carrey Slams California School Vaccine Legislation: It's 'Poisoning More Children'." *Hollywood Reporter.* Retrieved on September 19, 2016 at: www.hollywoodreporter.com/news/jim-carrey-slams-school-vaccine-806187.
65 Cited in Frank Bruni. July 5, 2015. "California, Camelot and Vaccines." *The New York Times,* SR3.
66 Robert Kennedy Jr., ed., 2014. *Thimerosal: Let the Science Speak: The Evidence Supporting the Immediate Removal of Mercury—a Known Neurotoxin—from Vaccines.* New York: Skyhorse Publishing.
67 Dawn Richardson. August 5, 2016. "The Fallout from California SB227: What Happens Next?" *National Vaccine Information Center.* Retrieved on September 20, 2016 at: www.nvic.org/nvic-vaccine-news/august-2015/sb277-fallout-what-happens-next.aspx.
68 Lisa McLaughlin. August 6, 2015, response to the story by Dawn Richardson. August 5, 2015.

69 Cited by Jeremy B. White. September 30, 2015. "California Referendum Falls Short in Internal Count." *Sacramento Bee.* Retrieved on September 20, 2016 at: www.sacbee.com/news/politics-government/capitol-alert/article37144386.html.

70 Quoted in Ariana Eunjung Cha. May 25, 2016. "7 Things about Vaccines and Autism that the Movie 'Vaxxed' Won't Tell You." *Washington Post.* Retrieved on September 20, 2016 at: www.washingtonpost.com/news/to-your-health/wp/2016/05/25/7-things-about-vaccines-and-autism-that-the-movie-vaxxed-wont-tell-you/.

71 F. DeStefano, T.K. Bhasin, W.W. Thompson, M. Yeargin-Allsopp, and C. Boyle. February 2004. "Age at First Measles-Mumps-Rubella Vaccination in Children with Autism and School-Matched Control Subjects: A Population-Based Study in Metropolitan Atlanta." *Pediatrics.* Vol.113(2):259–266.

72 Cited in Emily Willingham. August 6, 2015. "A Congressman and a CDC Whistleblower and an Autism Tempest in a Trashcan." *Forbes.* Retrieved on September 20, 2016 at: www.forbes.com/sites/emilywillingham/2015/08/06/a-congressman-a-cdc-whistleblower-and-an-autism-tempest-in-a-trashcan/#192a5cfa385e.

73 Robert F. Kennedy, Jr. July 14, 2015. "The CDC's Latest Tuskegee Experiment and the Link Between Autism in Black Americans and Vaccine." Retrieved on September 21, 2016 at: www.ora.tv/offthegrid/article/2015/7/14/robert--kennedy-jr-cdc-latest-tuskegee-experiment--link-african-american-autism--vaccines.

74 Quoted in Jeremy Gerard. March 30, 2016. "Axed 'Vaxxed' Docu Sets Downtown NYC Premier." *Deadline Hollywood.* Retrieved on September 20, 2016 at: http://deadline.com/2016/03/robert-de-niro-vaxxed-tribeca-film-festival-statement-1201726799/.

75 Jeremy Gerard. March 30, 2016. "Axed 'Vaxxed'."

76 Interview with Jenny McCarthy, Frontline. March 23, 2015. "Jenny McCarthy: 'We're Not An Anti-Vaccine Movement . . . We're Pro-Safe Vaccine.'" Retrieved on September 21, 2016 at: www.pbs.org/wgbh/frontline/article/jenny-mccarthy-were-not-an-anti-vaccine-movement-were-pro-safe-vaccine/. See also: McCarthy's 2007 *Louder than Words: A Mother's Journey in Healing Autism.* New York: Plume/Penguin.

77 Frontline interview with Jenny McCarthy. Emphases added.

78 Michael Hilzik. January 27, 2015. "Jenny McCarthy: Anti-Vaxxer, Public Menace." *The Los Angeles Times.* Retrieved on September 21, 2016 at: www.latimes.com/business/hiltzik/la-fi-mh-jenny-mccarthy-antivaxxer-public-menace-20150127-column.html.

79 Dr. Mercola's website suggests, among other things, that a broccoli-sprout compound may improve the symptoms of autism. Retrieved on September 21, 2016 at: http://articles.mercola.com/sites/articles/archive/2014/10/27/broccoli-sprouts-autism.aspx.

80 Barbara Loe Fisher. September/October, 2004. "In the Wake of Vaccines." *Mothering Magazine.* Retrieved on September 21, 2016 at the site for the National Vaccine Information Center: www.nvic.org/vaccination-decisions/wakeofvaccines.aspx.

81 Lorna Wing. 1981. "Asperger's Syndrome: A Clinical Account." *Psychological Medicine.* Vol.11:115–129. See also her extended review of the literature about Asperger's: Lorna Wing. April 1993. "The Definition and Prevalence of Autism: A Review." *European Child and Adolescent Psychiatry.* Vol.2(2):61–74.

82 John Donavan and Caren Zucker. 2016. *In a Different Key: The Story of Autism.* New York: Crown.

83 Steve Silberman. 2015. *NeuroTribes: The Legacy of Autism and How to Think Differently about People Who Think Differently.* New York: Avery/Penguin.

84 John Donavan and Caren Zucker. 2016. *In a Different Key.*

85 Daniel Smith. May 19, 2016. "Call a Kid a Zebra." *London Review of Books,* pp.11–15.

86 Bruno Bettelheim. 1959. "Joey: A 'Mechanical Boy'." *Scientific American.* Vol.200(3):116–120. See also: Bettelheim. 1972. *The Empty Fortress: Infantile Autism and the Birth of the Self.* New York: Free Press.

87 Steven Shapin. January 25, 2016. "Seeing the Spectrum." *The New Yorker*, pp.65–69.

88 John Donavan and Caren Zucker. 2016. *In a Different Key.*

89 Raanan Raz, et al. March 15, 2015. "Autism Spectrum Disorder and Particulate Matter Air Pollution before, during and after Pregnancy: A Nested Case-Control Analysis with the Nurses' Health Study II Cohort." *Environmental Health Perspectives.* Vol.123(3):264–270.

90 *Science Daily.* September 1, 2016. "Autism Severity Linked to Genetics, Ultrasound, Data Analysis Finds." Retrieved on September 22, 2016 at: www.sciencedaily.com/releases/2016/09/160901152140.htm. The original article from which the statement about the link between ultrasounds and autism is: Sara Jane Webb, Michelle M. Garrison, Raphael Bernier, Abbi M. McClintic, Bryan H. King, and Pierre D. Mourad. August, 2016. *Autism Research.* DOI 10.1002/aur.1690. Retrieved on September 22, 2016 at: http://onlinelibrary.wiley.com/doi/10.1002/aur.1690/full.

91 Kevin Helliker. September 20, 2016. "Study Raises New Questions about Fetal Ultrasounds." *Wall Street Journal*, p.D2.

92 Matthew Perrone and Ben Wieder. September 20, 2016. "'Echo Chamber' Shaped Policy: Lobbying Group's Efforts Trumpeted Access, Downplayed Addiction." Center for Public Integrity and the *Missoulian*, pp.C1,3.

The Body as the Last Line of Defense

6

The Fight against GMOs

Consider:

- All food contains chemicals and DNA.
- We could eliminate mosquito-borne diseases like Dengue fever, malaria, and Zika by genetically modifying mosquitoes to make them sterile.
- Those who accept the science of climate change often reject the science of GMOs.
- GMO crops are not a risk to human health; what we spray on GMO crops may be.
- Whether or not we accept the science of GMOs or of climate change, most of us cannot explain the science.
- Emotions affect our perception of risk.
- We accept scientific findings when they conform to our existing beliefs.

As a corporate leader of a major organic food company told me, "People are funny about their food."[1] Some of us want to know what we are eating; others do not care. Diet books and cook books are constant best sellers. Many of us seize on new diets like the Atkins Diet, the grapefruit diet, the Paleo diet, or the South Beach Diet, not just to lose weight but to take control of our lives and our health. Yet we don't want to work very hard at it because we're too busy to cook a meal that consists of real food, or too tired to exercise. We ignore the advice doctors have been giving for years about diet and exercise. There are easier solutions offered by scores of bloggers and websites that do two primary things. They create fear about what we are eating and offer solutions, usually for a price, about what to eat and what to avoid: in other words, to take control of our health.

If we are funny about our food, we are also funny about science. One food blogger, who calls herself the "Food Babe," says that "there is no acceptable level of any chemical to ingest, ever."[2] Yet, we drink two chemicals every day, dihydrogen monoxide, better known as H_2O or water. All of our food is made up of chemicals. A survey conducted in 2015 by two Oklahoma State University professors asked people if they supported mandatory labeling of foods that contained GMOs. A strong majority, 82.28%, said they did. The same group was also asked if they supported mandatory labeling for food containing DNA. Almost the same percentage (80.44%) said they did. *All food contains DNA.*[3]

The findings do not necessarily suggest that those polled were too dumb to know that food contains DNA. Rather, as a writer for the *Los Angeles Times* suggested, people have some awareness that GMOs result from tinkering with DNA and saw the questions as similar.[4] Social movement organizations devoted to promoting organic foods have worked to denounce the genetic modification of food, frequently making claims that are not supported by scientific findings, and demonizing those who argue GMOs are essential to our food supply. We cannot ignore the fact that *the agro-industrial complex gives Americans the cheapest food in the world*. According to the U.S. Department of Agriculture, the average American spends only 6.6% of their total income on food; the country that runs as a close second, Singapore, spends 6.7%. The Japanese, however, spend more than twice as much as we do, 14.1%, and the Russians four times as much, 28.4%. In less developed countries like Pakistan the figure is 41.4% and in Nigeria it is 56.6%.[5] Potentially, GMOs are an answer to the problem of hunger wherever it exists.

Yet the food problem is a complex one and it differs by country. While Americans have the cheapest food in the world it comes at a cost. Federal regulations that mandate the use of biofuels in gasoline encourage the overproduction of GMO corn where high yields are driven by the intensive use of fertilizers (nitrogen, phosphorus, and potassium) and herbicides (principally Monsanto's Roundup or glyphosate). Over 50% of all soy and corn grown in the United States is feed to livestock and poultry, and more is shipped to Europe to feed European animals. Cheap food (beans, corn, beef, chicken, pork, rice, sugar, wheat) also makes it possible for fast-food restaurants to operate profitably and for Americans to load up on fat and carbohydrates.

One of the enduring debates about GMOs is whether or not they are needed to feed the world's hungry and growing populations, or whether more traditional forms of agriculture are sufficient. Like many things, it depends. The solution proffered for countries where agricultural production lags is often to boost the food supply by relying on the same techniques, crops, and chemicals as employed in the United States; that is, using high concentrations of fertilizers, herbicides, pesticides, and genetically modified crops that will tolerate these chemicals. Here, too, things are more complicated. In Sub-Saharan Africa hunger can be driven by war that makes it impossible to grow food. There may also be inadequate infrastructure such as roads to transport crops to market and no facilities to store excess grain. Finally, shifting away from the production of a diversity of crops can raise the risk of the collapse of the food system in the event of a drought or other catastrophic event such as a blight that affects an entire crop. Sometimes industrialized agriculture which makes use of GMOs to boost the food supply is a solution to the problem of hunger; sometimes it is not.

The debates about the wisdom of growing GMO crops revolve around a number of issues. Are they safe? Does their use destroy traditional farming systems that produce a variety of foods? Do they destroy the environment? Are GMOs a new form of colonialism in which our system of agriculture is imposed on developing countries? Are GMOs more or less healthy than organic foods? What risks does globalization of the food supply pose, where a few companies control or own most of the seeds, herbicides, and pesticides? Do GMOs destroy family farms and the organic food industry in their drive for profit?

The organic food industry and its advocates argue that GMOs are not a boon to humanity but a bane. Their collective answers to these questions have been that GMOs pose grave risks to human health and the environment. The evidence offered for the negative effects of GMOs draws on science but does so selectively. Anti-GMO activists also make a demand on science that cannot be met. Science cannot prove beyond all doubt that something *cannot* happen.

What Is Science?

Why should we care about science? Because it is the best way we have of predicting outcomes. We should care about science because there is a real world which operates according to its laws. Rejection of science limits our ability to assure we can provide sufficient, safe, and nutritious food for growing populations or to assure we can solve problems like climate change. Rejection of science leads to political divides where one side regards science as simply another ideology and the other sees it as a "truth" which must be acted on. I put "truth" in quotation marks to signify that doubt is inherent in the scientific enterprise. There is always more to discover. The incomplete nature of scientific knowledge does not mean, however, that opinions and ideologies can substitute for it.

> Science is treated by many as just another system of belief.

Science by its very nature is never, ever certain. As the famous philosopher of science Karl Popper reasoned, all scientific theories must be capable of being falsified or they are not science.[6] It does not matter how many experiments we conduct, nothing is ever proved for certain because one more experiment could contradict our theory. As science develops, it challenges received wisdom about how the world works and our place in it. It is *disruptive* and can *diminish* our understanding about our own cosmic significance. After all, if the whole world operates in terms of scientific principles, what is the meaning of our own lives and actions?

Scientific theories are not easily tossed aside or disproved because *they are based on careful observations over time, and because they explain how and why things work the way they do*. Science is cumulative building on itself, as one researcher after another tries to refine a theory or refute it.[7] There are good reasons, then, to trust science.

Yet, no matter how careful and well-developed a scientific theory is, *science cannot prove a negative*. It is impossible to say that something will *never* happen or that a theory can *never* be disproved. As I'll explain in the following, those opposed to the use of GMOs in our food supply demand that the makers of non-organic herbicides and pesticides prove that they will never be harmful (prove the negative) to human health or will never seriously disturb ecosystems into which they are released. We can assume based on numerous studies that

> Science cannot prove something will never happen.

they are not harmful, but it is impossible to prove they will never be. This is called the **precautionary principle**: you guard against risk by trying to rule out all possible harms. We cannot, however, rule out all risk.

The Science of GMOs

Most of us are familiar with Gregor Mendel's experiments with peas. Over several years Mendel cross-pollinated peas which differed in terms of the size of the pea, the characteristics of the pod, and the color of the flower and the pod. In doing so, he created new hybrids, the result of the crossing of two genetically different peas to get one much like those in our gardens and supermarkets today. These hybrids are "natural" in the sense that there is nothing inserted into their genes that wasn't already there in nature. Getting a "better" pea (or cow or chicken) this way is, however, a slow process.

To speed up the motor of evolution researchers can expose seeds to radiation and to chemicals in order to create genetic mutations. As Pierre Lagoda, head of plant breeding at the International Atomic Energy Agency, explained about the use of radiation to stimulate mutations:

> We are mimicking nature in this. We're concentrating time and space for the breeder so he can do the job in his lifetime. We concentrate on

how often mutants appear — going through 10,000 to one million — to select just the right one.[8]

Scientists then choose those seeds that produce plants with desired characteristics. Many of these mutations have found their way into our food supply. Between 1930 and 2014 more than 3,200 mutant plant varietals were released; today 1,000 of them are being grown as crops. Again, there is nothing in the new varietal that wasn't there in nature in the first place; evolution has simply been sped up with radiation and naturally occurring (not synthesized) chemicals.[9] The downside, as Lagoda noted, is that it takes time and sometimes thousands of trials to create plants with new beneficial characteristics. New tools are now available to get the characteristics we want with just a few tries.

> New technologies will allow us to wipe out malaria, modify the food we eat, and edit the human embryo.

We now have the technology to rewrite the code of life. A revolutionary gene-editing tool, CRISPR (clustered regularly interspaced short palindromic repeats), allows biogeneticists to clip and snip an organism's DNA to produce desirable characteristics or eliminate undesirable ones. It's referred to as a gene-drive technology because it "drives" which genes get passed down to future generations. We no longer have to wait, through the tedious process of selective breeding, to get hogs with leaner meat or tomatoes that both taste good and can be harvested mechanically. We do not have to save the biggest seeds of corn from the fall harvest to plant in the spring; we can change the genetic code of corn to produce larger ears. CRISPR allows us to add or delete any sequence in the vast array of the genes that make an organism what it is. But what is important to note is that the technology doesn't add something that wasn't already present in nature.

Once the genetic code has been altered by CRISPR, it passes down through succeeding generations. As the science writer Michael Specter explains, this means we could eventually wipe out malaria. By altering the DNA of a mosquito to block the parasite for malaria, every time a mosquito bred this new trait it would be passed down to succeeding generations until eventually all mosquitoes would possess it and malaria would vanish.[10] The technology can also create sterile mosquitoes to release into the environment which would eventually wipe out all mosquitoes, eliminating not only malaria but Dengue fever and the Zika virus which causes microcephaly. Using CRISPR we can genetically engineer pigs to make their organs (heart, kidneys, and skin) more suitable for use in human transplantations.[11] Cancer researchers are now genetically engineering immune cells in the human body to kill cancer cells. A 1-year-old girl, Layla, was saved from leukemia by this therapy, when all other treatments failed.[12]

Part of the controversy over altering the genetic code of humans or plants and animals, even if it is to cure a disease or produce more bountiful crops, is that it is not "natural." The MIT professor of biology Keven Esvelt argues that it is wrong to assume that "the natural and [the] good are the same thing":

> When nature does something that hurts us, we respond with chemistry and physics. We spread toxic pesticides that kill problematic pests, and often kill most of the other insects in the area as well. To get rid of mosquitoes, we use bulldozers to drain swamps. It works but it also destroys wetlands and many other species.[13]

Why, he reasons, would we take these brutal actions when we could, by editing the gene of a pest, program it to avoid fruits and vegetables? One answer is that insects or viruses could be turned into biological weapons by the same means they are turned into harmless ones.[14] It is not always clear what the results of gene editing will be. Genes can also be transmitted to a similar species. Targeting one species of mosquito for elimination could lead to the elimination of another. But progress in the field of gene editing is extremely rapid. This technology can make crops more nutritious, drought resistant, or allow them to flourish in salt water. It can create better varieties of wheat or rice within days or weeks, rather than decades. The United States Department of Agriculture has already certified CRISPR-modified mushrooms and is likely to approve modified corn because no external DNA was added; unwanted DNA was simply "snipped" out.[15] More and more GMOs are likely to find their way to supermarket shelves. Many are already there. Most of the soy (94%), corn (88%), and canola oil (90%) we consume have been genetically modified, as have sugar, zucchini, yellow squash, and Hawaiian papayas. Do these pose a problem to our health?

Take the case of genetically modified corn. There is a naturally occurring pesticide in the soil Bt (Bacillus Thuringiensis) which for years was touted as a natural pesticide and is still used by organic farmers. The spores from Bt were sprayed over fields principally to control corn borers without harming beetles, flies, wasps, or bees.[16] The downside was that Bt did not last very long and could be degraded by rain. In response, biotechnology companies isolated the naturally occurring gene for the pesticide and inserted it directly into the genes of corn. So far so good, as Bt is a naturally occurring pesticide that plants evolved to protect themselves against insects. *Virtually all of the plants we eat have naturally occurring insecticides*, including peas and tomatoes and, as with Bt corn, there is *no* evidence that they are harmful to us.

> There is little evidence that GMO crops are harmful. What is sprayed on them may be.

The plot changes, however, when GMOs were engineered to be tolerant of the herbicide glyphosate, or Roundup. Glyphosate is a small molecule that inhibits an enzyme (EPSPS) in plants which is essential for the production of the amino acids necessary for growth. Spray glyphosate on a growing plant and it will die. To make it possible to spray fields of soy or corn with glyphosate, and kill weeds but not corn or soy plants, the seeds needed to be engineered to be Roundup ready. To do this and still get the plants to grow, scientists program the seeds to produce an alternative form of the same enzyme (EPSPS). Roundup ready corn and soy beans have the *same* basic genetic makeup as those that are not Roundup ready.[17] A study published in 2012, which summarized studies that had tracked the effect of GMO diets on people's health over several generations, concluded that "GM plants are nutritionally equivalent to their non-GM counterparts and can be safely used in food and feed."[18]

Should we trust this data? Or is residual glyphosate in the fields a health hazard?

Deniers

In spite of the rigor and openness of science, not everyone wants to accept the findings of scientists. Those who wish to challenge science do so in a number of ways. One line of attack is to claim that the science of whatever is in question is uncertain, and to sow doubt and mistrust among the public. This has been a well-honed strategy of climate deniers. In the case of those who oppose GMOs, the claim is made that we can never be certain of the long-term effects of consuming GMO crops. They might be cancerous. A similar challenge to science is to argue that something is risky. Humans are by nature risk-averse. We really don't like to take chances or, if we do take chances, we tend to discount the actual risks involved, if we are favorably disposed toward something.[19] A person who takes satisfaction from smoking will reason: "What can just one cigarette hurt?" Furthermore, how we evaluate a perceived risk depends not just on what we think about something but also about how we *feel* about it. For example, we *understand* that using pesticides in our garden will mean that bugs will not eat our vegetables but we may *believe* or feel that it is risky to use pesticides because they are poison and will kill harmless insects and that the risk to our health is not worth the risk of using them. If, on the other hand, our feelings toward using pesticides and herbicides are positive because it saves time and energy and we'll get a greater bounty from our garden, then we will judge the risks to be low.[20] *Our emotions drive our perception of risk.* So does trust.

The science of GMOs is not clear to the average citizen; most of us are not able to develop firm conclusions about either their benefits or harms. Therefore, *we use trust as an heuristic device to assess risk.* We judge something to be less risky if we trust the source. Part of the battle over climate change or the food industry is over the issue of trust.

There is a wide gap between scientists and non-scientists in the United States in terms of their beliefs about eating genetically modified foods. Eighty-eight percent of all scientists who belong to the American Association for the Advancement of Science (AAAS) believe GMOs are safe to eat, while only 37% of the public does.[21] You might think that it would be reasonable for the general public to trust scientific consensus but you would be wrong. If we already believe that GMOs are a danger, we will reject the science. One writer responding to the results of this poll suggested that the 88% were being paid through "some kind of funds, sponsorship, or work" for "BIG FOOD," so they could not respond honestly. The same writer also reported knowing that *all* animals fed GMOs got cancer and died. Another believed "gene splicing is a very dangerous thing."[22]

There seems to be a veritable legion of trolls who respond to any published information about whether or not GMOs are beneficial or harmful. Nathanael Johnson, a writer for the online magazine *Grist*, spent six months writing about GMOs and then reflected on his own experience. He was overwhelmed by responses from groups like GM Watch which ginned up menacing pictures of him surrounded by clouds of darkness. He was constantly attacked as being a paid mouthpiece for the biotech industry. His "crime" was to present the research as he understood it. In his words, "people weren't taking issue with the facts I'd presented. What seemed to bother them was my failure to interpret the evidence in a way that fit into a larger narrative."[23] That narrative relates to our views of corporate America.

> Debates about the safety of GMOs are really debates about the power of corporate America over our lives.

As the sociologist John Lang argues, the controversies surrounding GMOs serve as proxies for larger debates about the role of technology in our lives, globalization, corporate greed, and corporate responsibility.[24] Taking a stand against GMOs is about taking a stand against the agro-industrial complex and the corporatization of American society. It is about our desire to control our own bodies, what we eat, who we eat it with, and the stories we share. The battle against GMOs, and what we suspect may be happening to our food supply, is also a story about the need to build community. Farmers' markets aren't just about getting fresh vegetables; they are about connecting us to the people who grow our food, people we want to trust. They are also a chance to connect with our like-minded friends who are shopping at the same time. *Our bodies can seem to be the last line of defense in the struggle for autonomy in a capitalist world system.* In this context, whether we reject science or accept it has less to do with truth and more to do with our existing beliefs.

We are now picking and choosing scientific information that fits with the narratives we already have. As the science writer George Johnson has noted, we have entered *an era of alternative truths*:

> On one front after another, the hard-won consensus of science is (now) expected to accommodate personal beliefs, religious or otherwise, about the safety of vaccines, G.M.O crops, fluoridation or cellphone radio waves, along with the validity of global climate change. Like creationists with their "intelligent design," the followers of these causes come armed with their own personal science, assembled through Internet searches that inevitably turn up the contortions of special interest groups.[25]

Who Are You Going to Trust?

Creating fear and mistrust is important to those who want to reject science. In what has been referred to as the Séralini affair, the French molecular biologist, Gilles-Eric Séralini, published a paper that received worldwide attention and caused people to distrust regulators who were telling them GMOs were safe. A long-time critic of GMOs, Séralini claimed to have data which showed that rats that were fed genetically modified corn and glyphosate, the main ingredient in Monsanto's Roundup, contracted large cancerous tumors. The original article, published in *Food and Chemical Toxicology* in 2012, was eventually withdrawn by the editors because of serious flaws in the data.[26] A main reason was that the species of rats Séralini used for his study normally develop cancerous tumors.

> Trust plays a critical role in whether or not we accept or reject the science of GMOs.

Judy Hoy of Stevensville, Montana believes that numerous studies, including Séralini's, have clearly demonstrated the harmful effects of Roundup or glyphosate and, for the "sake of newborns now and all future generations of newborns," it should be banned. According to Hoy, it disrupts the:

> . . . development of craniofacial bones, tooth development, thymus, hearts, male reproductive organs and other organs (and) is causing many wildlife species to decline precipitously and many have gone extinct. Glyphosate is in mother's milk, in air, surface water and on plants.[27]

In 2016 the prestigious National Academies of Sciences, Engineering, and Medicine, whose mission it is to provide "non-partisan, objective guidance for decision makers on pressing issues," released its report on GMOs. The 20 scientists who contributed to the report concluded that GMOs are *not* a threat to human health, specifically those crops sprayed with Monsanto's Roundup or glyphosate.[28] To discredit the conclusions of the report, those opposed to GMOs pointed out that six out of the 20 scientists who contributed to the report had ties to the biotech industry. The Academies defended the report, noting that the conclusions and the recommendations of each scientist were based on hard facts.[29]

The U.S. Department of Health and Human Services publishes an extensive list of those substances *known* to cause cancer in humans and those which might *possibly* cause cancer. Drinking alcohol in excess is a known cause of breast cancer, as well as colorectal cancer, cancer of the larynx, liver, and esophagus. We know smoking tobacco causes cancer. Sun lamps and tanning beds can cause skin cancer and cataracts. Glyphosate, however, is *not* listed by the U.S. government as either a known cancer-causing agent or one that might possibly cause cancer.[30] The Environmental Protection Agency (EPA) declares glyphosate safe for humans to use and "practically nontoxic to fish, aquatic invertebrates, and honeybees."[31]

In March of 2015 the World Health Organization's International Agency for Research on Cancer (IARC) issued a report that drew international attention for two reasons. First, it identified *bacon, ham, sausage and hot dogs as known causes of colorectal cancer*, and noted that there was the possibility they also caused pancreatic and prostate cancer. Second, it identified glyphosate as having the *potential* to cause cancer, not that it was a *known* cause of cancer. Glyphosate was deemed less dangerous than bacon and hotdogs.[32] On the basis of this report a number of anti-GMO organizations demanded their governments take action to ban glyphosate.[33]

In 1986 Californians passed a ballot initiative, "The Safe Drinking Water and Toxic Enforcement Act," which required that the public be notified of any substance released into the environment that caused cancer, birth defects, or other reproductive harm. The Act further required the list to be updated annually and made available to the public. There are now 800 different substances listed, but in 2016 glyphosate was not among them.[34] At present, glyphosate is used by California farmers on 250 different crops. However in 2017, relying on the findings from the IARC, the State of California acted to require Monsanto to provide a warning label on Roundup as a possible cancer threat.[35]

The drive to provide warning labels in California is driven by intense lobbying on behalf of the organic food industry and bolstered with personal stories. Teri McCall, who is part of a national class-action suit against Monsanto, believed her husband, who died of cancer in 2015, would have lived if there had been warning labels. Her husband Jack had sprayed Roundup on the weeds in his orchards for 30 years. There were other California farmers who had used Roundup as long as Jack McCall but had not contracted cancer.[36] If one farmer used it and was stricken by cancer, while another user was not, what does that mean?

There are numerous stories offered by pro-organic advocates that tell about young women who grew up healthy on a farm but later developed cancer, which they attributed to Monsanto's spray. A woman born today in the United States has a 12.4% chance of getting breast cancer; she also has a 87.6% of not getting breast cancer.[37] This is true whether or not she lives in a rural area or an urban area, and is true whether or not she grew up in proximity to the use of agricultural pesticides and herbicides. The incidence of getting breast cancer is the same.[38] Why then do we demonize GMO foods?

> Both pro- and anti-GMO advocates rely on myths to support their cause.

Myths about GMOs

A headline in the *Huffington Post* proclaimed, "Tests Show Monsanto Weed Killer in Cheerios."[39] Monsanto is frequently portrayed as an evil corporation intent on making money at the expense of farmers and consumers. Headlines, such as this one, serve to keep alive myths and stories that may not be rooted in fact.

One of the anti-GMO myths which has gained significant traction is the claim that 250,000 or more cotton farmers in India committed suicide because of Monsanto's genetically engineered cotton seeds. No less a personage than Prince Charles claimed thousands of Indian farmers were killing themselves because they were "fooled" into planting GM cotton. The London *Daily Mail* claimed things were even worse than Prince Charles feared. The paper opened with a story about one victim whose cotton crop had failed two times in a row:

> Shankara, respected farmer, loving husband and father, had taken his own life. Less than 24 hours earlier, facing the loss of his land due to debt, he drank a cupful of chemical insecticide.
>
> The children were inconsolable. Mute with shock and fighting back tears, they huddled beside their mother as friends and neighbors prepared their father's body for cremation on a blazing bonfire built on the cracked, barren fields near their home.[40]

It's a moving story, but there was no spike in suicide rates because Indian farmers were using GMO seeds. Ian Plewis, a statistician at the University of Manchester in England, looked at the suicide rates for the major cotton-growing regions in

India and found they were actually *lower* than for their non-farming neighbors. In fact, their suicide rate (just under 30 per 100,000) was about the same as it was for farmers in France and Scotland. GM cotton is *not* the cause of these suicides.[41] What does cause farmer suicide in India is a banking system that confiscates a farmer's land when they cannot pay their loans.[42] However, the story of farmers killing themselves was such a powerful one that India's Supreme Court made positive propaganda for itself by recommending a ten-year ban on field trials of GM crops.[43]

Monsanto has also been blamed for the outbreak of the Zika virus in Brazil in 2016, and the ensuing 4,000 cases of microcephaly in infants. Argentina-based doctors working for the University Network of Environment and Health published an online article which claimed a pesticide manufactured by a Japanese company, Sumitomo, was the real culprit. It caused microcephaly, not the virus spread by mosquitoes. The doctors also claimed in their article that Sumitomo was a subsidiary of Monsanto. None of these statements were true but the story was quickly spread on Facebook and Twitter by those who oppose GMOs, and on websites like *Natural News*.[44]

Mike Adams, the editor of *Natural News*, who refers to himself as the "health ranger," suggested that Zika was not caused by mosquitoes—that was a hoax dreamed up by companies to sell more of their toxic chemicals, the actual cause of Zika.[45] He had previously offered up a number of "facts" about GMOs. His first was that "every grain of GM corn contains poison." He wasn't referring to the glyphosate sprayed on the corn; he was referring to Bt, which is a natural pesticide. If Bt can kill a corn borer, he reasoned, it might kill you or your child. His second point was that GMOs "have never been safely tested for human consumption," and that a child being fed corn flakes might in the future develop cancer, diabetes, or even Alzheimer's. Third, farmers are being reduced to the equivalent of slaves because they are forced to buy new expensive seeds every year and, as proof of this, he noted that "farmer suicides have skyrocketed in India."[46]

Those who favor the use of GMOs also have their own myths. The most prominent one is that in order to feed the world's growing populations we must abandon traditional methods of farming with small plots and diversified crops and turn to the use of genetically modified seeds and the use of fertilizers, herbicides, and pesticides; otherwise we'll starve. Nyasha Mudukuti, a pro-GMO advocate from Zimbabwe, stated, "My country's government would rather see people starve than let them eat genetically modified food."[47] Her concerns stemmed from a prolonged drought in her country which had devastated crops, coupled with a refusal by the minister of agriculture to accept any food aid that contained GMOs. She regarded the rejection of GMO food as a humanitarian outrage, as well as a rejection of science. Like many other advocates, she believed that GMOs were beneficial for the environment because farmers could plant high-yield crops that needed less water, and grow more food on less land.

The data about the actual benefits of GMOs tell a somewhat different story. Twenty years ago when most European countries banned GMOs, the United States and Canada embraced them. Therefore, a comparison between crop yields in the United States and Canada and the EU can serve to illuminate whether or not GMOs were essential to increasing world food sources. A study by *The New York Times* found that there was no discernible advantage to using GMO crops; yields per acre were the same as conventional crops.[48]

Being for or against GMOs is more complicated than whether or not they will provide us with more food. The issues involve the concentration of the production of the world's food supply into the hands of a few corporations; issues about whether a corporation has the moral right to patent genes; and about whether or not the profit motive is one that benefits humankind. The reality is that for most people, our food supply is not in our hands. Ten of the world's most powerful food and beverage companies (among them such notable names as Coca-Cola, Danone, General Mills, Kellogg, and Mars) control most of the retail trade in the world and buy their raw products from large corporate farms which in turn rely on the seeds, herbicides, and pesticides of just six firms—BASF, Dow Chemical, Bayer, DuPont, Monsanto, and Syngenta.[49] It is a model of agriculture that leaves out the small farmer, on whom a third of the population depends for food. The fight against this model, at least in the United States and Europe, is not just about helping us live healthier and happier lives; it is also about profit.

The Commodification of Dissent: The Organic Food Movement

Social movements frequently involve demands for justice and freedom. For a movement to successfully change policy, it must inform concerned citizens and mobilize them for action. People can be mobilized in a number of ways: by playing on their fears and anger, their need to feel they are part of a community of activists, or by making the movement relevant to their specific needs. *Social movement entrepreneurs* who head up organizations seeking change use all of these techniques and play on peoples' emotions to keep them committed and to keep funds flowing. These funds go to a small cadre of professional organizers or, sometimes, to just one person. Social media has proven to be an inexpensive way to build what may be illusory momentum where people commit to no more than making a small donation, signing a petition, or pledging to boycott some product. Movement members are offered special insights into the machinations of the corporate world, the alleged poisoning of our food systems, or other secrets discovered by the organization.

There is no guarantee that a social movement organization is democratic, even if it professes to be in pursuit of values we associate with democracy, e.g., freedom and social justice. Online members do not get to vote on an organization's goals or actions. Leaders of *social movement organizations* (SMOs), though, pay close attention to which issues focus the attention of their supporters and which causes they support with their donations.

There is a dense web of interconnectivity between organizations that focus on the same issue. In the case of the organic food movement, they draw on the same sources and cite one another to reinforce their position. Many cite the Séralini study to claim GMOs cause cancer. Though organics account for only 4% of the total food market, it is still a big business. Organic sales have grown steadily at a pace of about 10% a year over the past five years and in 2015 accounted for $43 billion in total sales.[50] Certified organic products command a price premium which means there is strong economic incentive to protect the branding of organics. For some products, it is also essential for export purposes to assure that a product marketed as organic is not contaminated by GMOs. Lundberg Family Farms in California, which grows several varieties of organic rice, supported a California initiative to ban GMOs, fearing their own crops would be contaminated by cross-pollination. Had they been contaminated the crops could not have been sold in Japan, one of their biggest markets. The California Farm Bureau, along with producers of GMO crops, mounted a well-funded counteroffensive which resulted in the initiative's defeat. The Farm Bureau argued that banning GMOs would drive up the cost of food and that GMOs were perfectly safe to eat.

As noted earlier, acceptance of scientific information depends on whether or not one trusts the messenger. It also depends on how the information is framed in terms of risk and our assessment of risk depends on our emotions. One of the largest of the SMOs behind the drive to support organics plays on their supporters' fears and emotions to consolidate their support.

The Organic Consumers Association

The Organic Consumers Association (OCA) is the largest organic SMO in the country, intent on bolstering support for the organic food industry. Let's look now at their actions and communications to identify themes, the evidence they provide for them, and the issues with which they use to mobilize people, raise funds, and convince their readers to support their causes.[51]

OCA was founded in 1998 as part of a backlash against the intentions of the U.S. Department of Agriculture (USDA) to weaken regulations for organic food.

The same year, the EU required labeling of foods containing GMOs. Headquartered in Finland, Minnesota, OCA serves as an advocate for coops, natural food stores, and farmers' markets. They claim to have 850,000 people in their database to which they send a constant stream of alerts. These alerts intensify when the OCA is focused on thwarting or supporting a specific piece of legislation. They have a diverse platform which calls for, among other things, a total transformation of American agriculture from industrial to organic, changes in farm subsidies to support organics, support for Fair Trade, a global moratorium on GMOs, a phase-out of concentrated animal food operations, and the provision of universal health care with a focus on nutrition and wellness, energy independence, and renewable energy.[52] This broad-based approach allows them to *bridge* or connect their efforts to other SMOs that are not solely focused on organic foods.

OCA operates primarily as a non-profit organization. According to their 2014 tax filings, they had an income of about $3.3 million, one-third of which was paid out in salaries and benefits.[53] The bulk of their funds in 2014 went to support unsuccessful efforts to ban GMOs in states like California, Oregon, and Washington. Only a small portion of their expenses are covered by dues and subscriptions; most income comes from fund raising, foundations, and unnamed donors or organizations that contributed a total of $1.14 million. Dr. Mercola's organization (which sells various nostrums to "cure" ailments from cancer to an upset stomach) appears to be the chief donor, as Mercola has provided fund-raising matches of up to $250,000.

OCA is headed by Ronnie Cummins who has served as President and Executive Director since its inception. Cummins is a lifelong professional activist and one well regarded within the food movement. Cummins previously served as the director of Jeremy Rifkin's Beyond Beef Campaign, and the Pure Food Campaign, which later became the OCA. He also served as director of Jerry Rifkin's anti-technology movement, Foundation on Economic Trends.[54] Cummins has been vocal in expressing his goal of undermining corporate agriculture. When OCA was launched, Cummins announced a "Millions against Monsanto" campaign.[55] In their 2000 book, *Genetically Engineered Food: A Self-Defense Guide for Consumers*, Cummins and Ben Lilliston argued that the technologies being used to create GMOs were unpredictable, had not been tested for their safety, and people were unwittingly consuming them, because they were everywhere in our food supply. The solution for the consumer was to shop wisely and campaign at the grassroots level for labeling.[56]

Cummins' declared role at OCA was to drive the demand for organics from a 4.2% market niche to become the dominant force in American food and farming and to get GMOs out of the nation's food supply.[57] While 4.2% of the market for food seems small, it is not in dollar terms. In 2015 around $45 billion was spent on organic foods. More rapidly growing than organics has been consumer demand for products with no GMOs. If a product has no GMOs, food companies have been quick to make that information available to the public in a bright label, "No GMOs."

There have been intensive campaigns by organic food producers and health-food advocates to accurately label our food so that consumers can make "wise" choices. If we judge by increasing rates of obesity and the declining health of Americans, whether or not they look for "No GMO" labels, most people are not making wise food choices. The reasons are multiple: shoppers can't afford the extra cost of organic foods; they may not be available; people are in a hurry and don't have time to read the small print on a label; their children want sugared or frosted flakes for breakfast instead of oatmeal; fast food is cheap and fills you up; and so forth. We have an abundance of cheap foods, high in calories and low in nutritional value. Healthy and nutritious food is available, organically labeled or not, but not everybody can afford it and not everybody takes responsibility for their own health.

Rather than scientific proof, personal stories posted on health-food sites recount how a person "discovered" that once they stopped eating junk food, they felt a surge of energy and their health improved. (Of course this is possible.) The documentary *Supersize Me* chronicles what happened when Morgan Spurlock ate nothing but McDonald's food for 30 days, three times a day. He gained 24 pounds, experienced mood swings, and sexual dysfunction. Once he stopped his experiment, it took him 14 months to lose the weight with the help of his girlfriend, a vegan chef.

The stories told by those who radically change their diets are similar to those told by alcoholics or drug addicts who manage to control their addictions. People frequently self-diagnose by attributing their poor health to "hidden" ingredients in their food. Those who suffer digestive disorders sometimes attribute the disorder to the Bt gene inserted into the corn they ate. They claim to have "leaky gut syndrome" or an "uneasy" stomach because of Bt, the natural insecticide. Their reasoning is that if Bt ruptures the intestinal tract of larvae and kills it, it must be doing something similar when they swallow it.[58] The real rate of gluten intolerance in the general population runs from 1–2%, yet the shelves of organic grocery stores are filled with "gluten-free" products.[59] Once people stop eating lots of refined carbohydrates, they feel better; so they reason they must have been gluten intolerant.

> The themes and strategies used by SMOs to affect change are very similar, regardless of the cause pursued.

We are using food as medicine to try and cure the ailments of modern society—stress, a lack of exercise and sleep. Our poor health, like being economically poor, is seen as our fault, something for which we need to take full responsibility. There are many things to be afraid of and over which we may have little control— our job, climate change, health care costs, whether we can pay for our education or that of our children's, or whether a relative in the military will come home safely. So, we turn to the things we can control and be certain about—"pure" foods. We do so, even when there is little evidence, as a study by researchers at Stanford's School of Medicine found, that organic foods provide any health or nutritional benefits that are not found in conventional foods.[60] In addition, many who buy organic are unaware that organic growers use natural pesticides that carry some of the same risks as non-organic ones.[61] So how then are people convinced to buy organic and to shun GMOs?

Major Themes and Strategies

The themes and strategies to mount a successful campaign to affect some change are remarkably similar in modern SMOs. Focusing on those used by the OCA can help us better understand and recognize how they are employed in other organizations and to raise questions about which strategies might be successful in future mobilizations:

- Assess blame for destroying peoples' health and the environment.
- Assert your trustworthiness and by implication the lack of it in others.
- Create fear.
- Be disruptive and outrageous to call attention to the cause.
- Ground demands in fundamental values such as freedom and justice.
- Seize political opportunities when they arise.
- Claim success no matter what the outcomes of mobilizing efforts are.
- Bridge or link to the causes of related groups.

These actions or strategies are melded together in the OCA and other modern movements, but I will treat them individually for purposes of illustration.

Assessing Blame

There is an enemies' list and Dow, the Koch Brothers, Monsanto, and Syngenta are on it. For almost two decades Monsanto has been the whipping boy for the OCA. If they can take down Monsanto, they will have made a major advance in ridding the food supply of GMO foods and increasing the sale of organics. Monsanto, along with Dow Chemical, has also been accused of causing millions of Vietnamese children to be born with birth defects, because of Agent Orange, a combination of two widely available weed killers (2, 4-D and 2, 4, 5-T) and used as a defoliant in the Vietnam War. It was supposed to eliminate the possibility of North Vietnamese soldiers hiding under the jungle canopy. Millions of gallons were sprayed on the Vietnamese as well as our own troops. In a review of the literature dealing with Agent Orange, the American Cancer Society concluded there was sufficient evidence to indicate that it could have caused four types of cancer: soft-tissue sarcoma, non-Hodgkin lymphoma, Hodgkin disease, and leukemia. It took intense lobbying by veterans groups before the Department of Defense admitted the reality of this connection and was willing to pay disability benefits.

The global Swiss company Syngenta produces agrochemicals and seeds and their planned 2017 merger with Monsanto will make them the largest producer in the world of herbicides, pesticides, and the owner of patents on the major GMO crops such as corn and soybeans. There is evidence to suggest that Syngenta's neonicotinoid pesticides are responsible for the collapse of bee populations.[62]

Where do the Koch Brothers come in? They own firms that manufacture nitrogen, an essential component in plant growth, along with phosphorus and potassium. Organic farmers use composted chicken manure, which contains relatively high concentrations of nitrogen. There are also nitrogen-fixing plants such as legumes and some forms of maize. Nitrogen does not, like phosphorus and potassium, occur in a physical form that can be mined. It must be manufactured through an energy-intensive process which combines nitrogen in the air with hydrogen. The eventual products are urea, ammonia, and nitrates. Agroindustrial firms use synthetic nitrogen because, while expensive, it is easy to apply to crops with predictable results. Nitrogen pollution of streams and lakes, as noted earlier, is a serious problem.

Whatever the specific firm, the reality is that there are real concerns about its products and their effect on our health and the environment. These concerns may be exaggerated to capture the attention of consumers and health advocates. One of the most effective ways of doing so is to talk about how a specific individual or group was harmed.

Assert Your Trustworthiness or the Opposition's Lack of It

The general story about producers of pesticides and herbicides, whether Monsanto or Syngenta, is that they cannot be trusted. As proof of their dishonesty, anti-GMO advocates argue that they are attempting to control our food supply, are only interested in profit, and are not producing healthy food. Their greed is supposedly evident because they package together seed and chemical sales, "forcing" farmers into using their high-priced products. Other anti-GMO arguments are: corporations are responsible for displacing indigenous people in the Amazon by farmers planting GMOs; corporate farming is simply a new form of imperialism; and any food shortages that exist in the world are due to politics and economics, so we don't need GMOs.

OCA has worked since its inception to require the labeling of all food products both in terms of their origin and in terms of their contents. In 2014, they thought their efforts to achieve a national standard gained momentum when the State of Vermont passed legislation to take effect in July of 2016 forcing disclosure of whether or not foods contained GMOs. A number of companies, including Campbell's Soup, General Mills, Mars, and Kellogg complied before the law took effect. They simply added to the bottom of the labels already required by the U.S. government the phrase, "made with genetically engineered products." Cheese, which Vermont makes a lot of, was exempted because it contains the GMO chymosin (rennin), an enzyme found in the stomachs of ruminants and used for centuries to coagulate milk. (Most of the world's cheese is made with chymosin.) Meat from animals fed with GMOs was also exempted. The passage of Vermont's labeling laws set off alarm bells among GMO producers and the Grocery Manufacturers Association. State-by-state labeling laws, they claimed, would confuse consumers and raise the price of groceries.

Pro-GMO forces engaged in intensive lobbying to prevent other states from enacting laws similar to Vermont's. Their goal was to pass a federal law that would prevent such labeling. At the same time, over 700 anti-GMO organizations became part of the campaign Just Label It. Among the organizations were such well-known firms as Stonyfield Organic, Nature's Path, Organic Valley, and Annies.[63] The Just Label It campaign had public opinion on their side because polls showed that upwards of 90% of Americans wanted to know what was in their food. What the anti-GMO groups did not have was the support of politicians and the *resources* of the pro-GMO forces.

Using language crafted by food companies, Representatives Mike Pompeo (R-Kansas, who became Director of the CIA in the Trump administration) and G.K. Butterfield (D-North Carolina) introduced legislation that would make labeling voluntary and would block states from requiring labeling. The Just Label It campaign and OCA referred to this as the DARK Act (Deny Americans the Right to Know). The legislation also made the Department of Agriculture, not the FDA which regulates all food stuff other than eggs and meat, responsible for determining which of 24,000 food products would need to be labeled. The legislation passed the House in 2015 and similar legislation was introduced in the Senate by Pat Roberts (R-Kansas) and Debbie Stabenow (D-Michigan).

By one estimate, over $100 million was spent trying to sway the votes of Congress.[64] The resulting "compromise" bill signed into law in 2016, which will go into effect in 2018, gave producers three choices. They could provide a label; provide a website or phone number where people could get information on the contents of a package; or they could provide a QR code that could be scanned with a Smartphone, if the consumer wanted to learn more. (The QR code is the unreadable square black box found on all packages.) To those in the organic food movement it was clear their elected representatives had abandoned them; Big Food was in league with Big government. OCA summed up the entire effort in three words: "Sold Out Again!" They were, however, not just sold out by Congress they were also, as OCA reported, sold out by "Organic Traitors," who had embraced the "compromise."[65] Just as there was big government, there are big organic food distributors like Whole Foods, Stonyfield, and United Natural Foods, the largest distributor of wholesale natural and organic foods in the United States and Canada. This betrayal had the advantage of making it seem to OCA's supporters that they were the only organic group to be trusted. A new report would add credibility to OCA's efforts and their claims about collusion between government and industry forces.

> The organic food movement lost the battle to label foods containing GMOs because of the power of the GMO lobby.

The New York Times reported in March 2017 that unsealed documents in a federal court raised questions about Monsanto's Roundup and its safety. Monsanto was being sued by a group of claimants who believed they were dying from non-Hodgkin lymphoma as a result of their exposure to Roundup. The documents included emails between federal regulators in the EPA and Monsanto. The emails suggested that Monsanto had ghostwritten research they attributed to academics. A Monsanto executive had emailed other company officials and suggested they could simply write the research which showed glyphosate did not cause cancer and pay academics to put their names on papers. "We would," he reasoned, "be keeping the cost down by us doing the writing and they would just edit & sign their names so to speak." In addition, the emails indicated that Jess Rowland, a senior EPA official, had worked to stifle a review of the main ingredient in Roundup, glyphosate, which was supposed to have been conducted by the U.S. Department of Health and Human Services. Rowland suggested to a Monsanto executive that if he could kill the review, "I should get a medal."[66]

The response from OCA to this story was immediate. They noted that "Monsanto's cancerous truth" had been revealed which proved "Monsanto knew all along that its flagship herbicide causes cancer." Furthermore, as OCA argued, the information proved there was collusion between large corporations and politicians.[67]

Create Fear

The ocean pout is an ugly, eel-like fish which I would not want to eat. It grows rapidly. On the other hand, I love salmon. So what could be wrong with taking genes from the ocean pout and combining them with those of the salmon to create a salmon that grows much more rapidly? According to a ruling by the Food and Drug Administration (FDA) there was no reason for concern. But from the perspective of the OCA and others in the organic food movement, what has been created is a "Frankenfish"; the first genetically modified animal approved for human consumption. The clever naming (or *framing*) of this monstrous new food is designed to frighten. The OCA argued that Aquabounty, the inventor of this new super fish, knew that the fish has the potential to increase allergies. They asked, "do we really want to eat a fish that contains elevated levels of the growth hormone . . . linked to prostate, breast and colon cancers?"[68] The answer for most of us would be "No." There is, however, no scientific evidence to suggest this is true.

> Outrageous and disruptive behavior is an effective tool in creating positive attention for a cause.

OCA reported that in a village in Argentina, surrounded by GMO soy crops, children are born with birth defects and degenerative diseases of unknown origin:

> One little girl has large brownish-black spots all over her face and body— marks she's had since birth. Another is slowly wasting away from an undiagnosed degenerative disease thought to be genetic, aggravated by exposure to herbicides. Many of the children are deformed in one way or another. Many of the elders are dying from cancer.[69]

Villagers hide in their homes when tractors spraying Roundup appear. Again, it is a powerful story but not one yet backed up by science linking the diseases of villagers with Roundup. A May 2017 headline from the OCA proclaimed, "Fracking Kills Babies."[70] It takes a close reading of the actual story on which the headline is based to understand just how tenuous this claim is.[71]

Be Disruptive and Outrageous

Attacking Monsanto for two decades is old news. The solution? Attack an organic icon like Ben & Jerry's ice cream and accuse them of poisoning Vermont's waterways, being responsible for animal abuse, bankrupting farmers, and contributing to global warming by "stripping the soil of its ability to draw down and sequester carbon."[72] Should you stop eating Chunky Monkey?

The OCA and one of its partners, Regeneration Vermont, claimed that between 1999 and 2012 cornfields were sprayed with over 2.5 million pounds of metolachor, atrazine, and simazine, all potential human carcinogens. Dairy cows were thus consuming dangerous toxins which *might* be in their milk and your ice cream. Further, the runoff from industrialized dairy farms was polluting waterways. So much milk was being produced in "factory" dairies that farmers were going broke.[73] The solution offered was to boycott Ben & Jerry's until they supported the organic dairy industry; which they already did.

OCA with its allies, Beyond Pesticides and Moms Across America, sued General Mills and its Nature Valley subsidary for "false and misleading representations and omissions" of its Nature Valley granola bars. They also sued Jessica Alba's Honest Company because they claimed her baby food did not meet organic standards.[74] The suits generate attention but little relevant action on the part of those organizations targeted.

It certainly sounded ominous when OCA announced they were going to put Monsanto on trial for crimes against humanity on October 16, 2016 in The Hague, home of the Dutch Government and the International Criminal Court. OCA, along with other like-minded groups, planned a Monsanto Tribunal that would judge the allegations against Monsanto and assess the damages they caused. The Tribunal intended to rely on the Principles of Business and Human Rights adopted by the UN in 2011 and on the statutes that created the International Criminal Courts. It was noted that, while the Tribunal could not impose penalties, "its final verdicts will serve as the foundation for future legal cases not only against Monsanto, but also Bayer, Syngenta, Dow and others."[75]

As official sounding as this was, the Tribunal was an assembly of anti-biotech activists who had denounced Monsanto for their "seed monopoly," for intimidating scientists who did not agree with them, and for harassing farmers who refused to buy their seeds, or whose crops had been contaminated with pollen from Monsanto crops. Ronnie Cummins at a press conference told Monsanto, "You are trying to poison us all, you know, in order to pursue maximizing profits."[76] The "trial" made for great theatre and it brought together activists from around the world, but there was nothing official about it.

Appeal to Fundamental Values Such as Freedom

Consumers have a *right* to products they deem to be healthy for themselves and their families. Some states prohibit the sale of raw milk, because of concerns about pasteurization but, as OCA argues, that limits people's freedom. Raw milk, it argues, is full of anti-microbial and immune-supporting components and is safe to drink.[77] We have a *right* to know where our food comes from, how it is processed, whether or not it contains GMOs, and whether it has been contaminated by herbicides and pesticides. We, not corporations or the government, should be in control of our health and our bodies. Not many would argue with this position but it is not one grounded in science.

Seize Political Opportunities

One of the central theoretical perspectives in social movement theory argues that the success of a social movement depends on the ability of an organization to seize *political opportunities* when they arise.[78] In the United States these opportunities most frequently occur at election time, when there is competition between elites and political parties. Political candidates may help to create legitimacy for a group, as the Democratic Candidate Bernie Sanders did when he chose to meet with members of the Black Lives Matter movement in 2016. Hillary Clinton also acknowledged their concerns. Under the Obama administration, the Department of Justice acted to demand changes in police training and practices in those cities where African-Americans had been shot and killed by the police (see Chapter 3). Though there was political opportunity following Vermont's decision to label food, *counter mobilization* by pro-GMOs forces limited that opportunity.

The Presidency of Donald Trump provided the OCA, as well as many other groups across America, many new opportunities to mobilize (see Chapter 7). The OCA announced on the day of Trump's inauguration brand-new initiatives: #ConsumerRevolution and #PoliticalRevolution, with two distinct platforms. The first involved continued efforts to get real labels on food and to support the organic food industry. The second, Political Revolution, involved backing candidates who supported the consumer revolution and those who were in favor of such programs as "Medicare for all." Ronnie Cummins played on the fear factor when he told his readers on the day Trump took the oath of office:

> We will witness the swearing in of a president who has signaled loud and clear his intent to maximize the profits of giant corporations—like Exxon Mobil, BP, and Monsanto and Bayer . . . —on a scale never before seen in our lifetimes. Public and environmental health be damned.[79]

He also warned against the news that Georgia's former governor, Sonny Perdue, would be nominated as the new USDA Secretary of Agriculture. Perdue was labeled "another millionaire climate-denier," and a "cheerleader for the worst of the worst agribusiness corporations." This would mean that "Perdue will have no interest in protesting the interest of rural farmers, farm workers or consumer from the routine poisoning of our food, water and air by factory farms, pesticides and GMOs."[80]

Readers were warned that with Trump's election we could expect the legislative agenda of the Competitive Enterprise Institute (CEI) to be implemented, which would gut food, health and environmental regulations, repudiate the Paris Climate Agreement, eliminate funding for activist research, and promote GMOs.[81] Alarm was also expressed that the Department of Energy would be led by a climate denier, Rick Perry, former governor of Texas. People were asked to call or write their Senators opposing the nomination of Perry as well as that of Scott Pruitt to head up the EPA. Pruitt, former Attorney General of Oklahoma, had consistently sued the very agency he was being asked to head.[82] OCA urged the Senate not to approve Betsy DeVos as Secretary of Education because, it was claimed, she would not support school gardens or farm to cafeteria programs.[83] All of those the OCA opposed were ultimately confirmed by the Senate and many of OCA's worries were soon realized.

Scott Pruitt, head of the EPA, rejected the findings of his own experts and reversed a recommendation by the Obama administration to ban all uses of a class of widely used pesticides. Chlorpyrifos (sold under brand names such as Dursban, Lorsban, and Warhawk) have been linked to learning and memory declines among farm workers and young children, as well as autoimmune disorders. Pruitt claimed that the science was unsettled and the EPA needed to study it some more. He asserted that now farmers could operate with regulatory certainty. "By reversing the previous administration's steps to ban one of the most widely used pesticides in the world, we are returning to using sound science in decision making—rather than predetermined results."[84] Whether by intention or not, Pruitt was using the same logic as climate deniers; the science was "not settled," since science never is.

> To keep members engaged in the long struggle for social change an organization needs to claim it is making progress.

When a movement is faced with defeat on many of its efforts—to derail the nomination of Cabinet nominees, to get labels on food, to roll back climate change—how do you keep movement members engaged? You declare success anyway and/or change direction.

Claim Success and Change Direction

You claim your organization is the one responsible for the good things that have happened. In the case of OCA, they claimed success for: educating a critical mass of consumers about the environmental and health hazards of GMOs; of doubling the demand for organic food; forcing multi-billion-dollar junk food conglomerates to start labeling their food; and alerting millions of consumers about why they can't trust the mass media, regulatory agencies, or the scientific establishment.[85] By one measure, they have reason to claim success. The Harris Poll, which ranks the 100 most visible companies in the United States, found that Monsanto ranked almost last at 96th, even below the ranking for the Koch Industries at 86th.[86]

How do you declare success in the face of defeat? You tell people the battle has just begun and that new allies have arrived to help in the battle. A March 2017 fund-raising appeal let supporters know that:

> Mercola.com, our ally in the battle against Monsanto, has stepped up with a triple match offer to help us reach our goal by midnight tonight . . . I don't have to tell you that the future looks bleak under the Trump administration—unless each and every one of us steps up to help.[87]

You also find new enemies and related causes. During the last two-and-a-half years (2015–July 2017) OCA has claimed that multi-national chicken producers were driving farmers into bankruptcy. Whole Foods was misleading consumers by using the term "responsibly grown." WebMD and Big Pharma were in league and WebMD was a shill for Monsanto.[88] Bill and Melinda Gates and their foundation were helping to fund a propaganda campaign that promotes GMOs and pesticides.[89] Dr. Oz was called out for referring to organic consumers as elitists and snobs. M&Ms are made with bioengineered ingredients. The list goes on.

You assert you are making progress. The goals of the OCA are, as noted earlier, diverse and require action over an extended period of time to restore resilience and biodiversity, to achieve social justice, and to assure passage of laws that get GMOs out of the food supply. Leaders need to give followers hope:

> Our adversaries in this battle are powerful and ruthless, but they are not invincible. Thanks to you, we're already forcing food companies to clean up their acts, to label or reformulate their products, or to add organic products to their lines. We're doing this by tarnishing their brands, by exposing the GMOs, pesticides and drug residues in their products, and by undermining their profits.[90]

OCA spent four-and-a-half years fighting for labels but lost when the Senate passed a bill that made labeling voluntary. Cummins wrote that it would be easy to give into despair. "But," he said, "let's not give Monsanto the satisfaction. Because the truth is, while we may not always be able to win in a policy arena awash in corporate money, we, as consumers, still have tremendous power to influence the marketplace." He suggested a Gandhi-type resistance and provided a list of companies that could be boycotted.

Bridge or Link to Other Popular Causes

The organic food movement does not stand alone. It claims to be part of a larger resistance movement that seeks to regain control over our lives, our food, and to create a more just world. OCA is not just anti-GMO but part of global efforts to reverse the effects of climate change, restore the health of soils, and create a more just world. The OCA supports justice for farm workers. OCA has thus urged a boycott of Driscoll foods because they buy from the grower, Sakuma, who allegedly mistreats their workers. The groups to which OCA attempts to **bridge** their causes and efforts are numerous and diverse: Friends of the Earth, Dr. Mercola, Moms across America, Truth in Labeling, U.S. Right to Know, Just Label It, Organic Center, Fair World Project, OCA Español, Via Organics, Organic Retail and Consumer Alliance, Greenpeace, Union of Concerned Scientists, Cornucopia Institute, and the Carbon Underground. The intention of casting such a wide net is strategic. It sends the message "we are all in this together."

No movement wants to be left behind when another captures national attention. To remain relevant they will try to link their message with that of a like-minded group in the spot-light When the Standing Rock Sioux and 300 Native Nations gathered to protest against the Dakota Access Pipeline, OCA called on their supporters to give to the cause. They argued, rightfully, that the tribes were standing against a corporation that was going to contribute to global warming and the destruction of the environment.[91] The Standing Rock Sioux were portrayed as brothers and sisters in a fight to resist corporate America.

The Food Movement as a Resistance Movement

Where, when, and how do you take a stand against forces that might seem invincible? What do you do when you are suspicious that the pharmaceutical industry really doesn't have your best interests at heart, or that corporate food giants and your elected representatives have teamed up against you? Where do we find, or create, freedom and autonomy in the 21st century? Our faith in the state to solve our problems has suffered a decline.[92] How do we prevent, to borrow a phrase from the Frankfurt School theorist Walter Benjamin, a continued *descent into barbarism?*[93] We turn to groups and organizations that share our existing beliefs and reaffirm our sense of dignity and purpose.

As I argued in Chapter 1, movements of cultural defiance and resistance are characterized by, among other things, an expression of moral outrage and demands for justice and dignity. Movements of defiance rely on **moral reasoning**, in which we divide decisions into those that are right and those that are wrong. Moral reasoning is not the same as scientific reasoning, which often yields to it. We close ourselves off from contradictions, reinforced by social media, and in the case of the organic food movement we demand the freedom to control our own bodies.

I have dwelt on the science of GMOs and the use of it that is made by both pro- and anti-GMO forces. As I hope to have demonstrated, each group claims to have science on their side. Science is appropriated to support ideological positions, which I see as a descent into alternative truths which limits our ability to solve real problems. *The science of GMOs is actually irrelevant because the real battle is over corporate food systems, not what is in our corn flakes.* Organics now make up slightly over 4% of the food people buy and the market for "No GMO" products is growing rapidly. But what this means is that 96% of the food we buy contains GMOs and most people don't care and it doesn't affect their health. What does affect their health are poor diets and a lack of exercise. But there is precious little reference to that in the hundreds of OCA posts that tell people how to manage their health, because the goal is to stoke fear and make the buying of organic food a **moral choice**. The data do not at this point suggest it is a scientific choice.

I want to make it clear I'm not opposed to the market for organic foods, farmers' markets, non-GMO foods, eggs from free-range chicken, or grass-fed beef. We eat them all in our family. Like a number of others, we follow the advice of the food-writer Michael Pollan who has said, if you want to take control of your health, it's simple: "Eat Real Food!"[94] Taking care of your own health and paying attention to what you eat is a positive thing. Rejecting science is not. GMOs have an important role to play in providing nutritious and inexpensive food. New gene-editing technologies may make it possible to engineer plants so they don't need herbicides or pesticides sprayed on them, or at the least to reduce the amounts needed. We should not close off options, nor should we move blindly ahead proclaiming the virtue of everything created in a lab.

The **strategies** used by the organic food movement—assessing blame, asserting trustworthiness, creating fear, seizing political opportunity, and so forth—are used by any number of SMOs to build and sustain support. As we saw in the previous chapter, all of these strategies are used by the anti-vaccine movement, along with assertions about the right to control our own bodies. Militias spread conspiracy theories with the intention of claiming that they alone are trustworthy. Blame is assessed with the federal government and politicians held responsible for the situation in which people find themselves. The danger of these tactics is that they reduce the opportunity to work toward a democratic future.

Notes

1 Scott G. McNall. March 6, 2017. Telephone interview with Ben and Jerry's Ice Cream.
2 Quoted in James Hamlin. February 11, 2015. "The Food Babe: Enemy of Chemicals." *The Atlantic*. Retrieved on March 10, 2017 at: www.theatlantic.com/health/archive/2015/02/the-food-babe-enemy-of-chemicals/385301/.
3 Jason Lusk and Susan Murray. January 16, 2015. "Food Demand Survey." Vol.2(9). Oklahoma State University. Retrieved on March 10, 2017 at: http://agecon.okstate.edu/faculty/publications/4975.pdf.
4 Karin Klein. March 10, 2017. "Are Americans Really Dumb Enough to Worry about Food Containing DNA?" *Los Angeles Times*. Retrieved on March 10, 2017 at: www.latimes.com/nation/la-ol-gmo-food-dna-20150119-story.html.
5 United States Department of Agriculture. August 17, 2016. "Food Expenditures." Retrieved on March 17, 2017 at: www.ers.usda.gov/data-products/food-expenditures/.
6 Karl R. Popper. 1934/1959. *The Logic of Scientific Discovery*. London and New York: Routledge.
7 Thomas Kuhn. 1962. *The Structure of Scientific Revolutions*. Chicago: University of Chicago Press.
8 Quoted in William J. Broad. August 28, 2007. "Useful Mutants, Bred with Radiation." *The New York Times*. Retrieved on March 23, 2017 at: www.nytimes.com/2007/08/28/science/28crop.html.
9 Wikipedia. 2017. "Mutation Breeding." Retrieved on March 23, 2017 at: https://en.wikipedia.org/wiki/Mutation_breeding.
10 Michael Specter. January 2, 2017. "Rewriting the Code of Life." *The New Yorker*, pp.334–343.
11 *The Economist*. October 17, 2015. "CRISPR/Cas9 Gene Editing Technology: No Pig in a Poke," p.82.
12 Michael LePage. November 14, 2015. "Layla's Gene-Editing Legacy." *New Scientist*, p.10.
13 The quotations are cited in Michael Specter. January 2, 2017. "Rewriting the Code of Life," p.38.
14 Jan van Aken and Edward Hammond. June, 2003. "Genetic Engineering and Biological Weapons." *EMBO Reports*. Vol.4(1):57–60. Retrieved on March 21, 2017 at: www.ncbi.nlm.nih.gov/pmc/articles/PMC1326447/.
15 Alexandra Ossola. September 6, 2016. "CRISPR-Modified Corn May Soon Be Ready for Market." *Popular Science*. Retrieved on March 23, 2017 at: www.popsci.com/crispr-modified-corn-may-soon-be-ready-for-market.
16 Ric Bessin. Nd. "Bt-Corn: What It Is and How It Works." Department of Entomology, University of Kentucky. Retrieved on March 21, 2017 at: https://entomology.ca.uky.edu/ef130.
17 Michael Eisen. June 12, 2012. "#GMOFAQ How Bt Corn and Roundup Ready Soy Work, and Why They Should Not Scare You." Michael Eisen is a University of California Biologist who blogs about genomes, among other things. Retrieved on March 22, 2017 at: www.michaeleisen.org/blog/?p=1135. There is more than one form of Bt; each form of which kills specific insects. Some bioengineered foods may have more than one form of Bt.
18 Chelsea Snell, Aude Bernheim, Jean-Baptiste Bergé, Gérard Pascal, Alan Paris, and Agnès Ricroch. March, 2012. "Assessment of the Health Impact of GM Plants Diets in Long-Term and Multigenerational Animal Feeding Trials: A Literature Review." *Food and Chemical Toxicology*. Vol.50(3–4):1134–1148.
19 The literature on how humans deal with risk is extensive and stems from the initial work of Daniel Kahneman and Amos Tversky. 1984. "Choices, Values, and Frames." *American*

Psychologist. Vol.39:341–350. For a detailed bibliography of risk aversion see: https://en.wikipedia.org/wiki/Risk_aversion_(psychology).

20 Ali Siddiq Alhakami and Paul Slovic. 1994. "A Psychological Study of the Inverse Relationship between Perceived Risk and Perceived Benefit." *Risk Analysis*. Vol.14 (6):1085–1096.

21 Cary Funk. January 29, 2015. "5 Key Findings on What Americans and Scientists Think about Science." *Pew Research Center*. Retrieved on March 20, 2017 at: www.pewresearch.org/fact-tank/2015/01/29/5-key-findings-science/.

22 Comments posted on the Pew Research Center site in response to the article. "5 Key Findings on What Americans and Scientists Think about Science." Retrieved on June 13, 2017 at: www.pewresearch.org/fact-tank/2015/01/29/5-key-findings-science/.

23 Nathanael Johnson. January 9, 2014. "What I Learned from Six Months of GMO Research: None of It Matters." *Grist*. Retrieved on April 3, 2017 at: http://grist.org/food/what-i-learned-from-six-months-of-gmo-research-none-of-it-matters/.

24 John T. Lang. 2016. *What's So Controversial about Genetically Modified Food?* Glasgow, Great Britain: Reaktion Books.

25 George Johnson. August 25, 2015. "The Gradual Extinction of Accepted Truths." *The New York Times*, D6.

26 Barbara Casassus. November 28, 2013. "Study Linking GM Maize to Rat Tumors Is Retracted." *Nature*. Retrieved on March 20, 2017 at: www.nature.com/news/study-linking-gm-maize-to-rat-tumours-is-retracted-1.14268.

27 Judy Hoy. June 9, 2015. "Pesticides, Herbicides: Stop Using Roundup, Glyphosate." Letter to the editor, *Missoulian*, B5.

28 National Academies of Sciences, Engineering and Medicine. 2016. *Genetically Engineered Crops: Experiences and Prospects*. Washington, D.C.: National Academies Press.

29 Tom Philpott. March 5, 2017. "Just One Small Problem with This Major Report on GMO Safety." *Mother Jones*. Retrieved on March 9, 2017 at: www.motherjones.com/environment/2017/03/gmo-report-national-academies-conflict-of-interest.

30 U.S. Department of Health and Human Services. November 3, 2016. "14th Annual Report on Carcinogens." Retrieved on March 7, 2017 at: https://ntp.niehs.nih.gov/pubhealth/roc/index-1.html#toc1.

31 U.S. Environmental Protection Agency. October, 2016. "Glyphosate." Retrieved on March 9, 2017 at: www.epa.gov/ingredients-used-pesticide-products/glyphosate.

32 World Health Organization. International Agency for Research on Cancer. January 26, 2017. "IARC Monographs on the Evaluation of Carcinogenic Risk to Humans." Retrieved on March 7, 2017 at: http://monographs.iarc.fr/ENG/Classification/index.php.

33 The European Food Safety Authority (EFSA) concluded that it was not warranted to list glyphosate as a carcinogen. GMWatch. November 3, 2016. "German Toxicologist Accuses EU Authorities of Scientific Fraud to Enable the Conclusion that Glyphosate Is Not to Be Considered a Carcinogen." Retrieved on March 9, 2017 at: www.gmwatch.org/news/latest-news/17307-german-toxicologist-accuses-eu-authorities-of-scientific-fraud-over-glyphosate-link-with-cancer.

34 California Environmental Health Hazard Assessment . January 2017. "Proposition 65." Retrieved on March 7, 2017 at: https://oehha.ca.gov/proposition-65.

35 Scott Smith. January 27, 2017. "Warning Label on Roundup Could Be Coming Soon in California." *Associated Press*. Retrieved on March 22, 2017 at: www.usnews.com/news/news/articles/2017-01-27/california-fights-monsanto-on-labels-for-popular-weed-killer.

36 Smith. January 27, 2017.

37 National Cancer Institute. September 24, 2014. "Breast Cancer Risk in American Women." Retrieved on March 17, 2017 at: www.cancer.gov/types/breast/risk-fact-sheet.

38 Lawrence S. Engel, et al., January 15, 2005. "Pesticide Use and Breast Cancer Risk among Farmers' Wives in the Agricultural Health Study." *American Journal of Epidemiology.* Vol.161(2):121–135; Jane A. Mcelroy, et al., July 5, 2006. "Risk of Breast Cancer for Women Living in Rural Areas from Adult Exposure to Atrazine from Well Water in Wisconsin." *Journal of Exposure Science and Environmental Epidemiology.* Vol.17:207–214; Peggy Reynolds, Susan E. Hurley, Robert B.Gunier, Sauda Yerabati, Thu Quach, and Andrew Hertz. August 2005. "Residential Proximity to Agricultural Pesticide Use and Incidence of Breast Cancer in California, 1988–1997." *Environmental Health Perspectives.* Vol.113(8):993–1000.

39 Carey Gillam. November 14, 2016. "Tests Show Monsanto Weed Killer in Cheerios, Other Popular Foods." *Huffington Post.* Retrieved on April 11, 2017 at: www.huffingtonpost.com/carey-gillam/tests-show-monsanto-weed_b_12950444.html.

40 Andrew Malone. November 2, 2008. "The GM Genocide: Thousands of Indian Farmers Committing Suicide after Using Genetically Modified Crops." *Daily Mail.* Retrieved on March 23, 2017 at: www.dailymail.co.uk/news/article-1082559/The-GM-genocide-Thousands-Indian-farmers-committing-suicide-using-genetically-modified-crops.html.

41 Ian Plewis. March 12, 2014. "Hard Evidence: Does GM Cotton Lead to Farmer Suicide in India?" *Conversation.* Retrieved on March 23, 2017 at: http://theconversation.com/hard-evidence-does-gm-cotton-lead-to-farmer-suicide-in-india-24045.

42 Keith Kloor. Winter, 2014. "The GMO Suicide Myth." *Discovery*, pp.65–70. Retrieved on March 23, 2017 at: https://blogs.discovermagazine.com/collideascape/files/2014/01/GMOsuicidemyth.pdf.

43 *The Economist.* March 13, 2014. "GM Crops, Indian Farmers and Suicide: GM Genocide?" Retrieved on March 23, 2017 at: www.economist.com/blogs/feastandfamine/2014/03/gm-crops-indian-farmers-and-suicide.

44 Dan Mitchell. February 16, 2016. "How Monsanto Got Stung by a Zika Virus Conspiracy Theory." *Fortune.* Retrieved on March 27, 2017 at: http://fortune.com/2016/02/16/monsanto-zika-virus-conspiracy/.

45 Mike Adams, February 11, 2016. "Zika HOAX Exposed by South American Doctors: Brain Deformations Caused by Larvicide Chemical Linked to Monsanto: GM Mosquitoes a 'Total Failure.'" *Natural News.* Retrieved on March 27, 2017 at: www.naturalnews.com/052943_Zika_virus_hoax_larvacide_chemical_GM_mosquitoes.html.

46 Mike Adams. July 27, 2014. "The Agricultural Holocaust Explained: the 10 Worst Ways GMOs Threaten Humanity and our Natural World." *Natural News.* Retrieved on March 27, 2017 at: www.naturalnews.com/046194_agricultural_holocaust_GMOs_environmental_destruction.htm.

47 Nyasha Mudukuti. March 11, 2016. "We May Starve, But at Least We'll Be GMO Free." *Wall Street Journal*, p.A15.

48 Danny Hakim. October 30, 2016. "Doubts about a Promised Bounty." *The New York Times*, pp.A1, 22–23.

49 Oxfam, February 26, 2013. "Behind the Brands: Food Justice and the 'Big 10' Food and Beverage Companies." Retrieved on April 4, 2017 at: www.oxfam.org/en/tags/behind-brands.

50 Organic Trade Association. 2016. "U.S. Organic Sales Post New Record of $43.3 Billion in 2015." Retrieved on March 13, 2017 at: www.ota.com/news/press-releases/19031.

51 I have tracked the mailings and alerts from the OCA for over 2.5 years (2015–April 2017).

52 Organic Consumers Association. 2017. Home Page. Retrieved on March 24, 2017 at: www.organicconsumers.org/about-oca.

53 Organic Consumers Association. 2017. "2014 990 Tax Filing." Retrieved on March 24, 2017 at: www.organicconsumers.org/sites/default/files/2014_oca_990.pdf.

54 See Jerry Rifkin. 2017. *Foundation for Economic Trends.* Retrieved on March 24, 2017 at: www.foet.org/about-foet.html.

55 Cited in *Activist Facts*. 2017. "Ronnie Cummins." Retrieved on March 24, 2017 at: www.activistfacts.com/person/1431-ronnie-cummins/.

56 Ronnie Cummins and Ben Lilliston. 2000. *Genetically Engineered Foods: A Self-Defense Guide for Consumers*. Boston, Massachusetts: De Capo Press.

57 Ronnie Cummins. August 2, 2012. "Open Letter to the Organic Community: The California Ballot Initiative to Label GMOs." *Common Dreams*. Retrieved on March 24, 2017 at: www.commondreams.org/views/2012/08/02/open-letter-organic-community-california-ballot-initiative-label-gmos.

58 Dr. Axe. 2017. "7 Signs and Symptoms You Have Leaky Gut." Retrieved on March 28, 2017 at: https://draxe.com/7-signs-symptoms-you-have-leaky-gut/.

59 Annalisa Copannolo, et al., 2015. "Non-Celiac Sensitivity among Patients Perceiving Gluten-Related Symptoms." *Digestion*. Vol.92(1):8–13. Retrieved on March 28, 2017 at: www.ncbi.nlm.nih.gov/pubmed/26043918.

60 Michelle Brandt. September 3, 2012. "Little Evidence of Health Benefits from Organic Foods, Study Finds." *Stanford Medicine*. Retrieved on March 28, 2017 at: https://med.stanford.edu/news/all-news/2012/09/little-evidence-of-health-benefits-from-organic-foods-study-finds.html/.

61 Christie Wilcox. September 24, 2012. "Are Lower Pesticide Residues a Good Reason to Buy Organic? Probably Not." *Scientific American*. Retrieved on March 28, 2017 at: https://blogs.scientificamerican.com/science-sushi/pesticides-food-fears/.

62 Damian Carrington. September 22, 2016. "Pesticide Manufacturers' Own Test Reveal Serious Harm to Honeybees." *The Guardian*. Retrieved on March 28, 2017 at: www.theguardian.com/environment/2016/sep/22/pesticide-manufacturers-own-tests-reveal-serious-harm-to-honeybees.

63 Just Label It. 2016. "Partners." Retrieved on March 30, 2017 at: www.justlabelit.org/partners-center/partners/.

64 Rob Coleman. February 25, 2016. "Food Lobby Spends $101 Million in 2015 to Avert GMO Labeling." *Environmental Working Group*. Retrieved on March 30, 2017 at: www.ewg.org/research/lobbying-anti-labeling-groups-tops-100m.

65 Ronnie Cummins. June 28, 2016. "Organic Traitors Team up with Monsanto and GMA on DARK Act." *Organic Consumers Association*. Retrieved on March 30, 2017 at: www.organicconsumers.org/essays/organic-traitors-team-monsanto-and-gma-dark-act.

66 Danny Hamkim. March 14, 2017. "Monsanto Weed Killer Roundup Faces New Doubts on Safety in Unsealed Documents." *The New York Times*. Retrieved on March 29, 2017 at: www.nytimes.com/2017/03/14/business/monsanto-roundup-safety-lawsuit.html.

67 Ronnie Cummins. March 15, 2017. "Monsanto's Cancerous Truth." *Organic Consumers Association*, pp.1–2.

68 Zack Kaldveer. 2017. "Five Ways the FDA Has Failed Consumers on Genetically Engineered Foods." *Organic Consumers Association*. Retrieved on March 30, 2017 at: www.organicconsumers.org/news/five-ways-fda-has-failed-consumers-genetically-engineered-foods.

69 *Organic Consumers Association*. September 29, 2016. "People Must Know." Retrieved on March 30, 2017 at: www.organicconsumers.org/newsletter/organic-bytes-526-what-has-monsanto-done-argentinas-children/people-must-know.

70 *Organic Consumers Association*. May, 2017. "Fracking Kills Babies." Retrieved on June 13, 2017 at: www.organicconsumers.org/newsletter/organic-bytes-549-epa-protects-corporations-who-will-protect-you/fracking-kills-babies.

71 Christopher Busby and Joseph J. Mangano. April, 2017. "There's a World Going on Underground—Infant Mortality and Fracking in Pennsylvania." *Journal of Environmental Protection*. Vol.8(4):381–393.

72 *Organic Consumers Association.* January 5, 2017. "Ben & Jerry's #DirtyDairy." Retrieved on March 30, 2017 at: www.organicconsumers.org/bytes/organic-bytes-536-ben-jerrys-dirtydairy-and-consumer-fraud.

73 Will Allen and Michael Colby. 2017. "Vermont's Industrial Dairying: Marketing vs. Reality." *Regeneration Vermont.* Retrieved on March 30, 2017 at: http://regenerationvermont.org/vermonts-industrial-dairying-marketing-vs-reality/.

74 *Organic Consumers Association.* August 23, 2016. "OCA Sues General Mills-Owned Subsidiary"; and August 29, 2016, "Tell Jessica Alba and Honest Co.: No Fake Baby Formula!" Retrieved on March 30, 2017 at: www.organicconsumers.org/press/non-profits-sue-general-mills-false-and-misleading-use-%E2%80%98natural%E2%80%99-0, and www.organicconsumers.org/node/1027636.

75 Ronnie Cummins. October 16, 2016. "No Kangaroos Here." *Organic Consumers Association.* Retrieved on March 30, 2017 at: www.organicconsumers.org/bytes/organic-bytes-527-no-kangaroos-world-food-day.

76 Quoted in Kavin Senapathy. December 7, 2015. "No, Monsanto Is Not Going on Trial for Crimes Against Humanity." *Forbes.* Retrieved on March 30, 2017 at: www.forbes.com/sites/kavinsenapathy/2015/12/07/no-monsanto-is-not-going-on-trial-for-crimes-against-humanity/2/#56290f3221d2.

77 *Organic Consumers Association.* 2017. "Healthy Raw Milk: It's Our Right." Retrieved on March 30, 2017 at: www.organicconsumers.org/campaigns/healthy-raw-milk.

78 For a review of the relevant literature on social movements and political opportunity see: David S. Meyer. 2004. "Protest and Political Opportunities." *Annual Review of Sociology.* Vol.30:124–145. See also: Doug McAdam, Sidney Tarrow, and Charles Tilly. 2001. *Dynamics of Contention.* New York: Cambridge University Press.

79 Ronnie Cummins. January 20, 2017. "Ronnie's Inauguration Day Message." *Organic Consumers Association.* Retrieved on March 31, 2017 at: www.organicconsumers.org/essays/ronnie%E2%80%99s-inauguration-day-message.

80 Ronnie Cummins, January 20, 2017. "Ronnie's Inauguration Day Message."

81 Ronnie Cummins. December 30, 2016. "I'm Going to Break the Rules Today." *Organic Consumers Association.* Retrieved on March 31, 2017 at: www.organicconsumers.org/news/im-going-break-rules-today. See the Competitive Enterprise Institute's Legislative Agenda, *Free to Prosper* at: https://cei.org/agendaforcongress-2017.

82 *Organic Consumers Association.* 2017. "Tell the Senate: Don't Let Monsanto Run the USDA and the EPA!" Retrieved on March 31, 2017 at: https://action.organicconsumers.org/o/50865/p/dia/action3/common/public/?action_KEY=19679.

83 Alexis Baden-Meyer. February 2, 2017. "Love School Gardens? Call Your Senators!" *Organic Consumers Association.* Retrieved on March 31, 2017 at: https://action.organicconsumers.org/content_item/oca-email?email_blast_KEY=1365607.

84 Quoted in Eric Lipton. March 29, 2017. "E.P.A. Chief, Rejecting Agency's Science, Chooses Not to Ban Insecticide." *The New York Times.* Retrieved on March 31, 2017 at: www.nytimes.com/2017/03/29/us/politics/epa-insecticide-chlorpyrifos.html?_r=0.

85 Ronnie Cummins. July 31, 2016. "Corporate Money Defeats GMO Labeling—What Would Gandhi Do?" *Organic Consumers Association.* Retrieved on March 31, 2017 at: www.organicconsumers.org/essays/corporate-money-defeats-gmo-labeling%E2%80%94what-would-gandhi-do.

86 Harris Poll. February 18, 2016. "The Harris Poll Releases Annual Reputation Rankings for the 100 Most Visible Corporations in the U.S." Retrieved on April 4, 2017 at: www.theharrispoll.com/business/Reputation-Rankings-Most-Visible-Companies.html.

87 Ronnie Cummins. March 31, 2017, "Less than 24 Hours." *Organic Consumers Association.* Retrieved on March 31, 2017 at: www.inboxdb.com/less-than-24-hours-873021/.

88 Dr. Mercola. January 19, 2016. "WebMD—the Latest Shill for Monsanto." *Organic Consumers Association.* Retrieved on March 31, 2017 at: www.organicconsumers.org/news/webmd-%E2%80%94-latest-shill-monsanto.

89 *Organic Consumers Association.* January 28, 2016. "The Science of Deceit." Retrieved on March 31, 2017 at: www.organicconsumers.org/sites/default/files/organicbytes497.pdf.

90 Ronnie Cummins. December 22, 2015. "And the Earthworms Will Dance." *Organic Consumers Association.* Retrieved on March 31, 2017 at: www.organicconsumers.org/news/and-earthworms-will-dance.

91 Kathleen Paul. December 9, 2016. "Can We Bring the Buffalo Home?" *Organic Consumers Association.* Retrieved on March 31, 2017 at: www.organicconsumers.org/essays/standing-rock-can-we-bring-buffalo-home.

92 Jürgen Habermas. 1975. *Legitimation Crisis.* Boston, Massachusetts: Beacon.

93 Walter Benjamin. 1940/1969. *Illuminations.* Hannah Arendt, ed.; Harry Zohn, trans. New York: Schocken.

94 Michael Pollan. January 23, 2017. "How to Eat: Diet Secrets from Michael Pollan (and Your Great Grand-Mother)." *Houston Chronicle.* Retrieved on April 4, 2017 at: http://michaelpollan.com/reviews/how-to-eat/.

The Revolution Will Not Be Tweeted, But It Can Be Organized

7

Consider:

- Today's mass movements take on similar characteristics because they must solve the same problems.
- Dissent is being turned into a commodity.
- New social movements of defiance and resistance are value-based movements that arise in response to the dissolving of traditional bonds of solidarity—faith, family, community.
- Movements of defiance and resistance are attempts to create moral communities.
- Localized social movements spring up in response to a well-defined grievance but most are fragile and fade quickly away.
- Social media provide useful tools for alerting people to opportunities but there is little evidence they generate long-term commitment and sacrifice.
- Embracing a strategy of "Go big or go home!" enhances the likelihood that volunteers will commit to a project.
- Movement success depends on embracing two different strategies: face-to-face organizing coupled with mass mobilization.

My wife, son, and I squeezed into the line of marchers that had assembled in the rain in Washington, D.C. on Saturday, April 22, Earth Day, 2017 to march for science. We were about 50 feet behind the front of the line, following a little boy of about 10 who was leading a call and response chant. He shouted: "What does democracy look like?" Those around him responded: "This is what democracy looks like!" We could hear other marchers in the crowd chanting "Ho-ho, hey-hey, I support the EPA." In spite of the cold and rain, the March for Science drew 70,000 to 100,000 people to the nation's capitol and tens of thousands more to sister marches across the country. People came to stand up for science and protest attacks on their profession and their integrity.

The idea for the march was spawned on Reddit immediately following the Women's March on January 21, 2017, the day after Trump's inauguration. Someone on the site worried about how to respond to a new administration they feared would be hostile to science. The answer came back: "A march of scientists on Washington." The idea for a march was picked up by Jonathan Berman, a postdoctoral fellow from the University of Texas Health Sciences Center. A Facebook page was quickly created, and after just one day there were 300,000 followers, a website, and a Twitter handle. Berman was joined online by a science writer and health communicator from New York City, Caroline Weinberg. Weinberg's inspiration for a science march came from the Women's March. Weinberg thought, "How hard could it be to organize a march for science?" She and Berman reasoned they could reach out to academics at local universities to get a crowd. Their immediate goal was to dramatize the fact that politicians were not making decisions based on science and they wanted to raise the alarm about Trump's proposed budget cuts for the Environmental Protection Agency and the National Institutes of Health.[1] What happened exceeded their expectations.[2] On the eve of the march, they had raised over $1 million, through the sale of merchandise and donations, and 100 different scientific and environmental organizations endorsed their efforts.

Like any major protest, the event drew people with differing agendas. Even though the organizers had made it clear they did not want to politicize the march and detract from its non-partisan message about the need to support science, there were speakers and participants who took aim at Trump. One carried a sign which read "Real Science, Not Fake President." Another proclaimed: "Politicians can evolve!" Two women carried signs made up of photographs of their cats solving problems with the heading, "My cat does better science than your administration."

The issue of women in science was on full view. Three young women carried signs proclaiming, "If boys will be boys, then women will be physicists." Several marchers held hand-made signs asking: "Got the plague? Neither do I. Thank science!" Other slogans included "Science not silence," "There is no Planet B." Parents pushed strollers with small girls holding signs saying "Future STEM student." One informed us: "My parents are scientists." One little blond girl was dressed in a yellow and black honey-bee outfit. Her mother was worried about the collapse of bee colonies. Some marchers wore white lab coats; others wore pink "brain" hats, knitted

> Scientific facts are being treated as just another opinion.

from designs provided on the web. Science teachers, researchers, students, and concerned citizens massed in support of science, as well as other issues. Black Lives Matter activists marched behind a banner noting that climate change would affect them more than other ethnic groups. The crowd, however, was overwhelmingly white (80%) and made up primarily of Democratic voters (98% by one estimate).[3]

Some of those marching were doing so for the first time, because they saw science under threat. It was not just the proposed budget cuts that concerned them; it was that science was being treated as just another opinion to be challenged by alternative facts.[4] Scientists find the rise of the anti-vaccination movement and the denial of climate change as dumbfounding and dangerous.[5] In the United States, 42% of people polled believe that God created humans in our present form less than 10,000 years ago.[6] Scientists see these beliefs as a challenge to their professional integrity, as well as the methodology of their disciplines, which accepts the fact that there is always a level of uncertainty. Scientists believe there are real facts and scientific laws in the world that are not the product of power or social status. Gravity and evolution are facts, even though 42% of Americans do not believe in evolution. Giraffes really are taller than ants.[7] As the philosopher of science, Robert P. Crease, has noted:

> Scientific facts aren't scattered around . . . like sticks and stones, waiting to be spotted and gathered. They are produced by an infrastructure of laboratories that earn credibility by exposing their findings to repeated checks . . . The system is not perfect, but constant scientific scrutiny is the principal reason we can trust its conclusions.[8]

Other participants had previously marched for other issues. Some, including one man I saw, wore pink pussy hats left over from the Women's March. One woman told us, "I've been marching since 1967!" Another wore a t-shirt that said, "I can't believe I'm still protesting this crap!" Students, researchers, and science leaders were marching for both personal and political reasons. In a parallel event in Morgantown, West Virginia, Amanda Stover marched because she lost a family member to a heroin overdose and wanted to assure that funds would continue for studying the link between addiction and suicide.[9] Most were marching, as a University of Delaware study revealed, to encourage policies based on science (97%), to encourage the public to support science (93%), and to oppose political attacks on science (93%).[10]

When we returned to our home in Montana, we were greeted with numerous emails celebrating the event and talking about "next steps." Groups that had endorsed the march sent out congratulatory notes to their members and posted photographs of participants on their websites. The Audubon Society showed a woman in a stocking cap holding a sign which announced: "It's time to give a flock. Stand for science based conservation." Another sponsor, the climate change group 350.org, explained that the Saturday march had been about respecting science and told us that the march to be held on the following Saturday, April 29, the Peoples Climate March, was about acting on the basis of science. It would be, the organizers noted, a march for climate, justice, and jobs. The Climate March of April 29 was followed on May 1 by marches around the country advocating for immigrants and workers. I went to a picnic in support of labor on the same day. In short, in the aftermath of Trump's election and inauguration, there were scores of protests in Washington D.C. and in cities large and small across the country, about a wide range of issues and which continue to plague us. Can these large-scale mobilizations translate into effective actions or bring about real social change? There is a remarkable sameness to how people are being mobilized for action. Protesters on the right and left are offered cookie-cutter plans for ways to mobilize, alert their friends, and raise money. There are so many that collectively they run the risk of dissipating protest energy that might bring about actual change.

From March to Movement

The team that stood behind the March for Science made it clear ahead of time that they wanted to build on the march and create a permanent organization that would advocate for science. After the march, they sent emails to those on their distribution lists. One of the first urged us to protest actions being taken by the new head of the EPA, Scott Pruitt, a climate denier. We were asked to "Stand up for science and tell the EPA leadership: Don't delete the facts." Pruitt had ordered the removal of climate change data from the EPA website, removed scientists from review boards, and replaced them with representatives from the industries whose pollution the agency is supposed to regulate. The action requested was to send a postcard or make a phone call to our federal representatives. Donations were solicited to support the effort.

The American Association for the Advancement of Science (AAAS), a major force behind the march, also sent out emails urging its members to donate so that "evidence and not ideology" would be the driving force behind public policy decisions. The AAAS also provided a set of net-based tools to keep people engaged. A series of training tools was offered to help members create their own plans for engaging with federal, local, and state officials. Interested members could sign up for weekly chats on social media and receive alerts about policy issues. The goal of the AAAS was to lead a unified group of scientific societies to assure that public decision-makers understood the science they needed to make informed policy choices.[11] Dissent is being increasingly managed with sophisticated online tools. Embedded within these tools is an understanding that *the power of protest depends on building direct connections between participants.*

How to turn a march into a movement that can accomplish its objectives is a challenge faced by all groups seeking change. The Women's March drew 500,000+ to Washington D.C. and millions more to 650 companion marches around the United States and in more than 50 other countries.[12] It began as a Facebook effort but it was a technology platform, Action Network, which made it possible for the movement to spread the word and make sure mundane activities were taken care of, such as where to show up and when. Action Network was built by progressives to create social movements that would not be one-off events but would have real staying power. Action Network offers online tools for creating petitions, alerting people to events, creating fund raisers, and developing letter writing campaigns.[13] Action Network's tools were also used to organize protests against the Keystone XL pipeline, the Dakota Access Pipeline, and to organize wage protests against Wal-Mart.[14]

> Sophisticated technology tools have been developed to mobilize and organize protests.

After the Women's March, its organizers identified ten actions to take in 100 days. Step two, after marching, was to organize what were termed "huddles." There were over 5,000 events people could attend scattered in neighborhoods across the country. A detailed *Huddle Guide* was provided which gave step-by-step actions to make the event a success and to build on the energy created by the national march. Among the guidelines offered were: getting 10–15 of your friends together, finding a place to meet, registering your huddle with the national group, choosing a group facilitator, and a reminder to bring post-its and blank paper. An agenda was even provided with suggested amounts of time dedicated for introducing people, watching a video provided by Action Network, deciding what to do next, and writing postcards to senators.[15]

I attend a huddle, of sorts, in Missoula, Montana; a progressive community with a number of active organizations on the left and a handful on the right. The purpose of the meeting was to decide what the next steps would be after 10,000 people marched on the state capitol in Helena. Over 400 people filled the Union Bar and Grill and more lingered on the sidewalk outside. The organizers of the huddle spoke briefly about the need for unity, not working at cross purposes, the importance of raising money for continued efforts, and explained why they were not going to merge their efforts with those of previously existing and long-standing social justice organizations in the community. We were then told to break into groups depending on whether or not we wanted to raise money, hold events, or meet with members of the American Civil Liberties Union (ACLU) team who were there to advise us about what to do if we were arrested during protests.

After some back-and-forth conversation, it was decided that people would assemble under or by a sign held by a group with whom we wanted to make a connection. I chose to stay with a small group trying to organize a local chapter of the Democratic Socialists of America (DSA), although I could have chosen to meet with Greenpeace, 350.org, Missoula Rising, a group that deals with violence against women and hate speech, or any number of other groups seeking to expand their ranks. I stayed with the DSA group because I liked the fact that they identified themselves as "Berniecrats." Their stated goal was to move the Democratic Party to the left. This was to be accomplished in part by establishing rapid response teams at the local level that could march and picket when alerted to do so by the national DSA organization. They were operating with a Tea Party model—where resistance to all things proposed by the Democratic Party was the norm—to one where all things proposed by the Republican Party would be defied. (As noted later, they were not the only organization that adopted this model.)

A meeting was called for the following Saturday to get the group started and to form a local chapter. The meeting was facilitated by two people who had extensive experience in lobbying, working on the Bernie Sanders' campaign, and working for the state-wide and national DSA. An agenda was created for the public meeting and people were assigned roles. One person was to explain the relationship of the DSA to electoral politics; another explained how to form a chapter; and one spoke about rapid response teams. We were also instructed to identify organizations with which we could ally locally and share email lists for action alerts. Early alerts that followed from the DSA asked people to rally in front of the local office of our Republican Senator (Daines) to demand he vote against the confirmation of various Trump nominees for cabinet-level positions.

About 20 people came to the first public meeting and after making introductions, people were asked why they were there and what they hoped the DSA would accomplish. The list was long: support Planned Parenthood; protect Roe vs. Wade; mobilize for economic justice; learn more about the meaning of democratic socialism; develop a support network for striking workers; advocate for Medicare for all; convince Trump voters that democratic socialism was a viable alternative; support public K-12 education; and so forth. Numerous suggestions were offered about other groups with which the DSA might affiliate, including national groups such as Indivisible and Our Revolution as well as local groups like Big Sky Rising and Missoula Rising. A local group of college students representing the International Workers of the World (IWW) came seeking to collaborate with the DSA and gain support for an upcoming May Day event, and for the protests they and other students were leading against planned tuition increases at the University of Montana.

In addition to this list of potential projects, several people spoke to their emotional needs. They wanted to create a sense of community. One young man said he needed to find a group of people he could talk to about the state of his country, because nobody at his workplace wanted to listen to him about what was wrong and what needed to be done. A woman told us she felt traumatized in the aftermath of Trump's election and needed to find a group of people who shared her feelings. Several spoke to the need to do something, anything, to fight back. One woman, who said she was unemployed, wanted to create events at which people who shared common beliefs could get together for potlucks and conversation. A carpenter wanted to engage in actions that would reflect her values and those of the group.

It was then time to break into small groups to address issues that had been raised, as well as practical matters; for example, what needed to be done to form a chapter; which projects the DSA should tackle; the creation of a reading group to share ideas and learn more about democratic socialism. One breakout group was made up mostly of women who had been involved in social justice issues and who belonged to Missoula organizations that pursued a range of issues from climate change to immigrant rights. Long-term activists, their response to any idea proposed by somebody outside of their circles was, "We've tried that before; that won't work." None of them returned to future meetings. By the end of the meeting, a reading group had been formed; a small group had the responsibility for tackling the paperwork associated with starting a chapter; and it had been agreed the DSA would work to support the May Day event proposed by the students. Left open was the question about what specific project, or projects, the group as a whole would embrace. That would come later.

Another Saturday meeting followed two weeks later. Again, about 20 people came but at least half were new to the group. Once again there were introductions and people were asked why they came and what they hoped the DSA might do. Some wanted to re-educate Trump voters, which lead to a discussion about how that could be done. A biology major wanted to use the DSA to create a left wing of the Democratic Party. A self-identified old-time unionist said he wanted to do whatever worked. A student and former prisoner on parole spoke about the need to address unjust laws, ineffective drug wars, and corrupt law enforcement. Others believed the group should focus on and lobby for specific pieces of legislation. The owner of an organic juice bar and café said what we needed to do was focus on health care and engage in guerrilla actions that made it clear who we were and what we stood for. Others raised questions about whether we were in it for the long game, or the short game; meaning, were we trying to transform capitalist society, or simply protesting

> All social movements must solve two basic problems: who is a member and what will the group do?

against a new administration. At one point a discussion about gun legislation began and an argument broke out with two people claiming that people should not discuss guns if they did not know the difference between a clip and a magazine. A young woman from the East coast said she did not "get all this talk about guns." She did not return to succeeding meetings. It was the first time the larger group became aware that there were pro-gun advocates among potential members, and it produced an awkward silence before the conversation moved on to other topics.

People drifted in and out and turnover was high from one meeting to the next. People were, without exactly knowing it, trying to solve two basic problems all new groups must solve: Who is a member and what exactly is the group trying to do?

Who Belongs?

The discussions among the group of DSA recruits, and the churn in who attended the meetings, is typical of new groups emerging to challenge existing political and economic realities. The sociologist Kathleen Blee studied over 60 emerging grassroots organizations in Pittsburg between 2003–2007.[16] The 60 collectively tackled a wide range of different issues: LBGT rights, the war in Iraq, guns, drugs, violence, the environment, animal rights, and school reform. Most were small and many were ephemeral. They lasted for a brief period of time with a burst of intensive activity and then slowly faded away. Blee's work is unique and invaluable, as most studies of social movements focus on those which have been successful. Doing so blinds us to the dynamics of group formation and development; we don't see *what caused* a group to succeed, or to fail. She tells us that today we are looking at new forms of organization where people strive to create a sense of community not provided by ties of occupation, place, or class. Instead recruits come from a diversity of backgrounds, where they must struggle to create a sense of commonality or a core of true believers. As groups form, boundaries are continually challenged, as members actively reflect on who they are and what they want to accomplish. Groups sometimes dissolve into one another and "activists migrate from one to the other,"[17] as people seek out those who share their values.

When the newly forming Missoula chapter of the DSA was asked to identify other like-minded groups in the community, 20 were named including SALAM (standing alongside American's Muslims), the Jeannette Rankin Peace Center, 350 Montana, and the Missoula Central Labor Council. With the exception of the newly emergent group, SALAM, most groups were of long-standing and had credibility in the community. The time any given individual has to devote to participating in any one group is limited. Multiple groups have the effect of narrowing the ranks to those who provide leadership and sometimes, unintentionally, causing protest groups to be less democratic. Overlapping memberships and a community dense with options means that should a nascent group stumble and implode, members can easily move to another group, which means loyalty and group cohesion can be hard to maintain.

As Blee points out, many emergent groups are fragile. They flame up in response to one issue (opiate addiction, contamination of local waterways with toxins, police shootings of unarmed civilians, and school shootings) then fade away as people grow weary of continuing a battle they believe they cannot win. They are fragile, because at the beginning one or two individuals can destroy group cohesiveness by dominating the discussions and diminishing the contributions of others. New social movement organizations are also fragile because key leadership positions may remain unfilled. In the case of the Missoula DSA, organizing efforts were threatened when one leader left for graduate school in another state and when other leaders had to deal with health and financial issues.

> Protest groups need to be understood as ways to create a collective imagination about what is possible.

All emergent groups have similar problems to solve. A principle one is membership. This may seem simple but it is not, and involves more than paying dues (sometimes required, sometimes not) and showing up. Small groups create cultures and emergent movements are places where, to use Blee's words, "people work collectively to understand their world, decide what is just or unjust, and express their values."[18] *Protests and the groups that give rise to them need to be understood as ways to create a collective imagination about what is possible.*[19] To create a shared imagination a group needs not just anybody as a member but the "right" kind of member. When a group takes the first step toward organization, people frequently come with a few friends; some stay, some do not. Initial meetings are "getting to know one another" events in which people explain what they care about and group leaders explain what the intent and purpose of the group is. Over time there is both the deepening of a group culture and a winnowing away of those who do not share the group's collective vision until the group becomes "people like us." If there are new recruits they must abide by the norms already established by a moral community.

Groups well established come to a point where recruitment of new members ceases to be a goal unless they are faced with what they deem to be a new moral crisis. To turn back to Chapter 3, Black Lives Matter, the three women who are credited with first creating the movement were very clear about the "right" kind of member. They emphasized they were not just another civil rights movement and certainly not one to be dominated by men. Members needed to be committed not just to issues of racial equality but committed to a woman-centered movement focused on the needs and rights of the LGBT community. They resisted attempts by political organizations to take over the purpose of their movement, as well as their members. They defended the **moral borders** of their organization. The militia group described in Chapter 4, who took over the Malheur Wildlife Refuge in Oregon, required its members to commit to the possibility of arrest, violence, and even death. One man (LaVoy Finicum) was killed by law enforcement officers as he tried to escape apprehension, and several involved in the standoff were tried for crimes committed both in Nevada and Oregon. The "right" kind of member demonstrated their credibility by being members of well-established militia groups. Some members had stood with the Bundys when federal officials tried to take their cattle for non-payment of grazing fees.

Some long-standing activist groups serve the same functions as a family. They provide rules for behavior and often provide a sense of certainty and acceptance in an uncertain world. They share memories of how they backed down the police in Ferguson, Missouri. They tell stories about sexual harassment or assault. A number of protesters in the Battle in Seattle, Chapter 2, went on to lead other similar protests together. The Bundy family and their friends told stories about how they came together and routed federal agents trying to take their cows. Groups create a **shared history**. They protest and engage in acts of defiance in celebration of this shared history and their common humanity. *Acts of defiance are an expression of a need for belonging and an expression of trust.* The development of trust is central because it is the glue that holds families, friends, and communities together.

Membership, then, involves more than joining; it involves dedication to a cause and embracing a faith. Those who dissent from the norms of a moral community will be pushed out because dissent is a form of betrayal.[20] Betrayal is a rejection of a community of believers. After the arrests of those occupying the Malheur Wildlife Refuge, some pled guilty instead of standing with the handful of men who chose to face a jury trial. The Bundy Ranch Facebook page quickly dropped these men from consideration and

> Today's institutions are characterized by temporariness, vulnerability, and inclination to constant change.

later referred to some of them as "government informants." They were not part of the "family," and no longer to be trusted. Likewise, "keyboard warriors," who urged the men to make a last stand, were not seen as worthy members of the group.

Numerous scholars have wondered why bonds of solidarity (faith, family, community) no longer hold in modern society. The sociologist Zygmunt Bauman uses the term *liquid modernity* to describe the situation in which change is so rapid that no major social institutions have time to solidify. Today's institutions, in Bauman's words, are characterized by "temporariness, vulnerability and inclination to constant change." We humans are never settled in our identities but constantly struggling to become modern, a task which can never be completed. We are not attached to anything permanent; the only certainty is uncertainty.[21] This is, frankly, an intolerable psychological situation and is one of the factors that drive people to seek community in cultures of defiance and resistance.

Bargaining and Negotiating What Is to Be Done

Another problem all social movement organizations need to solve is which specific project they are going to embrace.[22] Like membership, this too is an iterative process, changing over time when barriers are encountered or new crises emerge. The national organization founded by the environmental writer and activist Bill McKibben, 350.org, had as its original goal the need to keep the level of carbon emissions in the atmosphere below 350 parts per million (ppm), because levels higher than that would lead to a doomsday scenario. It was thought to be the point (350 ppm) beyond which Earth's atmosphere would reach a point of no return and global warming would ultimately threaten human life. The action proposed was to roll back the use of fossil fuels and to keep existing supplies in the ground. CO_2 buildup, however, has continued to climb and has now reached 400 ppm. But 350.org did not admit defeat; instead, they changed the project, which is now "freeze new fossil fuel development." The national organization also pushed for the development of renewable forms of energy such as solar and wind power. When new technologies like fracking were developed to squeeze more oil and gas out of existing fields, 350.org turned its attention to the dangers of fracking. Local chapters of 350.org., which often respond to issues closer to home, now embrace a wide range of projects. On university campuses, 350.org chapters have pushed trustees to divest from fossil fuels. In the Missoula chapter of 350.org a temporary project was to raise money for the Dakota Access Pipeline protests, as well as transport food, fuel, and winter clothing to those protesters hanging on through the cold winter months. Fund-raising efforts were undertaken by the local group to help cover the legal costs of four men who turned off pipelines carrying oil from the tar sands of Canada. Local chapters of 350.org organized parallel marches for science in their community. All of these efforts were consonant with the larger mission of 350.org, which was to transition to a green-energy economy. Groups need to be nimble in identifying projects that will keep members engaged and provide both the reality and the feeling that what the group and its members are doing matters.

As I noted earlier, when the local chapter of the DSA was forming, initial meetings were devoted to the many things that people wanted to do, some of which they were already engaged in doing by virtue of their membership or participation in *other* groups. Those women who were active in Planned Parenthood and wanted the DSA to create an agenda that would focus on protecting women's right to choose eventually drifted away from the group, because reproductive rights never became the group project and because there was already a local Planned Parenthood group to pursue that agenda. This is part of the normal bargaining and negotiating that goes on between potential members in the early days of group formation. What did become the focus of the local DSA was a result of the interplay of several different factors.

Those who played central roles in forming the local chapter referred to themselves as "Berniecrats," which in their case meant, among other things, lamenting the fact that the Democratic National Committee (DNC) had supported Clinton instead of Sanders. They remained silent in meetings to form the chapter on the broad goals of the national organization which stated: "Democratic Socialists of America share a vision of a humane international social order based on equitable distribution of resources, meaningful work, a healthy environment, sustainable growth, gender and racial equality, and non-repressive relationships."[23] Had potential members been asked to identify projects that were consonant with the mission of the national organization a different project might have emerged. What did become a central project for the group was "Medicare for All." This became the answer to the question: What do we do? It did so for an anomalous reason. Ryan Zinke, Montana's sole representative, had been tapped to become Secretary of the Interior and a special election was underway to choose a replacement. When it was announced that Bernie Sanders, who continued to stump for this idea, was coming to support the Democratic candidate for the House seat, it seemed "logical" to embrace this idea. It also resonated with two of the women in the group who had a professional interest in health care and had been working with other newly formed groups in the community to pursue this project. There was a potential to choose any number of other interests because the DSA supports a widely diverse set of interests: labor, religion, youth, anti-racism, feminism, LGBT rights, and environmental justice. The choices that groups make at the outset of their formation have a profound effect on what happens next.

Why did Black Lives Matter choose to pursue issues relevant to the LBGT community, even though the precipitating incident was the shooting of Michael Brown by a white policeman in Ferguson, Missouri? Because one of the founders identified herself as queer and another was married to a transgendered male. Why did militia members decide to try and take over the Malheur Wildlife Refuge? Because members of the Bundy family were able to rally neighbors and militia members to their ranch in Nevada and take back their cattle, and they believed they could use the same tactics to demand the return of federal lands to local control. They chose to make a stand in Oregon because two local ranchers were going to do jail time and they felt they could rally the local community to their side. Once they made that decision, they were stuck with the possibility of being arrested. Why is there an anti-vaccination movement? In part, because Andrew Wakefield

> Social movements and the organizations that give rise to them are path dependent.

published a fraudulent article claiming that autism was linked with vaccinations, which provided an answer to a question parents were desperate for. In the language of social movement theory, social movements and the organizations that give rise to them are *path dependent*, which is a way of saying that what happens first determines what happens later.[24] How an issue is framed for potential recruits, who shows up at a meeting, and who assumes leadership all determine the eventual outcome.

Outcomes of social action are not predetermined. Actors with will and intent run up against circumstances that cause them to change plans or projects. The anti-GMO movement driven by the Organic Consumers Association (OCA) lost the labeling battle. Instead of continuing that battle, they turned immediately to challenging the EPA's 2017 decision *not* to ban Dow's "brain-damaging pesticide," chlorpyrifos, and broadened their mission to include the improvement of soils. Groups may also change direction when a new crisis emerges which can cause the group to reconsider its goals and strategies.

Social and Historical Context

The insurgent campaign of Bernie Sanders was driven in part by increasing gaps in income and wealth that had deepened sharply over three decades. Issues which Sanders embraced had come to the fore during the Occupy Wall Street Movement of 2011. The impact of neoliberal free trade agreements on working men and women were front and center during the 1999 Battle for Seattle. Long simmering issues created the historical context that gave rise to a populist campaign on the left. But as we know, they also gave rise to one on the right which provided a new context for mobilization.

In the aftermath of Trump's election, sales of older dystopian novels exploded. Sinclair Lewis' 1935 novel, *It Can't Happen Here*, imagined what the United States would have been like if a fascist had defeated Franklin D. Roosevelt for President. George Orwell's *1984* portrayed a world constantly at war and a society in which its citizens were monitored and manipulated by its government and public opinion was shaped by what we would now call alternative facts. Readers also sought out Margaret Atwood's 1985 *The Handmaid's Tale* in which a totalitarian theocracy controlled women's bodies for the greater good of society. In the first 100 days of his Presidency, Trump issued a blizzard of Executive Orders that were intended to roll back many of Obama's initiatives. For a time, each generated opposition on the left and celebration among supporters on the right.

The election of Donald Trump caused both membership and fund raising to spike in established groups such as Planned Parenthood, the League of Women Voters, the Southern Poverty Law Center, and the DSA. The ACLU raised $24 million in just three days, far more than the $4 million it receives in a typical year.[25] National Public Radio stations urged listeners to contribute so they could get real news. Where local affiliates of these national groups existed, they too saw a surge in membership and activity. Mass demonstrations took place—the Women's March, the March for Science, and the Climate March—which drew on support from existing social movement organizations. Whatever the organization, they were all saying "trust us" to lead the fight. Trust is essential in promoting collective and coordinated action and groups compete among themselves for who is the most trustworthy and relevant.[26]

One of the first new social movement organizations to emerge in the aftermath of the election was Indivisible. A group of former White House staff members came together to produce a guide, based on the strategies and success of the Tea Party efforts.[27] (See Chapter 4.) Accordingly, they advocated attending town hall meetings of Republican office holders to protest positions they had taken, to attend local political events to make sure their issues stayed in front of the public, to show up at district offices of representatives, and to make coordinated calls to Congress. In short, Indivisible wanted people to do everything possible to embarrass lawmakers who had taken positions contrary to theirs, such as repealing Obamacare. If success was measured in terms of the publicity garnered by these actions, they achieved their goals because the events were closely covered by all media outlets. Harassment was so intense that some Republican representatives abandoned the notion of holding public meetings and chose, instead, to hold public "call-ins" where questions could be monitored and the conversation controlled. Yet, despite the number of protests and demands to maintain the Affordable Care Act (ACA), House Republicans voted in May of 2017 to repeal significant portions of the Act.[28]

Our Revolution, another national group, also sought to capture this insurgent energy. Our Revolution was spun out of the Bernie Sanders' campaign. It focused on electoral politics and sought to elect progressive Democratic candidates to office and thereby move the Democratic Party to the left. It spawned a number of statewide and local groups and in Montana there were several: Big Sky Rising,

Montana Rising, Flathead Rising, and Missoula Rising. One of the difficulties faced by Our Revolution was that it was closely linked with the Democratic Party and the DNC, not surprising considering the focus on electoral politics and the desire to elect Democrats. The group of which I was a member, DSA Missoula, was approached by Our Revolution to sign a memorandum of understanding to work with them, which DSA decided to do. It was seen by those involved in our discussion as an effort on the part of Our Revolution to develop legitimacy among the leftist groups that had emerged in the aftermath of the election. The Democratic Party also tried to claim the label of the resistance asking for donations to fight Trump's agenda and support health care, working families, immigrants, the environment, and children.

The historic occasion of the election of a populist candidate from the right provided an opportunity for scores of previously existing organizations to reach out to their members, as well as recruit new ones. New mobilizations, like the Women's March and the March for Science, were turned into *social movement organizations* whose general thrust was to challenge the Trump administration. There was intense competition among groups for relevance. The Climate March in Washington, D.C. and in local communities was seen by the founder of 350.org, Bill McKibben, as a way "to build a new progressive idea about what must be done should people ever regain power in our country."[29] The outpouring of protest was not limited to groups on the left; Tea Party rallies were held to counter anti-Trump demonstrations. Supporters carried signs which claimed "Trump will make America great again." Debbie Dooley, who co-founded the first national Tea Party Rally in 2009, said the Tea Party demonstrations were a response to a deluge of phone and email requests she received to "do something, anything, in response to the scores of anti-Trump protests taking place around the country."[30]

We can think of many of the actions of the Trump administration as a form of *counter mobilization* against the left. One of the first actions of Trump's Attorney General, Jeff Sessions, was to challenge the legitimacy of consent decrees that had been reached with cities like Baltimore and Chicago to reform their police departments. These agreements were made possible because President Obama and his Department of Justice pursued active investigations of the departments in question and demanded change. Historical circumstances and context made it possible for groups like Black Lives Matter to advance part of their agenda. The historical circumstances that put former Senator Jeff Sessions (R-Alabama) in charge of the Department of Justice allowed him to take the opposite tack, claiming that consent decrees undermined the respect for the police and therefore increased crime. He also vowed to renew the "war on drugs" and hand out the maximum sentence allowed under the law. As we saw in Chapter 1, the war on drugs was and is a thinly disguised attack on urban minorities.

Levels of Commitment and Engagement

Having tailor-made opportunities for engagement does not necessarily lead to a deep commitment. Let me take an organization to which I belong, the Citizens Climate Lobby (CCL), as an example. The CCL is fully funded by two entrepreneurs who had previously used their resources to support a program of micro-loans in Bangladesh. They then realized their efforts to raise Bangladeshi out of poverty would be meaningless if large sections of the country were underwater due to global warming. They created the CCL to lobby Congress, through local groups, to support a carbon fee and dividend program. (Fees charged for the use and consumption of all products containing carbon would be returned on a per-capita basis to households.) A website was created, state-wide coordinators were identified, and step-by-step instructions were provided about how to form a local chapter. A forum for monthly online meetings was developed and materials offered to help educate people about climate change. Leaders of local chapters were encouraged to learn and use the materials provided so they could give presentations to local groups and attract new members. Eighteen volunteer activities were identified. Under the heading of chapter development one could mentor a new member to serve as Secretary, Fundraiser, Outreach, or Media Coordinator. If one chose to be a fundraiser, they were expected to raise money, become a donor, or reach out to potential donors.[31]

> Every opportunity for engagement will not lead to the kind of commitment that can bring about real change.

There was difficulty in getting the group off the ground because attendance at meetings was low. The organizer hired a part-time person to serve as secretary and to keep track of who came to meetings. This meant some of the volunteer positions were not filled and it meant that, other than the organizer, nobody had skin in the game. The mission of CCL was not one that animated people who were already committed members of other groups that were dealing with environmental and climate change issues. And some thought the focus of CCL was inappropriate. At a meeting with the Missoula chapter of 350.org some were adamant that a free-market solution to climate change was misdirected; we needed to create alternatives to capitalism.

New groups in a community dense with existing volunteer organizations face several difficulties. They need to distinguish themselves from other groups to attract new members and, if they are focused on long-term goals, they need to build commitments that will endure. Yet, many of today's protests are one-off events where people can be quickly mobilized for a march or some other activity that involves a limited time commitment.

There is little about signing one more petition or marching in one more parade that binds people together and allows them to make the deep investments of time and energy that allow them to take actions characteristic of **cultures of defiance and resistance** (see Chapter 1). *Dissent manufactured and pre-programmed is not a recipe for engagement.* To take a counter example, the Civil Rights Movement of the 1960s is rightly pointed to as one of the most important collective actions ever taken in American history. Those who marched in the South, tried to register voters, risked their lives—by meeting violent aggression with non-violence—shamed Congress and jolted the federal government into action. They drew on networks of trust rooted in local churches and organizations that trained people how to work together. They kept pushing for change even when churches were burned down and members of their groups were jailed or murdered.

Consider, too, those who gathered (2016–2017) to protest the Dakota Access Pipeline at the Standing Rock Sioux Reservation in North Dakota. Native American activists from a number of tribes, as well as First Nation Peoples from Canada, came together to oppose a pipeline that had already destroyed culturally significant burial sites and would carry oil under a lake. Any rupture of the pipe would threaten the water supply of the Dakota and Lakota peoples of the Standing Rock Sioux Tribe. The protests were also about the larger issue of Native sovereignty: the right to protect and control their own land. Activists were pepper-sprayed, shot with rubber bullets, attacked by dogs, and doused with water in below freezing temperatures.[32] They stayed through life-threatening wind chills and heavy snow and only left when forced to do so by the police. They even stayed after President Trump, reversing Obama's decision to block the project, gave the go-ahead for completion of the pipeline. Though the Sioux lost their battle over the pipeline they deepened conversations about tribal sovereignty and social justice among other tribes; a discussion not likely to go away.

> Framing is part of the process by which a collective imagination is created.

Framing and Bridging

Many demands for social change frame the issue broadly in order to capture as large a membership as possible. *Framing* is part of the process by which a collective imagination is created. As the sociologist Doug McAdam notes, *framing* is "the conscious, strategic efforts by groups of people to fashion shared understanding of the world and of themselves that legitimate and motivate collective action."[33] A frame shapes how we think about an issue and therefore shapes the actions we think are necessary. The demand may be framed as a desire for social justice or freedom from oppression, as was the case with both Civil Rights protesters and those at Standing Rock. Social justice, however, is an exceptionally broad category which can be expanded infinitely. After all, who doesn't support social justice?

Demands for social justice come in many forms. In the case of those who marched in Seattle (Chapter 2), the demand for justice involved withdrawal from the World Trade Organization (WTO); they linked their message with labor organizations concerned about the outsourcing of manufacturing jobs. For the militants who took over the Wildlife Refuge, they framed their demand for justice as returning federal lands to states and counties and opening up federal lands for ranching, mining, and logging. They attempted to link their message to all patriotic groups on the right, who espoused values of freedom: freedom from government control over their lives and the freedom to bear arms. The Women's March in January 2017 was framed initially as "Women's rights are human rights" and came to include a range of related issues: abortion rights, racism, immigrant laws, and demands for equal pay.

Normally social movement organizations work independently, even when they try to link their goals and messages to other groups. They do so for obvious reasons: they depend on loyal supporters to fund the organization and to swell their numbers so their message has credibility with policy makers. When faced with a common foe or crisis, this strategy may change and cooperation becomes a defensive strategy. Potential recruits then do not gravitate to just one group that may reflect their values, but several. A reporter for *The New York Times* followed the paths of several people in the wake of Trump's victory. A man from Rhode Island, Justin Boyan, was concerned with the issue of climate change but had never done much about it. After the election, he began to volunteer with Working Families, which focused on income inequality. He then went to the Women's March on Washington and protested at the capitol in his home state against Trump's travel ban on immigrants from Muslim countries. Boyan's protest activity was facilitated by social media, as he moved from one event to another.

Working Families later joined with MoveOn.org, an established group on the left, to create weekly "Resist Trump Tuesdays." Meetup.com, a website to facilitate community gatherings and events, created more than a thousand local groups called #Resist Meetups to encourage political activism.[34] Progressive activists who were interested in stopping gun violence, public education, women's rights, worker's rights, electoral politics, and climate change found themselves marching together. Many of these events were organized through Facebook and their related service, Messenger. What is unknown is whether this fusion of dissenting groups will bring about political, social, or economic change.

Some groups are extremely nimble when it comes to claiming that they stand for the same things as another group. In this form of *bridging* the intent is to capture the attention and possibly the membership of another group. The OCA has bridged to the issues of climate change, regenerative agriculture (which rebuilds soil to boost yield), the Standing Rock protests, Mexican and indigenous farmers, opposition to corporate agriculture, and websites that sell health products.

Another reason for *bridging* to another group's mission and message is that, if another group generates considerable interest, nobody wants to be left out. Black Lives Matter activists claimed, with justification, that their interests linked to those of the Women's March and, as I noted, they marched for science because they correctly claimed that climate change would have a differential effect on minority populations. The failure of a group to *bridge* their efforts to those of a popular movement, even a temporary one, risks marginalizing their group.

Well-established groups will also try to take over new groups. As we saw in Chapter 3, the Baptist preacher Al Sharpton appeared at virtually every major protest and demonstration involving the shooting of unarmed African-Americans by the police. His group, the National Action Network, organized and led national demonstrations that sometimes appropriated the ground-work and organizing of Black Lives Matter activists. In addition, Black Lives Matter contended with the NAACP and the Urban League for who "owned" emerging protest activity in Ferguson, Missouri. The DNC worked hard to corral the wave of protest activity among those opposed to a Trump Presidency. With multiple groups competing for members and using the same online tools for mobilization and organizing, what strategies and efforts are likely to be successful in actually changing policy?

Can Mass Mobilization from the Bottom Up Become Successful?

The Marxist theorist Rosa Luxemburg (1877–1919) believed in the revolutionary potential of mass strikes. This put her at odds with those, like Lenin, who believed it was essential to create a strong organizational structure or political party first, if a revolution was to succeed. Luxemburg argued instead "that the mass strike appears as the natural means to recruit, organize and prepare the widest proletarian layers for revolutionary struggle."[35] The issue of whether or not mass protests, as opposed to a strong organization, are critical for movement success is still relevant.

The 2016 presidential campaign offers an opportunity to consider the usefulness for social change and the predictive power of one of the most notable and important theories about social movements: that of Frances Fox Piven and Richard Cloward's 1977 classic, *Poor People's Movements: Why They Succeed, How They Fail.*[36] The two authors lay out an argument similar to Luxemburg's. They claim that movements from the bottom up succeed when they are *not* captured by existing political parties and organizations like unions, and fail when they are. The reason they fail, according to Piven and Cloward, is that organizers waste time trying to build and sustain an organization rather than capitalizing on dissent. One needs to seize the historical moment. In her 2006 work, *Challenging Authority*, Piven extends this argument noting that there are extraordinary moments in history when people "rise up in anger and hope, defy the rules that ordinarily govern their lives, and, by doing so, disrupt the working of the institutions in which they are enmeshed."[37] Piven sees history as punctuated by a series of disruptive outbreaks which erupt quickly and then can just as quickly dissipate. At The People's Summit, held in June, 2016, Piven extended her theory to the pro-Sanders' insurgency.

Upwards of 3,000 Sanders supporters had come to Chicago to share ideas and to figure out how diverse groups and causes—Black Lives Matter, the Fight for $15, immigration, climate, LGBT, labor, united students against sweatshops, anti-poverty, anti-war, anti-bigotry—could all work together and win electoral power. Following the logic of her earlier work, Piven argued in a speech at the Summit that the country was experiencing a "movement moment," cautioning that: "Movements and electoral politics nourish each other. But electoral politics can also smother movements."[38] She advised resisting any attempt by the DNC to capture the movement for fear it would crush the insurgency. Once Trump was elected, she argued that something more than signing petitions and marching in parades needed to be done to challenge his Presidency. What people needed to do was to "defy the rules that ensure their cooperation" and acquiescence. People needed to be mobilized to strike and "throw sand in the gears of the institutions that depend on their cooperation."[39] But how are they to do this on their own?

The work of the community organizer and political activist, Saul Alinsky, is sometimes posed against that of Piven and Cloward. In his classic *Rules for Radicals*, Alinsky argues for a style of organizing that involves a one-on-one personal relationship between the organizer and the person or group of people to be organized.[40] The goal is to help people build community-based organizations. Piven and Cloward take a different view, writing, "A disruptive strategy does not require that people affiliate with an organization and participate regularly. Rather, it requires that masses of people be mobilized to engage in disruptive action."[41] They go on to add that if people mobilized for a welfare disruption it would be more effective if they demanded relief and caused a government crisis rather than joining a welfare organization to advocate on their behalf. This, of course, begs the question of how such efforts would be sustained and how they would be channeled to affect government policy. The major criticisms of Piven and Cloward's theories come from resource mobilization theorists who argue organizational strength is essential for movement success.[42] As an example, research on the Civil Rights Movement demonstrated the key role Black community organizations, such as churches, played in sustaining the movement.[43]

Looking back at Occupy Wall Street (Chapter 2), we see that a mass movement arose and then collapsed. There was no organization to sustain the effort and there was no distinct project that would have changed national economic policies. However, five years later when Sanders announced his candidacy and Trump stormed through the Republican primaries, the issue of income inequality returned. So, too, did the issue of outsourcing manufacturing jobs to other countries come back into focus—the point of the 1999 demonstrations in Seattle. The *timing* of mass mobilizations matters. It mattered that it was a presidential election year; otherwise the issue of trade agreements and income inequality would not have been rallying cries or resonated with voters. The historical context which saw a continued decline in the fortunes of working Americans set the stage for a revolt.

Sanders' campaign serves as a "test" of which theoretical framework best explains mobilization as well as which strategies are likely to be most effective in an internet age. Two veterans of internet activism, Becky Bond and Zack Exley, took on the daunting task of organizing Sanders' supporters in every state that did not have an official campaign office. They combined two different strategies: the Alinsky model of reaching out on a one-to-one basis and the Piven and Cloward model of mass mobilization around one or two big issues—

> You will not get a revolution unless you ask for one.

free college education and Medicare for all. Sanders did not have a ten-point plan about fracking; it was "No Fracking!" The *framing device*—big uncomplicated issues—shaped the campaign. At the end of the campaign, more than 100,000 volunteers had made 75 million telephone calls. These were not robo-calls; people spoke to one another and callers talked about why they were supporting Sanders. They also sent 8 million text messages, organized 100,000 volunteer events, and were responsible for turning out supporters for 1,000 mass meetings.[44] In the end, Sanders received 13.2 million votes in the Democratic primaries, compared to Clinton's 16.9 million. And he did it relying on volunteers.

Bond and Exley compare their model of "big" organizing with the "small" organizing of professional consultants and paid campaign staff who use sophisticated algorithms to channel dissent into one of the major parties. Small organizing focuses on incremental change, while big organizing focuses on revolutionary change. As they say, "You won't get a revolution if you don't ask for one."

> [T]he key to big organizing is that you don't just ask people to pay staff at an organization to do something big . . . You ask people to be part of something big. Because doing something big is only possible if everyone is doing it together.[45]

This is, as they admit, hard work and for it to succeed a plan was needed. Somebody needs to steer the ship. The campaign used what I referred to as a *spoke-and-hub model* in discussing the 1999 demonstrations in Seattle against the WTO in Chapter 2. There was a central plan and small teams of committed volunteers were free to figure out how best to accomplish the goal. This combination of strategies (one-on-one organizing combined with coordination from a central committee) makes it possible to respond to a crisis (in this case the outcome of an election) with a burst of activity. Some believe that Bond and Exely "set the standard for how progressives should organize for decades to come."[46] Non-violent civil resistance of the kind described by Piven and Cloward can and has been an extremely effective strategy when it comes to changing policies; far more so than violent resistance.[47] Nevertheless, there remains the problem of sustaining a slim organizational staff to mobilize people for future action. This can take on the character of a full-time business where the intent is primarily to raise money for a small staff. Change is not the goal; raising funds is.

The Commodification of Dissent

I was told I could be a "citizen scientist" by writing to the President and letting him know why I marched for science. In May 2017, the March for Science sent out a notice for Mother's Day urging recipients to give the gift of Mother Earth by donating to Cool Effect. Instead of roses, mothers would receive a notice telling them they were protecting a rare Peruvian orchid. A portion of the fee would support the March for Science. Because of other email lists to which I subscribed and groups to which I belonged, I received a steady stream of opportunities beginning in late 2016 and continuing into 2017 to march, sign a petition, donate, hold a meeting, or send a postcard to an elected representative. I usually received at least two emails a week from CREDO giving me an opportunity to sign a petition or take some action such as: "Save the EPA," "Get Trump to release his taxes," "We need Medicare for all," "Investigate the collusion between Monsanto and the EPA."

I learned about CREDO when a friend relayed an electronic petition to me, asking that I add my name. I did and immediately received solicitations to change my cell phone carrier to CREDO. CREDO sells phones and cell phone services. I was told that if I switched my carrier to CREDO I could get $100 off a Smartphone. CREDO was formed as a business with the intention of using a portion of the profits to support progressive causes. According to their website they donate $150,000 a month to progressive groups such as Planned Parenthood, the Rainforest Action Network, the ACLU, and the National Gay and Lesbian Task Force.[48] If I was one of their subscribers, I could choose which of these organizations would receive money.

In Chapter 1, I described the Tea Party as a fake, *astro-turf organization*, not a real grassroots organization. Though there was real grassroots anger and resentment directed against Obama, the Tea Party was bankrolled by Republican Party activists who wanted conservative Republicans elected to office who would support shredding the social safety net, roll back banking controls, and reduce taxes. Party activists poured funds into Tea Party activities both to foment and to capture dissent on the right. Fox News, serving as a *social movement organization* for the Republican Party, publicized the Tea Party's activities and fanned its growth.

The anti-vaccination movement described in Chapter 5 has been sustained by those selling false hope and "cures" for autism. Websites like Dr. Mercola's offer nostrums with no known benefits in the pursuit of profit. Discredited "scientists" seek speaking fees and hawk their books and videos. Unsuccessful in defeating a California law that requires all healthy children attending school to be vaccinated, anti-vaccine activists turned their attention on vulnerable immigrant communities. Andrew Wakefield and his supporters targeted the Somali-American community in Minneapolis, turning up at community meetings and reaching out to the community with the message: "Remember measles is just a five-to-seven-day disease. Autism is forever!" The result was an epidemic of measles among children in the Somali community.[49] Profit and the cynical manipulation of others were driven by ideology and the profit motive.

Of course any *social movement organization* needs resources to drive home its message and mobilize people, if it is to change policies. Both conservative and progressive lobbying groups spend millions shaping government policy on issues related to the environment, health care, and taxes. To counter such efforts, resources in the form of numbers and money must be raised. Once you have signed a petition or donated in support of a group such as Planned Parenthood you will receive notices of rallies around the country and the tools to organize a rally in your own community, if you are so inclined. You will be asked regularly to donate to the cause. At the other end of the spectrum, fund-raising efforts take on the characteristics of a cottage industry. The Bundy Ranch sold belt buckles, t-shirts, and other paraphernalia and held small fund-raising events to pay legal costs associated with the arrest of friends and family members.

Many so-called grassroots organizing campaigns create a false sense of belonging through the use of social media. Social movement theorists are well aware of the importance of creating a sense of collective identity. Feeling that you are part of something bigger than yourself is a way to deal with feelings of isolation and anomie. Many commercial organizations understand this and use social media to create a collective identity. Marketing campaigns for Uber or Airbnb are not just about getting a cheap ride or place to sleep. They aim, as the writer for *The New Yorker* Nathan Heller tells us, to make it seem as though we are the right kind of people because we use these services.[50] When we call Uber we are part of a tech-savvy vanguard participating in the "sharing" economy. The political groups to which we are connected electronically constantly tell us that only we and our donations are standing in the way of Armageddon. The sites used by militias, which offer a range of combat gear for sale, tell us we are part of a special group defending the 2nd Amendment and freedom. Commercial firms and non-profits use the same techniques to create a sense of community.

Many of the social movement organizations vying for our attention and support are not democratic groups, even though they may use the rhetoric of freedom and democracy. It is difficult to hold leaders accountable, especially in the case of movements that exist primarily as online organizations. Elections are not held and members do not vote for the leaders or the agenda of the OCA; it is run by Ronnie Cummins. Stewart Rhodes is head of Oath Keepers. He founded the group, controls its website postings, and decides which protests to support. He told his online followers not to support the takeover of the Malheur Wildlife Refuge. There are few restraints on internet-based groups, although the Media Mobilizing Project (MMP) out of Philadelphia monitors social justice groups to hold leaders accountable for their decisions.[51]

> When we choose a group to join we are making a judgment about whether or not this is where people like us belong.

On the other hand, there are those who have suggested that social media can support greater democracy and activism. Todd Wolfson, who writes about the cyber left, has described the internet as a system with horizontal, non-hierarchical structures that operate with leaderless governance and are focused on radical democratic approaches to social change.[52] Yet even though the internet has the potential for open-sourced democracy we seem to use it to cluster ever more tightly together.

Social Media

We are tribal people. We vote as tribes and act as tribes. We seek out like-minded people who share the same values we do. When we choose a group to join or a political party to vote for we are making a judgment less about ideology, than we are about whether this is where people like me belong.[53] Social media greatly facilitates this process. As the sociologist Victoria Carty has so ably demonstrated, new technologies have changed the way social movements unfold, how they recruit new members, how they are sustained, and how they can be used to fan the flames of discontent.[54] There is, literally, a group for everyone.

At any given moment, there are around 1 billion websites in the world, and upwards of 88 million in the United States. They come and go at a rapid rate; old ones are shut down and new ones created hourly. They span, as every reader knows, virtually everything. We can buy and sell on the web, check out potential partners, shop, and look up information on Wikipedia. We can find groups that support white supremacist causes, the environment, the humane treatment of animals, and efforts to save whales or elephants. We can send Tweets to our Facebook friends about what we've found online and Snapchats to show them what we are doing , eating, or wearing.

Most people do not venture far across the web.[55] Instead we concentrate on a few sites that meet our needs, whether it is for politics or shopping. In short, social media is used not to open up our minds to new and challenging perspectives but to reinforce what we already believe. Readers of Breitbart News or the Drudge Report are not reading *The New York Times* and people who watch CNN are not watching Fox News. As I noted in Chapter 5 on the anti-vaccine campaigns, social media functions to limit our understanding of events and limits the choices we think we have.

Much has been made of the rise of "alternative" facts. Truth is, in fact, hard to find on the internet. In his *True Enough*, the writer Farhad Manjoo argued that the internet would usher in a "post-fact" age.[56] The 2016 campaign and its aftermath have proven him right. We are now inundated with false information, outright lies, distortions, and conspiracy theories on a daily and sometimes hourly basis. There is such a flood of "information" that it is difficult to stop and check which statements are true and which are not. And some of the information is downright dangerous. In response to stories that circulated on the internet during the 2016 Presidential campaign, a North Carolina man walked into a Washington, D.C. Comet Ping Pong pizza parlor with a gun to "self investigate" a rumor he got off the internet. The rumor was that Hillary Clinton and her campaign chief were running a child-sex ring from the restaurant's backrooms. The retired general, Michael Flynn, who was tapped to be Trump's head of national security, did not pick up his gun, but shared online stories with others that claimed Hillary was engaged in pedophilia.[57] It was not for that reason that he lost his job; it was for his failure to tell the truth about his contacts with Russian diplomats. We are simply blind to information that does not reinforce our existing beliefs and the internet provides the blinders.

Web-based movements are composed of people loosely connected to one another with a few key individuals providing the information on which the others rely or what gets posted or re-Tweeted.[58] The rise of the alt-right during the 2016 campaign spurred Jonathon Morgan and his colleagues at New Knowledge to identify the most radical extremists among a network of 27,000 accounts associated with the alt-right. They wanted to know just how dangerous and widespread these groups were. The 3,500 they identified as the most extreme used Nazi symbols, proclaimed "white pride," were anti-Semitic and homophobic. They embraced conspiracy theories, picked up on Trump's claims that President Obama had founded the Islamic State, and supported the idea that Black Lives Matter activists were terrorists. In studying the spread of information among members of this network, what Morgan found was that only ten people accounted for most of the information. These ten were the most radical and it was their posts that sustained the network.[59] The "information" they provided was sent, not by a dense network of close friends, but between a widely dispersed network of online acquaintances. Thus, just a few people can create the illusion of a broad-based "movement." The network that makes up the alt-right is a classic example of the strength of weak ties, where new information comes from and spreads between acquaintances.[60] There is, of course, fierce competition between online groups for attention, which lessens the ability of any one group to affect actual change.

As we saw in the case of the militias, in the takeover of the Malheur Wildlife Refuge several groups competed online for attention. The Oath Keepers vehemently condemned the action and argued that the occupation was ill-conceived and led by hotheads. Online "keyboard warriors" also tried to stake their claims on who "owned" the issue of taking back public lands for the purpose of mining, ranching, and logging. Tweets, Facebook postings, and emails were sent out to diverse networks asking potential allies to come to the Refuge and participate. Some messages urged people to come armed. The small number who actually showed up suggests that in spite of literally thousands of social media posts few choose to engage in a highly risky activity. Some of the occupiers were, after all, saying they would fight to the death. The majority of those who were involved in the occupation, with the exception of one or two people, already knew one another and had been involved in similar activities. So, while there appeared to be a wide and diverse audience of sympathizers, this did not result in on-the-ground support.

There is limited evidence that social media campaigns can bring about significant social change. In July of 2015, a Minnesota dentist killed an iconic lion in Zimbabwe named Cecil. The dentist's guide had lured Cecil from a protected area by dragging meat, which the lion followed, to where he could be shot. People for the Ethical Treatment of Animals (PETA) wanted the dentist, Walter J. Palmer, hanged.[61] Over a million people signed petitions demanding justice for

Cecil. They wanted the dentist jailed. PETA created a Halloween costume of Cecil mauling the dentist. Sales were brisk. In support of Cecil, three airlines said they would no longer transport hunting trophies from Africa. However, in spite of these divergent efforts, the population of lions in Africa continues its catastrophic decline. As the environmental writer Richard Conniff has pointed out, the reason is that trophy hunting isn't the problem. The problem is that growing African populations are killing the game that lions used to eat.[62] To solve this problem, people would need to contribute substantial effort and money to set up protected reserves for the lions and find a way to feed the people who were killing the lions' prey. Online support for a cause does not mean people are willing to commit to the hard and complex work of change.

Beginning in the 2004–2005 college year, a number of students on campuses across the country wore t-shirts with the slogan "Save Darfur." This was in response to a brutal civil war that had broken out in 2003 in Darfur, a western region of Sudan. It was a humanitarian tragedy. Upwards of 2.3 million people were eventually displaced and 300,000 killed.

The initial response in the United States and other Western nations was overwhelming. Ann Brown, writing for the Save Darfur Coalition and the Genocide Intervention Center, claimed they had a combined membership list of over 800,000, with a nationwide student movement.[63] A number of actions were undertaken by the Coalition, including asking 1 million people to send similarly worded postcards to President George Bush to support a stronger UN peacekeeping force in Darfur to protect civilians. A divestment campaign was organized, rallies with political figures and celebrities were held, and a former Marine Captain toured the country to explain in words and pictures what was happening in Darfur. However, as of this writing (2017), outbreaks of violence and incidents of genocide continue.

Today, few college students are aware of the continuing conflict and not much has changed. One reason is that much of the support for the Save Darfur campaign was online support, which often doesn't actually require people to *do* anything. The sociologist Kevin Lewis and his colleagues Kurt Gay and Jens Meierhenrich carefully analyzed the donation activity of 1.1 million Facebook users who claimed to support the Save Darfur cause. Most supporters gave nothing to the cause and only a handful "recruited" another person to the cause. Less than $100,000 was raised from Facebook followers, meaning that on average supporters gave less than 10 cents each. As the researchers found, just a handful of people were active in recruiting and donating. They also found that interest in the overall effort declined rapidly to the point of invisibility. The massive online numbers created the *illusion of activism* rather than the real thing.[64]

Occupy Wall Street brought literally hundreds of thousands of people into the streets, not only in the United States but in Western Europe. Facebook and Twitter were used extensively to alert participants and video streams were sent from cell phones so that people could see both the numbers involved and record the actions of police. Mainstream media also provided extensive coverage of the sit-ins, which helped to publicize the efforts. In local communities the occupations took on a diverse and sometimes celebratory character. Environmentalists, social justice advocates, those interested in local politics, and students set up tent encampments, which also attracted some of the homeless and some with drug and alcohol problems. However, as research on Twitter feeds demonstrated, the movement "tended to elicit participation from a set of highly interconnected users with pre-existing interests in domestic politics and foreign social movements."[65]

In the case of the Occupy movement, after a certain point, social media engagement dropped steeply, as it did in the occupation of the Malheur Wildlife Refuge. Just what social media can do to mobilize people and affect change is controversial. As I have argued in the cases discussed earlier, social media can be used to mobilize people who are *already* loosely connected to one another and share the same values.

Some of the greatest controversy about whether or not social media can affect social change relates to the Arab Spring of 2011, and the overthrow of corrupt leaders in Egypt and Tunisia, the ouster and death of the Libyan leader, Muammar Gaddafi, and the attempted overthrow of Syria's Bashar al-Assad. There were strong claims made that the Arab Spring was a Twitter and Facebook revolution and as we know now, it was not an enduring one.[66] Thomas L. Friedman, writing for *The New York Times* from Cairo, asserted the mass demonstrations in Tahrir Square were "started by youth and enabled by Facebook and Twitter."

> Social media serves to mobilize people who are already loosely connected to one another.

It was a "total do-it-yourself revolution. This means anyone in the neighborhood can copy it."[67] Friedman was not alone in his overly optimistic assessment of the ease by which people can be mobilized for sustained and successful action.

The Project on Information Technology and Political Islam, headquartered at the University of Washington, asserted that authoritarian rule had been challenged by average citizens emboldened by digital media. Their assumptions are worth quoting at length:

> [The] successful challengers were 20-year-olds and 30-year-olds who never experienced open debate and democratic discourse except as mediated through online forums and social computing. On the ground, tech-savvy activists and students leaders are actively learning how non-violent civic action has meaning and sustained political outcomes. Moreover they are designing new tools and repurposing existing tools

in ways unintended and unexpected . . . Large numbers of people with large numbers of devices on multiple digital platforms are behind these new discursive practices.[68]

They were, perhaps, premature in their evaluation of the positive role of social media. The Muslim Brotherhood which came into power in Egypt was ousted from power by the military when a former general, Abdel Fattah el-Sisi, became president in 2014. In Yemen the leader who fled returned to power amidst civil war; Libya disintegrated into warring factions; and the protests in Syria led to the brutal oppression of those who opposed the Assad regime. Only the Tunisian revolution was successful.

The writer and journalist Evgeny Morozov argued that in the case of the Arab Spring, Facebook and Twitter were simply tools used by people who had already been organized. Because activists were at risk, they met secretly and offline to develop strategy. There were many such events, some attended by Morozov, and as he argues, they belie the idea that the "protests were organized by random people doing random things online." Networks came together that had been funded by Western governments and foundations such as George Soro's Open Society Foundation.[69] The Muslim Brotherhood also had a well-developed organization and, although publicly denying support for the mass demonstrations, played a central role in planning, inciting, and steering them.[70]

The writer Malcolm Gladwell has argued caution in making claims for the use of Facebook and Twitter as a means of bringing about social change.[71] As with Morozov, he sees social media simply as tools which can be used by activists. In critiquing the role of social media in *real* social change, Gladwell suggests that social media alone are not sufficient to generate the level of commitment needed. He draws on the work of the Stanford sociologist, Doug McAdam, to make this point. McAdam wondered who, out of all of those students who had applied to go to the South in 1964 to register voters, actually went. It was, as potential participants knew, a risky business and many dropped out. The best predictor of who went and who stayed home was the number and closeness of their *prior* relationships with one another: *the strength of their real-time ties.*[72]

As noted earlier, another sociologist, Aldon D. Morris, has contributed to our understanding of what lies behind a successful movement like the one for civil rights. In his careful analysis and interviews with Black activists, Morris shows that the Civil Rights Movement was the result of a slow and gradual organization of Black communities in the South. It had its deepest roots in African-American churches and the Baptist preachers who provided leadership throughout the struggle for equality.[73] A similar point is made by Zeynep Tufekci, who describes herself as a techno-sociologist studying the effects of social media on politics. She reminds us that Facebook was not available to Civil Rights protesters.

To organize the Montgomery, Alabama boycott, "they had to mimeograph 52,000 leaflets by sneaking into a university duplicating room and working all night, secretly. They then used the 68 African-American organizations that criss-crossed the city to distribute those leaflets by hand."[74]

The larger message is that a core leadership with resources and human ties is essential for movement success; social media are just one means of communicating with potential followers.

Today's Movements of Defiance and Resistance

We are witnessing the rise of *cultures of defiance and resistance* on both the left and right that are rooted in opposition to the dominant culture of neoliberal capitalism and the elites who support it. Whether it is the person trying to protect their children's bodies from vaccines or the militant demanding that federal lands be returned to local control, these movements are part of a larger struggle against all forms of domination, exploitation, and oppression.[75] These new movements are class based because, whether on the left or right, they are about taking a stand against what people perceive to be assaults on their values and way of life. They are an attempt to maintain dignity in the face of declining opportunities. They are about the continued concentration of wealth in the hands of the 1%, while many others face the threat of bankruptcy because they don't have health care or can't afford even $500 to deal with an emergency. These movements represent the voices of the minority men and women who are trapped in urban neighborhoods where there are few jobs and the men are often locked away in prisons. And, yes, they are sometimes driven by anger and rage.

People are challenging politics as usual, driven by moral shock and outrage at the circumstances in which they find their country and themselves. They are demanding that their values be honored, whether they are about faith, family, patriotism, or local community. Moral outrage, driven by sexual, economic, political, and cultural discrimination, has given rise to movements that say "Enough!" On the left and right people are demanding and seeking new ways of relating to one another through the movements themselves. Some of them will have the potential to develop into broad-based struggles for democracy; others will support authoritarian trends and continued discrimination.

Today's cultures of defiance and resistance bear a resemblance to the movements of the 1960s and 1970s, when people looked for ways and places to stand in opposition to a bureaucratic society that seemed to have penetrated every aspect of their lives and offered "freedom" only through consumption. The answer to domination then was part of what Herman Marcuse referred to as *The Great Refusal*.[76] We need to reject institutions that control our lives and destroy our sense of common purpose.

Opposition to the way things are continues to build, but we are now a divided nation. Political elites have fostered a climate of resentment by using class, race, and gender to divide Americans from one another. Non-college educated white men believe their declining fortunes are the results of "others," e.g., professors, immigrants, minorities, and sometimes women. Well-educated coastal elites simply do not "get" Middle America—their economic concerns or their values. Movements of defiance and resistance can bind us closer to one another or create fissures based on class, race, and gender. Finding and executing an agenda that benefits all Americans is a challenge, but a worthy one. You, the reader, are in a position to choose which out of the many that exist you will support.

You Say You Want a Revolution?

I said earlier that if you really want to change things you need to "Think big or go home!" Let me back away from that thought for a moment and talk about how you would even begin. There are important lessons to be learned from the different groups covered in this book. Let me list a few of them:

- The *spoke-and-hub model* works. There needs to be a central plan and small, autonomous groups must be trusted and given the authority to execute the plan.
- For a group to have staying power it needs to create a shared sense of purpose and community. It does this by embracing a common project and acting together, in person, to implement that project.
- Big movements require the adoption of elements of both the Alinksy model and that of Piven and Cloward, that is, one-on-one organizing coupled with the mass strike or protest.
- Social media tools are useful to bring together people who already share similar ideas.
- You don't have to reinvent the wheel.

What I mean by the last sentence is that there are hundreds of social movement organizations already working to cause change. Find out what they are doing in your community and, if it is what you want to do, join. Once a group is well established you are not likely to change its goals or directions. You need to support what they are already doing or risk being expelled from the group. If you want to be involved with a national group simply Google resistance.org, CREDO, Indivisible, or MoveOn.org. If you read about a group that captures your attention, just look for them online. They will be there.

Let's assume you want to start your own group. Use the suggested tools from a group like Indivisible which walk you step-by-step through what you need to do, after you assemble a small group of people who share your values. If you can't find a small group of people, then use MeetUp.org. The site will give you a list of all groups that exist in your community, what they do, and when they meet. You can post a request to form a group listing the reasons why you want to meet other people who share your values.

I have three more recommendations for getting you involved:

- Read Kathleen Blee's *Democracy in the Making*. As I noted earlier, hers is the most complete account of why small groups seeking to bring about change succeed or fail. Her discussion of the ways in which people seek to create a collective sense of purpose and how this can be sabotaged is important to understand.
- Becky Bond and Zack Exley's *Rules for Revolutionaries: How Big Organizing Can Change Everything* is equally important. They offer 22 different rules or lessons they learned as a result of organizing volunteers for Sanders' campaign. The advice is practical and even though focused on large electoral efforts, provides a framework for understanding and contextualizing all change efforts.
- Heed the words of the feminist and revolutionary Emma Goldman (1869–1910): "People have only as much liberty as they have the intelligence to want and the courage to take."[77]

Notes

1 Sarah Kaplan. January 25, 2017. "Are Scientists Going to March on Washington?" *Washington Post*. Retrieved on May 2, 2017 at: www.washingtonpost.com/news/speaking-of-science/wp/2017/01/24/are-scientists-going-to-march-on-washington/?utm_term=.08c211ffeeb1.
2 Lindzi Wessel. April 14, 2017. "On Eve of Science March, Planners Look Ahead." *Science*. Vol.356(6334):118.
3 Tim Appenzeller. April 28, 2017. "An Unprecedented March for Science." *Science*. Vol.356(6336):356–357.
4 Sarah Kaplan. April 24, 2017. "Science March Organizers Try to Galvanize Fervor into Full-Blown Movement." *Washington Post*, A4.
5 Caitlin Gibson. April 24, 2017. "'Science' Is in This Guy's Name." *Washington Post*, C1,3.
6 Frank Newport. June 2, 2014. "In U.S., 42% Believe Creationists View of Human Origins." *Gallup*. Retrieved on May 10, 2017 at: www.gallup.com/poll/170822/believe-creationist-view-human-origins.aspx.
7 The statement is attributed to David Detmer in Helen Pluckrose. March 27, 2017. "How French 'Intellectuals' Ruined the West: Postmodernism and Its Impact, Explained." *Areo Magazine*. Retrieved on May 8, 2017 at: https://areomagazine.com/2017/03/27/how-french-intellectuals-ruined-the-west-postmodernism-and-its-impact-explained/.
8 Robert P. Crease. April 27, 2017. "Why Does Alec Baldwin Hate Science?" *Wall Street Journal*, A17.

9 Science staff. April 28, 2017. "Meet the Marchers." *Science*. Vol.356(6336):358–359.

10 University of Delaware Center for Political Communication. April 18, 2017. "March for Science Participants Seek Evidence-Based Policies and Public Support for Science." Retrieved on May 2, 2017 at: www.udel.edu/content/dam/udelImages/udaily/2017/April/pdf/march-for-science-study-2017.pdf.

11 Email received from AAAS on May 2, 2017. "Evidence isn't optional."

12 It is difficult to estimate the size of crowds, because with large numbers people mill about, come early or late to a protest, and so forth. Some have estimated that 750,000 women marched in Washington.

13 Action Network. May, 2017. "On-line Organizing Tools." Retrieved on May 3, 2017 at: https://actionnetwork.org/.

14 Emily Peck and Ryan Grim. January 26, 2017. "Progressives Have a Secret Weapon in the Fight against Trump." *Huffington Post*. Retrieved on May 3, 2017 at: www.huffingtonpost.com/entry/action-network-womens-march_us_5888cdc7e4b098c0bba7dbb2.

15 Women's March Network. 2017. "First, We Marched, Now We Huddle." Retrieved on May 3, 2017 at: www.womensmarch.com/100/action2/.

16 Kathleen M. Blee. 2012. *Democracy in the Making*. New York: Oxford University Press.

17 Blee. 2012, p.13.

18 Blee. 2012, p.31.

19 Cecilia Güemes. 2017. "Neoliberal Welfare Policy Reforms and Trust: Connecting the Dots." *Journal of Iberian and Latin American Research*. Vol.23(1):18–33.

20 For a discussion of how thick relationships form and why a rejection of them is regarded as an act of betrayal see: Avishai Margalit. 2017. *On Betrayal*. Cambridge, Massachusetts: Harvard University Press.

21 Zygmunt Bauman. 2000. *Liquid Modernity*. Malden, Massachusetts: Polity Press, p.82.

22 These are not the only two hurdles that movements must overcome to be successful. Doug McAdam lists six: recruit members, sustain morale and commitment, generate media coverage, mobilize the support of the public, limit the control options of one's opponents, and ultimately shape public policy. Doug McAdam. 1996. "The Framing Function of Movement Tactics: Strategic Dramaturgy in the American Civil Rights Movement," in Doug McAdam, John D. McCarthy, and Mayer N. Zald, eds. *Comparative Perspectives on Social Movements: Political Opportunities, Mobilizing Structures and Cultural Framings*. New York: Cambridge University Press, pp.339–340.

23 *Democratic Left*. Spring, 2017. "Building Democratic Socialist Power," Vol.XLIV(4), p.16.

24 Paul Pierson. 2000. "Increasing Returns, Path Dependence, and the Study of Politics." *American Political Science Review*. Vol.94(2):251–267.

25 Barbara Ortutay. February 13, 2017. "Trump Resistance Brews Online." *The Missoulian* (Associated Press), p.A8.

26 Cecilia Güemes. 2017. "Neoliberal Welfare Policy Reforms and Trust," p.18.

27 Indivisible. 2017. "The Guide." Retrieved on May 8, 2017 at: www.indivisibleguide.com/.

28 As of July, 2017, the Senate continued to work to repeal the ACA.

29 Missoula 350.org. April 27, 2017. Email alert, "A Test of Strength."

30 Debbie Dooley, cited in Josh Sanburn. March 2, 2017. "Meet the Tea Partiers behind the Rallies for President Trump around the U.S." *Time Magazine*. Retrieved on May 9, 2017 at: http://time.com/4688825/donald-trump-rallies-tea-party-spirit-america/.

31 Citizens Climate Lobby. 2017. "Help Us Solve Climate Change." Retrieved on May 9, 2017 at: http://citizensclimatelobby.org/?gclid=CLr75eXL49MCFcKOfgodAZYCQw.

32 *Democracy Now*. September 4, 2016. "Video: Dakota Access Pipeline Company Attacks Native American Protesters with Dogs and Pepper Spray." Retrieved on May 10, 2017 at: www.democracynow.org/2016/9/4/dakota_access_pipeline_company_attacks_native. See also: Derek Hawkins. November 16, 2016. "Police Defend Use of Water Cannons on

Dakota Access Protesters in Freezing Weather." *Washington Post*. Retrieved on May 10, 2017 at: www.washingtonpost.com/news/morning-mix/wp/2016/11/21/police-citing-ongoing-riot-use-water-cannons-on-dakota-access-protesters-in-freezing-weather/?utm_term=.c174602acb09.

33 Doug McAdam. 1999. *Political Process and the Development of Black Insurgency, 1930–1970*, 2nd ed. Chicago, Illinois: University of Chicago Press, Introduction.

34 Yamiche Alcindor. February 17, 2017. "Liberal Activists Join Forces against a Common Foe: Trump." *The New York Times*. Retrieved on May 10, 2017 at: www.nytimes.com/2017/02/14/us/politics/protesters-resist-trump.html?_r=0.

35 Rosa Luxemburg. 1906. *The Mass Strike, the Political Party, and the Trade Unions*. Chapter 7. Marxist Archives. Retrieved on May 16, 2017 at: www.marxists.org/archive/luxemburg/download/mass-str.pdf.

36 Frances Fox Piven and Richard Cloward. 1977. *Poor People's Movements: Why They Succeed, How They Fail*. New York: Random House.

37 Frances Fox Piven. 2006. *Challenging Authority: How Ordinary People Change America*. New York: Rowan and Littlefield, dust jacket blurb.

38 Rose Ann De Maro. June 24, 2016. "People's Summit." Retrieved on May 12, 2017 at: www.thepeoplessummit.org/2016/06/24/2467/.

39 Frances Fox Piven. January 18, 2017. "Throw Sand in the Gears of Everything." *The Nation*. Retrieved on May 12, 2017 at: www.thenation.com/article/throw-sand-in-the-gears-of-everything/.

40 Saul Alinsky. 1971. *Rules for Radicals*. New York: Vintage.

41 Piven and Cloward. 1977. *Poor People's Movements*, p.284.

42 J. Craig Jenkins. 1983. "Resource Mobilization Theory and the Study of Social Movements." *Annual Review of Sociology*. Vol.9:527–553.

43 Aldon Morris. 1986. *The Origins of the Civil Rights Movement*. New York: Simon and Schuster.

44 Becky Bond and Zack Exley. 2016. *Rules for Revolutionaries: How Big Organizing Can Change Everything*. White River Junction, Vermont: Chelsea Green Publishing, p.xv.

45 Bond and Exley. 2016, p.14.

46 Kenneth Pennington cited in Lizzie Crocker. November 16, 2016. "How to Plan the Political Revolution that Could Stop President Trump." *The Daily Beast*. Retrieved on May 13, 2017 at: www.thedailybeast.com/articles/2016/11/16/how-to-plan-the-political-revolution-that-could-stop-president-trump.

47 This is especially true when considering the effectiveness across societies. See Erica Chenoweth and Maria J. Stephan. 2011. *Why Civil Resistance Works: The Strategic Logic of Nonviolent Conflict*. New York: Columbia University Press.

48 CREDO. 2017. "Winning Together." Retrieved on May 9, 2017 at: https://credoaction.com/.

49 Maggie Fox. May 8, 2017. "Measles Outbreak in Minnesota Caused by Vaccine Skeptics." *NBC News*. Retrieved on May 9, 2017 at: www.nbcnews.com/health/health-news/measles-outbreak-minnesota-caused-vaccine-skeptics-n756246.

50 Nathan Heller. May 15, 2017. "The Gig Is Up: Many Liberals Have Embraced the Sharing Economy. But Can They Survive It?" *The New Yorker*, pp.52–63.

51 Media Mobilizing Project. 2017. Retrieved on May 16, 2017 at: https://mediamobilizing.org/.

52 Todd Wolfson. 2014. *Digital Rebellion: The Birth of the Cyber Left*. Urbana-Champaign, Illinois: University of Illinois Press.

53 Christopher H. Achen and Larry M. Bartels. 2016. *Democracy for Realists: Why Elections Do Not Produce Responsive Government*. Princeton, New Jersey: Princeton University Press.

54 Victoria Carty. 2015. *Social Movements and New Technology*. Boulder, Colorado: Westview. Carty provides a careful analysis of the role of social media played in a diverse range of

social movements including the Tea Party, MoveOn.org, the Arab Spring, and Occupy Wall Street.

55 Adrienne La France. September 30, 2015. "How Many Websites Are There?" *The Atlantic*. Retrieved on July 5, 2016 at: www.theatlantic.com/technology/archive/2015/09/how-many-websites-are-there/408151/.

56 Farhad Manjoo. 2008. *True Enough: Learning to Live in a Post-Fact Society*. New York: Wiley.

57 Faiz Siffiqui and Susan Svrluga. December 5, 2016. "N.C. Man Told Police He Went to D.C. Pizzeria with Gun to Investigate Conspiracy Theory." *Washington Post*. Retrieved on May 16, 2017 at: www.washingtonpost.com/news/local/wp/2016/12/04/d-c-police-respond-to-report-of-a-man-with-a-gun-at-comet-ping-pong-restaurant/?utm_term=. d05e8a9432c7.

58 Victoria Carty. 2015. *Social Movements and New Technology*, p.67; Doug McAdam and Ronnelle Paulsen. 1993. "Specifying the Relationships between Social Ties and Activism." *American Journal of Sociology*. Vol. 99(3):640–667.

59 Jonathon Morgan. September 26, 2016. "These Charts Show Exactly How Racist and Radical the Alt-Right Has Gotten This Year." *Washington Post*. Retrieved on May 15, 2017 at: www.washingtonpost.com/news/the-intersect/wp/2016/09/26/these-charts-show-exactly-how-racist-and-radical-the-alt-right-has-gotten-this-year/?utm_term=. a6b059dedc36.

60 Mark S. Granovetter. 1973. "The Strength of Weak Ties." *American Journal of Sociology*. Vol.78(6):1360–1380.

61 PETA. 2015. "Cecil's Death Highlights Cowardice of Hunting." Retrieved on July 5, 2016 at: www.peta.org/blog/cecils-death-prompts-call-to-ban-trophy-hunt-imports-to-u-s/.

62 Richard Conniff. July 3, 2016. "Any Tweets Won't Help African Lions." *The New York Times*. Sunday Review, p.7.

63 Ann Brown. November 1, 2010. "Advocacy Groups Save Darfur Coalition and Genocide Interventional Network Announcement." Retrieved on July 5, 2016 at: http://standnow.org/2010/11/01/advocacy-groups-save-darfur-coalition-and-genocide-intervention-network-announce-merger/.

64 Kevin Lewis, Kurt Gay, and Jens Meierhenrich. February, 2014. "The Structure of Online Activism." *Sociological Science* 1:1–9.

65 Michael D. Conover, Emilio Ferrara, Filippo Menczer, and Alessandro Flammini. May 29, 2013. "The Digital Evolution of Occupy Wall Street." *Plos/One*. Retrieved on July 8, 2016 at: http://journals.plos.org/plosone/article?id=10.1371/journal.pone.0064679.

66 Joel Beinin makes a different claim. He points out, correctly, that real revolutions can take a long time to unfold and that the conditions that gave rise to the outbreaks in 2011 are still present and will create pressures for change. Joel Beinin. January 1, 2014. "The Arab Uprisings Have Not Failed: They Are Continuing." *Mobilizing Ideas*. Retrieved on May 15, 2017 at: https://mobilizingideas.wordpress.com/2014/01/01/the-arab-uprisings-have-not-failed-they-are-continuing/.

67 Thomas L. Friedman. February 11, 2011. "Postcard from a Free Egypt." *The New York Times*. Retrieved on July 7, 2016 at: www.nytimes.com/2011/02/11/opinion/11-web-friedman.html?_r=0.

68 Center for Communication and Civic Engagement. 2011. "The Project on Information Technology and Political Islam." Seattle: University of Washington. Retrieved on July 7, 2016 at: http://ccce.com.washington.edu/projects/pitpi.html.

69 Evgeny Morozov. March 7, 2011. "Facebook and Twitter Are Just Places Revolutionaries Go." *The Guardian*. Retrieved on July 7, 2016 at: www.theguardian.com/commentisfree/2011/mar/07/facebook-twitter-revolutionaries-cyber-utopians. See also his: *The Net Delusion: The Dark Side of Internet Freedom*. New York: Public Affairs/Perseus Press. There he argues that the net can and is used by governments to limit freedom.

70 Lt. Col. (ret.) Jonathan D. Halevi. August 16, 2012. "Intelligence Document Reveals Muslim Brotherhood Role in Egyptian Revolution." Jerusalem Center for Public Affairs. Retrieved on July 9, 2016 at: http://jcpa.org/intelligence-document-reveals-muslim-brotherhood-role-in-egyptian-revolution/. The information comes from a leaked document taken from the offices of Egyptian intelligence. Some have argued that the document was created by Egyptian intelligence to justify the repression of the Brotherhood.

71 Malcolm Gladwell. October 4, 2010. "Small Change: Why the Revolution Will Not Be Tweeted." *The New Yorker.* Retrieved on July 6, 2016 at: www.newyorker.com/magazine/2010/10/04/small-change-malcolm-gladwell.

72 Doug McAdam. 1990. *Freedom Summer.* New York: Oxford University Press.

73 Aldon D. Morris. 1986. *The Origins of the Civil Rights Movement: Black Communities Organizing for Change.* New York: Free Press.

74 Zeynep Tufekci. February, 2015. "Online Social Change: Easy to Organize, Hard to Win." *TED Talk.* Retrieved on May 15, 2017 at: www.ted.com/talks/zeynep_tufekci_how_the_internet_has_made_social_change_easy_to_organize_hard_to_win.

75 For an elaboration of this point see Chris Dixon. 2014. *Another Politics: Talking Across Today's Transformative Movements.* Berkeley, California: University of California Press.

76 Herbert Marcuse. 1964. *One Dimensional Man.* Boston, Massachusetts: Beacon.

77 Emma Goldman. 1910. *Anarchism and Other Essays.* New York: Mother Earth Publishing.

Index